Requirements for Certification

Requirements for Certification

of Teachers, Counselors, Librarians, Administrators

for Elementary and Secondary Schools

Eighty-Seventh Edition, 2022–2023

Edited by
Alain Park

The University of Chicago Press
Chicago and London

The University of Chicago Press, Chicago 60637

Eighty-seventh edition 2022
Published annually since 1935
International Standard Book Number-13: 978-0-226-82415-4 (cloth)
International Standard Book Number-13: 978-0-226-82416-1 (e-book)
DOI: https://doi.org/10.7208/chicago/9780226824161.001.0001
International Standard Series Number: 1047-7071
Library of Congress Catalog Card Number: A43-1905

♾ This paper meets the requirements of ANSI/NISO Z39.48-1992 (Permanence of Paper).

Contents

Introduction to the Eighty-Seventh Edition
2022–2023

With the publication of this eighty-seventh edition, it may prove useful to ask why a physical book on certification requirements remains so widely used and needed. After all, isn't most of this information available online in some form or other? The answer, in a word, is accessibility.

Unlike the sprawling internet, this volume provides a concise yet detailed summary of relevant information that in many cases is not available in a standardized form on the websites of individual state offices. The quality and presentation of said information on the internet can also vary greatly from website to website. With an array of online application forms, automated systems, and literally hundreds of pages of legislative regulations reproduced verbatim, it can be a significant challenge to unearth a clear, consistent overview of certification. Our aim is to provide the reader with exactly that vantage point.

Our compilation provides a "balcony view" of current information on certification requirements for all fifty states and the District of Columbia. This enables readers to access and compare information about different certificates or endorsements within a state or about a single certificate or endorsement across states. Updated annually and presented in a clear and concise format, this book provides a fresh overview for teachers, counselors, librarians, and administrators, as well as any who aspire to join their ranks. This eighty-seventh volume strives to remain an essential service to both the public and the professionals who continue to need this information.

As in previous years, state certification saw more movement toward automated online application processes. While this move is likely welcomed by many users, it also has the effect of further embedding and obscuring valuable information that this book seeks to make accessible. The COVID-19 pandemic also continues to alter the policies of many offices as they deal with office closures, deadline adjustments, staff response delays, or even certification deferrals. As of the writing of this introduction, pandemic-related changes remain, and those seeking certification are strongly encouraged to search out any adjustments to the certification process that may still be in place.

Requirements for Certification had its inception in the Board of Vocational Guidance and Placement (now Career Advancement) at the University of Chicago. The original study was made by Robert C. Woellner, professor of education and head of the Board, and M. Aurilla Wood, placement counselor. The digest continued under the direction of Elizabeth H. Woellner until her retirement in 1983. Produced only in mimeograph form its first year, the digest was published and made available for sale by the University of Chicago Press in 1935 and has appeared in annual editions since that time.

The publication of this volume would not be possible without the meticulous aid and generosity of the state certification officers who go above and beyond to help us ensure that this book is accurate and complete. We trust that these efforts will bear fruit for the certification professionals and for those who seek access to their knowledge.

Alabama

Stages and Titles of Teaching Certificates

I. Class B Professional Educator Certificate (valid 5 years*)
   A. Issued on basis of a bachelor's degree and completion of all other requirements for issuance
II. Class A Professional Educator Certificate (valid 5 years*)
   A. Issued on basis of a master's degree and completion of all other requirements for issuance
III. Class AA Professional Educator Certificate (valid 5 years*)
   A. Issued on basis of an education specialist (EdS) degree resulting from completion of an approved, planned sixth-year program of at least 30 semester hours of post-master's graduate credit and completion of all other requirements for issuance
IV. Class A Professional Leadership Certificate (valid 5 years*)
   A. Issued on basis of a master's degree and completion of all other requirements for issuance
V. Class AA Professional Leadership Certificate (valid 5 years*)
   A. Issued on basis of an EdS degree resulting from completion of an approved, planned sixth-year program of at least 30 semester hours of post-master's graduate credit and all other requirements for issuance

*Valid from the date of issuance through the remainder of the same scholastic year, and thereafter, for the next 5 consecutive scholastic years.

Requirements for Teaching Certificates

I. Teaching certificates available include:
   A. Pre-Kindergarten (Birth–Age 4)
   B. Early childhood education (P–3)
   C. Early childhood special education (P–3)
   D. Elementary education (K–6)
   E. Collaborative special education teacher (K–6)
   F. Middle level (4–8)
   G. High school (6–12)
   H. Collaborative special education teacher (6–12)
   I. Elementary-secondary (P–12)
   J. Special education (P–12 for hearing impairment, visual impairment, or gifted)
II. Certificates are endorsed in specific teaching field(s).
III. The Educator Certification Chapter of the Alabama Administrative Code adopted March 10, 2016, contains all current information applicable to earning a certificate in

Alabama and is accessible via the following link: https://www.alabamaachieves.org/teacher-center/teacher-certification/ (under Administrative Code)

or

If the link does not work, go to https://www.alabamaachieves.org/ and click on Teachers & Administrators: Teacher Center: Teacher Certification. Administrative Code.

IV. Specific Teaching Certificates and Their Requirements
- A. Class B Professional Educator Certificate
    1. Earn a bachelor's degree from a regionally accredited senior institution, *and*
    2. Meet academic requirements in teaching field for which certification is sought through 1 of the following options:
        a. Alabama State Board of Education–approved program, *or*
        b. Valid professional educator certificate issued by another state, the District of Columbia, a US territory, or the Department of Defense Education Activity (DoDEA) at the bachelor's degree level, *or*
        c. Educator preparation program in another country at the bachelor's degree level, *or*
        d. Valid certification by the National Board for Professional Teaching Standards (NBPTS) in a teaching field in which Alabama offers comparable certification; see Rule 290–3-2-.27 in document accessible via link at III, directly above.
- B. Class A Professional Educator Certificate
    1. Earn a master's degree from a regionally accredited senior institution, *and*
    2. Meet academic requirements in teaching field for which certification is sought through 1 of the following options:
        a. Alabama State Board of Education–approved program, *or*
        b. Valid professional educator certificate issued by another state, the District of Columbia, a US territory, or DoDEA at the master's degree level, *or*
        c. Educator preparation program in another country at the master's degree level, *or*
        d. Valid NBPTS Certification in a teaching field in which Alabama offers comparable certification; see Rule 290–3-2-.27 in document accessible via link at III, directly above.
- C. Class A Professional Educator Certificate: Alternative Class A Approved Program
    1. Earn a master's degree from a regionally accredited senior institution, *and*
    2. Meet Alabama State Board of Education–approved program requirements

specified in Rule 290–3-3-.42 of the Educator Preparation Chapter of the Alabama Administrative Code accessible via the following link: https://www .alabamaachieves.org/teacher-center/teacher-preparation/ (under Administrative Code). If the link does not work, go to https://www.alabamaachieves.org/ and click on Teachers & Administrators: Teacher Center: Teacher Preparation: Administrative Code.

D. Class AA Professional Educator Certificate

   1. Earn an EdS degree from a regionally accredited senior institution resulting from completion of an approved, planned sixth-year program of at least 30 semester hours of post-master's graduate credit,
and

   2. Meet academic requirements in teaching field for which certification is sought through 1 of the following options:

      a. Alabama State Board of Education–approved program,
or

      b. Valid professional educator certificate issued by another state, the District of Columbia, a US territory, or DoDEA at the EdS level,
or

      c. Educator preparation program in another country at the EdS level,
or

      d. Valid NBPTS Certification in a teaching field in which Alabama offers comparable certification; see Rule 290–3-2-.27 in document accessible via link at III, directly above.

Administrative/Supervisory Certificates and Their Requirements

I. Class A Professional Leadership Certificate

  A. Earn a master's degree from a regionally accredited senior institution,
and

  B. Meet requirements in administration through 1 of the following options:

   1. Alabama State Board of Education–approved program in Instructional Leadership (note: prior to admission to the program, the applicant must have had at least 3 full years of full-time, acceptable professional educational experience in a P–12 setting, to include at least 1 full year of full-time P–12 classroom teaching experience) (Instructional Leadership certification allows one to serve as an administrator and/or supervisor),
or

   2. Valid professional educator certificate in administration issued by another state, the District of Columbia, a US territory, or DoDEA at the master's degree level, and 3 full years of full-time acceptable professional educational experience in a P–12 setting, to include at least 1 full year of full-time P–12 classroom teaching experience.

  C. Meet requirements in supervision through a valid professional educator certificate in supervision issued by another state, the District of Columbia, a US territory, or DoDEA at the master's degree level, and 3 full years of full-time acceptable professional educational experience in a P–12 setting, to include at least 1 full year of full-time P–12 classroom teaching experience.

II. Class AA Professional Leadership Certificate

A. Earn an EdS degree from a regionally accredited senior institution resulting from completion of an approved, planned sixth-year program of at least 30 semester hours of post-master's graduate credit,
    and

B. Meet requirements in administration through 1 of the following options:

1. Alabama State Board of Education–approved program in Instructional Leadership (Instructional Leadership certification allows one to serve as an administrator and/or supervisor),
    or

2. Valid professional educator certificate in administration issued by another state, the District of Columbia, a US territory, or DoDEA at the EdS level, and 3 full years of full-time acceptable professional educational experience in a P–12 setting, to include at least 1 full year of full-time P–12 classroom teaching experience.

C. Meet requirements in supervision through a valid professional educator certificate in supervision issued by another state, the District of Columbia, a US territory, or DoDEA at the EdS level, and 3 full years of full-time acceptable professional educational experience in a P–12 setting, to include at least 1 full year of full-time P–12 classroom teaching experience.

Support Services Certificates and Their Requirements

I. Class A Professional Educator Certificate for Library Media, School Counselor, School Psychometrist, or Sport Manager

A. Earn a master's degree from a regionally accredited senior institution,
    and

B. Meet academic requirements in support area for which certification is sought through 1 of the following options:

1. Alabama State Board of Education–approved program,
    or

2. Valid professional educator certificate issued by another state, the District of Columbia, a US territory, or DoDEA at the master's degree level,
    or

3. Valid certification by the NBPTS in the support area.

    a. See Rule 290–3-2-.27 in document accessible via link at Requirements for Teaching Certificates, III, above.

4. An option for school counseling is to verify compliance with the Council for Accreditation of Counseling and Related Educational Programs (CACREP) approach.

    a. See Rule 290–3-2-.22 in document accessible via link at Requirements for Teaching Certificates, III, above.

C. Verify 2 full years of full-time acceptable professional educational experience in a

P–12 school system. Applicants through the Alabama State Board of Education–approved program option must have completed the 2 full years of experience before admission to the program. Applicants through the CACREP approach do not have to meet this requirement.

II. Class A Speech-Language Pathology Professional Educator Certificate
   A. Earn a master's degree from a regionally accredited senior institution,
   B. Meet academic requirements in speech-language pathology through completion of a master's degree–level speech-language pathology program that was accredited by the Council on Academic Accreditation (CAA) of the American Speech-Language-Hearing Association (ASHA) at the time of program completion,
   C. Verify satisfactory performance on the CAA-prescribed Praxis subject test(s), *and*
   D. Verify a valid speech-language pathology license issued by any state's board of examiners in speech-language pathology.

III. Class AA Professional Educator Certificate for Library Media or School Counselor
   A. Earn an EdS degree from a regionally accredited senior institution resulting from completion of an approved, planned sixth-year-level program of at least 30 semester hours of post-master's graduate credit, *and*
   B. Meet academic requirements in support area for which certification is sought through 1 of the following options:
      1. Alabama State Board of Education–approved program, *or*
      2. Valid professional educator certificate issued by another state, the District of Columbia, a US territory, or DoDEA at the EdS level, *or*
      3. Valid certification by the NBPTS in the support area.
         a. See Rule 290–3-2-.27 in document accessible via link at Requirements for Teaching Certificates, III, above.
   C. Verify 2 full years of full-time acceptable professional educational experience in a P–12 school system.

IV. Class AA Professional Educator Certificate for School Psychologist
   A. Earn an EdS degree from a regionally accredited senior institution resulting from completion of an approved, planned sixth-year-level program of at least 30 semester hours of post-master's graduate credit, *and*
   B. Meet academic requirements in school psychology through 1 of the following options:
      1. Alabama State Board of Education–approved program, *or*
      2. Valid school psychologist professional educator certificate issued by another state, the District of Columbia, a US territory, or DoDEA at the EdS level, *or*
      3. Verification of compliance with the Nationally Certified School Psychologist (NCSP) approach.

a. See Rule 290–3-2-.28 in document accessible via link at Requirements for Teaching Certificates, III, above.

C. Verify 2 full years of full-time acceptable professional educational experience in a P–12 school system. Applicants through the NCSP approach do not have to meet this requirement.

Alabama Educator Certification Assessment Program

I. Applicants for an Alabama professional educator certificate, professional leadership certificate, or alternative approach certificate must meet the requirements of the Alabama Educator Certification Assessment Program (AECAP) as a precondition for certification.
   A. AECAP consists of subject area assessments and a performance assessment.
      1. Subject area assessments consist of Alabama State Board of Education–approved tests from the Praxis Subject Assessment series, administered by ETS.
      2. The performance assessment, which became effective Fall 2018, is the Educative Teacher Performance Assessment (edTPA), administered by Pearson Education, Inc.

Out-of-State Reciprocity

I. Professional educator and professional leadership certification in Alabama is not offered reciprocally on the basis of educator preparation programs completed at non-Alabama institutions.
II. Alabama professional educator and professional leadership certification is only considered reciprocally on the basis of holding a valid professional educator or professional leadership certificate issued by another state, the District of Columbia, a US territory, or DoDEA, and if Alabama offers comparable certification.

Certificates

Requirements for the following certificates are available at https://www.alabamaachieves.org/teacher-center/teacher-certification/ (under Administrative Code).

I. Career and Technical Education, including Health Science and specific technical education program areas, for grades 6–12
II. Alternative Certificate Approaches
III. Early Childhood Development (Birth–Age 4)
IV. Dyslexia Therapist
V. Higher Education Transitional
VI. Speech-Language Pathology Assistant
VII. Speech-Language Pathology Temporary

Alaska

Initial Teacher Certificates

I. Initial/2- and 3-Year Teacher Certificate (valid 2 years; not renewable, but may be extended to a third year if Alaska studies and Alaska multicultural coursework are turned in before interim deadline)
   A. Requirements for Initial 2-Year Certification—Candidate:
      1. Has completed a bachelor's degree from a regionally accredited university;
      2. Has completed a state-approved teacher preparation program;
      3. Has passing scores on an approved basic competency exam (BCE) (for details, consult https://education.alaska.gov/teachercertification/praxis);
      4. Has passing scores on an approved Content Area Exam (for details, consult https://education.alaska.gov/teachercertification/contentareaexams);
      5. Has never held an Initial or Provisional Alaska teacher certificate;
      6. Is not eligible for reinstatement of a Professional or Master teacher certificate; *and*
      7. Has completed the 4 mandatory trainings during the 5 years prior to receipt of application.
      8. For the 1-year extension, official transcripts—showing the completion of 3 semester hours of an approved Alaska studies course and the completion of 3 semester hours of an approved Alaska multicultural course—must be received by the Teacher Certification office prior to the expiration date of the Initial certificate.
         a. An applicant who has satisfied the Alaska studies and Alaska multicultural coursework requirements at the time of application will be issued an Initial/3-Year teacher certificate.
II. Initial/Out-of-State Teacher Certificate (valid 1 year; may be extended twice for a total of 3 full years; end dates of extensions are June 30 and December 31 of the given year)
   A. Requirements—Candidate:
      1. Has completed a bachelor's degree from a regionally accredited university;
      2. Has never held an Alaska teacher certificate; *and*
      3. Holds a current, valid out-of-state teacher certificate at the time the applicant's contract for instructional services begins in an Alaska public school district.
         a. Out-of-country certificates will not be accepted.
      4. To extend the 1-year certificate for an additional year, the applicant must obtain passing scores on an approved basic competency exam.
      5. To extend the 2-year certificate for an additional year, the applicant must:
         a. Complete 3 semester hours of an approved Alaska studies course; *and*
         b. Complete 3 semester hours of an approved Alaska multicultural course.

6. Endorsements placed on an Initial/Out-of-State teacher certificate will reflect the endorsements on the applicant's out-of-state certificate.
    a. If an applicant holds more than 1 valid out-of-state certificate, the applicant must choose which out-of-state certificate to submit with the Initial application.

III. Initial/Program Enrollment Teacher Certificate (valid 1 year; may be reissued twice for a total of 2 1-year extensions)
    A. Requirements—Candidate:
        1. Has completed a bachelor's degree from a regionally accredited university;
        2. Is enrolled in a state-approved teacher preparation program;
            a. Program enrollment may not be used for individuals enrolled in special education programs; rather, they must complete their program prior to applying for the Initial certificate.
        3. Has been offered a certified teaching position by an Alaska public school district;
        4. Has obtained passing scores on an approved basic competency exam (for details, consult https://education.alaska.gov/teachercertification/praxis);
        5. Has obtained passing scores on an approved Content Area Exam;
        6. Has included the Proof of Program Enrollment form in the application packet, completed by the correct university official;
            and
        7. Has obtained from the hiring district a completed District Request & Assurance form, signed by the district superintendent or human resources director, attesting to the applicant's 5 years of subject matter experience (can include undergraduate coursework).
        8. For the first 1-year extension, the certificate holder must submit the following items to the Teacher Certification office prior to expiration date of the Initial Proof of Program Enrollment teaching certificate:
            a. An updated Proof of Program Enrollment form;
                and
            b. An updated transcript showing progress toward the completion of a state-approved teacher preparation program.
        9. For the second 1-year extension, the certificate holder must submit the following:
            a. A State-Approved Program Verification form;
            b. Official transcripts showing 3 semester hours of an approved Alaska studies course and 3 semester hours of an approved Alaska multicultural course.
                and
            c. Transcripts showing completion of the teacher preparation program.

IV. Initial/Reemployment Teacher Certificate (valid 1 year; nonrenewable and not eligible for extension)
    A. Requirements—Candidate:
        1. Has never held a Reemployment teacher certificate in Alaska;
            and
        2. Has held an Alaska teacher certificate that was valid for at least 2 years.

3. The most recent Alaska teacher certificate held by candidate must have expired more than 1 year prior to the date of application.

4. Endorsements placed on an Initial/Reemployment certificate will reflect the endorsements on the applicant's previous Alaska teacher certificate. No endorsements may be added or removed during the life of the Reemployment certificate.

5. An applicant who has held a Reemployment certificate is no longer eligible for another Initial certificate, but must apply for a Professional teacher certificate to continue teaching.

6. An applicant is eligible to apply only for the Professional 5-year certificate and will not qualify for another Initial certificate unless the applicant meets every requirement for the Professional *except* 2 full years of certified, full-time equivalent (FTE) teaching experience. Under that circumstance, the applicant must apply for the Second Initial certificate.

B. Additional Requirements

1. Special Education—applicants who wish to teach special education to children with disabilities must, in addition to meeting other requirements for teacher certification, secure an endorsement based upon completion of an approved teacher-training program in special education.

   a. Preschool Special Education—those who wish to teach preschool children with special needs and who are not eligible for an endorsement in preschool special education must have completed at least 6 semester hours in early childhood special education in addition to holding a teaching certificate with a special education endorsement. This does not constitute an endorsement in Early Childhood Special Education.

2. Gifted—applicants who wish to teach gifted children must, in addition to meeting requirements for teacher certification, have completed at least 6 semester hours in gifted education. This does not constitute an endorsement.

3. Vocational Education—applicants who wish to teach vocational trades must have an endorsement in vocational education or a Type M Limited Certificate.

V. Second Initial Teacher Certificate (valid 3 years; nonrenewable)

A. Requirements—Candidate:

1. Has held an Initial or Provisional teacher certificate;

2. Has passing scores on an approved basic competency exam (for details, consult https://education.alaska.gov/TeacherCertification/praxis.html);

3. Has completed a teacher preparation program as verified by a State-Approved Program Verification form;
   and

4. Presents official transcripts showing 3 semester hours of approved Alaska studies coursework; 3 semester hours of approved Alaska multicultural coursework; and 6 semester hours of coursework completed in the 5 years prior to application (recency credit).

5. If the applicant has held a Professional or regular Type A teacher certificate, the certificate must have expired more than 1 year prior to the date of application.

Professional and Master Teacher Certificates

I. Professional Teacher Certificate (valid 5 years; renewable)
   A. Requirements—Candidate:
      1. Has completed a bachelor's degree from a regionally accredited university;
      2. Has completed a state-approved teacher preparation program;
      3. Has passing scores on an approved basic competency exam (BCE) (for details, consult https://education.alaska.gov/teachercertification/praxis);
      4. Has passing scores on an approved Content Area Exam;
      5. Has completed 3 semester hours of an approved Alaska studies course;
      6. Has completed 3 semester hours of an approved Alaska multicultural course;
      7. Has completed 6 semester hours of college coursework within the 5 years prior to application;
      8. Has 2 years of teaching experience in a state-approved or accredited school while holding a teaching certificate;
         and
      9. Has completed the 4 mandatory trainings during the 5 years prior to receipt of application.
   B. Renewal requirements: Prior to the expiration date of the certificate, applicant must:
      1. Earn 6 semester hours of renewal credit taken during the life of the certificate being renewed.
         a. A minimum of 3 semester hours must be upper-division or graduate credit.
         b. The remaining 3 semester hours may be:
            i. Either lower-division or upper-division credits as shown on official transcript;
            ii. Continuing education units (CEUs) as defined at https://education.alaska.gov/teachercertification/non-academic-credit-CEU-info;
            iii. Nonacademic credits (for which applicant must receive pre-approval and must pre-pay), as outlined at https://education.alaska.gov/TeacherCertification/forms/Non-Academic-Credit-Workshops.docx.
         c. The 6 renewal credits earned must be:
            i. Related to the certificated person's employment at the time of renewal, if that employment requires a certificate;
            ii. Related to the certificated person's endorsements;
               or
            iii. A required element of a program that will lead to an endorsement under 4 AAC 12.395 that the certificated person seeks to acquire.
      2. Present verification of current employment in an Alaska public school district in a position requiring a certificate;
         a. If an applicant is not employed in this capacity at the time of renewal, a fingerprint card will be required.
      3. Complete application and pay all fees; fees are nonrefundable.
         and

        4.   Complete mandatory training as shown at https://education.alaska.gov/teachercertification/mandatorytraining.

   C.   Additional Requirements—See Initial Teacher Certificates, IV, B, 1–3, above.

II.   Master Teacher Certificate (valid 10 years; renewable)

Note: All endorsements for which an applicant was eligible on a Professional teacher certificate can be added to this certificate, in addition to the endorsement for National Board Certification.

   A.   Requirements—Candidate must:
1. Meet all requirements for the Professional certificate;
2. Hold a current Initial or Professional certificate;
3. Hold current National Board Certification issued by National Board for Professional Teaching Standards (NBPTS);
4. Complete application and pay all fees, all of which are nonrefundable; *and*
5. Have completed the 4 mandatory trainings during the 5 years prior to receipt of application (for applications on and after June 30, 2017).

   B.   Renewal requirements—Candidate must:
1. Hold a current, renewed National Board Certification;
2. Have completed 6 semester hours of renewal credit taken during the life of the Master certificate being renewed, of which a minimum of 3 semester hours must be upper-division or graduate credit;
3. Present verification of employment in an Alaska public school district in a position requiring a certificate;
   a. If an applicant is not employed in this capacity at the time of renewal, fingerprint cards will be required.
   and
4. Complete application and pay all fees; fees are nonrefundable.
5. The 6 renewal credits earned must be:
   a. Related to the certificated person's employment at the time of renewal, if that employment requires a certificate;
   b. Related to the certificated person's endorsements; *or*
   c. A required element of a program that will lead to an endorsement under 4 AAC 12.395 that the certificated person seeks to acquire.
6. If the requirements to renew a Master certificate have not been met, an applicant must meet all current renewal requirements for the Professional certificate.

   C.   Additional Requirements—See Initial Teacher Certificates, IV, B, 1–3, above.

Administrative Certificates

I.   Type B Administrative Certificate (valid 5 years; renewable)

   A.   Requirements—Candidate:
1. Has at least 3 years of experience as a certificated teacher or special service provider;

2. Has completed an approved teacher-education program in school administration;
3. Has completed a master's or higher degree from a regionally accredited institution;
4. Has completed a state-approved, university-based educator preparation program;
5. Has completed 6 semester hours or 9 quarter hours of credit earned during the 5-year period preceding the date of application;
   a. See Provisional Type B Administrator certificate, directly below.
6. Has completed 3 semester hours of approved Alaska studies and 3 semester hours of approved multicultural education/cross-cultural communications;
   a. See Provisional Type B Administrator certificate, directly below.
7. Has completed application packet, which includes a signed and notarized application, the State-Approved Program Verification form, official transcripts, 2 sets of completed fingerprint cards, and processing fees, all of which are nonrefundable;
   and
8. Has completed the 4 mandatory trainings during the 5 years prior to receipt of application (for applications on and after June 30, 2017). Note: Trainings are not required under the reemployment option for this certificate.

B. Renewal Requirements: Prior to the expiration date of the certificate, applicant must:
1. Have completed 6 semester hours of renewal credit taken during the life of the certificate being renewed, of which a minimum of 3 semester hours must be upper-division or graduate credit;
2. Present verification of current employment in an Alaska public school district in a position requiring a certificate;
   a. If an applicant is not employed in this capacity at the time of renewal, a fingerprint card will be required.
   and
3. Complete application and pay all fees; fees are nonrefundable.
4. The 6 renewal credits earned must be:
   a. Related to the certificated person's employment at the time of renewal, if that employment requires a certificate;
   b. Related to the certificated person's endorsements;
      or
   c. A required element of a program that will lead to an endorsement under 4 AAC 12.395 that the certificated person seeks to acquire.

II. Provisional Type B Administrator Certificate (valid 2 years; nonrenewable)
   A. This certificate is for applicants meeting all other requirements for certification, but who lack 6 semester hours of credit earned during the 5-year period preceding the date of application, or who lack 3 semester hours of credit in Alaska studies and/or 3 semester hours of credit in multicultural education or cross-cultural communications.
   B. In order to avoid a lapse in certification, the Provisional Type B Administrator certificate holder must submit official transcripts to the Teacher Certification office showing the completion of 3 semester hours of approved Alaska studies coursework

and the completion of 3 semester hours of approved Alaska multicultural coursework prior to the expiration date of the Provisional certificate.

    1. In addition, prior to the expiration date of their certificate, the Provisional certificate holder must apply for the 5-year Regular Type B Administrative certificate.

  C. Candidates must have completed the 4 mandatory trainings during the 5 years prior to receipt of application.

III. Superintendent Endorsement

  A. Requirements—Candidate:

    1. Has completed a State-Approved Program Verification form showing completion of an approved superintendency program from a regionally accredited university;

    2. Has at least 5 years of employment as a classroom teacher or administrator;

      a. At least 3 years must have been satisfactory employment as a teacher with a teaching certificate or comparable certificate issued by another state; and at least 1 year must have been satisfactory employment as an administrator with a Type B certificate or comparable certificate from another state.

      and

    3. Has completed the 4 mandatory trainings during the 5 years prior to receipt of application.

IV. Special Education Administrator Endorsement

  A. Requirements—Candidate:

    1. Has completed a State-Approved Program Verification form showing completion of an approved special education administrative program from a regionally accredited university;

    2. Has at least 3 years of employment as a certified special education teacher or school psychologist, with a teaching or special services certificate or comparable certificate issued by another state;

      and

    3. Has completed the 4 mandatory trainings during the 5 years prior to receipt of application.

V. Director of Special Education

  A. Requirements for applicants who wish to be employed solely as the administrator or director of special education and are not eligible for a special education administrator endorsement:

    1. Possess both a Type B certificate and a teaching certificate endorsed for special education or for a related services specialty. (This does not constitute an endorsement.)

      a. To be assigned as a classroom teacher in Alaska, applicant must have a valid teacher certificate (Initial, Professional, or Master), since the Type B certificate does not allow the holder to be a classroom teacher.

      b. Applicants who currently hold a valid Alaska teaching certificate and are applying for a Type B certificate are considered an initial applicant for the Type B.

2. Have completed the 4 mandatory trainings during the 5 years prior to receipt of application (for applications on and after June 30, 2017).

VI. Type C Special Services Certificate (valid 5 years; renewable)

A. Requirements—Candidate:

1. Has completed a program in a special service area;
2. Has a bachelor's or higher degree;
3. Has completed a state-approved, university-based preparation program;
4. Has completed 6 semester hours or 9 quarter hours of credit taken within the past 5 years;
5. Has completed 3 semester hours of approved Alaska studies and 3 semester hours of Alaska multicultural education/cross-cultural communications;
6. Has completed an application packet, which includes a signed and notarized application, a State-Approved Program Verification form, official transcripts, a fingerprint card, and fees, all of which are nonrefundable;
   and
7. Has completed the 4 mandatory trainings during the 5 years prior to receipt of application. Note: Trainings are not required under the reemployment option for this certificate.

B. Renewal Requirements: Prior to the expiration date of the certificate, applicant must:

1. Have completed 6 semester hours of renewal credit taken during the life of the certificate being renewed, of which a minimum of 3 semester hours must be upper-division or graduate credit;
2. Present verification of current employment in an Alaska public school district in a position requiring a certificate;
   a. If an applicant is not employed in this capacity at the time of renewal, a fingerprint card will be required.
   and
3. Complete application and pay all fees; fees are nonrefundable. (For Advanced Type C renewal applicants, a completed application includes a copy of the certificate showing renewed National Board Certification. The expiration date of the renewed Advanced Type C certificate will be the same as the National Board Certification expiration date.)
4. The 6 renewal credits earned must be:
   a. Related to the certificated person's employment at the time of renewal, if that employment requires a certificate;
   b. Related to the certificated person's endorsements;
      or
   c. A required element of a program that will lead to an endorsement under 4 AAC 12.395 that the certificated person seeks to acquire.

VII. Provisional Type C Special Services Certificate (valid 2 years)

A. This certificate is for applicants meeting all other requirements for certification, but who lack 6 semester hours of credit earned during the 5-year period preceding the date of application; or who lack 3 semester hours of credit in Alaska studies and/or 3 semester hours of credit in multicultural education or cross-cultural communications.

B. In order to avoid a lapse in certification, the Provisional Type C Special Services certificate holder must submit official transcripts to the Teacher Certification office showing the completion of 3 semester hours of approved Alaska studies coursework and the completion of 3 semester hours of approved Alaska multicultural coursework prior to the expiration date of the Provisional certificate.

    1. In addition, prior to the expiration date of their certificate, the Provisional certificate holder must apply for the 5-year regular Type C Special Services certificate.

  C. Candidates must have completed the 4 mandatory trainings during the 5 years prior to receipt of application.

VIII. Initial Special Services (Type C) Endorsements

  A. Endorsements under a Type C certificate include Audiology, Occupational Therapy, Physical Therapy, School Nursing, School Psychology, School Psychometry, School Social Work, Speech Pathology, School Counselor, and Library Science-Media.

    1. School Psychology Endorsement Requirements

      a. Candidate must also hold a master's or higher degree in school psychology; be recommended by an institution whose school psychology program has been approved by the National Association of School Psychologists (NCATE) or the American Psychological Association; and have completed a 1200-hour internship (with 600 of the hours in a school setting);

        or

        Be certified under the certification system of the National Association of School Psychologists.

    2. Speech, Language, or Hearing Endorsement Requirements

      a. Candidate must hold either a master's or higher degree with a major emphasis in speech-language pathology, audiology, or speech-language and hearing science;

        or

        Possess certification of clinical competence from the American Speech-Language-Hearing Association.

      b. Candidate must also be recommended for endorsement by an institution with a program approved by NCATE or the American Speech-Language-Hearing Association.

    3. Other Special Service Endorsement Requirements

      a. Candidates who wish to be employed to provide such services as speech or language pathology, school psychology, school counseling, orientation and mobility, psychometry, library and/or media services, or school nursing, must have a Type C Special Services certificate endorsed in the field of employment.

      b. A Type C certificate does not qualify the holder for assignment as a classroom teacher or school administrator.

IX. Reemployment Certificate—Type B and C (valid 1 year, effective the date the complete application packet is received in the office of Teacher Education and Certification; nonrenewable)

  A. Applicants who held a certificate that has been expired for over 12 months may be eligible for the Reemployment certificate. During the year of validity, the applicant must complete all current requirements for the Regular 5-year certificate and submit an application.

  1. See Administrative Certificates, I, Type B Administrative Certificate; and VI, Type C Special Services Certificate, above, for details.
B. After holding a Reemployment certificate, applicants are only eligible to apply for the Regular 5-year certificate and will not qualify for Provisional certification.
C. The endorsements on the Reemployment certificate will be the same as those on the applicant's expired administrative or special services certificate.
D. During the life of the Reemployment certificate no endorsements may be added or removed.

Other Certificates

For details, consult https://education.alaska.gov/teachercertification/certification.

  I. Retired (Lifetime) Certificate
 II. Type E Early Childhood Certificate
III. District-sponsored certificates
   A. Type M Limited Certificate
      1. Career and Technical Education
      2. Recognized Language Expert
      3. Junior Reserve Officer Training Corps (JROTC)
   B. Type I Limited Certificate (Instructional Aide)
   C. Type W Limited Certificate (World Language)

Arizona

Standard Professional Teaching Certificates

I. Standard Professional Teaching Certificates (valid for 12 years; may be renewed)
   A. Early Childhood (Birth–Grade 3 or Age 8)
   B. Elementary (K–8)
   C. Secondary (6–12)
   D. Mild/Moderate Disabilities (K–12)
   E. Moderate/Severe Disabilities (K–12)
   F. Hearing Impaired (Birth–Grade 12)
   G. Visually Impaired (Birth–Grade 12)
   H. Early Childhood Special Education (Birth–Grade 3 or Age 8)
   I. PreK–12 Art Education
   J. PreK–12 Dance Education
   K. PreK–12 Music Education
   L. PreK–12 Physical Education
   M. PreK–12 Theatre Education

II. Specific information on coursework and exam requirements for Standard Professional Teaching Certificates may be downloaded at http://www.azed.gov/educator-certification/forms-and-information/certificates/.

III. The requirements for a Standard Professional Teaching Certificate are:
   A. A valid Arizona Department of Public Safety IVP fingerprint clearance card
   B. A bachelor's or more advanced degree from an accredited institution
   C. One of the following:
      1. Completion of a teacher preparation program in the specified certification area from an accredited institution or a Board-approved teacher preparation program; or
      2. Completion of the specified Board-approved or accredited teacher education coursework or trainings and 2 years of full-time teaching experience in the specified certificate area.
   D. A passing score on the required Arizona Professional Knowledge Exam or qualification for an exam waiver. The Professional Knowledge Exam requirement may be waived with 1 of the following:
      1. A passing score on a substantially similar Professional Knowledge Exam from another state; or
      2. A National Board for Professional Teaching Standards certificate in the appropriate area; or
      3. Three years of full-time teaching experience in any state in the comparable area of certification.
   E. A passing score on the required Arizona Subject Knowledge Exam or qualification for an exam waiver. For Secondary Certificates: If an exam is not offered in the

subject area, 24 semester hours of coursework in the subject is required. The Subject Knowledge Exam requirement may be waived with 1 of the following:

1. A passing score on a substantially similar subject knowledge exam from another state or agency; or
2. A National Board for Professional Teaching Standards certificate in the appropriate area; or
3. A bachelor's, master's, or doctoral degree in the subject area; or
4. Three years of full-time teaching experience in any state in the appropriate subject area; or
5. Experience teaching courses relevant to the appropriate subject area for the last 2 consecutive years, and for a total of at least 3 years, at 1 or more accredited postsecondary institutions; or
6. Demonstration of expertise in the appropriate subject area through 5 years of relevant work experience.
7. If a Subject Knowledge Exam is not offered in a foreign language, a passing score of Advanced Low on the American Council for the Teaching of Foreign Languages (ACTFL) speaking and writing exams may substitute for 24 semester hours of coursework.
8. Verification of Native American Language proficiency from an official designated by the tribe may substitute for 24 semester hours of coursework.

F. The Standard Professional Visually Impaired Special Education, Birth–Grade 12 Certificate also requires demonstration of proficiency in Braille.

G. Within 3 years of the date of certificate issuance, Standard Professional, Early Childhood, and Elementary Certificates require completion of:
1. Three semester hours of college coursework or 45 hours of training in the science of reading instruction, including research-based systematic phonics; and
2. Three semester hours of college coursework or 45 hours of training in instructional practices and interventions to support students with reading difficulties, including dyslexia.

H. Within 3 years of the date of certificate issuance, all Standard Professional Teaching Certificates require:
1. A class or exam covering the provisions and principles of the constitutions of Arizona and the United States, unless the applicant is certified to teach an academic course on history, government, social studies, citizenship, law, or civics. In that case, the requirement must be completed in 1 year.

I. Educators who hold a valid comparable out-of-state teaching certificate and who are in good standing in their state may qualify for the equivalent Standard Professional Teaching Certificate under reciprocity rules. Teachers who qualify under reciprocity are exempt from all requirements except for the requirement to hold a valid Arizona Department of Public Safety IVP fingerprint clearance card and to complete the Arizona and US Constitutions requirements within the allowable time frame.

Additional Secondary Teaching Certificates

I. All certificates require a valid Arizona Department of Public Safety IVP fingerprint clearance card.

II. Specialized Secondary Certificate—Science, Technology, Engineering, or Mathematics (STEM), Grades 6–12 (valid for 12 years; may be renewed)

   A. Demonstration of expertise in a STEM subject through 1 of the following:

   1. A bachelor's, master's, or doctoral degree and 24 semester hours of relevant coursework in an academic subject that is specific to science, technology, engineering, or mathematics; or

   2. Teaching experience in science, technology, engineering, or mathematics for the last 2 consecutive years and for a total of 3 years, at 1 or more accredited postsecondary institutions

   B. Five years of verified work experience in science, technology, engineering, or mathematics.

III. Subject Matter Expert Standard Teaching Certificate, Grades 6–12 (valid for 12 years; may be renewed)

   A. A bachelor's degree.

   B. One of the following:

   1. Experience teaching the subject area of certification for the last 2 consecutive years, and for a total of 3 years, at 1 or more accredited postsecondary institutions; or

   2. A bachelor's, master's, or doctoral degree from an accredited institution in the specific subject area of certification; or

   3. Verification of expertise in the subject area of certification through 5 years of work experience relevant to the subject area.

   C. The Subject Matter Expert Standard Teaching Certificate requires passing the Arizona Professional Knowledge Secondary Exam, or qualification for an exam waiver, within 2 years from date of issuance of the certificate. Individuals who qualify with postsecondary teaching experience are exempt from this requirement.

Other Teaching Certificates

I. All certificates require a valid Arizona Department of Public Safety IVP fingerprint clearance card.

II. Detailed information on requirements to qualify for and maintain these certificates may be downloaded on the certification website at http://www.azed.gov/educator-certification/forms-and-information/certificates/.

III. Substitute Certificate, PreK–12 (valid for 6 years; may be renewed).

   A. The requirement is:

   1. A bachelor's degree

IV. Emergency Substitute Certificate, PreK–12 (valid for 1 school year or part thereof; nonrenewable)

   A. The certificate authorizes the holder to substitute teach only in the district that verifies that an emergency employment situation exists.

    B. The requirements are:
        1. A high school diploma, GED, or associate degree
        2. Verification from a district superintendent that an emergency employment situation exists

  V. Emergency Teaching Certificate, PreK–12 (valid for 1 school year or part thereof; nonrenewable)
    A. The certificate authorizes the holder to enter into a teaching contract only in the district that verifies an emergency employment situation exists.
    B. The requirements are:
        1. A bachelor's degree
        2. Verification from a district superintendent or charter school administrator that an emergency employment situation exists

  VI. Alternative Teaching, PreK–12 (valid for 2 years; may be extended yearly for no more than 2 consecutive years)
    A. The certificate entitles the holder to enter into a teaching contract while completing the requirements for an Arizona teaching certificate.
    B. The requirements are:
        1. A bachelor's degree
        2. Verification of enrollment in an Arizona Board of Education–approved alternative path to certification program or a Board-approved educator preparation program

  VII. Standard Adult Education Certificate (valid for 12 years; may be renewed)
    A. The certificate requires a bachelor's degree.

  VIII. Junior Reserve Officer Training Corps Teaching Certificate, Grades 9–12 (valid for 12 years; may be renewed). The requirements are:
    A. Verification from a school district that it offers an approved Junior Reserve Officer Training Corps program of instruction in which the applicant will be teaching
    B. Verification by the district that the applicant meets the work experience required through military service

  IX. Athletic Coaching Certificate, Grades 7–12 (valid for 12 years; may be renewed). The requirements are:
    A. Valid certification in first aid and CPR
    B. Completion of required training or coursework
    C. Verification of 250 hours of verified coaching experience in the sport to be coached

  X. International Teaching Certificate (valid for the length of the certificate holder's visa, not to exceed 12 years)
    A. The certificate is issued to teachers who are contracted through the foreign teacher exchange program.
    B. The requirements are:
        1. Verification that the applicant has completed teacher preparation in the home country or country of legal residence that is comparable to the requirements to qualify for an Arizona teaching certificate.
        2. A valid non-immigrating visa issued by the United States Department of State or United States Citizenship and Immigration Services for international teachers.

3.   Verification that the applicant has been contracted by an Arizona school through a foreign teacher program.

XI.   Native American Language Certificate, PreK–12 (valid for 12 years; may be renewed)

    A.   The certificate requires verification of proficiency in a Native American language by a person, persons, or entity designated by the appropriate tribe.

XII.   Student Teaching Intern Certificate, PreK–12 (valid for 1 year; may be extended for 1 year)

    A.   The certificate is optional and entitles the holder to perform teaching duties under the supervision of a program supervisor.

    B.   The requirements are:

        1.   Verification of enrollment in the culminating student teaching capstone experience of an Arizona Board of Education–approved educator preparation program (EPP). The program must have a Board-approved written supervision plan for student teachers.

        2.   A request for issuance of the Student Teaching Intern Certificate from the district or charter school superintendent and EPP

        3.   Verification that the applicant has completed coursework with a minimum GPA of 3.0 on a 4.0 scale, or the equivalent

        4.   A passing score on the required Arizona Professional Knowledge Exam

        5.   A passing score on the required Arizona Subject Knowledge Exam

XIII.   Classroom-Based Standard Teaching Certificate (valid for 12 years; may be renewed). The requirements are:

    A.   A bachelor's degree

    B.   Successful completion of an Arizona Board of Education–approved classroom-based alternative preparation program

    C.   Verification of satisfactory progress and achievement with students

    D.   Demonstration of subject knowledge proficiency by passing the required Arizona Subject Knowledge Exam or qualifying for a waiver of the exam requirement

    E.   Demonstration of professional knowledge proficiency by passing the required Arizona Professional Knowledge Exam requirement or qualifying for a waiver of the exam requirement

Endorsements

I.   Endorsements are posted to valid educator certificates. Each is automatically renewed with the certificate on which it is posted.

II.   Applicants who hold a valid, comparable endorsement from another state and are in good standing in that state may qualify to add the equivalent endorsement in Arizona under the rules of reciprocity.

III.   Detailed information on the requirements for endorsements may be downloaded from the certification website at http://www.azed.gov/educator-certification/forms-and-information/endorsements/.

IV.   Special subject endorsements, PreK–12

    A.   Special subject endorsements are issued in the areas of art, computer science, dance, dramatic arts, music, or physical education.

    B. The requirements are:
       1. An Elementary, Secondary, or Special Education Certificate
       2. One course in methods of teaching the subject at the elementary level and 1 course in methods of teaching the subject at the secondary level
       3. A passing score on the appropriate Arizona Subject Knowledge Exam, qualification for a waiver of the Subject Knowledge Exam requirement, or completion of 30 semester hours of coursework in the subject area which may include the methods courses

V. Mathematics Endorsement, K–8. The requirements are:
    A. An Elementary or Special Education Certificate
    B. Three years of full-time teaching
    C. Completion of 6 semester hours of specified mathematics education coursework
    D. One of the following:
       1. Eighteen semester hours of specified mathematics content coursework; or
       2. A passing score on the Arizona Subject Knowledge Middle Grades Mathematics Exam or qualification for an exam waiver

VI. Reading Endorsements, K–8. The requirements are:
    A. An Elementary, Special Education, or Early Childhood Certificate
    B. Three years of full-time teaching experience
    C. Three semester hours of a supervised field experience or practicum in reading for grades K–8
    D. One of the following:
       1. Twenty-one semester hours of specified reading coursework; or
       2. A passing score on the Arizona Subject Knowledge Reading Endorsement K–8 Exam or qualification for an exam waiver

VII. Reading Endorsement, 6–12. The requirements are:
    A. An Elementary, Secondary, or Special Education Certificate
    B. Three years of full-time teaching experience
    C. Three semester hours of a supervised field experience or practicum in reading completed for grades 6–12
    D. One of the following:
       1. Twenty-one semester hours of specified reading coursework; or
       2. A passing score on the Arizona Subject Knowledge Reading Endorsement 6–12 Exam or qualification for an exam waiver

VIII. Reading Endorsement, K–2. The requirements are:
    A. An Elementary, Secondary, Special Education, or Early Childhood Certificate
    B. Three years of full-time teaching experience
    C. Three semester hours of supervised field experience or practicum in reading for grades K–5
    D. Three semester hours of supervised field experience or practicum for grades 6–12
    E. One of the following:
       1. Completion of 24 semester hours of specified reading coursework; or
       2. A passing score on the Arizona Subject Knowledge Reading Endorsement K–8 and Reading Endorsement 6–12 Exams, or qualification for a waiver of the exam requirement

IX. Elementary Foreign Language Endorsement, K–8. The requirements are:
   A. An Elementary, Secondary, or Special Education Certificate
   B. Verification of proficiency in speaking, reading, and writing a language other than English, verified by an accredited institution. Native American language proficiency shall be verified by an official designated by the appropriate tribe.
   C. Three semester hours of courses in the methods of teaching a foreign language at the elementary level

X. Provisional Bilingual Endorsement, PreK–12
   A. The Provisional Bilingual endorsement is valid for 3 years and is nonrenewable.
   B. The requirements are:
      1. An Arizona Elementary, Secondary, Supervisor, Principal, Superintendent, Special Education, Early Childhood, Arts Education, or Career and Technical Education (CTE) Certificate; and
      2. Proficiency in a spoken language other than English

XI. Bilingual Endorsement, PreK–12. The requirements are:
   A. An Arizona Elementary, Secondary, Supervisor, Principal, Superintendent, Special Education, Early Childhood, Arts Education, or CTE Certificate
   B. Proficiency in a spoken language other than English
   C. Completion of a bilingual education program from an accredited institution or 18 semester hours of specified bilingual education courses
   D. A practicum in a bilingual program or 2 years of bilingual teaching experience

XII. Provisional English as a Second Language (ESL) Endorsement, PreK–12
   A. The Provisional ESL endorsement is valid for 3 years and is nonrenewable.
   B. The requirements are:
      1. An Elementary, Secondary, Supervisor, Principal, Superintendent, Special Education, Early Childhood, Arts Education, or CTE Certificate
      2. Six semester hours of ESL courses, including at least 1 course in methods of teaching ESL students

XIII. English as a Second Language (ESL) Endorsement, PreK–12. The requirements are:
   A. An Elementary, Secondary, Supervisor, Principal, Superintendent, Special Education, Early Childhood, Arts Education, or CTE Certificate
   B. Completion of an ESL education program from an accredited institution or 18 semester hours of specified ESL coursework
   C. Three semester hours of practicum or 2 years of verified ESL or bilingual teaching experience
   D. Second-language learning experience. For requirements, please refer to http://www.azed.gov/educator-certification/forms-and-information/endorsements/.

XIV. Provisional Gifted Endorsement, PreK–12
   A. The Provisional Gifted Endorsement is valid for 3 years and is nonrenewable.
   B. The requirements are:
      1. A valid Elementary, Secondary, Early Childhood, or Special Education Certificate
      2. One of the following:
         a. Ninety clock hours of verified in-service training in gifted education; or
         b. Six semester hours of courses in gifted education

XV.   Gifted Endorsement, PreK–12. The requirements are:
   A.   An Elementary, Secondary, Early Childhood, or Special Education Certificate
   B.   One of the following:
      1.   A minimum of 180 clock hours of verified in-service training in gifted education; or
      2.   Twelve semester hours of courses in gifted education. Up to 6 semester hours of coursework may be waived with district in-service training.

XVI.   Provisional Early Childhood Endorsement, Birth–Age 8 or Grade 3
   A.   The Provisional Early Childhood Endorsement is valid for 3 years and is nonrenewable.
   B.   The requirements are:
      1.   An Elementary or Special Education Certificate
      2.   A passing score on the Arizona Subject Knowledge Early Childhood Education Exam or qualification for a waiver of the exam requirement

XVII.   Early Childhood Endorsement, Birth–Age 8 or Grade 3. The requirements are:
   A.   An Elementary or Special Education Certificate
   B.   A passing score on the Arizona Subject Knowledge Early Childhood Education Exam or qualification for a waiver of the exam requirement
   C.   One of the following:
      1.   Completion of 21 semester hours of specified coursework; 4 semester hours of practicum or 1 year of teaching in Birth–PreK; and 4 semester hours of student teaching or 1 year of teaching in K–3
      2.   A passing score on the Arizona Professional Knowledge Early Childhood Exam or qualification for an exam waiver; 4 semester hours of practicum or 1 year of teaching in Birth–PreK; and 4 semester hours of practicum or 1 year of teaching in K–3
      3.   Three years of teaching experience in Birth–Grade 3 or Age 8

XVIII.   Library Media Specialist Endorsement, K–12. The requirements are:
   A.   An Arizona Elementary, Secondary, Early Childhood, or Special Education Certificate
   B.   A passing score on the Arizona Subject Knowledge Library Media Specialist Exam or qualification for a waiver of the Subject Knowledge Exam
   C.   One year of teaching experience

XIX.   Driver's Education Endorsement. The requirements are:
   A.   An Arizona teaching certificate
   B.   An Arizona driver's license
   C.   A 3-semester-hour course or 45 hours of training in safety education
   D.   A 3-semester-hour course or 45 hours of training in driver and highway safety education
   E.   A 3-semester-hour course or 45 hours of training in driver education laboratory experience
   F.   A driving record with less than 7 violation points and no revocation or suspensions within 2 years preceding the application

XX.   Cooperative Education
   A.   A Provisional or Standard CTE Certificate
   B.   A course in CTE

XXI. Computer Science Endorsement, PreK– 8. The requirements are:
  A. An Arizona Standard Professional Elementary, Middle Grades, Secondary, Special Education, or PreK–12 teaching certificate
  B. Nine semester hours of specified coursework in computer science
    1. Completion of a training program through an Arizona public local education agency or an accredited institution may substitute for the semester hours of coursework.
    2. Fifteen clock hours of training, or the equivalent competency-based credential, is equivalent to 1 semester hour of coursework.
XXII. Computer Science Endorsement, Grades 6–12. The requirements are:
  A. An Arizona Standard Professional Elementary, Middle Grades, Secondary, Hearing Impaired, Visually Impaired, Mild/Moderate Disabilities, Moderate/Severe Disabilities, or PreK–12 teaching certificate
  B. Twelve semester hours of specified coursework in computer science
    1. Completion of a training program through an Arizona public local education agency or an accredited institution may substitute for the semester hours of coursework.
    2. Fifteen clock hours of training, or the equivalent competency-based credential, is equivalent to 1 semester hour of coursework.
XXIII. Provisional Mild/Moderate Disabilities Endorsement, PreK–12
  A. The Provisional Mild/Moderate Disabilities Endorsement is valid for 3 years and is nonrenewable.
  B. The requirements are:
    1. An Arizona Standard Professional Early Childhood, Elementary, Middle Grades, Secondary, Visually Impaired, Hearing Impaired, Early Childhood Special Education, or Moderate/Severe Disabilities Certificate
    2. Three years of full-time teaching experience in PreK–12
    3. Six semester hours of specified coursework in special education
    4. Fifteen clock hours of practicum in mild/moderate disabilities special education, which may be included in the 6 semester hours of coursework
XXIV. Mild/Moderate Disabilities Endorsement, PreK–12. The requirements are:
  A. An Arizona Standard Professional Early Childhood, Elementary, Middle Grades, Secondary, Visually Impaired, Hearing Impaired, Early Childhood Special Education, or Moderate/Severe Disabilities Certificate
  B. Three years of full-time teaching experience in PreK–12
  C. Fifteen semester hours of specified coursework in special education
  D. Forty-five clock hours of practicum in mild/moderate disabilities special education, which may be included in the 15 semester hours of coursework
XXV. Provisional Moderate/Severe Disabilities Endorsement, PreK–12
  A. The Provisional Moderate/Severe Disabilities Endorsement is valid for 3 years and is nonrenewable.
  B. The requirements are:
    1. An Arizona Standard Professional Early Childhood, Elementary, Middle Grades, Secondary, Visually Impaired, Hearing Impaired, Early Childhood Special Education, or Mild/Moderate Disabilities Certificate

2. Three years of full-time teaching experience in PreK–12
3. Six semester hours of specified coursework in special education
4. Fifteen clock hours of practicum in moderate/severe disabilities special education, which may be included in the 6 semester hours of coursework

XXVI. Moderate/Severe Disabilities Endorsement, PreK–12. The requirements are:
   A. An Arizona Standard Professional Early Childhood, Elementary, Middle Grades, Secondary, Visually Impaired, Hearing Impaired, Early Childhood Special Education, or Mild/Moderate Disabilities Certificate
   B. Three years of full-time teaching experience in PreK–12
   C. Fifteen semester hours of specified coursework in special education
   D. Forty-five clock hours of practicum in moderate/severe disabilities special education, which may be included in the 15 semester hours of coursework

XXVII. Deaf/Hard of Hearing Endorsement, Birth–Grade 12. The requirements are:
   A. A valid Standard Professional Early Childhood, Elementary, Middle Grades, Secondary, Mild/Moderate Disabilities, Moderate/Severe Disabilities, Early Childhood Special Education, Specialized Special Education, Cross-Categorical Special Education, or Visually Impaired Certificate
   B. Three years of full-time teaching experience in PreK–12
   C. Twenty-one semester hours of specified coursework in special education and deaf/hard of hearing education
   D. Ninety clock hours of practicum in deaf/hard of hearing education, which may be included in the 21 semester hours of specified coursework
   E. American Sign Language (ASL) learning experience. If the applicant meets this requirement by passing a Board-approved exam in ASL, they shall qualify for a Deaf/Hard of Hearing endorsement with an ASL proficiency designation.

XXVIII. Visually Impaired Endorsement, Birth–Grade 12. The requirements are:
   A. A valid Standard Professional Early Childhood, Elementary, Middle Grades, Secondary, Mild/Moderate Disabilities, Moderate/Severe Disabilities, Early Childhood Special Education, Specialized Special Education, Cross-Categorical Special Education, or Hearing Impaired Certificate
   B. Three years of full-time teaching experience in PreK–12
   C. Twenty-one semester hours of specified coursework in special education and visually impaired education
   D. Ninety clock hours of practicum in visually impaired education, which may be included in the 21 semester hours of specified coursework
   E. Demonstration of proficiency in Braille

Administrative Certificates

I. All certificates require a valid Arizona Department of Public Safety IVP fingerprint clearance card.
II. An applicant who holds a valid, comparable administrative certificate from another state and is in good standing with that state may qualify for the equivalent Arizona certificate under reciprocity rules.

III. The Arizona Administrator Exam requirements may be waived with 1 of the following:
   A. A passing score on a substantially similar administrator exam from another state; or
   B. Three years of full-time experience as an administrator in any state, including Arizona
IV. Standard Professional Supervisor Certificate, PreK–12 (valid for 12 years; may be renewed). The requirements are:
   A. A valid Arizona Early Childhood, Elementary, Secondary, Special Education, Career and Technical Education certificate or other professional certificate
   B. A master's or more advanced degree from an accredited institution
   C. Three years of verified full-time teaching or related education services experience in PreK–12
   D. Completion of a program in educational administration consisting of a minimum of 18 graduate semester hours of educational administration courses teaching the knowledge and skills described in Arizona's Professional Administrative Standards (R7–2-603, available at http://azsbe.az.gov/sites/default/files/media/Item4GCloseArticle6.pdf), and 3 semester hours of school law and 3 semester hours of school finance
   E. A practicum in educational administration or 2 years of verified educational administrative experience in grades PreK–12
   F. A passing score on the Arizona Supervisor, Principal, or Superintendent Exam or qualification for a waiver of the exam requirement
V. Standard Professional Principal Certificate, PreK–12 (valid 12 years; may be renewed). The requirements are:
   A. A master's or more advanced degree from an accredited institution
   B. Three years of verified full-time teaching experience in grades PreK–12
   C. Completion of a program in educational administration for principals including at least 30 graduate semester hours of educational administration courses teaching the knowledge and skills described in Arizona's Professional Administrative Standards (R7–2-603, available at http://azsbe.az.gov/sites/default/files/media/Item4GCloseArticle6.pdf) and 3 semester hours of school law and 3 semester hours of school finance
   D. A practicum as a principal or 2 years of experience as a PreK–12 principal or assistant principal under the supervision of a certified principal
   E. A passing score on either the Principal or Superintendent portion of the Arizona Educator Proficiency Assessments (AEPA) or qualification for a waiver of the exam requirement
VI. Superintendent Certificate, PreK–12 (valid 12 years; may be renewed). The requirements are:
   A. A master's or higher degree, including at least 60 graduate semester hours from an accredited institution
   B. Completion of a program in educational administration for superintendents including at least 36 graduate semester hours of educational administrative courses teaching the knowledge and skills described in Arizona's Professional Administrative Standards (R7–2-603, available at http://azsbe.az.gov/sites/default/files/media/

Item4GCloseArticle6.pdf) and 3 semester hours of school law and 3 semester hours of school finance

C. Three years of verified full-time teaching or related education services experience in PreK–12

D. A practicum as a superintendent or 2 years of verified experience as a superintendent, assistant superintendent, or associate superintendent in grades PreK–12

E. A passing score on the Arizona Superintendent Exam requirement or qualification for a waiver of the exam requirement

VII. Arizona issues Interim Supervisor, Interim Principal, and Interim Superintendent Certificates to individuals who are enrolled in Board-approved administrator preparation programs and are working under the direct supervision of a certified administrator or county school superintendent. Interim administrative certificates are valid for 1 year and may be extended yearly for no more than 2 consecutive years. Specific requirements for these certificates may be downloaded at http://www.azed.gov/educator-certification/forms-and-information/certificates/.

Professional Non-Teaching Certificate (PreK–12)

I. All certificates require a valid Arizona Department of Public Safety IVP fingerprint clearance card.

II. An applicant who holds a valid, comparable professional non-teaching certificate in another state and is in good standing in that state may qualify for the equivalent Arizona professional non-teaching certificate under reciprocity rules.

III. Standard School Psychologist Certificate, PreK–12 (valid for 12 years; may be renewed). The requirements are:

A. A master's or more advanced degree from an accredited institution

B. One of the following:

1. Completion of a graduate program in school psychology, consisting of at least 60 graduate semester hours; or

2. Completion of a doctoral program in psychology and completion of a retraining program in school psychology from an accredited institution or a Board-approved program with a letter of institutional endorsement from the head of the school psychology program; or

3. Five years of experience as a full-time school psychologist within the last 10 years; or

4. A Nationally Certified School Psychologist Credential; or

5. Diploma in school psychology from the American Board of School Psychology

C. One of the following:

1. A letter from a university department head or designee verifying completion of a supervised internship of at least 1,200 clock hours with a minimum of 600 of those hours in a school setting; or

2. A letter from a district superintendent, personnel director, or designee verifying 3 years of experience as a certified school psychologist within the last 10 years

IV. Standard School Counselor Certificate, PreK–12 (valid for 12 years; may be renewed). The requirements are:

A. A master's or more advanced degree

B. One of the following:

1. Completion of a graduate program in guidance and counseling; or

2. Completion of a graduate program in counseling, social work, or psychology, with 6 semester hours of courses in any of the following areas: school counseling, college and career guidance, or academic advising; or

3. A valid license as an associate counselor, professional counselor, master or clinical social worker, or marriage and family therapist issued by the Arizona Board for Behavioral Health Examiners, with 6 semester hours of courses in any of the following areas: school counseling, college and career guidance, or academic advising; or

4. Completion of a graduate program in academic advising and 6 semester hours of courses in school counseling in any of the following areas: social and emotional development, mental health counseling, trauma and disaster counseling, multiculturalism in counseling, theories of counseling, foundations of school counseling, or child and adolescent counseling.

C. One of the following is required within 3 years of issuance of the Standard School Counselor, PreK–12 Certificate:

1. Completion of a supervised counseling practicum in school counseling (official transcript[s] required); or

2. Two years of verified full-time experience as a school guidance counselor; or

3. Three years of verified full-time teaching experience.

D. The 6 semester hours of coursework described above in IV, B, 2–4 must be completed within 3 years of the date of issuance of the Standard School Counselor, PreK–12 Certificate.

V. Standard Speech-Language Pathologist Certificate, PreK–12 (valid for 12 years; may be renewed). The requirements are:

A. A master's or more advanced degree in speech pathology or communication disorders

B. A minimum of 250 clinical clock hours supervised by a university or a speech-language pathologist with a certificate of clinical competence

C. A certificate of clinical competence, a passing score on the national exam in speech pathology, or a passing score on the Arizona Speech and Language Impaired Exam

VI. Standard School Social Worker, PreK–12 (valid for 12 years; may be renewed). The requirements are:

A. A master's or more advanced degree in social work

B. Completion of 6 semester hours of practicum in social work in a school setting or 1 year of full-time experience as a social worker in a setting which primarily serves children in PreK–12.

Career and Technical Education Certificates

I. Career and Technical Education (CTE) Certificates are issued in the areas of Agriculture, Business and Marketing, Education and Training, Family and Consumer Sciences, Health Careers, and Industrial and Emerging Technologies.

II. All certificates require a valid Arizona Department of Public Safety IVP fingerprint clearance card.

III. Standard Career and Technical Education Certificates, Grades K–12 (valid for 12 years; may be renewed). The requirements are:

    A. One of the following:
1. A bachelor's degree and 240 clock hours of work experience in the CTE area; or
2. A valid Arizona Provisional or Standard Teaching Certificate, verification of 1 year of teaching with satisfactory performance, completion of specified coursework, and 240 clock hours of work experience in the CTE area; or
3. Six thousand (6,000) clock hours of work experience in the CTE area; or
4. A bachelor's degree, completion of a teacher preparation program in the CTE area, and 240 clock hours of work experience in the CTE area

    B. A course or examination covering the provisions and principles of the Arizona and US Constitutions must be completed within 3 years from date of issuance.

    C. A passing score on the required Arizona Professional Knowledge Secondary Exam, or qualification for an exam waiver, must be completed within 3 years from date of issuance.

    D. Completion of specified CTE professional knowledge coursework must be completed within 3 years from date of issuance.

    E. An applicant who holds a valid, comparable CTE certificate from another state and is in good standing with that other state may qualify for the Standard CTE Certificate under reciprocity rules. Applicants who qualify under reciprocity are exempt from all requirements except for the requirements to hold a valid IVP fingerprint clearance card and to complete the Arizona and US Constitutions requirements within 3 years.

IV. Standard Specialized Career and Technical Education (CTE) Certificates, Grades K–12 (valid for 12 years; may be renewed). The requirements are:

    A. Demonstration of expertise in the specified CTE area through 1 of the following:
1. A bachelor's or more advanced degree in the specified CTE area; or
2. A bachelor's or more advanced degree and completion of 24 semester hours of coursework in the specified CTE area; or
3. An associate degree in the specified CTE area; or
4. An industry certification, license, or credential in the specified CTE area approved by the Arizona Department of Education CTE Program Specialist or Program Services Director

    B. Individuals who qualify for the Specialized CTE Certificate are exempt from the Arizona and US Constitutions and Professional Knowledge Exam requirements.

V. Detailed information on the requirements to qualify for and maintain a CTE Certificate may be downloaded at http://www.azed.gov/educator-certification/forms-and -information/certificates/.

Arkansas

Types of Licenses

I. Standard License (valid 5 years; renewable)
   A. Prerequisites
      1. Bachelor's or higher degree from an accredited institution
      2. Criminal background check by the Arkansas State Police and the FBI
      3. Child Maltreatment Central Registry Check
      4. Novice teachers must successfully complete Arkansas Department of Education (ADE) induction program.
      5. Completion of 7 hours of Preservice Professional Development
      6. Passing of content area exams
      7. Passing of pedagogy assessment
   B. Renewal Requirements
      1. Accrue 36 professional development hours during each year of the 5-year renewal cycle
         a. One 3-hour college credit course may count as 15 hours of professional development. No more than 18 hours may be completed through college credit coursework each year.
II. Alternative Route Licensure (provisional licensure valid for 2 to 3 years depending upon the program)
   A. These programs are designed to give talented and highly motivated applicants with college degrees in fields other than education an opportunity to obtain the proper credentials and become educators in Arkansas public schools.
      1. Prerequisites: See Standard License, I, A, 1–6, above.
      2. Complete application and supporting documents
      3. Ethics training
      4. Conversion to the standard license upon completion of the program and passing of pedagogy assessment

Levels and Areas of Licensure

I. Levels of Licensure are defined as the grade-age-level parameters of the educator license and include the following:
   A. Birth–Kindergarten: Integrated
   B. Kindergarten/Young Adulthood: Grades K–12
   C. Elementary (K–6)
   D. Middle Childhood/Early Adolescence: Grades 4–8
   E. Adolescence/Young Adulthood: Grades 7–12
   F. Postsecondary: Above Grade 12

II. Teacher Licensure Competency Areas are defined as the particular content field(s) of the teaching license.
   A. Areas include adult education; agriculture sciences technology (7–12); art (K–12); business technology (4–12); chemistry (7–12); drama/speech (K–12); early childhood instructional specialist (birth–K); early childhood special education (birth–K); English-language arts (4–8); English-language arts (7–12); family and consumer science (7–12); foreign language (K–12); geometry (7–12); gifted and talented education (K–12); industrial technology (K–12); library media specialist (K–12); life science (7–12); marketing technology (7–12); mathematics (4–8); mathematics (7–12); music-instrumental (K–12); music-vocal (K–12); physical education/health (K–12); physics (7–12); school counseling (K–12); school psychology specialist (K–12); science (4–8); social studies (4–8); social studies (7–12); special education (K–12); teachers of hearing-impaired students; teachers of visually impaired students (K–12).
   B. Exception areas include ancillary student services; dyslexia (K–12); educational examiner (K–12); educational leadership and supervision; professional and technical; reading specialist (K–12); special education; and Teaching English to Speakers of Other Languages (K–12).
      1. Applicants cannot test out of exception areas but must complete the program of study.
III. Adding Areas of Licensure
   Note: Questions about adding additional licensure areas may be directed to the Office of Educator Licensure via email (see Appendix 1).
   A. Prerequisites
      1. Hold a valid Standard Arkansas teaching license. See Types of Licenses, I, A and B, above.
   B. To add non-exception teaching areas within the same level of licensure or 1 grade-level span above or below initial level of licensure, an applicant must pass the State Board–required specialty area assessment(s).
   C. To add exception areas:
      1. Complete a State Board–approved performance-based program of study and testing for the area.
   D. Teachers may test out of content licensure areas within their level of licensure and 1 level above or below their initial level of licensure.
   E. To add an area of licensure or endorsement for which there is not a State Board–required specialty area assessment:
      1. Successfully complete an approved performance-based program of study and a currently approved pedagogy assessment.
   F. Special Situations
      1. The non-instruction student services areas of school psychology specialist and speech-language pathology shall have completed a master's degree in the area from an accredited program and the State Board–required assessment to be licensed.
      2. Teachers or administrators adding elementary (K–6), middle school or

secondary social studies to their valid standard license shall have completed a 3-credit-hour course in Arkansas history.

3. Elementary (K–6) and special education (K–12) teachers must pass the Foundations of Reading exam.
4. Additional areas/levels of licensure or endorsement shall be added to a valid standard license upon receiving documentation that all requirements have been met and upon receiving an application requesting the additional licensure area or endorsement.

Administrative Licensure

I. Levels of Licensure
    A. Building-Level Administrator—Principal, assistant principal, or vice principal (P–12)
    B. Curriculum/Program Administrator—A school leader responsible for program development and administration, and/or employment evaluation decisions. Each Curriculum/Program Administrator License is limited to 1 of the following areas:
        1. Special Education (P–12)
        2. Gifted and Talented Education (P–12)
        3. Career and Technical Education (P–12)
        4. Content Area Specialist (P–12)
        5. Curriculum Specialist (P–12)
        6. Adult Education (Postsecondary)
    C. District Level Administrator—Superintendent, assistant superintendent, or deputy superintendent (P–12)
II. Types of Licensure
    A. Standard Building or Curriculum Program Administrator License
        1. Have 3 years of experience in classroom teaching, in counseling, or in library media
        2. Hold a graduate degree that includes a program of study with an internship
            a. For candidates holding a graduate degree in an area other than educational leadership, the Arkansas institution of higher education will review their credentials to determine their individual needs.
        3. Participate in a mentoring experience upon first employment
            a. The mentor provided should have relevant experience sought by the new administrator, at least 3 years of administrator experience, hold a standard teaching license, and have completed the mentorship training.
            b. Districts shall submit their administrator mentoring plans to the Arkansas State Department of Education for approval.
        4. Successfully complete the School Leaders Licensure Assessment (SLLA) with the current cut-score approved by the State Board
    B. District Administrator License
        1. Hold a standard teaching license
        2. Have 3 years of classroom teaching experience and be licensed as a Building-

Level Administrator or Curriculum/Program Administrator with at least 1 year of administrator experience

3. Hold an advanced degree, or complete an advanced program of study above the master's degree, based on individual needs inclusive of an internship and portfolio development based on the Standards for District Level Administrator licensure

4. Successfully complete the School Superintendent Assessment (SSA) with the current cut-score approved by the State Board

Reciprocity

I. Eligibility to apply:

   A. Hold a valid or expired standard teaching license equivalent from another state with no deficiencies. The license must have been in good standing for the most recent 3 years of teaching if applicable.

   B. Have 3 years of teaching experience or complete content area testing for licensure areas. Arkansas testing will be assessed if deficient.

   C. Hold a degree from an institution that holds regional or national accreditation recognized by the United States Department of Education (USDOE). The education program must also hold national accreditation recognized by the USDOE or be State Board–approved for licensure in Arkansas.

II. A 3-hour Arkansas history course or approved professional development in Arkansas history will be required for Arkansas licensure when the licensure area is elementary, middle school social studies, or secondary social studies.

III. Provisional licensure is available for those required to complete testing or Arkansas history.

IV. For full details on exceptions to eligibility requirements as well as information on candidates from other countries, email the Office of Professional Licensure (see Appendix 1).

California

All multiple and single subject professional teacher preparation programs require candidates to pass an assessment of teaching performance in order to earn a teaching credential. For full details about the Teaching Performance Assessment (TPA), consult the website (see Appendix 1).

Teaching Credentials

I. Multiple Subject Teaching Credential—Commonly used in elementary school service
II. Single Subject Teaching Credential—Commonly used in secondary school service
III. Education Specialist Instruction Credential—Commonly used in special education settings
IV. Five-Year Preliminary Multiple Subject and Single Subject Teaching Credential (nonrenewable)
   A. Requirements for California-Trained Teachers
      1. Bachelor's or higher degree from regionally accredited college or university. A Professional Education degree is only acceptable for Multiple Subject Teaching Credentials.
      2. Teacher preparation program, including student teaching, completed at California college or university with a Commission-approved program
      3. California's basic skills requirement (BSR)*
      4. US Constitution (course or examination)
      5. Subject-matter competence by:
         Obtaining a passing score on appropriate subject-matter examination
         or
         Obtaining a letter from California college or university with approved subject-matter program
         or
         Completion of bachelor's degree or higher from a regionally accredited college or university in the statutory single subject sought (or Liberal Studies degree for Multiple Subject Teaching Credential)
         or
         Coursework evaluation from a Commission-approved teacher preparation program
      6. Completion of course in developing English language skills, including reading
      7. Completion of course in foundational uses of computers in educational settings
      8. Multiple Subject Teaching Credential only: all California-prepared applicants must pass Reading Instruction Competence Assessment (RICA)
   B. Requirements for Teachers Trained in Other States or US Territories
      1. Bachelor's or higher degree from regionally accredited college or university

2. Possession of comparable teaching credential (does not have to be valid at time of application)
3. Prior to or within first year of issuance of credential, candidate must satisfy the BSR*: see IV, A, 3, directly above.
    a. Unless the BSR* is satisfied within 1 year of issuance date of credential, credential will not be valid for employment in California's public schools until requirement is met.
4. There are 3 different routes under which an out-of-state-trained teacher may qualify for certification, and each route has specific renewal requirements.
    a. Route 1: Less than 2 years of out-of-state, full-time teaching experience
    b. Route 2:
        i. Two or more years of full-time teaching experience in a public or regionally accredited private school, *and*
        ii. Photocopies of performance evaluations from 2 separate years of the verified out-of-state teaching experience on which the candidate received ratings of "satisfactory" or better
    c. Route 3: Possess National Board for Professional Teaching Standards (NBPTS) Certificate (results in issuance of clear credential)
C. Requirements for Teachers Trained Outside of the United States
    1. The equivalent of a bachelor's or higher degree from a regionally accredited college or university located in the United States
    2. Completion of a comparable teacher preparation program, including student teaching, that is equivalent to a teacher preparation program from a regionally accredited college or university located in the United States
    3. Possession of, or eligibility for, a comparable teaching credential issued by the country in which the program was completed
    4. Prior to or within first year of issuance of credential, candidate must satisfy the BSR*
        a. See B, 3, a, above.
    5. Individuals trained outside of the United States must have their foreign transcripts evaluated by a Commission-approved agency prior to submission of their application packet.
V. Five-Year Clear Multiple Subject and Single Subject Teaching Credential (renewable every 5 years)
    A. Requirements for California-Trained Teachers
        1. See IV, A, 1–8, above.
        2. Completion of Commission-approved induction program with subsequent formal recommendation to the Commission for the credential by induction program sponsor
    B. Requirements for Teachers Trained in Other States or US Territories
        1. See IV, B, 1–4
        2. Complete renewal requirements associated with route under which preliminary teaching credential was issued
            a. Route 1:

    i. Complete Commission-approved induction program with subsequent formal recommendation by induction program sponsor

    ii. Earn a California English learner authorization

   b. Route 2:

    i. Earn a California English learner authorization

   c. Route 3

    i. Individuals who qualify based on NBPTS Certification are issued clear credentials.

 C. Requirements for Teachers Trained Outside of the United States

  1. See IV, C, 1–5, above.

  2. Completion of a course in developing English language skills, including reading (or passage of RICA for holders of Multiple Subject credentials only)

  3. US Constitution course or examination

  4. Subject-matter competence by:

   Obtaining a passing score on appropriate subject-matter examination

   or

   Obtaining a letter from California college or university with approved subject-matter program

   or

   Completion of bachelor's degree or higher from a regionally accredited college or university in the statutory single subject sought (or Liberal Studies degree for Multiple Subject Teaching Credential)

   or

   Coursework evaluation from a Commission-approved teacher preparation program

  5. Commission-approved induction program with subsequent final recommendation by induction program sponsor

  6. CPR training for adults, infants, and children

 D. Clear credentials are renewable every 5 years via the Commission's online renewal system or by paper application.

VI. Authorization for Service for Multiple Subject and Single Subject Teaching Credential

 A. Teacher authorized for multiple subject instruction may be assigned to teach in any self-contained classroom in preschool and grades K–12 and in classes organized primarily for adults.

 B. Teacher authorized for single subject instruction may be assigned to teach any subject in authorized fields in any grade level (preschool, grades K–12) and in classes organized primarily for adults.

  1. Statutory subjects available: agriculture, art, business, English, foundational-level general science, foundational-level mathematics, health science, home economics, industrial and technology education, mathematics, music, physical education, science (in 1 of these areas: biological sciences, chemistry, geosciences, or physics), specialized science (in 1 of the 4 science areas immediately prior), and social science, world language: English language development, world languages: languages other than English (specify)

VII. Five-Year Clear Specialist Instruction Credential—Covers specialist areas requiring advanced professional preparation or special competencies, including agriculture, early childhood education, gifted education, mathematics, reading and language arts, and health science

A. Requirements

    1. Valid prerequisite California teaching credential

    2. Professional preparation program in specialist area

    3. Recommendation of California college or university with specific, Commission-approved specialist program

        a. Applicants trained outside of California who meet requirements in VII, A, 1 and 2, directly above, may still be certified. Student teaching must have been completed, and applicant must provide photocopy of out-of-state credential listing a comparable authorization.

        b. Applicants for Mathematics Instructional Leadership Specialist Credential who trained out of state must apply through and be recommended by California college or university with Commission-accredited program, possess an English learner authorization, and verify 3 years of experience.

B. Authorization for Service

    1. Credential authorizes holder to teach in area of specialization in preschool and grades K–12 classes and in classes organized primarily for adults.

VIII. Five-Year Preliminary or Level I Education Specialist Instruction Credential—Available in following specialization areas: mild/moderate disabilities, moderate/severe disabilities, deaf and hard of hearing, visual impairments, physical and health impairments, early childhood special education, and language and academic development

A. Requirements for California-Trained Teachers

    1. Bachelor's or higher degree from regionally accredited college or university

    2. Professional preparation program in education specialist category completed at California college or university with Commission-approved program

    3. BSR*

    4. US Constitution course or examination

    5. Completion of course in developing English-language skills, including reading

    6. Passage of RICA

        a. RICA passage is not required for category of early childhood special education, nor is it required of those who hold a valid California teaching credential issued based upon possession of a bachelor's degree and completion of a teacher preparation program including student teaching.

    7. Verification of subject-matter competence (see IV, A, 5, above)

        a. Verification of subject-matter competence is not required for category of early childhood special education, nor is it required of those who hold a valid California clear or life general education teaching credential based upon possession of a bachelor's degree and completion of a teacher preparation program including student teaching.

    8. Formal recommendation of California college or university with Commission-approved program

B. Requirements for Teachers Trained in Other States, US Territories, or outside of the United States

      1.   See IV, B and C, above, with the addition to IV, B, 4, b, i, that the 2 or more years of full-time teaching experience in a public or regionally accredited private school must be in special education.

   C. Contact Commission on Teacher Credentialing (see Appendix 1) for full information on Preliminary, Level I, Clear, or Level II Education Specialist Instruction Credential requirements.

IX. Authorization of Service for Education Specialist Instruction Credential

   A. Authorizes holder to teach in area of specialization and at level listed on credential in following settings: special schools, home/hospital settings, correctional facilities, nonpublic schools and agencies, and resource rooms, special education settings, state hospitals, development centers, and alternative and nontraditional settings

Services Credentials

I. Five-Year Preliminary Administrative Services Credential (nonrenewable)

   A. Requirements for Individuals Prepared in California

      1.   Possession of valid clear California credential, which may be in teaching; designated-subjects teaching (if bachelor's or higher degree, conferred by a regionally accredited college or university, is held); pupil personnel services; librarian; health services school nurse; clinical or rehabilitative services; or speech-language pathology

      2.   Five years of successful, full-time experience in public or private schools of equivalent status in any of areas listed directly above in A, 1

      3.   Approved program of specialized and professional preparation in administrative services

         or

         Passing score on the California Preliminary Administrative Credential Examination (CPACE; valid for 10 years)

         or

         Approved administrative internship program from California college or university

      4.   BSR*

      5.   Recommendation of program sponsor with Commission-approved administrative services program

      6.   California-trained applicants must have offer of employment in administrative position from California school district, nonpublic school or agency, or county office of education

         or

         May apply for Certificate of Eligibility

   B. Common Requirements for Individuals Prepared in Other States or US Territories (see I, C, 1 and 2, below, for additional requirements)

      1.   Verify completion of bachelor's or higher degree from regionally accredited college or university

      2.   BSR*

         a.   The 1-year nonrenewable credential is available to an administrator, at the request of an employing agency, who prepared out of state if all requirements except the BSR* are complete.

3. Complete administrative preparation program in which candidate was issued, or qualified for, administrative services credential based upon that program

C. There are 2 different routes under which out-state-prepared administrators may qualify for preliminary certification.

1. Route 1: 5 or more years of out-of-state teaching experience

   a. Candidates who meet common requirements (see I, B, 1–3, above) and the additional requirements listed below will be academically eligible for the Preliminary Administrative Services Credential.

      i. Completion of a teacher preparation program in another state

      ii. Possession of or eligibility for the equivalent of a professional-level teaching credential issued by another state

      iii. Verification of 5 years of successful, full-time teaching experience in a public or private school of equivalent status located in another state

2. Route 2: Less than 5 years of out-of-state teaching experience

   a. Candidates who meet common requirements (see I, B, 1–3, above) and the additional requirements listed below will be academically eligible for the Preliminary Administrative Services Credential or Certificate of Eligibility.

      i. Possession of a clear or life teaching or services credential in California

      ii. Verification of 5 years of successful, full-time teaching and/or services experience in a public or private school of equivalent status located in California and/or another state

      iii. Verification of an offer of employment in an administrative position from a California employing agency (candidates who do not have an offer of employment in an administrative position may apply for a Certificate of Eligibility)

II. Five-Year Clear Administrative Services Credential

A. Requirements for California-trained Candidates

1. Preliminary credential (see I, A, 1–6, above)

2. Two years of successful full-time experience in position requiring preliminary credential

3. Completion of a Commission-approved induction program and subsequent formal recommendation to the Commission for the clear credential by the program sponsor

B. Requirements for out-of-state-prepared administrators

1. Possession of a preliminary credential (see I, C, 1 and 2, above)

2. Two years of successful, full-time experience while holding the preliminary credential

3. Completion of a Commission-approved induction program and subsequent formal recommendation to the Commission for the clear credential by the program sponsor

4. Candidates who qualify for a preliminary credential under Route 2 (see I, C, 2,

above) must also maintain possession of a California clear or life teaching or services credential.

   C. Candidates prepared outside of California may earn a clear credential without first holding a preliminary credential by:

      1. Meeting common requirements (see I, B, 1–3, above)

      2. Completing a teacher preparation program in another state

      3. Possessing a professional-level teaching credential issued by another state

      4. Verifying 5 years of successful, full-time teaching experience in a public or private school of equivalent status located in another state

      5. Verifying 3 years of successful, full-time administrative experience in a public or regionally accredited private school located in another state

      6. Submitting photocopies of performance evaluations from the last 2 years of verified out-of-state administrative experience with ratings of "satisfactory" or better

         a. Possessing a California teaching or services credential and verifying employment in an administrative position in California are not required of candidates who qualify via this option.

   D. The 1-year nonrenewable credential is available, at the request of the employing agency, to administrators who prepared out of state if all requirements except the BSR* are complete.

III. Authorization for Service

   A. An Administrative Services Credential authorizes the holder to provide various duties that may allow the holder to serve in a number of positions, including superintendent, associate superintendent, deputy superintendent, principal, assistant principal, dean, supervisor, consultant, coordinator, or in equivalent or intermediate-level administrative positions.

IV. Clear Teacher Librarian Services Credential

   A. Requirements

      1. Bachelor's degree from regionally accredited college or university

      2. Valid prerequisite California teaching credential (if it is a clear full-time designated-subjects teaching credential, the individual must also possess a baccalaureate degree from a regionally accredited institution and satisfy the BSR*)

      3. Completion of:

         a. Commission-approved teacher librarian services program and recommendation of California college or university where program was completed

           or

         b. Out-of-state teacher librarian services program consisting of 30 graduate semester units approved by appropriate state agency in state where program was completed

      4. BSR*

         a. The 1-year nonrenewable credential is available, at the request of an employing agency, to an individual who prepared out of state if all requirements except the BSR* are complete.

      5.   Possession of an English learner authorization

  B.   An individual who holds NBPTS Certification in the area of Early Childhood through Young Adulthood—Library Media may be issued a Clear Teacher Librarian Services Credential if the following requirements are also met:

      1.   Possession of a valid prerequisite California teaching credential (if it is a clear full-time designated-subjects teaching credential, the individual must also possess a baccalaureate degree from a regionally accredited institution and satisfy the BSR*)

      2.   Possession of an English learner authorization

  C.   Authorization for Service

      1.   Teacher Librarian Services Credential authorizes holder to assist and instruct pupils in choice and use of library materials; to plan and coordinate school library programs with instructional programs of school district; to select materials for school and district libraries; to conduct planned course of instruction for those pupils who assist in operation of school libraries; to supervise classified personnel assigned to school library duties; and to develop procedures for and management of school and district libraries.

      2.   The Special Class Authorization authorizes the holder to provide departmentalized instruction in information literacy, digital literacy, and digital citizenship to students in grades 12 and below, including preschool, and in classes organized primarily for adults. Individuals must satisfy all of the following requirements:

         a.   Hold a valid prerequisite California teaching credential as follows:

           i.   A valid 1-year nonrenewable, Clear, or Life Teacher Librarian or Library Media Services Credential

           ii.   Library Services Credential

           iii. Standard Elementary, Secondary, Early Childhood Education, or Junior College Teaching Credential with a specialized preparation minor in Librarianship

           iv. General Credential in Librarianship

         b.   Completion of a Commission-approved Special Class Authorization program of professional preparation

         c.   Recommendation from a Commission-approved Teacher Librarian Services program

V. Pupil Personnel Services Credential

  A.   Authorization for Services

      1.   Credential available in 4 different areas: school counseling, school social work, school psychology, and child welfare and attendance services

  B.   Requirements for School Counseling Authorization

      1.   A baccalaureate degree or higher, except in professional education, from a regionally accredited college or university

      2.   Post-baccalaureate study consisting of 48 semester units (30 semester units for out-of-state prepared) specializing in school counseling, including a supervised field experience

      3.   BSR*

a. The 1-year nonrenewable credential is available, at the request of an employing agency, to an individual who prepared out of state if all requirements except the BSR* are complete.

4. Recommendation of a California college or university with a Commission-approved School Counseling program
   a. Individuals who trained out of state must:
      i. Verify possession of, or eligibility for, the equivalent authorization in the state where the program was completed,
      and
      ii. Provide written verification from the college or university where the program was completed that the program included supervised field experience with school-age children in school counseling.

C. An individual who holds NBPTS Certification in the area of Early Childhood to Young Adulthood—School Counseling may apply directly to the Commission for a Clear Pupil Personnel Services Credential in School Counseling and is exempt from BSR* satisfaction and all other credential requirements.

D. Requirements for School Social Work Authorization
   1. A baccalaureate degree or higher, except in professional education, from a regionally accredited college or university
   2. Post-baccalaureate study consisting of 45 semester units specializing in school social work, including a supervised field experience
   3. BSR*
      a. The 1-year nonrenewable credential is available, at the request of an employing agency, to an individual who prepared out of state if all requirements except the BSR* are complete.
   4. Recommendation of a California college or university with a Commission-approved School Social Work program
      a. Individuals who trained out of state must:
         i. Verify possession of, or eligibility for, the equivalent authorization in the state where the program was completed,
         and
         ii. Provide written verification from the college or university where the program was completed that program included supervised field experience with school-age children in school social work.

E. Requirements for School Psychology Authorization
   1. A baccalaureate degree or higher, except in professional education, from a regionally accredited college or university
   2. Post-baccalaureate study consisting of 60 semester units specializing in school psychology, including a practicum and supervised field experience
   3. BSR*
      a. The 1-year nonrenewable credential is available, at the request of an employing agency, to an individual who prepared out of state if all requirements except the BSR* are complete.
   4. Recommendation of a California college or university with a Commission-approved School Psychology program

        a.   Individuals who trained out of state must:

            i.   Verify possession of, or eligibility for, the equivalent authorization in the state where the program was completed, *and*

           ii.   Provide written verification from the college or university where the program was completed that the program included a supervised field experience with school-age children in school psychology.

    F.   Child Welfare and Attendance Authorization. Contact the Commission (see Appendix 1) for full information

VI.   For detailed information on credentials in speech-language pathology and clinical or rehabilitative services, consult the website (see Appendix 1).

*Unless otherwise noted, for initial issuance all applicants must satisfy the BSR. This requirement does not apply to applicants who are having their credentials renewed, reissued, or upgraded. Applicants who prepared out of state may be issued a 1-year, nonrenewable credential pending satisfaction of the BSR if a California public school employer cannot find a fully credentialed person to fill the position and offers employment to the credential applicant.

Colorado

Applying for an Initial License

I. Initial License (valid 3 years; renewable). Requirements for applicant include:
   A. Hold an earned bachelor's or higher degree from a regionally accredited institution of higher education;
   B. Complete an approved teacher preparation program at a regionally accredited institution of higher education or a state-approved alternative teacher preparation program;
   C. Complete a student teaching/clinical experience that meets the requirements as outlined in Colorado Revised Statutes 23–1-121-(2)(d), available online at http://leg.colorado.gov/sites/default/files/images/olls/crs2018-title-23.pdf;
   D. Pass a fingerprint-based criminal history background check via the Colorado Bureau of Investigation;
   E. Submit a complete application for licensure, including copies of official transcripts, an approved program verification form, associated fees, and other supporting documentation to the Colorado Department of Education (CDE) Licensure Office (see Appendix 1);
   and
   F. Demonstrate subject matter knowledge necessary for teaching in the endorsement area.
      1. All elementary education teachers, including special education generalist teachers, must pass a Colorado State Board of Education (CSBE)–approved elementary education content exam and the approved teaching reading exam.
      2. All special education generalist teachers must also pass the CSBE-approved special education exam.
      3. All early childhood education teachers, including early childhood special education teachers, must pass the CSBE-approved early childhood education exam and the approved teaching reading exam.
      4. All early childhood special education teachers must also pass the CSBE-approved early childhood special education exam.
      5. Teachers of all middle school (grades 6–8), secondary (grades 7–12), and K–12 endorsement areas must hold an earned bachelor's or higher degree in the endorsement area;
      or
      Demonstrate 24 semester hours of applicable coursework as determined by a transcript review;
      or
      Pass the CSBE-approved assessment of content knowledge relevant to the area of endorsement.

II. Available Endorsement Areas for Colorado Educator Licenses
   A. Colorado issues 4 types of licenses—administrator, principal, special services provider, and teacher—with endorsements that indicate the age or grade level(s), subject area(s), or other areas of specialization that are appropriate to the applicant's preparation, training, and experience. They are typically granted in the major areas of specialization and only in those areas which constitute approved programs. Available endorsements include:
      1. Administrator (Grades K–12)
         a. Administrator (superintendent), Director of Special Education, Director of Gifted Education
      2. Principal (Grades K–12)
         a. School Principal
      3. Special Services Provider (Ages 0–21)
         a. School Audiologist; School Nurse; School Occupational Therapist; School Orientation and Mobility Specialist; School Physical Therapist; School Psychologist; School Social Worker; School Speech-Language Pathologist
         b. School Counselor (Grades K–12)
      4. Teacher
         a. Early Childhood Education (Ages 0–8); Early Childhood Special Education (Ages 0–8); Elementary Education (Grades K–6); Special Education Generalist (Ages 5–21)
         b. Grades K–12 include: Culturally & Linguistically Diverse Education;* Culturally & Linguistically Diverse–Bilingual Education Specialist;* Dance; Drama/Theater Arts; Health; Instructional Technology Specialist;* Instructional Technology Teacher; Music; Physical Education; Visual Arts; World Language (American Sign Language, French, German, Italian, Japanese, Latin, Mandarin Chinese, Russian, Spanish)
         c. Middle School (Grades 6–8) includes: Middle School Mathematics
         d. Secondary (Grades 7–12) includes: Agriculture and Renewable Natural Resources; Business/Marketing Education; English Language Arts; Family and Consumer Sciences; Mathematics; Science; Social Studies; Speech; Technology Education (Industrial Arts)
         e. Endorsements requiring approved graduate-level programs or a master's degree (depending on endorsement area sought) include: Early Childhood Special Education Specialist (Ages 0–8); Gifted Education Core (Grades PK–12);* Gifted Education Specialist, (Grades PK–12);* Reading Specialist (Grades K–12);* Reading Teacher (Grades K–12);* Special Education Specialist (Ages 5–21);* Special Education Specialist: Visually Impaired (Ages 0–21); Special Education Specialist: Deaf/Hard of Hearing (Ages 0–21); Teacher Librarian (Grades K–12)*
            *This endorsement cannot be issued as a stand-alone endorsement. It may only be added to an existing valid Colorado teacher license.
III. Applying for an Initial Special Services Provider (SSP) License
   A. Meet all requirements for applying for an initial license, I, A–E, above, except that the approved preparation program must be for the special services area of specialization.

B.   Meet additional requirements for specific special services licenses, including:
   1.   School Audiologist
      a.   Hold a doctor of audiology degree (AuD) or PhD in audiology;
      b.   Complete a minimum 8-week full-time practicum or internship in audiology in a school setting;
         and
      c.   Pass the CSBE-approved audiology exam.
   2.   School Counselor
      a.   Option 1:
         i.   Hold a master's degree in school counseling or social work;
         ii.   Complete a Council for Accreditation of Counseling and Related Educational Programs (CACREP)–accredited school counseling program;
         iii. Complete a minimum 100-clock-hour practicum and a minimum 600-clock-hour internship in a school setting;
             and
         iv.   Pass the CSBE-approved school counselor exam;
         or
      b.   Option 2:
         i.   Hold a master's degree in a clinical counseling domain or in social work;
             and
         ii.   Hold a valid Colorado Department of Regulatory Agencies–issued LPC, or an LSW or LCSW license;
         iii. Applicants who meet both requirements in i.–ii and who have been hired as school counselors in a Colorado school, district, or BOCES may be issued a Temporary Educator Eligibility (TEE) authorization, valid for 1 year and renewable twice with documented evidence of progress toward meeting the full requirements for the school counselor endorsement. While under the TEE, they must complete identified school counseling coursework and take and pass the CSBE-approved school counselor exam. Upon completion of requirements, the candidate may then apply to advance to an initial SSP license for school counselor.
   3.   School Nurse
      a.   Option 1:
         i.   Hold a bachelor of science or higher degree in nursing from an accepted institution of higher education;
             and
         ii.   Hold a valid Colorado registered nurse (RN) license issued by the Colorado Department of Regulatory Agencies or a nursing compact state;
         or
      b.   Option 2:

       i.   Hold a valid Colorado RN license issued by the Colorado Department of Regulatory Agencies or a nursing compact state;
           and

      ii.   Have 3 or more years of practical experience working with school-aged children;
           and

     iii.   Have completed an RN or bachelor of science in nursing (BSN) program recognized by the US Secretary of Education and a specialized accrediting agency, such as the Commission on Collegiate Nursing Education (CCNE) or the Accreditation Commission for Education in Nursing (ACEN).

4. School Occupational Therapist
   a. Complete an American Occupational Therapy Association (AOTA)–accredited occupational therapy program;
   b. Complete program-required practicum(s) and/or internship(s);
   c. Pass the national exam through the National Board for Certification in Occupational Therapy (NBCOT);
   and
   d. Hold a valid Colorado occupational therapist license issued by the Colorado Department of Regulatory Agencies.

5. School Orientation and Mobility Specialist
   a. Complete approved preparation program for school orientation and mobility specialists;
   b. Complete a minimum 320-clock-hour full-time practicum in a school setting;
   c. Pass the Academy for Certification of Vision Rehabilitation and Education Professionals (ACVREP) exam;
   and
   d. Hold a valid ACVREP orientation and mobility certificate.

6. School Physical Therapist
   a. Complete an American Physical Therapy Association (APTA)–accredited physical therapy program;
   b. Complete program-required practicum(s) and/or internship(s);
   and
   c. Hold a valid Colorado physical therapist license issued by the Colorado Department of Regulatory Agencies.

7. School Psychologist
   a. Complete a state-approved sixth-year specialist program (60 graduate semester hours) or doctoral program for school psychologist, serving children birth–21;
   b. Complete program-required practicum(s) and/or internship(s);
   c. Complete a minimum 1200-clock-hour internship or supervised field experience;
   and

        d.   Pass the CSBE-approved school psychologist exam or hold National Association of School Psychologists (NCSP) certification.

    8. School Social Worker

       a. Hold a master's degree in social work (MSW);

       b. Complete coursework in school and special education law, functional behavior assessment, and the development of behavioral intervention plans;

       c. Complete a minimum 900-clock-hour practicum in a school, social service agency, mental health clinic, or facility or other hospital setting;

       d. Complete at least 1 field experience with school-aged children; *and*

       e. Pass the Association of Social Work Boards (ASWB) master's, clinical, or advanced generalist exam.

    9. School Speech-Language Pathologist

       a. Hold a master's or higher degree in communication disorders or speech-language pathology;

       b. Complete an American Speech-Language-Hearing Association (ASHA)–accredited speech-language pathology program accredited by the Council on Academic Accreditation (CAA) in audiology and speech-language pathology of the ASHA;

       c. Complete a minimum 8-week full-time practicum or internship with children ages birth–21; *and*

       d. Hold ASHA certification or have passed the CSBE-approved speech-language pathology exam.

IV. Applying for an Initial Principal License

  A. Meet all requirements for applying for an initial license, I, A–E, above, except that the approved preparation program must be for principals.

  B. Meet additional requirements for principal license, including:

    1. Provide documented evidence of 3 or more years of full-time successful experience working as a licensed or certificated professional in a public or nonpublic elementary or secondary school in the United States; *and*

    2. Have a passing score on the CSBE-approved principal exam.

V. Applying for an Initial Administrator License

  A. Meet all requirements for applying for an initial license, I, A–E, above, except that the approved preparation program must be for administrators.

  B. Meet additional requirements for specific administrator licenses, including:

    1. Initial Administrator (Superintendent) License

       a. Complete an approved graduate program for school district administration at an accepted, regionally accredited institution of higher education; *and*

       b. Have a passing score on the CSBE-approved administrator exam.

    2. Initial Administrator (Director of Special Education) License

       a. Hold a master's or higher degree in special education from a regionally accredited institution of higher education;

      b.   Have a minimum of 2 years of experience working with students with disabilities;

      c.   Complete an approved program for the preparation of special education directors, including a supervised field-based experience, or complete an approved administrator preparation program.
and

      d.   Have a passing score on the CSBE-approved administrator exam. (Individuals who have not met the requirements for a special education generalist endorsement will also need to pass the exams required for that endorsement.)

3.   Initial Administrator (Director of Gifted Education) License

      a.   Hold a master's or higher degree in gifted education from a regionally accredited institution of higher education;

      b.   Have a minimum of 2 years of experience working with gifted students;

      c.   Complete an approved program for the preparation of gifted education directors, including a supervised field-based experience, or complete an approved administrator preparation program.
and

      d.   Have a passing score on the CSBE-approved administrator exam. (Individuals who have not met the requirements for a gifted education core endorsement will also need to pass the exam required for that endorsement.)

Moving from an Initial License to a Professional License

I.   Professional License (valid 7 years; renewable). Requirements include:

    A.   Complete a Colorado Department of Education–approved induction program.

        1.   Approved teacher induction programs are provided by Colorado school districts and Boards of Cooperative Services (BOCS) and include supervision by mentor teachers, ongoing professional development, ethics training, and performance evaluations. Individuals completing approved SSP induction programs must be mentored by licensed SSPs in the same specialty; principals and administrators completing induction must be mentored by licensed principals and administrators.

        2.   Educators must be serving in the role (e.g., a principal license-holder must be serving as a principal or assistant principal) to participate in induction.

    B.   Complete and submit an online license application.

        1.   Upload a copy of original induction certificate of completion into the application.

    C.   See more at http://www.cde.state.co.us/cdeprof/Licensure_provtoprof_faq.asp and http://www.cde.state.co.us/cdeprof/checklist-initialtoprofessionalteacher (the requirements and process described in the checklist are the same for advancing the other three license types).

Connecticut

To access Connecticut's most recent certification requirements changes, consult "News/Alerts Impacting Certification" at https://portal.ct.gov/SDE/Certification/Bureau-of-Certification.

Three-Tier Certification System Overview

I. Initial Educator Certificate (valid 3 years)
   A. Issued to applicants who meet all eligibility requirements and who have fewer than 2 full school years of appropriate successful teaching experience in the past 10 years.
II. Provisional Educator Certificate (valid 8 years)
   To qualify for the provisional educator certificate, an applicant must complete 1 of the following:
   A. Ten months of successful appropriate experience under the initial educator certificate or interim initial educator certificate in a Connecticut public school;
   and
   Successful completion of the teacher induction/mentoring program, as made available by the Connecticut State Board of Education;
   or
   B. Thirty months of successful appropriate experience within 10 years in an approved nonpublic school or nonpublic school approved by the appropriate governing body in another state;
   or
   C. Twenty months of successful appropriate experience within 10 years in a public school system under a valid certificate in another state.
III. Professional Educator Certificate (valid 5 years)
   To qualify for the professional educator certificate, an applicant must complete the following requirements:
   A. Thirty school months of successful appropriate experience in a Connecticut public or approved nonpublic school under the provisional educator certificate;
   and
   B. Any person who is issued a Connecticut educator certificate for the first time on or after July 1, 2018, will be required to complete a master's degree in an appropriate subject matter area in order to advance their provisional educator certificate to the professional educator certificate;
   or
   C. Additional course requirements, as prescribed by current Connecticut certification regulations. Specific course work requirements vary depending on endorsement.
      1. For certificate-specific requirements, consult http://www.sde.ct.gov/sde/lib/sde/PDF/Cert/regulations/regulations.pdf as well as Guide to Assessments for Educator Certification in Connecticut at http://www.ct.gov/sde/certtests.

IV. Interim Educator Certificate (valid 1 year or 3 years)
   A. The interim educator certificate may be issued at the initial or provisional level.
   B. A 1-year, nonrenewable interim certificate may be issued with a coursework deficiency.
   C. Out-of-state applicants who meet all certification criteria except Connecticut assessment requirements may be issued a 3-year, nonrenewable interim certificate with a deferral for testing.

First-Time Connecticut Certification

I. Requirements include:
   A. Successfully complete a state-approved planned program of general academic and professional education at a regionally accredited college or university;
      and
   B. Pass subject-specific tests, if applicable to the endorsement requested.
      1. For certificate-specific requirements, consult http://www.sde.ct.gov/sde/lib/sde/PDF/Cert/regulations/regulations.pdf as well as Guide to Assessments for Educator Certification in Connecticut at http://www.ct.gov/sde/certtests.

II. Eligibility Based on Teaching Experience
   A. Educators who have completed the equivalent of 2 school years of full-time teaching experience in the same school in the grade level and subject appropriate to the endorsement requested may waive the planned program requirement. However, all course work, degree, testing and any experiential requirements must still be met. To obtain such certification, educators must:
      1. Document no fewer than 20 school months of successful, appropriate full-time teaching experience in the same approved nonpublic school or an out-of-state public school under a valid certificate;
      2. Pass subject-specific tests for those endorsements where a test is required;
         and
      3. Successfully complete all required general academic and professional education course work for the endorsement areas sought.
         a. All course work must result in college-level credit awarded to official transcripts from regionally accredited colleges or universities.
      4. For certificate-specific requirements, consult http://www.sde.ct.gov/sde/lib/sde/PDF/Cert/regulations/regulations.pdf as well as Guide to Assessments for Educator Certification in Connecticut at http://www.ct.gov/sde/certtests.
      5. All candidates applying for a Connecticut educator certificate which requires completion of a bachelor's degree or advanced degree from a regionally accredited institution must submit official transcripts verifying completion of the degree, regardless of the basis of their certification.
         a. Only course work resulting in credit awarded to an official transcript of a regionally accredited college or university can be accepted to meet certification requirements.

III. Out-of-State Educators
   A. Connecticut participates in the National Association of State Directors of Teacher

Education and Certification (NASDTEC) Interstate Agreement (NIA). Under this agreement, to waive specific course work requirements, Connecticut may accept:

1. Completion of a state-approved educator preparation program at a regionally accredited college or university from another US state,
    or
2. A minimum of 30 months of successful full-time experience under the other state's valid educator certificate (at least equivalent to a Connecticut initial educator certificate), appropriate to the subject area being requested.
    a. To be considered, the experience must be completed within 10 years of the date of application for Connecticut certification.
    b. Out-of-state educators who taught successfully for at least 3 of the past 10 years under an appropriate certificate in another state may be exempt from Connecticut licensure assessments.
3. The interstate agreement does not exempt candidates from degree, testing and/or experiential requirements applicable to the requested certification endorsement.
    a. For certificate-specific requirements, consult http://www.sde.ct.gov/sde/lib/sde/PDF/Cert/regulations/regulations.pdf as well as Guide to Assessments for Educator Certification in Connecticut at http://www.ct.gov/sde/certtests.
    b. Educators are no longer required to take Connecticut licensure assessments if they have passed an out-of-state educator certification test that is determined to be equivalent to the corresponding Connecticut assessment.
4. Candidates who do not qualify for Connecticut certification under the terms of the interstate agreement must meet all of Connecticut's requirements for the endorsement requested, including course work.
5. Connecticut does not participate in the interstate agreement for administrative endorsements.
6. Assessment Exemptions. Effective July 1, 2009, amended as of July 1, 2013, educators may be exempt from Board-approved assessment requirements, including Praxis II subject knowledge tests, Connecticut Foundations of Reading Test, Reading Specialist Test, Early Childhood Test, and/or ACTFL OPI and WPT, if they meet the following criteria:
    a. Hold a valid certificate in another state that is equivalent to at least a Connecticut initial educator certificate and fulfill 1 of the following:
        i.   Have 3 years of successful appropriate experience in the same state (in the same approved nonpublic school or public school system, in the endorsement requested) in the past 10 years;
             or
        ii. Hold a master's degree in the academic subject area for which Connecticut certification is being requested. Pedagogical degrees in the subject area, such as those for elementary education, special education or physical education, do not meet the requirements of the exemption.
7. Assessment Deferral
    a. Out-of-state applicants who meet all certification criteria except Connecticut assessment requirements may be issued a 3-year, nonrenewable interim certificate with a deferral for testing.

              b.   To maintain certification and obtain subsequent certificates, the applicant must complete all required tests before the expiration date of the certificate.

              c.   All applicants who are eligible for a deferral of testing requirements will automatically be issued an interim certificate once all requirements other than testing have been met.

IV.   Foreign credentials for certification

    A.   Applicants who completed any education required for certification outside of the United States must have their credentials evaluated by an agency currently approved by the Connecticut State Department of Education and meet current certification requirements, including course work and assessments, as appropriate.

        1.   To access a list of approved agencies, consult http://www.sde.ct.gov/sde/lib/sde/pdf/cert/obtaining1109aw.pdf.

    B.   In addition to credential evaluations, applicants must submit:

        1.   Original course-by-course analysis, completed by 1 of the approved agencies, of all college- or university-level course work including general academic, subject area and program preparation course work completed outside of the United States;
            and

        2.   ED 126 Statement of Successful Professional Experience, verifying completion of K-12 teaching/service completed within the past 10 years in foreign public schools or approved nonpublic schools, along with a copy of the certificate or license authorizing this service.

            a.   Foreign experience must be verified by the superintendent or head of the school district, or by the ministry of education or other authorized agency.

            b.   If the verification of teaching experience or the teaching license or authorization is printed in a language other than English, the original document must be accompanied by a notarized translation.

Delaware

In Delaware, educators are required to hold both a License and a Certificate.

Licensure

I. Initial License (valid 4 years; issued to applicants with 0 – 4 years of teaching experience)
    A. In-State Requirements
        1. Bachelor's degree from regionally accredited college or university.
        2. Complete 1 of the following:
            a. An approved student teaching program.
            b. An approved alternative route to licensure and certification program.
            c. Ninety-one days "in lieu of student teaching" of long-term substitute teaching experience in 1 assignment in a Delaware public/charter school within the same academic year before application for licensure, with supporting evidence of satisfactory performance evaluations
                NOTE: The first certificate under this option may not be in a core content area (math, English/language arts, social studies, science, or elementary) or in special education.
        3. Disclose any criminal conviction history.
    B. Out-of-State or Lapsed Requirements
        1. Out-of-State: Department of Education may issue:
            a. Initial License to an applicant who is currently licensed as an educator in another jurisdiction with less than 4 years of credentialed teaching experience. The applicant must also meet requirements for certification.
            b. Continuing License to an applicant who has 4 years or more of verified credentialed teaching experience under a full and valid out-of-state credential with attestation/proof of a minimum of 2 satisfactory summative evaluations during that license period.
        2. Lapsed: An applicant who previously held a Delaware Initial License that has been expired for more than 5 years will be treated as a new applicant and must meet all current requirements in law and regulation. In addition to an Initial License, applicants must also apply for a Standard Certificate in the appropriate area; see Standard Certificate below. This may apply for both the Initial License and the Continuing License.
    C. Preparations for Continuing License Application
        Before expiration of Initial License, applicant must:
        1. Complete mentoring and other prescribed professional development activities.
        2. Receive no more than 1 unsatisfactory annual evaluation, as defined by the Delaware Performance Appraisal System.
        3. Disclose any criminal conviction history.

II.   Continuing License (valid 5 years; renewable and extendable upon proof of exigent
      circumstances for up to 3-year leave of absence)
      A.   General Requirements
           1.   Successfully complete requirements for Initial License (see I, A, directly above).
           2.   Receive no more than 1 unsatisfactory annual evaluation, as defined by the
                Delaware Performance Appraisal System, during period of Initial License.
           3.   Hold current and valid educator license in another jurisdiction with evidence of
                completing 4 or more years of successful teaching experience and 2 successful
                summative evaluations.
      B.   Delaware Certificates issued prior to July 2, 2001
           1.   Continuing License may be issued to educator who holds a Delaware Certificate
                issued prior to July 13, 1971, or who previously held a valid Delaware Standard
                or Professional Status Certificate that has expired.
           2.   As a condition of maintaining the original license, the educator shall
                successfully complete 1 year of an approved mentoring program required of
                educators within their first year of employment.
      C.   Continuing License Renewal (valid 5 years; renewable)
           1.   Fulfill 90-clock-hour requirement for professional growth:
                a.   At least 45 hours every 5 years must be in activities related to educator's
                     work with students or staff.
                b.   Professional development hours must take place during term of Continuing
                     License.
                c.   See Department of Education (Appendix 1) for detailed options.
                d.   Disclose any criminal conviction history.
III. Advanced Licensure (valid 5 years; renewable)
      A.   Requirements
           1.   Application by holder of National Board of Professional Teaching Standards
                Certification or equivalent program approved by Professional Standards
                Board.
      B.   Renewal
           1.   Renewable for up to 10 years provided that educator maintains proficiency
                under program for which license was first issued.
           2.   If holder does not renew the Advanced License, a Continuing License will be
                issued upon expiration of the Advanced License.

Alternative Routes to Teacher Licensure and Certification Program

I.   Candidates participating in an Alternative Routes to Teacher Licensure and Certification
      Program (ARTC) shall be issued an Initial License of no more than 4 years' duration.
      Emergency Certificates for content areas may be of no more than 3 years' duration.
      Certificates of Eligibility for special education areas may be of no more than 3 years'
      duration, and candidates must be actively participating in a state-approved Alternative
      Routes to Certification Certificate of Eligibility program.
II.   Requirements for ARTC Candidates
      A.   Hold a bachelor's degree from a regionally accredited college or university, with

a major appropriate to the instructional field desired, which shall be no less than 24 credit hours appropriate to the instructional field.

B. Obtain and accept an offer of employment in a position that requires licensure and certification in the instructional field desired and remain continuously employed full-time in that position.

C. Obtain acceptable health clearance under Department regulations and an acceptable criminal background check clearance.

D. Achieve a passing score on an examination of content knowledge, such as Praxis II, in the instructional field desired, if applicable and available.

E. Maintain satisfactory progress toward the completion of all ARTC program requirements.

F. Provide 2 summative evaluations using a state-approved system, with not more than 1 unsatisfactory summative evaluation.

III. Components of the Alternative Routes Program
   A. Seminar and practicum that include the following:
      1. Formal instruction or equivalent professional development required by ARTC program established by regulation or law.
      2. Introduction of basic teaching skills through supervised teaching experiences with students.
      3. Components that are integrated and include an orientation to the policies, organization, and curriculum of the employing district or charter school.
   B. Completion of at least 200 hours of formal instruction, or equivalent professional development approved by the Department, addressing at a minimum:
      1. Curriculum
      2. Student development and learning at all levels
      3. The classroom and the school
   C. ARTC participants may be granted hours for formal instruction or equivalent professional development successfully completed prior to entry into the ARTC program or during the seminar and practicum.

Standard Certificate

I. Issued to an educator who holds a valid Delaware Initial, Continuing, or Advanced License; or a Standard or Professional Status Certificate issued prior to August 31, 2003, who has met the below requirements.

II. Preliminary Requirement
Satisfy at least 1 of the following:
   A. Certification from the National Board for Professional Teaching Standards in area of certification.
   B. Meeting the requirements of the relevant Department or Professional Standards Board regulations for obtaining a Standard Certificate in area of certification.
   C. Graduation from an educator preparation program approved by the National Council for Accreditation of Teacher Education (NCATE) or the Council for the Accreditation of Educator Preparation (CAEP), or from a Delaware-approved educator preparation program using National Association of State Directors of

Teacher Education and Certification (NASDTEC) or NCATE (CAEP) standards, with a major or its equivalent in area of certification.

D. Satisfactory completion of an Alternative Routes to Teacher Licensure and Certification Program or other Department-approved alternative educator preparation programs.

E. Bachelor's degree from a regionally accredited college or university in non-content area—including 15 credit hours or their equivalent in professional development related to the area of certification, of which at least 6 credit hours must focus on pedagogy—selected by the applicant with the approval of the employing school district or charter school.

III. Additional Requirements

A. Meet or exceed Praxis II scores and/or required coursework or additional certificate requirements.
NOTE: Some certifications require Praxis II only, and some certifications require Praxis II and coursework and/or degree, along with teaching experience.
or

B. Hold a valid and current license/certificate in certification area from another state.

Early Childhood Teacher Standard Certificate (Birth–Grade 2)

I. Issued to an educator who holds a valid Delaware Initial, Continuing, or Advanced License; or a Standard or Professional Status Certificate issued by the Department prior to August 31, 2003.

II. Requirements

A. See Standard Certificate, I, II, and III, above.

Elementary Teacher Standard Certificate (Grades K–6)

I. Issued to an educator who holds a valid Delaware Initial, Continuing, or Advanced License; or a Standard or Professional Status Certificate issued by the Department prior to August 31, 2003.

II. Requirements

A. See Standard Certificate, I, II, and III, above.

Administration

I. School Principal/Assistant Principal

A. Educational Requirements
Satisfy at least 1 of the following requirements:

1. Master's or doctoral degree with a major or its equivalent in PreK–12 in educational leadership, offered by an NCATE (CAEP) specialty organization–recognized educator preparation program or state-approved educator preparation program where the state approval body employed the appropriate NASDTEC or NCATE (CAEP) specialty organization standards, at a regionally accredited college or university.

    2.   Master's or doctoral degree in any content area from a regionally accredited college or university and 1 of the following:

        a.   Satisfactory completion of an alternative routes for licensure or certification program for school principals as provided in 14 Del.C. 1260–1266.

        b.   Satisfactory completion of a Department-approved educator preparation program for school principals as provided in 14 DE Admin. Code 290 Approval of Educator Preparation Programs.

B. Experience Requirements

    1.   Minimum of 5 years of experience as an educator with satisfactory annual summative evaluations or the equivalent thereof on a state-approved educator evaluation system under a state credential in any PreK–12 public school setting or an equivalent setting as approved by the Department.

C. Praxis II Requirements

The applicant shall have achieved a passing score on 1 of the following examinations:

    1.   A passing score of 160 on the School Leaders Licensure Assessment (ETS Code #6011).

    2.   A passing score of 160 on the School Superintendent Assessment (ETS Code #6021).

    3.   A passing score of 151 on the School Leaders Licensure Assessment (ETS Code #6990).

    4.   A passing score of 162 on the School Superintendent Assessment (ETS Code #6991).

II. Certified Central Office Personnel

A. Education Requirements

Satisfy at least 1 of the following requirements:

    1.   Master's or doctoral degree with a major or its equivalent in PreK–12 in educational leadership, offered by an NCATE (CAEP) specialty organization–recognized educator preparation program or state-approved educator preparation program where the state approval body employed the appropriate NASDTEC or NCATE (CAEP) specialty organization standards, at a regionally accredited college or university.

    2.   Master's or doctoral degree in any content area from a regionally accredited college or university and 1 of the following:

        a.   Satisfactory completion of an alternative routes for licensure or certification program for central office personnel as provided in 14 Del.C 1260–1266.

        b.   Satisfactory completion of a Department-approved educator preparation program for central office personnel as provided in 14 DE Admin. Code 290 Approval of Educator Preparation Programs.

        c.   Hold a School Principal and Assistant School Principal Standard Certificate (14 DE Admin. Code 1591).

           and

           Satisfactory completion of an *additional* 9 graduate-level credit hours in PreK–12 educational leadership from a regionally accredited college or university or the equivalent in professional development approved by the Department.

NOTE: The additional 9 graduate-level credit hours must have been completed *after* the applicant earned his or her master's or doctoral degree.

B.   Experience Requirements

1.   Minimum of 5 years of experience as an educator with satisfactory annual summative evaluations or the equivalent thereof on a state-approved educator evaluation system under a state credential in any PreK–12 public school setting or an equivalent setting as approved by the Department.

C.   Praxis II Requirements

The applicant shall have achieved a passing score on 1 of the following examinations:

1.   A passing score of 146 on the Educational Leadership: Administration and Supervision Assessment (ETS Code #5412).

2.   A passing score of 160 on the School Leaders Licensure Assessment (ETS Code #6011).

3.   A passing score of 160 on the School Superintendent Assessment (ETS Code #6021).

4.   A passing score of 151 on the School Leaders Licensure Assessment (ETS Code #6990).

5.   A passing score of 162 on the School Superintendent Assessment (ETS Code #6991).

III.   Superintendent or Assistant Superintendent

A.   Educational Requirements

Satisfy at least 1 of the following additional education requirements:

1.   Doctoral degree with a major or its equivalent in PreK–12 in educational leadership offered by an NCATE (CAEP) specialty organization–recognized educator preparation program or state-approved educator preparation where the state approval body employed the appropriate NASDTEC or NCATE (CAEP) specialty organization standards, at a regionally accredited college or university.

2.   Master's or doctoral degree in any content area from a regionally accredited college or university and 1 of the following:

a.   Satisfactory completion of an alternative routes for licensure or certification program for superintendents as provided in 14 Del.C 1260–1266.

b.   Satisfactory completion of a Department-approved educator preparation program for superintendents as provided in 14 DE Admin. Code 290 Approval of Educator Preparation Programs.

c.   Hold a Certified Central Office Personnel Standard Certificate (14 DE Admin. Code 1592) or a Special Education Director Standard Certificate (14 DE Admin. Code 1594) that was issued by the Department.

and

Satisfactory completion of an *additional* 9 graduate-level credit hours in PreK–12 educational leadership from a regionally accredited college or university or the equivalent in professional development approved by the Department.

NOTE: The additional 9 graduate-level credit hours must have been completed *after* the applicant was issued his or her Certified Central Office Personnel Standard Certificate or Special Education Director Standard Certificate.

B. Experience Requirements

Minimum of 7 years of education experience.

1. Minimum of 5 years of experience as an educator with satisfactory annual summative evaluations or the equivalent thereof on a state-approved educator evaluation system in any PreK–12 public school setting or an equivalent setting as approved by the Department.

    and

2. Minimum of 2 years of full-time leadership experience with satisfactory annual summative evaluations or the equivalent thereof on a state-approved educator evaluation system in any PreK–12 public school setting or an equivalent setting as approved by the Department working in any of the following areas:

    a. School Principal or Assistant School Principal.
    b. Certified Central Office Personnel Administrator.
    c. Special Education Director.
    d. Other instructional leadership position.

C. Praxis II Requirements

The applicant shall have achieved a passing score on 1 of the following examinations:

1. A passing score of 160 on the School Superintendent Assessment (ETS Code #6021).
2. A passing score of 162 on the School Superintendent Assessment (ETS Code #6991).

IV. Special Education Director

A. Education Requirements

Satisfy at least 1 of the following education requirements:

1. Master's or doctoral degree with a major or its equivalent in special education leadership offered by an NCATE (CAEP) specialty organization–recognized educator preparation program or state-approved educator preparation program where the state approval body employed the appropriate NASDTEC or NCATE (CAEP) specialty organization standards, at a regionally accredited college or university.

2. Master's or doctoral degree in special education offered by an NCATE (CAEP) specialty organization–recognized educator preparation program or state-approved educator preparation program where the state approval body employed the appropriate NASDTEC or NCATE (CAEP) specialty organization standards, at a regionally accredited college or university.

    and

    Satisfactory completion of alternative routes for licensure or certification program for leaders as provided in 14 Del.C 1260–1266.

3. Master's or doctoral degree in any content area from a regionally accredited college or university.

and

Satisfactory completion of a Department-approved educator preparation program for special education directors as provided in 14 DE Admin. Code 290 Approval of Educator Preparation Programs.

4. Master's or doctoral degree with a major or its equivalent in PreK–12 educational leadership offered by an NCATE (CAEP) specialty organization–recognized educator preparation program or state-approved educator preparation program where the state approval body employed the appropriate NASDTEC or NCATE (CAEP) specialty organization standards, at a regionally accredited college or university.

and

Thirty graduate-level credit hours from a regionally accredited college or university in special education taken either as part of a degree program or in addition to it, or the equivalent in professional development preapproved by the Department.

B. Experience Requirements

Minimum of 5 years of 1 of the following experience requirements in any PreK–12 public school setting or an equivalent setting as approved by the Department:

1. Teaching special education students under a state credential with satisfactory annual summative evaluations or the equivalent thereof on a state-approved educator evaluation system.
2. Working with special education students as a school psychologist, speech pathologist, or audiologist under a Delaware Standard or Professional Status Certificate.
3. Working with special education students as an educational diagnostician or special education coordinator.
4. Supervising staff who teach special education students with satisfactory annual summative evaluations or the equivalent thereof on a state-approved educator evaluation system.
5. Any combination of the types of experiences prescribed above that totals a minimum of 5 years.

C. Praxis II Requirements

The applicant shall have achieved a passing score on 1 of the following examinations:

1. A passing score of 146 on the Educational Leadership: Administration and Supervision Assessment (ETS Code #5412).
2. A passing score of 160 on the School Leaders Licensure Assessment (ETS Code #6011).
3. A passing score of 160 on the School Superintendent Assessment (ETS Code #6021).
4. A passing score of 151 on the School Leaders Licensure Assessment (ETS Code #6990).
5. A passing score of 162 on the School Superintendent Assessment (ETS Code "#6991).

Guidance Counselor

I. Elementary School Counselor
   A. Requirements
      1. Holds a valid Delaware Initial, Continuing, or Advanced License or a Standard or Professional Status Certificate issued prior to August 31, 2003.
      2. Has met the requirements as set forth in 14 DE Admin. Code 1505 Standard Certificate.
      3. Has satisfied the following additional requirements:
         a. Completed a master's degree from a regionally accredited college or university with a major or its equivalent in elementary school counseling from an educator preparation program approved or recognized by the Council for Accreditation of Counseling and Related Educational Programs (CACREP) or a state where the state approval body employed the appropriate standards.
            or
            Satisfactorily completed a Department-approved educator preparation program in elementary school counseling.
            or
            Holds a master's degree from a regionally accredited college in any field; and has satisfactorily completed 39 credits of graduate coursework or the equivalent in professional development as approved by the Department in the areas of: Introduction to School Counseling & Theories (3 credits); Human Behavior and Child Development (3 credits); Ethical Issues in School Counseling (3 credits); College & Career Readiness K–12 (3 credits); Testing, Measurements, and Research in School Counseling (3 credits); The Counselor as Consultant (3 credits); Special Education Law & the School Counselor's Role (3 credits); Group Counseling (3 credits); Individual Counseling Skills & Strategies (6 credits); Family Counseling (3 credits); and Principles and Practices of a School Counseling Program (6 credits).
         b. Has completed 700 hours of clinical experience in an elementary-school setting under the direct supervision of a State Department of Education–certified Elementary School Counselor.
         c. Achieves a passing score on an examination of content knowledge, such as Praxis II, for Professional School Counselor.
II. Secondary School Counselor
   A. Requirements
      1. Holds a valid Delaware Initial, Continuing, or Advanced License or a Limited Standard, Standard, or Professional Status Certificate issued prior to August 31, 2003.
      2. Has met the requirements as set forth in 14 DE Admin. Code 1505 Standard Certificate.
      3. Has satisfied the following additional requirements:
         a. Completed a master's degree from a regionally accredited college or

university with a major or its equivalent in elementary school counseling from an educator preparation program approved or recognized by the CACREP or a state where the state approval body employed the appropriate standards.
or
Satisfactorily completed a Department-approved educator preparation program in secondary school counseling.
or
Holds a master's degree from a regionally accredited college in any field; and has satisfactorily completed 39 credits of graduate coursework or the equivalent in professional development as approved by the Department in the areas of: Introduction to School Counseling & Theories (3 credits); Human Behavior and Child Development (3 credits); Ethical Issues in School Counseling (3 credits); College & Career Readiness K–12 (3 credits); Testing, Measurements, and Research in School Counseling (3 credits); The Counselor as Consultant (3 credits); Special Education Law & the School Counselor's Role (3 credits); Group Counseling (3 credits); Individual Counseling Skills & Strategies (6 credits); Family Counseling (3 credits); and Principles and Practices of a School Counseling Program (6 credits).

b. Has completed 700 hours of clinical experience in a secondary-school setting under the direct supervision of a State Department of Education–certified Secondary School Counselor.

c. Achieves a passing score on an examination of content knowledge, such as Praxis II, for Professional School Counselor.

School Psychologist

I. Licensure Requirements
A. The Department shall issue a Standard Certificate as a School Psychologist to an applicant who has met the following:
1. Holds a valid Delaware Initial, Continuing, or Advanced License or Standard or Professional Status Certificate issued by the Department prior to August 31, 2003.
2. Has met the requirements for licensure in Delaware and presents proof of a valid and current license or certificate as a school psychologist.
3. Has satisfied either of the following additional education and internship requirements:
a. The applicant shall have received an Educational Specialist (EdS) degree, the equivalent of an EdS degree, or a doctoral degree through a program approved by the National Association of School Psychologists (NASP) at a regionally accredited college or university; or a doctoral degree in school psychology through a program approved by the American Psychological Association (APA) at a regionally accredited college or university;
and
The applicant shall have completed a supervised, culminating,

comprehensive field experience of at least 1,200 hours, 600 hours of which must have been completed in an educational setting in an institution or agency that is approved by the applicant's graduate program or the Department, completed at or near the end of formal training, through which the applicant had the opportunity to integrate and apply professional knowledge and skills acquired in prior courses and practica as well as to acquire new competencies consistent with training program goals;
or

b. The Department may issue a School Psychologist Standard Certificate to an applicant who holds a Nationally Certified School Psychologist (NCSP) certificate from NASP that is in good standing;
and

The applicant shall have achieved a passing score of 147 on the Praxis Subject Assessment—School Psychology (ETS Test Code # 5042).

School Social Worker

I. Requirements
   A. The Department shall issue a Standard Certificate as a School Social Worker to an applicant who has met the following:
      1. Holds a valid Delaware Initial, Continuing, or Advanced License or Standard or Professional Status Certificate issued by the Department prior to August 31, 2003.
      2. Has met the requirements for licensure in Delaware and presents proof of a valid and current license or certificate as a school social worker from another state or jurisdiction whose requirements are substantially similar.
      3. Has satisfied the following requirements:
         a. Master's degree in Social Work (MSW) from a regionally accredited college or university.
         b. License to practice as a LCSW (licensed as a clinical social worker) or LMSW (licensed as a master's social worker) issued by the Delaware Board of Social Work Examiners that is in good standing.
         c. Two years of full-time work experience as a social worker as approved by the Department. Post-degree supervised clinical social work experience completed in order to obtain an LCSW license shall count as work experience.

School Library Media Specialist

I. Licensure Requirements
   A. The Department shall issue a Standard Certificate as a School Library Media Specialist to an applicant who has met the following:
      1. Holds a valid Delaware Initial, Continuing, or Advanced License or Standard or Professional Status Certificate issued by the Department prior to August 31, 2003.

2. Has met the requirements for licensure and presents proof of a valid and current license or certificate as a school library media specialist.
3. Has satisfied at least 1 of the following additional education requirements:
    a. Holds a master's or doctoral degree from a regionally accredited college or university in an American Library Association–approved program in School Library Media.
    b. Holds a master's or doctoral degree from a regionally accredited college or university in any area.
       and
       Has completed a Department-approved School Library Media program that meets American Library Association standards.

District of Columbia

Teaching Licenses/Credentials

For a list of documents required to apply for each credential, see https://osse.dc.gov/page/teacher-certification.

I. Initial Teacher Credential (valid 3 years; nonrenewable)
    A. Option 1, for those currently enrolled in an approved teacher preparation program—candidate:
        1. Holds a completed bachelor's degree;
        2. Has successfully passed the Praxis CORE, Pre-Professional Skills Test (PPST), or other accepted alternate basic skills exam;
        3. Has successfully passed the Praxis II subject content exam in the area of the credential;
        4. Is admitted into an Office of the State Superintendent of Education (OSSE)-approved teacher licensure program, or a teacher licensure program approved in another state accepted by OSSE, in the area of the credential; *and*
        5. Is employed or contracted as a teacher by a local education agency (LEA) operating in the District of Columbia.
    B. Option 2, for those who hold a valid license from another state and have demonstrated effective teaching performance experience—candidate:
        1. Holds a completed bachelor's degree;
        2. Has successfully passed the Praxis CORE, PPST, or other accepted alternate basic skills exam;
        3. Has successfully passed a corresponding subject content exam in another state or has passed the DC-required Praxis II exam;
        4. Has documentation satisfactory to OSSE to confirm that the candidate:
            a. Has completed at least 2 years of effective full-time teaching experience in another state as measured by a summative evaluation rating; *or*
            b. Has completed 2 years of effective or equivalent teaching experience as measured by the student growth component of an evaluation rating. The experience shall be completed within the previous 5 years, and the final year shall show a rating of Effective or higher; *and*
        5. Holds a valid teaching credential, in good standing, issued from another state accepted by OSSE.
    C. Option 3, for those currently employed or contracted as teachers by an LEA operating in the District of Columbia—candidate:
        1. Holds a completed bachelor's degree;

2. Has successfully passed the Praxis CORE, PPST, or other accepted alternate basic skills exam;

3. Has successfully passed the Praxis II subject content exam in the area of the credential;

4. Is employed or contracted as a teacher by an LEA operating in the District of Columbia;
    and

5. Has a written request for issuance of an Initial Teacher Credential addressed to OSSE from the employing LEA.

II. Standard Teacher Credential (valid 4 years; renewable; may be used for interstate reciprocity with other US states, territories, and the Department of Defense Dependents Schools. For a list of documents required to apply, see https://osse.dc.gov/page/teacher-certification)

A. Option 1, for those who have completed an approved teacher licensure program—candidate:

1. Holds a completed bachelor's degree;

2. Has completed an approved teacher licensure program in the corresponding subject area;

3. Has successfully passed the Praxis CORE, PPST, or other accepted alternate basic skills exam;

4. Has successfully passed the Praxis II subject content exam in the area of the credential;
    and

5. Has successfully passed the Praxis II Principles of Learning & Teaching (PLT) exam for the grade level of the credential.

B. Option 2, for those who hold or have held a DC Initial Teacher Credential and demonstrate effective teaching performance experience within a DC LEA—candidate:

1. Holds or has held a DC Initial Teacher Credential;

2. Has completed at least 2 years of effective or equivalent full-time teaching experience while holding the initial credential at an LEA in the District of Columbia within the previous 5 years, as demonstrated by the applicant's summative evaluation rating from the employing LEA; the performance evaluation reviews must have been conducted by the same LEA and the evaluation system must have been accepted by OSSE;
    and

3. Has successfully passed the Praxis II PLT exam for the grade level of the credential.

C. Option 3, for those who hold a valid teaching license and demonstrate effective teaching performance experience in another state—candidate:

1. Holds a completed bachelor's degree;

2. Holds a valid full teaching credential from another reciprocal state;

3. Has successfully passed the Praxis CORE, PPST, or other accepted alternate basic skills exam;

4. Has successfully passed a corresponding subject content exam in another state or has passed the DC-required Praxis II exam;

5. Has successfully passed a corresponding pedagogy exam in another state or has passed the DC-required Praxis II exam;
   and

6. Has completed at least 2 years of effective or equivalent full-time teaching experience in another state, as measured by a summative evaluation rating of 2 years of effective or equivalent teaching based upon the student growth component of an evaluation rating. The experience shall be completed within the previous 5 years, and the final year shall show a rating of Effective or higher.

D. Option 4, for those who are currently employed as teachers within a DC LEA that does not require a license, but who demonstrate effective teaching performance experience—candidate:

1. Holds a completed bachelor's degree;

2. Has successfully passed the Praxis CORE, PPST, or other accepted alternate basic skills exam;

3. Has successfully passed the Praxis II subject content exam in the area of the credential;

4. Has successfully passed the Praxis II PLT exam for the grade level of the credential;

5. Has completed at least 2 years of effective or equivalent full-time teaching experience at an LEA in the District of Columbia within the previous 3 years, as demonstrated by the applicant's summative evaluation rating from the employing LEA. The performance evaluation reviews must have been conducted by the same LEA and the evaluation system must have been accepted by OSSE;
   and

6. Is currently employed as a "teacher of record" with a DC LEA.

Service Provider Credentials

For a list of documents required to apply for each credential, see https://osse.dc.gov/page/school-service-provider-certification#required.

I. School Counselor—candidate:

A. Holds a completed master's degree in school counseling education from an approved licensure program;
   or
   Holds a completed master's degree in counseling and has completed graduate-level coursework in each area listed below. A letter grade of "C" or higher is required.

1. Counseling children and adolescents
2. Multicultural counseling
3. Counseling students with exceptionalities
4. Crisis and trauma counseling and interventions
5. Career development and vocational education counseling

      6.   Testing assessments and measurements

      7.   Legal and ethical issues for school counselors

  B. Has successfully completed at least 300 hours of supervised school-based field, practicum, or internship experience as part of the degree program. Field experience may also be met by one of the following:

      1.   A degree in school counseling from a program approved by the Council for Accreditation of Counseling and Related Educational Program (CACREP) or a valid National Certified Counselors (NCC) credential issued by the National Board for Certified Counselors (NBCC);

         or

         Appropriate documentation verifying at least 2 years of full-time teaching experience or 1 year of full-time experience as a school counselor.

      2.   A passing score for the DC-required school counselor content exam or a comparable exam in another state where a school counselor license is held.

II. School Librarian—candidate:

  A. Holds a completed master's degree in school library media from an approved licensure program or a completed master's degree in library science and has completed graduate-level coursework in each area listed below. A letter grade of C or higher is required.

      1.   Cataloging and classification

      2.   Selection and use of media for children

      3.   Instructional media design and development/production

      4.   Information sources, services, and instruction

      5.   School library organization

      6.   Integration of technology into the curriculum

  B. Has completed directed field experience in a school library with an experienced library media specialist

    or

    Has completed 2 years of school-based teaching experience

    or

    Has completed 1 year of experience as a school librarian;

  C. Has achieved a passing score for the DC-required library media specialist content exam

    or

    Has passed a comparable exam in another state where a school library media specialist license is held.

III. Additional Service Provider Licenses: visit the Educator Licensure and Accreditation website at https://osse.dc.gov/page/school-service-provider-certification for full details on the following licenses:

  A. School Audiologist

  B. Reading Specialist

  C. School Psychologist

  D. School Social Worker

  E. School Speech Pathologist

Administrative Services Credentials

For a list of documents required to apply for administrative services credentials, see https://osse.dc.gov/page/principal-and-assistant-principal-certification.

I. Initial Administrator Credential (available to applicants who do not meet current requirements for a standard credential; valid 2 years; nonrenewable)—candidate:
   A. Holds a completed bachelor's degree;
   B. Has completed an approved program that leads to a state certification in school leadership and supervision;
      or
      Holds a valid full principal license in another state;
      or
      Holds a completed master's degree or higher;
   C. Has completed at least 2 years of school-based teaching, instructional leadership, or pupil services experience. Substitute teaching experience does not apply.
II. Standard Administrator Credential (valid 4 years; renewable)—candidate:
   A. Holds a completed bachelor's degree;
   B. Has completed an approved program that leads to a state certification in school leadership and supervision;
      or
      Holds a completed master's degree or higher;
   C. Has completed 4 years of school-based teaching, instructional leadership, or pupil services experience. Substitute teaching experience does not apply.
   D. Has passing scores for the DC-required school leadership licensure exam.

Teacher, Service Provider, and Administrator Licensure Renewal Requirements

I. Option A: Renewal by Performance Evaluation Rating (available to applicants currently employed by a DC LEA)
   A. Performance evaluation reviews must have been conducted while applicant was an employee of a DC LEA that administers an official educator performance evaluation system accepted by OSSE for the purposes of obtaining a state educator credential.
   B. Performance evaluation reviews must have been administered by the same DC LEA during the applicable renewal cycle of the credential being renewed.
   C. Applicant must have achieved at least an Effective or equivalent performance rating for at least 3 school years of the 4-year validity term of the credential. The ratings must be achieved based upon a summative or student growth component of the evaluation system.
   D. The assignment area of the performance evaluation review must have been conducted for the same assignment area of the credential being renewed.
   E. For a list of documents required for renewal, see https://osse.dc.gov/page/option-renewal-performance-evaluation-ratings.
II. Option B: Renewal by Completion of Professional Development Training Activity Hours
   A. Applicants must submit documentation verifying satisfactory completion of the

equivalent of 120 hours of professional development (PD) training activities completed within the 4-year term of the credential being renewed.

B. The equivalent of 120 hours equals 120 actual clock hours of instruction/activity time completed, or 8 college credit hours, or a combination of both. One college credit hour equals 15 clock hours.

C. A minimum of the equivalent of 60 hours must be directly related to the content area of the credential being renewed. The additional hours may align with any of the areas in the table on the website linked in letter E, below.

D. The hours may be accrued by completion of college coursework or completion of training activities delivered by the employing local education agency, national education organizations, related industry organizations, and/or accredited PD provider organizations.

E. For required content of PD training activities and required documentation, see https://osse.dc.gov/page/option-b-%E2%80%93-renewal-completion-professional-development-training-activity-hours.

Florida

The Bureau of Educator Certification at the Florida Department of Education determines individualized eligibility and testing requirements for certification. After an application for certification is on file, the Bureau will issue the applicant an Official Statement of Status of Eligibility (SOE). This statement will indicate individualized eligibility and testing requirements; these may include the Florida Teacher Certification Exams (FTCE) or, for candidates seeking certification in educational leadership, the Florida Educational Leadership Exam (FELE). Contact the Bureau (see Appendix 1) for complete information.

Types of Certificates

I. Professional Certificate Eligibility Requirements
   A renewable professional certificate, valid for 5 school years, may be issued to an applicant who meets all of the following:
   A. Files a completed application, including official degree transcripts and a complete fingerprint report that has been cleared by the Florida Department of Law Enforcement and the FBI;
   B. Holds a bachelor's or higher degree from an accredited or approved institution of higher learning;
   C. Has received a passing score on the Florida General Knowledge Test;*
   D. Has received a passing score on the Florida Professional Education Test;*
   E. Has received a passing score on the Florida developed or Florida approved subject area examination for each subject or field to be shown on the certificate;*
   F. Meets professional preparation requirements (see V, below);
      and
   G. Successfully demonstrates professional education competencies identified by Florida statutes and administrative rules.
   *Note: There are other available options for satisfying the requirements for each mastery area (I, C–E.); see section 1012.56, Florida Statutes.

II. Restricted Professional Certificate Eligibility Requirements
   A renewable professional certificate, valid for 5 school years, may be issued to an applicant who meets all of the professional certificate eligibility requirements (see I, above), except C. An applicant who holds the restricted professional certificate may not be assigned to a classroom as the teacher of record. The restricted professional certificate can only be issued in the following subject areas:
   A. Educational Media Specialist
   B. School Counseling
   C. School Psychology
   D. School Social Work
   E. Speech Language Impaired

III. Temporary Certificate Eligibility Requirements

A nonrenewable, temporary certificate, valid for 3 school years, may be issued to an applicant who submits a complete application package requiring background screening, a certificate issuance request from an employer, official transcripts, and satisfies the subject specialization in A, B, or C:

A. Has an acceptable major in a single subject in which Florida offers certification or meets specialization requirements in the subject;
   or

B. For subjects requiring only a bachelor's degree, has received a passing score on the Florida-developed or Florida-approved subject area examination for each subject or field to be shown on the certificate;
   or

C. Has obtained a 2.5 grade point average on a 4.0 scale in the course analysis of the initial subject shown on the certificate.

IV. Professional Certificate Renewal

A. Completion of 6 semester hours of appropriate college credit, or 120 approved Florida in-service (staff-development) points or training/course work related to the educational goals and performance standards outlined in Florida statutes during each 5-year validity period

   1. Beginning July 1, 2014, credit must include 1 semester hour or 20 approved Florida in-service (staff-development) points in teaching students with disabilities.

   2. For educators holding a certificate with a beginning validity date of July 1, 2020, or later, at least 2 college credits, 40 in-service (staff development) points, or a combination thereof must be completed in evidence-based instruction and interventions for students with characteristics of dyslexia, including the use of explicit, systematic, and sequential approaches to reading instruction, developing phonological and phonemic awareness, and decoding and implementing multisensory intervention strategies. This requirement applies to educators renewing in any of the following coverage areas, regardless of teaching assignment:

      a. Elementary Education (K–6)
      b. Prekindergarten/Primary Education (Age 3–Grade 3)
      c. Elementary Education (1–6)
      d. Primary Education (K–3)
      e. English (1–6)
      f. Middle Grades English (5–9)
      g. Middle Grades Integrated Curriculum (5–9)
      h. English (6–12)
      i. Reading (K–12)
      j. Reading Endorsement
      k. English for Speakers of Other Languages (ESOL) (K–12)

V. Professional Preparation Requirements for Academic, Administrative, Degreed Career and Technical, and Specialty Class Coverages (PreK–12)

A. Completes an undergraduate teacher education program at an institution approved by the Florida State Board of Education or another state;

or
B.   Possesses a valid full-time standard teaching certificate issued by another state or by the National Board for Professional Teaching Standards;
     or
C.   Professional Preparation (for applications received beginning January 1, 2016)
     1.   Completes a minimum of 15 semester hours in the following professional education areas:
          a.   Classroom management with a focus on creating safe learning environments in which effective teaching and learning can take place by promoting a physically, emotionally, socially, and academically secure climate for students;
          b.   Child and adolescent development, including theories and principles of learning;
          c.   Educational assessment practices that include analysis and application of data from statewide standardized assessments and other multiple sources to improve instruction and learning;
          d.   Effective instructional techniques, strategies, and materials to meet the needs of diverse learners, including students with disabilities;
          e.   For certificate subject coverages classified by rule as academic or degreed career and technical, applications of research-based instructional practices in reading;
               and
          f.   Instructional strategies for teaching students of limited English proficiency, including instruction in the English language and development of the student's mastery of the 4 language skills of listening, speaking, reading, and writing.
     2.   Completes practical experience in teaching, satisfied by 1 of the following methods:
          a.   One year of full-time teaching experience in an approved elementary or secondary school,
               or
          b.   Six semester hours earned in a college student teaching or supervised internship completed in an elementary or a secondary school in which the candidate demonstrates ability to positively impact student learning growth with a diverse population of students.
     3.   The requirements of professional preparation in C, 1, directly above, are not applicable and shall not be required for school social work or speech-language impaired certification.
D.   For other options, see http://www.fldoe.org/teaching/certification/general-cert-requirements/professional-preparation-edu-competenc.stml.

Elementary Education, Preschool Education, and Prekindergarten Education

I.   General Requirements
     A.   General and professional preparation. See Professional Certificate Eligibility, above.

II. Specific Subject Requirements
   A. Elementary Education: Bachelor's or higher degree with a major in elementary education that includes teaching reading at the K–6 level
   B. Preschool Education: Bachelor's or higher degree with a major in preschool education (birth–age 4)
   C. Prekindergarten/Primary Education: Bachelor's or higher degree with a major in prekindergarten/primary education (age 3–grade 3)
   D. Florida offers alternative plans for certification in the subject fields:
      1. Elementary Education: https://www.flrules.org/gateway/RuleNo.asp?title=CERTIFICATION&ID=6A-4.0151
      2. Preschool Education: https://www.flrules.org/gateway/RuleNo.asp?title=CERTIFICATION&ID=6A-4.0141
      3. Prekindergarten/Primary Education: https://www.flrules.org/gateway/RuleNo.asp?title=CERTIFICATION&ID=6A-4.0142

Middle Grades (5–9)

I. General Requirements
   A. General and professional preparation. See Professional Certificate Eligibility, above.
II. Specific Requirements
   A. Middle Grades English: a bachelor's or higher degree major in English, or a bachelor's or higher degree in another subject or field and 18 semester hours in English, including specific courses in grammar and composition above the freshman level, speech, and 9 semester hours of literature
   B. Middle Grades Mathematics: a bachelor's or higher degree major in mathematics, or a bachelor's degree in another subject or field and 18 semester hours in mathematics, including specific courses in calculus (pre-calculus/trigonometry), geometry, probability or statistics
   C. Middle Grades General Science: a bachelor's or higher degree major in general science, or a bachelor's or higher degree in another subject or field and 18 semester hours in science with associated lab experience, including specific courses in biology, earth-space science/earth science, and chemistry or physics
   D. Middle Grades Social Science: a bachelor's or higher degree major in social science, or a bachelor's or higher degree in another subject or field and 18 semester hours in social science, including specific courses in Western civilization (or European, Asian, African, Latin American, or Middle Eastern history), economics, United States government, geography, and 6 semester hours in United States history

Secondary School (6–12)

I. General Requirements
   A. General and professional preparation. See Professional Certificate Eligibility, above.
II. Special requirements for subject fields: agriculture, biology, business education, chemistry, drama, earth-space science, English, family and consumer science, marketing, mathematics, physics, social science (general), and engineering and technology education

A. For all subject fields, applicants may qualify by having a bachelor's or higher degree with a major in the field.

B. Florida offers alternative plans for certification in the subject fields:

1. A bachelor's or higher degree in another subject or field with 30 semester hours of specified courses in the field for which certification is being sought. For details on specific course distributions for each subject, visit https://www.flrules .org/gateway/ChapterHome.asp?Chapter=6A-4.

2. For mathematics and separate areas in science, applicants may also qualify by a third certification plan. (See https://www.flrules.org/gateway/ChapterHome.asp ?Chapter=6A-4.)

All Grades (K–12)

I. General Requirements

A. General and professional preparation. See Professional Certificate Eligibility, above.

II. Special requirements for subject fields: art, computer science, dance, English for speakers of other languages, exceptional student education, health, hearing impaired, humanities, music, physical education, reading, speech-language impaired, visually impaired, and world languages. (See https://www.flrules.org/gateway/ChapterHome.asp ?Chapter=6A-4.)

A. For subject fields except reading and speech-language impaired, applicants may qualify by having a bachelor's or higher degree with a major in the field. For reading and speech-language impaired, applicants may qualify by having a master's degree or higher with a graduate major in the field.

B. Florida offers alternative plans for certification in the subject fields, except for English for speakers of other languages and humanities.

1. For all subject fields except reading and speech-language impaired, applicants may qualify by having a bachelor's or higher degree with a major of 30 semester hours of specified courses in the field for which certification is being sought. (For details on specific distributions, visit https://www.flrules.org/gateway/ ChapterHome.asp?Chapter=6A-4.)

2. For world language specializations in Arabic, Chinese, Farsi, French, German, Greek, Haitian Creole, Hebrew, Hindi, Italian, Japanese, Portuguese, Russian, Spanish, and Turkish, applicants may also qualify by 3 additional certification plans. For Latin, applicants may qualify by 1 additional plan. (See https://www .flrules.org/gateway/RuleNo.asp?title=CERTIFICATION&ID=6A-4.0243.)

3. For reading, in some cases, applicants may qualify by having at least a bachelor's degree major with 30 semester hours to include specified course work and a supervised reading practicum. (For details on specific distributions, visit https://www.flrules.org/gateway/RuleNo.asp?title=CERTIFICATION&ID=6A -4.0291.)

4. For speech-language impaired, applicants may qualify by having a master's or higher degree major or 60 semester hours to include specified course work and a supervised clinical practice. (For details on specific distributions, visit https://www.flrules.org/gateway/RuleNo.asp?title=CERTIFICATION&ID=

6A-4.0176.) Other options include holding a valid license in speech-language pathology issued pursuant to Chapter 468, Part I, Florida Statutes, or holding a valid certificate of clinical competence issued by the American Speech-Language Hearing Association.

Administration

I. General Requirements
    A. General and professional preparation. See Professional Certificate Eligibility, above.
II. Educational Leadership, Level One Certificate
    A. Holds a master's or higher degree from an accredited institution
    B. Documents successful completion of the Florida Educational Leadership Core Curriculum (see https://www.flrules.org/gateway/RuleNo.asp?title= CERTIFICATION&ID=6A-4.0082 for specific areas) through 1 of the following plans:
        1. Successful completion of a Florida Department of Education–approved preservice program in educational leadership offered by an accredited institution;
        2. A graduate degree major in educational administration, administration and supervision, or educational leadership awarded by an approved institution;
        3. A graduate degree with a major in a subject other than educational administration, administration and supervision, or educational leadership, and successful completion of a Department of Education–approved modified Florida program in educational leadership offered by an accredited institution;
        4. A graduate degree with a major in a subject other than educational administration, administration and supervision, or educational leadership awarded by an accredited institution, and 30 semester hours of graduate credit in each of the Florida-specified principal leadership standard areas and an internship or a course with associated field experience in educational leadership.
            or
        5. Successful completion of an educational leadership training program approved by the Florida Department of Education and offered by a Florida public school district.
III. School Principal, Level Two Certificate
    A. Holds a valid professional certificate covering educational leadership, school administration, or school administration/supervision;
        and
        Documents successful performance of the duties of school principalship;
        and
        Demonstrates successful performance of the competencies of the school principalship, which shall be verified by the Florida district school superintendent.

Educational Media Specialist (PreK–12)

I. General Requirements
  A. General and professional preparation. See Professional Certificate and Restricted Professional Certificate Eligibility, above.
II. Specialization Requirements
  A. Bachelor's or higher degree with a major in educational media or library science, *or*
  B. Bachelor's or higher degree with 30 semester hours in educational media or library science, including the following areas:
     1. Management of library media programs
     2. Collection development
     3. Library media resources
     4. Reference sources and services
     5. Organization of collections
     6. Design and production of educational media

School Counseling (Grades PreK–12)

I. General Requirements
  A. General and professional preparation. See Professional Certificate Eligibility and Restricted Professional Certificate Eligibility, above.
II. Specialization Requirements
  A. Master's or higher degree with a graduate major in guidance and counseling or in school counseling that includes a minimum of 600 clock hours of supervised internship experience serving school-aged students in a PreK, elementary, or secondary school setting; *or*
  B. Master's or higher degree with a graduate major in counseling other than guidance and counseling or school counseling (e.g., mental health counseling) that includes a minimum of 600 clock hours of supervised internship experience with school-aged children and their families, with at least 9 semester hours of graduate credit to include the following areas:
     1. Student appraisal and evaluation methods in PreK, elementary, and secondary schools, including interpretation and analysis of standardized tests and other assessment results that assist students in career exploration, academic skills, and personal and social skill development;
     2. College and career planning for PreK, elementary, and secondary school students, including college and career exploration, and knowledge of financial aid and financing of postsecondary education options;
     3. Principles, philosophy, organization, and administration of a comprehensive school counseling program in PreK, elementary, and secondary schools; *and*
     4. Consultation skills and techniques for conferring with groups such as agencies, teachers, and parents.

Note: Applicants pursuing this plan must be assigned a mentor during the first 2 years of employment as a school counselor.

Note: Noncitizens, resident aliens, and refugees may be issued a certificate on the same basis as citizens of the United States, provided they meet exact and specific qualifications established by the Florida State Board of Education. Proof of eligibility to work in the United States is required for noncitizens.

Georgia

Certification Classification

I. Categories
- A. Renewable (except for the Life certificate, professional certificates are valid 5 years, during which educator must satisfy standard renewal requirements)
    1. Performance-Based Professional
        a. Issued to teachers who are evaluated on the statewide evaluation system and leaders who have completed Georgia Professional Standards Commission (GaPSC)–approved performance-based Educational Leadership programs
        b. Not issued in service fields
        c. Indicates completion of all professional and Georgia-specific requirements for certification in the field
    2. Standard Professional
        a. Issued to those meeting professional requirements for certification who are not evaluated on the statewide evaluation system or do not meet the requirements for the Performance-Based Professional
        b. Indicates completion of all professional requirements for certification in the field
        c. May initially be issued without completion of all Georgia-specific requirements
    3. Advanced Professional
        a. Issued to teachers with expert classroom practice as evidenced by teaching experience and 1 of the following: advanced degree in a teaching field beyond the initial preparation program; a valid professional certificate in Curriculum and Instruction or Instructional Technology; or a valid National Board for Professional Teaching Standards (NBPTS) Certification
        b. Not issued in service or leadership fields; indicates completion of all professional and Georgia-specific requirements for certification in the field
    4. Lead Professional
        a. Issued to qualified teachers who promote, support, and expand opportunities for teacher leadership in grades P–12, as evidenced by teaching experience, completion of related education/training, and successful completion of a Teacher Leadership assessment
        b. Not issued in service or leadership fields
        c. Indicates completion of all professional and Georgia-specific requirements for certification in the field
    5. Life: issued prior to July 1, 1974; remains valid for current holders
    6. Certificate of Eligibility (no longer issued after January 1, 2020)
        a. Issued to individuals meeting all requirements for a particular certificate

with the sole exception of employment by a Georgia local unit of administration (LUA)
   b. Issued to individuals renewing their certificates who do not have at least 1 year of experience in Georgia
   c. May be converted to the specified certificate upon employment
7. Retired Educator Certificate (initial certificate is valid for 30 years and may be renewed for 10-year validity periods)
   a. Issued to individuals previously holding professional Georgia certification who have retired as verified by the Georgia Teacher's Retirement System
   b. Acceptable for short-term substitute teaching only

B. Non-Renewable (valid for up to 5 years; except for the Pre-Service certificate, issuance must be requested by an employing Georgia LUA)
   1. Pre-Service (valid 5 years, issued at the request of an educator preparation provider, may be extended)
      a. Issued to candidates enrolled in state-approved educator preparation programs and participating in field and clinical experiences in Georgia schools
      b. Requires exposure to the Georgia Code of Ethics for Educators and successful state background check
      c. Authorizes the holder to participate in supervised field experience, clinical practice, student teaching, or residency work in Georgia schools
   2. Five-Year Induction (valid for 5 years, but may be issued for less than 5 years in some circumstances)
      a. Issued to individuals who complete a state-approved educator preparation program and have less than 3 years of successful teaching experience
      b. Indicates that all professional requirements for certification in the field have been met except the Georgia-specific requirement for 3 years of teaching experience to earn professional certification
   3. Three-Year Induction (valid for 3 years)
      a. Issued to individuals holding the Five-Year Induction certificate who are assigned to teach out-of-field; outstanding requirements for the Five-Year Induction certificate may include content assessment or approved program completion
      b. May only be requested by a Georgia LUA
   4. One-Year Induction (valid for 1 year)
      a. Issued to individuals who meet all requirements for the Five-Year Induction certificate with the exception of passing the content knowledge assessment
      b. May only be requested by a Georgia LUA
   5. Provisional Certificate (formerly known as the Induction Pathway 4 Certificate; maximum validity is 3 years, with the exception of certain career and technical fields)
      a. Issued at the request of an employing Georgia LUA to those meeting minimum education and testing requirements who have not met professional requirements for certification
   6. Non-Renewable Professional (validity period depends on the certificate)

a. Three-Year Non-Renewable Professional teaching fields or endorsements are issued to professionally certified educators teaching out-of-field; outstanding requirements for renewable professional certification may include content assessment or approved program completion.

b. Non-Renewable Professional leadership certificates are issued for 3 years to those employed in a leadership position; outstanding requirements for renewable professional certification include passing GaPSC leadership assessments and completion of a GaPSC-approved leadership program.

    i. Tier I Educational Leadership: issued to individuals who hold a bachelor's degree or higher and are placed in entry-level leadership positions below principal at the building level, and district-level positions that do not supervise principals. The GaPSC-approved program is completed at the master's level.

    ii. Tier II Educational Leadership: issued to individuals who hold at least a master's degree and are placed in advanced-level leadership positions that supervise other leaders. The GaPSC-approved program is completed at the education specialist degree or higher.

c. Non-Renewable Professional service certificates are issued for 3 years to individuals who have not met certain requirements for renewable professional certification in a service field; outstanding requirements for renewable professional certification may include content assessment, approved program completion, or completion of a higher degree.

d. One-Year Non-Renewable Professional certificates may also be issued to individuals lacking standard renewal requirements, or to individuals who meet all requirements for a professional certificate with the exception of passing the content knowledge assessment.

e. May only be requested by a Georgia LUA.

7. International Exchange (valid for 3 years; may be extended in some circumstances): issued at the request of an employing Georgia LUA to educators certified in other nations who wish to teach in Georgia schools

8. Waiver (valid for up to 1 year; may be extended in some circumstances): issued at the discretion of the GaPSC to educators who have not satisfied all certification requirements

9. Military Support Certificate

a. Standard Professional Military Support Certificate (valid for 5 years; renewable)

    i. Issued to employed Georgia educators who held a valid renewable professional certificate and were called to active military duty. The certificate may be renewed for the full 5-year validity, even if renewal requirements have not been met.

b. Military Support Provisional Certificate (issued to veterans and military family members enrolled in the Troops to Teachers program). The maximum usable validity is 3 years, issued in 1-year increments; individuals have a modified timeline for completion of requirements.

    i. Initial Issuance: bachelor's degree or higher, unless Georgia does not require a bachelor's degree for the specific field; complete the Georgia Assessments for the Certification of Educators (GACE) Educator Ethics–assessment; for Career and Technical Specializations, individuals must meet specific eligibility requirements

  ii.   Year 2 Issuance: attain a passing score on the GACE content assessment (if available for the field, except Special Education consultative fields); verify enrollment in a state-approved educator preparation program leading to certification

  iii. Year 3 Issuance: attain a passing score on the GACE Program Admission Assessment or meet exemption

  iv.   Completion Requirements: verify completion of a state-approved educator preparation program; for Career and Technical Specializations, complete any outstanding industry testing/licensure requirements as outlined in the appropriate rules; for Special Education consultative fields, pass the GACE content assessment (if available in the field)

II. Types

A. Adjunct (valid for 1 year, renewable)

  1. Issued at the request of an employing Georgia LUA to individuals with specific knowledge, skills and experience in various professions

  2. Authorizes the holder to provide instruction for up to 50 percent of the school day in specific subjects in grades 6–12 only

B. Clearance (valid for up to 5 years, renewable): issued at the request of the employing Georgia LUA to educators who satisfactorily complete fingerprint and criminal background check requirements and do not have a certificate that is currently revoked or suspended in Georgia or any other state

C. Educational Interpreter: issued to individuals who serve as sign language interpreters in schools

D. Leadership: issued in fields that prepare an educator to administer or supervise a Georgia LUA, school, or school program

E. Non-Instructional Aide: issued to eligible individuals hired to perform routine non-instructional tasks; has no assigned level

F. Paraprofessional (valid for 5 years, renewable): issued to eligible individuals hired as paraprofessionals; requires passing an assessment or meeting a minimum education level of an associate's degree or completion of 60 semester hours of college course work; has no assigned level

G. Permit (initial permit is valid for 3 years; subsequent permits may be extended for 5 years upon completion of specific requirements): issued at the request of an employing Georgia LUA to individuals with specific experience in the teaching fields of performing arts (Art, Music, Dance, and Drama); Foreign Languages; JROTC; Career, Technical, and Agricultural Education (CTAE) specializations; Healthcare Science; Engineering and Technology; and the position of superintendent

H. Service: issued in fields that prepare an individual to provide support services to students, school personnel, and school operations

I. Support Personnel: issued at the request of an employing Georgia LUA to individuals who serve in positions of leadership over support functions in the LUA; has no assigned level

J. Teaching: issued in fields that prepare an educator to teach subject matter offered as part of school curriculum

III. Certificate Fields

A. Teaching Fields

1. Early Childhood: Birth through Kindergarten; Elementary Education (P–5); Special Education General Curriculum/Elementary Education (P–5)

2. Middle Grades (Grades 4–8): Language Arts; Math; Reading; Science; Social Science

3. Secondary (Grades 6–12): Behavioral Science; Biology; Chemistry; Earth/Space Science; Economics; English; Geography; History; Mathematics; Physics; Political Science; Science; Speech

4. Career, Technical, and Agricultural Education (Grades 6–12): Agriculture; Business; Engineering and Technology; Family and Consumer Sciences; Healthcare Science; Marketing; Career and Technical Specializations; Computer Science

5. P–12 Fields: Art; Dance; Drama; English for Speakers of Other Languages (ESOL); Gifted P–12; Health; Health and Physical Education; Music; Reading Specialist

6. Special Education (Grades P–12): Special Education Adapted Curriculum; Behavior Disorders; Deaf Education; Special Education General Curriculum; Learning Disabilities; Physical and Health Disabilities; Special Education Preschool (Ages 3–5); Visual Impairment

7. Foreign Languages (Grades P–12): American Sign Language; Arabic; Chinese (Mandarin); Farsi; French; German; Greek (Classical); Hebrew; Hindi; Italian; Japanese; Korean; Latin; Portuguese; Russian; Spanish; Swahili; Turkish; Urdu

B. Service Fields: Audiology; Curriculum and Instruction; Instructional Technology; Literacy Specialist; Media Specialist; School Counseling; School Nutrition Director; School Psychology; School Social Work; Speech and Language Pathology; Teacher Leadership

C. Leadership Fields: Educational Leadership Tier I; Educational Leadership Tier II; Superintendent

D. Endorsements: Agricultural Education (P–5); Autism; Birth through Age 5; Career Exploration; Career Technical Instruction; Coaching; Computer Science; Coordinated Career Academic Education; Culinary Arts; Dramatic Writing Micro-endorsement; Dual Immersion Elementary Education; Dyslexia; ESOL; Gifted In-Field; Intervention Specialist; K–5 Mathematics; K–5 Science; Middle Grades; Multi-Tiered System of Supports (MTSS) Facilitator; Online Teaching; Personalized Learning; Positive Behavior Intervention and Supports (PBIS); Reading; Safety and Driver Education; Special Education Deaf Education; Special Education Physical and Health Disabilities; Special Education Preschool Ages 3–5; Special Education Transition Specialist; Special Education Visual Impairment; STEM education; Student Support Team Coordinator; Teacher Leader; Teacher Support and Coaching; Urban Education; Work-Based Learning. Each endorsement requires a prerequisite certificate and may be added by completing course work within an approved college or staff development endorsement program.

IV. Certificate Levels
   A. Indicate the highest degree level recognized by the GaPSC that has been awarded to the certificate holder, according to the following guidelines:
      1. Level 1 (Selected Career, Technical, and Agricultural Education fields only): completion of a high school diploma or the GED equivalent
      2. Level 2 (Selected Career, Technical, and Agricultural Education fields only): completion of an associate's degree or GaPSC-determined equivalent
      3. Level 4: completion of a bachelor's degree or GaPSC-determined equivalent; a bachelor's degree is the minimum degree requirement for teaching certification except for selected Career, Technical, and Agricultural Education fields
      4. Level 5: completion of a master's degree or GaPSC-determined equivalent
      5. Level 6: completion of an education specialist degree or GaPSC-determined equivalent or completion of a minimum of 36 semester hours of course work and comprehensive examinations required for a level 7 doctoral degree
      6. Level 7: completion of a Ph.D., Ed.D. or GaPSC-determined equivalent
   B. An educator who earns an advanced degree in Educational Leadership may be assigned Leader Level in addition to a general certificate level; a leader level is used for placement on the state salary schedule only if the holder is employed in a designated leadership position

V. Renewal Requirements
   A. Standard renewal requirements for employed Georgia educators may be fulfilled by successful completion of a Professional Learning Plan (PLP) or Professional Learning Goals (PLG) established by the educator with oversight by his/her supervisor during the validity period of the certificate.
   B. Standard renewal requirements for non-employed Georgia educators may be fulfilled by completion of 1 of the following options within 5 years of the date of renewal:
      1. Six semester hours of college course work
      2. Ten Georgia Professional Learning Units earned through an approved provider
      3. Ten approved Continuing Education Units
      4. One hundred hours of Bright from the Start (BFTS)–approved training
      5. One full year of acceptable educator experience earned in another state while holding a valid professional certificate issued by that state
      6. Retaking and passing the GACE content assessment in the field(s) of certification
      7. For some service fields, a valid state or national licensure
      8. A valid National Board for Professional Teaching Standards (NBPTS) certification
   C. Educators employed by a Georgia LUA at the time of renewal must undergo a criminal record check.
   D. Renewal Cycle
      1. Georgia certificates usually have a beginning date of July 1 and an ending date of June 30.

2. Valid certificates may be renewed after December 1 of the year preceding the ending validity date of the calendar year in which the certificate expires.

Routes to Teaching Certification

I. Traditional Route to Induction Certification
   A. Requirements:
      1. Hold at least a bachelor's degree, except for certain Career, Technical, and Agricultural Education fields
      2. Complete all requirements of state-approved certification program, including field experience or clinical practice
      3. Complete applicable Special Georgia Requirements, including content assessment
   B. Certification program may lead to a degree (bachelor's or advanced) or may be a certification-only post-baccalaureate program
   C. Five-Year Induction certificate will be issued upon completion of the state-approved certification program and applicable Special Georgia Requirements
   D. Requirements to convert from Induction to Professional certification will include 3 years of successful teaching experience
II. Interstate reciprocity
   A. Requirements:
      1. Hold a renewable, professional teaching certificate in another US state
      2. Complete applicable Special Georgia Requirements, including content assessment and the Educator Ethics assessment if educator has fewer than 3 years of experience
   B. Five-Year Induction or Standard Professional certificate will be issued depending on the years of acceptable experience
III. Alternative Route to Certification: Georgia offers a nontraditional certification preparation program known as Georgia Teacher Academy for Preparation and Pedagogy (GaTAPP).
   A. Admission Requirements:
      1. Content assessment or degree major in the teaching field
      2. Employment by a Georgia LUA
      3. Minimum of a bachelor's degree
      4. Basic skills assessment
      5. Educator Ethics assessment
   B. Program Framework:
      1. Candidate Support Team trained in Coaching Standards and GaTAPP Assessments
      2. School-based Administrator
      3. School-based Mentor
      4. Provider Supervisor
      5. Content Specialist (May be dual role for existing member)
      6. Individualized based on Candidate Performance Assessment Data

  7.   Job-embedded Clinical Practice
  C.   Provisional certificate is issued upon employment.

Special Georgia Requirements

I.   Content Knowledge
  A.   The Georgia Assessments for the Certification of Educators (GACE) are the accepted content assessments for most certification fields.
    1.   GACE content assessments have 2 passing levels: Induction and Professional; until further notice, all passing scores earned on GACE assessments will be treated as Professional level scores even if the official score report reflects an Induction level score.
    2.   The Praxis exam is the state-approved content assessment for the field of Speech and Language Pathology, and the proficiency exams offered by the American Council on the Teaching of Foreign Languages (ACTFL) are the state-approved content assessments for foreign language fields in which there is no GACE exam available.
    3.   Georgia does not have a content assessment for the fields of Audiology, Dance, Drama, School Nutrition Director, School Social Work, Speech, Physical and Health Disabilities, Special Education Preschool, Visual Impairment, and some foreign language fields. In fields for which there is no state-approved or state-accepted content assessment, passing a content assessment for certification is not required.
  B.   The following individuals are required to pass the GACE content assessment for the desired certification field at the Induction level or higher, unless meeting exemption criteria:
    1.   Applicants seeking a Five-Year Induction certificate
      a.   A Georgia LUA may request a One-Year Induction certificate for those who meet all requirements for the Five-Year Induction certificate except the content knowledge assessment.
    2.   Applicants seeking a professional certificate in a teaching, service, or leadership field
    3.   Applicants for the Provisional certificate
      a.   Applicants for Provisional certification in Special Education Consultative fields are not required to pass the content assessment but must satisfy this requirement before the certificate can be converted.
      b.   Applicants for Provisional certification who are enrolled in a GaTAPP program may not be required to pass the content assessment if content knowledge has been verified in another way, such as a degree major in the field.
    4.   Applicants seeking an initial permit in a foreign language field
  C.   The following applicants may be exempt from passing the GACE content knowledge assessment(s):
    1.   Out-of-state certificate holders applying for initial Georgia certification who have worked in the same certificate field for 5 years at any time in their careers

or have passed the out-of-state content assessment required for issuance of the out-of-state certificate field

2. Individuals holding valid National Board for Professional Teaching Standards (NBPTS) Certification in the specific field, with the exception of the Middle Grades Generalist Field

3. Individuals seeking certification in a field for which the GaPSC has not adopted a content assessment

II. Standards of Conduct
   A. An applicant for certification in Georgia must comply with the ethical standards of the profession.
   B. An FBI background check (fingerprint) is required for employment in Georgia public schools and a Georgia criminal history check is required every 5 years for certificate renewal.
   C. Applicants for certification must respond to background check questions on the application form.

III. Special Education course
   A. Certification in a teaching field, leadership field, or the service fields of Media Specialist and School Counseling requires completion of an approved course in the identification and education of children who have special educational needs
   B. May be satisfied by NBPTS Certification
   C. May be issued prior to completion of this requirement; the course must be completed as part of requirements to renew or convert the certificate
   D. Out-of-state certificate holders applying for initial Georgia certification who have worked in the same certificate field for at least 5 years at any time in their career may be exempt from this requirement.

IV. Ethics Assessment
   A. The Educator Ethics Assessment is required for issuance of a Five-Year Induction or a Provisional certificate
   B. The Ethics for Educational Leadership Assessment is required for issuance of Educational Leadership Tier I; for Educational Leadership Tier II if it was not previously passed for Tier I; and to extend the Superintendent Permit.

V. Pedagogy Assessment
   A. The Education Teacher Performance Assessment (edTPA) was previously required for issuance of the Five-Year Induction certificate or conversion of the Provisional certificate, but as of July 1, 2020, the GaPSC no longer requires this assessment for certification.
   B. The Performance Assessment for School Leaders (PASL) is required for those who complete a GaPSC-approved Educational Leadership Tier II certification program.
      1. The PASL is not required for those completing the obsolete Building and System Level program or those coming from out of state with leadership certification.

Leadership Certificate Requirements

I. Tier II Performance-Based Educational Leadership
   A. Issued to Georgia educators who completed the previously approved Building Level or System Level Educational Leadership program

    B. Issued to Georgia educators who complete a state-approved Tier II Performance-Based Educational Leadership program

    C. Qualifications

        1. Complete a GaPSC-approved program at the education specialist level or higher

        2. Meet applicable Special Georgia Requirements, including GACE content assessment

    D. Non-Renewable Professional issued at the request of an employing Georgia LUA to the following individuals:

        1. Those holding an expired Georgia Performance-Based Educational Leadership certificate but not meeting renewal requirements (valid 1 year)

        2. Those holding a master's degree or higher and employed in a leadership position that supervises other leaders (valid 3 years)

  II. Tier II Standard Professional Educational Leadership

    A. Issued to Georgia educators who completed a state-approved Educational Leadership program by September 30, 2009, and have fulfilled Special Georgia Requirements, including content assessment

    B. Issued to out-of-state educators holding professional leadership certification that meet 1 of the following requirements along with fulfilling Special Georgia Requirements, including content assessment:

        1. Have completed a leadership preparation program at the education specialist level or higher

        2. Have completed a leadership preparation program at the master's degree level and have at least 3 years of acceptable leadership experience

    C. Non-Renewable Professional (valid 1 year): issued at the request of an employing Georgia LUA to those holding an expired Georgia Tier II Standard Professional Educational Leadership certificate but not meeting renewal requirements

  III. Tier I Standard Professional Educational Leadership

    A. Issued to Georgia educators who complete a state-approved Tier I Educational Leadership program and have fulfilled Special Georgia Requirements, including content assessment

    B. Issued to educators applying to Georgia by reciprocity who completed a state-approved Educational Leadership program at the master's degree level and have fewer than 3 years of educational leadership experience while holding a professional certificate in another state

    C. Non-Renewable Tier I Professional issued at the request of an employing Georgia LUA to the following individuals:

        1. Those holding an expired Georgia Tier I Standard Educational Leadership certificate but not meeting renewal requirements (valid 1 year)

        2. Those holding a bachelor's degree or higher and employed in a leadership position that does not supervise other leaders (valid 3 years)

Certificate Level Upgrade Requirements

  I. Accreditation Requirements: colleges/universities offering advanced degrees leading to upgrades must meet at least 1 of the following criteria at the time of admittance:

A. Approved by the GaPSC
B. Accredited by the National Council for Accreditation of Teacher Education (NCATE), the Teacher Education Accreditation Council (TEAC) or the Council for the Accreditation of Educator Preparation (CAEP)
C. Hold a Carnegie Classification of Research University-Very High Research Activity (RU/VH) or Research University-High Research Activity (RU/H)

II. Certificate and Degree Requirements
   A. The following certificates may be upgraded:
      1. Renewable, professional certificates; includes Standard Professional, Performance-Based Professional, Advanced Professional, and Lead Professional
      2. Five-Year Induction certificate
   B. The field or degree major of the advanced degree program must be closely related to a field in which the educator is certified.
      1. The certificate field must be one that is currently offered by the GaPSC.
      2. If the certificate field in which the educator completes an advanced degree is not a leadership field, the resulting level upgrade will apply to all fields held.
      3. An educator who earns an advanced degree in Educational Leadership may be assigned a Leader Level in addition to a general certificate level; a leader level is used for placement on the state salary schedule only if the holder is employed in a designated leadership position.
   C. The certificate level may not be upgraded by completing an initial certification program in a field in which the educator has already completed such a program.
   D. An educator may upgrade and add a new field simultaneously by completing an advanced degree that leads to certification in a new field and fulfilling any applicable Special Georgia Requirements.
      1. Educators who upgrade and add the field of School Counseling must complete a GaPSC-approved School Counseling program or a Council for Accreditation of Counseling and Related Educational Programs (CACREP)–accredited school counseling program.

III. Grandfathering Timelines: Advanced degrees started as late as January 2013 may fall under less rigorous requirements; please visit www.gapsc.com for more information.

Hawaii

Licenses

I. Standard License
   A. This is a National Association of State Directors of Teacher Education and Certification (NASDTEC) Stage 3 License whose requirements include that the individual:
      1. Hold a minimum of a bachelor's degree,
      2. Complete a State-approved Teacher Education Program, *and*
      3. Meet all jurisdiction-specific requirements of the issuing Member Jurisdiction.
   B. Routes to Obtain the Standard License
     Note: All routes require completion of the Standard License application online at hawaiiteacherstandardsboard.org.
      1. Applicants who will complete an Educator Preparation Program (EPP) prior to licensure but do not hold a teaching license in any state must submit:
        a. Verification of completion of preparation program,
        b. Verification of meeting basic skills and content knowledge expertise, *and*
        c. Verification of at least 3 out of the past 5 years of satisfactory full-time teaching in Hawaii or another state.
      2. Applicants who hold a current, valid National Board for Professional Teaching Standards (NBPTS) Certificate and a current, valid out-of-state teaching license must submit:
        a. Copy of current, valid NBPTS Certificate,
        b. Copy of current valid out-of-state license, *and*
        c. Verification of at least 3 out of the past 5 years of satisfactory full-time teaching in Hawaii or another state.
      3. Applicants who hold a current, valid out-of-state teaching license with the Meritorious New Teacher Candidate (MNTC) designation must submit:
        a. Copy of current, valid out-of-state license with the MNTC designation, *and*
        b. Verification of at least 3 out of the past 5 years of satisfactory full-time teaching in Hawaii or another state.
      4. Applicants who hold a teaching license issued for the first time in another state since July 1, 2006, must submit:
        a. Hawaii Teacher Standards Board (HTSB) Form OS3009 or a copy of the out-of-state license, if that state's licensing agency does not have a public license look-up, *and*

        b.   Verification of at least 3 out of the past 5 years of satisfactory full-time teaching in Hawaii or another state.

    5.   Applicants who have held a valid, unrevoked teaching license from another state for at least 3 out of the past 5 years must submit:

        a.   HTSB Form OS3009 or a copy of the out-of-state license, if that state's licensing agency does not have a public license look-up,

        b.   Verification of basic skills and content knowledge expertise using Hawaii or options from state that issued license,
           and

        c.   Verification of at least 3 out of the past 5 years of satisfactory full-time teaching in Hawaii or another state.

    6.   For applicants who are recommended by a Hawaii preparation program under an alternative method for preparation, the Hawaii EPP will submit to the HTSB verification of the preparation program completion, basic skills and content knowledge.

        a.   Applicants must submit verification of at least 3 out of the past 5 years of satisfactory full-time teaching in Hawaii or another state.

    7.   Applicants who completed a non-US teacher education program must submit:

        a.   National Association of Credential Evaluation Services (NACES) evaluation of foreign transcript providing evidence of completion of a teacher preparation program,

        b.   Verification of basic skills and content knowledge expertise,
           and

        c.   Verification of at least 3 out of the past 5 years of satisfactory full-time teaching in Hawaii or another state.

II. Provisional License (valid 3 years; nonrenewable)

    A. This is a NASDTEC Stage 2 License for applicants who have not yet met the jurisdiction-specific requirements for a Stage 3 license. Requirements include that the individual:

       1.   Hold a minimum of a bachelor's degree,

       2.   Complete a State-approved EPP,
          and

       3.   Submit verification of meeting basic skills and content knowledge.

III. Career and Technical Education (CTE) Limited Standard License: teachers holding this license may only be assigned to the content field on their license and may not add any additional fields to the license.

    A. Applicants must apply online at http://www.hawaiiteacherstandardsboard.org and submit:

       1.   An official transcript showing completion of an associate's degree from a regionally accredited college;

       2.   Documentation of a minimum of 3 years of industry experience in the content field;

       3.   Evidence of 1 of the following ways to meet content knowledge:

        a.   Content test in the field,
          or

b.   Current valid national industry certification in the content field,
      or

c.   Current valid industry license in the content field,
      or

d.   Thirty hours of course work in the content field;
      and

4.   Evidence of 1 of the following:

a.   Fifteen hours of pedagogy course work from a state-approved EPP in the grade level of the license,
      or

b.   Twelve hours of pedagogy course work from a state-approved EPP in the grade level of the license and a passing score on the Principles of Learning and Teaching (PLT) exam in the appropriate grade level of the license.

IV. Advanced License

   A. This is a NASDTEC Stage 4 License whose requirements include that the individual:

      1. Hold a minimum of a master's degree or the equivalent,

      2. Has completed an approved EPP,
      and

      3. Has met any jurisdiction-specific requirements beyond those required for the Stage 3 License of the issuing Member Jurisdiction.

   B. Routes to obtain the Advanced License

      1. For teachers who have held a Standard License in Hawaii or another state and have at least 5 years of experience within the past 8 years in Hawaii or another state:

a.   Submit the Advanced License application;

b.   Submit 1 of the following with application:

    i.   An official transcript verifying a master's, specialist, or doctoral degree from a regionally accredited institution in an area relevant to the teaching field for which license is sought or a field that improves the practice of teaching (examples of which include but are not limited to curriculum and instruction, technology, reading, and teacher leadership), and this degree must be different from the one used to obtain a Standard License;
      or

    ii.   Verification of a valid NBPTS Certificate and a current, valid out-of-state teaching license (Hawaii-licensed teachers do not need to submit a copy of the Standard License or NBPTS Certificate if it was earned while a Hawaii-licensed teacher);
      or

    iii. Verification of being designated a teacher leader by the Hawaii Department of Education, a Hawaii Charter School, or a member school of the Hawaii Association of Independent Schools;
      and

c.   Submit the Verification of Qualifying Experience for Advanced License to document satisfactory full-time teaching experience in the state which issued the Standard License for 5 out of past 8 years.

V. Documentation and Verification Procedures for Basic Skills and Content Knowledge
Note: For a list of tests and scores, consult http://hawaiiteacherstandardsboard.org/content/licensure-test-categories/.

A. Basic Skills
   1. Basic skills licensure tests in reading, writing, mathematics (applicants licensed out of state may use those tests to meet this requirement);
      or
   2. Bachelor's degree from a regionally accredited institution;
      or
   3. SAT in reading and mathematics and writing (for tests taken after March 2016; for tests taken before March 2016, Praxis score for writing can be used in lieu of SAT writing score);
      or
   4. ACT in reading and mathematics and writing.

B. Content Knowledge
   1. Licensure test in the content field (applicants licensed out of state may use those tests to meet this requirement);
      or
   2. Content major in the content field from a bachelor's degree from a regionally accredited institution;
      or
   3. Thirty credit hours of course work in the content field, 15 of which must be upper-division courses, from a regionally accredited institution;
      or
   4. Advanced degree (master's, specialist, doctorate) in the content field from a regionally accredited institution;
      or
   5. NBPTS Certification in the content field.
      or
   6. Elementary education (K–6) only: A total of 36 semester hours, including 9 semester hours in each of the following core content areas: language arts, mathematics, science, social studies. At least 3 semester hours in each of the core content areas must be upper-division level.

Idaho

For the most current information, visit the "Rules Governing Uniformity" section of the "Rules of the Board Governing Education" at https://adminrules.idaho.gov/rules/current/08/080202.pdf. Additional details are available at the Certification website: http://www.sde.idaho.gov/cert-psc/.

General Requirements for All Teachers and Administrators

I. Standard Instructional Certificate (valid 5 years; 6 semester credit hours required every 5 years for renewal)
    A. Hold a baccalaureate degree from an accredited college or university
    B. Have a minimum of 20 semester credit hours, or 30 quarter credit hours, in the philosophical, psychological, and methodological foundations; in instructional technology; and in the professional subject matter, including at least 3 semester credit hours, or 4 quarter credit hours, in reading and its application to the content area
        1. Credit hours must include at least 6 semester credit hours, or 9 quarter credit hours, of student teaching in the grade range and subject areas as applicable to the endorsement
    C. Complete an approved teacher preparation program
    D. Receive an institutional recommendation from an accredited college or university specifying the grade ranges and subjects for which applicant is eligible to receive an endorsement
        1. Those seeking endorsement in a secondary grade range must complete preparation in at least 2 fields of teaching: 1 consisting of at least 30 semester credit hours or 45 quarter credit hours; and a second consisting of at least 20 semester credit hours or 30 quarter credit hours.
            a. Preparation of not less than 45 semester credit hours or 67 quarter credit hours in a single subject area may be used in lieu of the 2 teaching field requirements.
    E. Meet or exceed the qualifying score on the state board–approved content area and pedagogy assessments, i.e., Praxis II test(s). See http://www.ets.org/praxis/idaho/requirements.
        1. Applicants for certificates in Administration or Pupil Personnel Services are exempt from this requirement.
II. Out-of-State Applications
    A. The State Department of Education or the Division of Career Technical Education, as applicable, is authorized to issue a non-renewable 3-year interim certificate to applicants who hold a valid certificate or license from another state or other entity that participates in the National Association of State Directors of Teacher Education

and Certification (NASDTEC) Interstate Agreement, or engaged in an alternate route to certification.

B. An educator who has graduated from a foreign institution and holds a valid teaching credential may be issued a non-renewable, 3-year interim certificate.

1. Determination of eligibility for certification will be made by the State Department of Education.

2. All other procedures in effect at the time must be followed at the time of application.

III. Alternative Authorizations, Non-Traditional Routes, and Emergency Provisional Certificate Details and Requirements

A. Alternative Authorization—Teacher to New Certification (valid 1 year; may be renewed for 2 additional years with evidence of satisfactory progress toward completion of an approved alternative route preparation program). This option allows school districts to request additional certification when a professional position cannot be filled by someone with the correct certification and/or endorsement.

1. Candidate must hold a baccalaureate degree and a valid Idaho instructional certificate before applying.

2. School district must provide supporting information attesting to the ability of the candidate to fill the position.

3. Candidate must participate in an approved alternative route preparation program through a participating college or university and the employing school district.

a. Candidate must complete a minimum of 9 semester credit hours annually to maintain eligibility for renewal.

b. Participating college or university shall provide procedures to assess and credit equivalent knowledge, dispositions, and relevant life/work experiences.

B. Alternative Authorization to Endorsement (candidates must meet all requirements of the applicable option)

1. Option I: An official statement from the college of education of competency in a teaching area or field is acceptable in lieu of courses for a teaching field if the statement is:

a. Created in consultation with the department or division of the accredited college or university in which the competency is established, and

b. Approved by the director of teacher education of the recommending college or university.

2. Option II: By earning national board certification in content-specific areas, teachers may gain endorsement in a corresponding subject area.

3. Option III: By earning a graduate degree in a content-specific area, candidates may add an endorsement in that area to a valid instructional certificate.

4. Option IV: Content area assessment and mentoring. An endorsement may be added by successfully completing a state board–approved content area assessment within the first year of authorization and a 1-year state board–approved mentoring component.

C. Alternative Authorization—Content Specialist (valid 1 year; may be renewed for

2 additional years). This alternative authorization allows a local education agency to request an instructional certificate for an individual who possesses distinct content knowledge so that the individual can teach in an area of need identified by the local education agency.

1. Candidate must hold a baccalaureate degree or have completed all the requirements of a baccalaureate degree except the student teaching portion.
2. The local education agency shall ensure the candidate is qualified to teach in the area of identified need. The candidate shall meet or exceed the state qualifying score on the appropriate state board–approved content or pedagogy assessment or demonstrate content knowledge through a combination of employment experience and education.
3. A consortium comprised of a state board–approved educator preparation program, a local education agency representative, and the candidate shall determine the preparation needed to meet the Standards for Initial Certification. This plan must include mentoring, a minimum of 1 classroom observation by the mentor per month, and annual progress goals.
4. The candidate must complete a minimum of 9 semester credit hours (or its equivalent of accelerated study) in education pedagogy prior to the end of the first year of authorization, with the number of required credits specified in the consortium-developed plan.
5. The candidate must enroll in and work toward completion of the alternative route preparation program through a participating college or university (or other state board–approved certification program) and the employing school district. Program attendance, participation, and completion are conditions of annual renewal.

D. Non-Traditional Routes to Certification (e.g., American Board for Certification of Teacher Excellence; Teach for America; College of Southern Idaho; Lewis-Clark State College). To complete this non-traditional route, the candidate must earn interim certification (valid 3 years; available to candidates only once) by:

1. Holding a baccalaureate degree or higher from an accredited institution of higher education
2. Completing a state board–approved program
3. Passing state board–approved pedagogy and content knowledge exams
4. Completing the Idaho Department of Education background check
5. Completing a 2-year teacher mentoring program during the term of the interim certificate
6. Adhering to all laws and rules governing conduct, discipline, and professional standards under any Idaho certificate
7. Obtaining a valid renewable Idaho Educator Credential during the 3-year interim certification term

E. Emergency Provisional Certificate (valid 1 year; cannot be renewed)

1. In declared emergencies, the state board may authorize the issuance of provisional certificates based on not less than 2 years of college training.

IV. Interim Certificates

1. To receive an interim certificate (specific to certain endorsement areas),

current Idaho teachers (including those pursuing alternate authorizations, non-traditional routes, and reinstatements) and teachers coming from out of state must complete:

    a.   A state board–approved Idaho Comprehensive Literacy course or assessment

       or

    b.   An approved secondary equivalent.

  2. To receive an interim certificate with an All Subjects (K–8) endorsement, any mathematics endorsement, Exceptional Child Generalist endorsement, Blended Early Childhood/Early Childhood Special Education endorsement, or administrator certificate, current Idaho teachers and administrators (including those pursuing alternate authorizations, non-traditional routes, and reinstatements) and teachers or administrators coming from out of state must complete:

    a.   A state board–approved Teaching Mathematical Thinking course

       or

    b.   Another State Department of Education–approved alternative course.

V. Career and Technical Education

  A. The Idaho State Division of Career and Technical Education is authorized to determine whether applicants meet requirements for instructing or administering professional-technical programs at the secondary and postsecondary levels. For additional information on CTE certification and endorsements, please see https://cte.idaho.gov/educators/ and https://adminrules.idaho.gov/rules/current/08/080202.pdf.

VI. Renewal of Certification

  A. All 5-year clear credentials may be renewed upon completion of at least 6 semester credit hours of college courses within the 5-year period of validity. Educators working in an Idaho public school can derive 3 credits from participation in district-approved in-service. For administrators, 3 of the credits must be in the Framework for Teacher Evaluation.

VII. Criminal History and Background Check

  A. All individuals who work in Idaho public schools and have unsupervised contact with children, whether or not they hold certificates or are applying for certification, are required to have results of a criminal history check on file with the State Department of Education. Please see the Background Investigation Check website at https://www.sde.idaho.gov/cert-psc/bic/ for details and current information.

VIII. Administrator Certificates (valid 5 years; 6 semester credit hours required every 5 years to renew)

  A. Every person who serves as a superintendent, a director of special education, a secondary school principal, or principal of an elementary school with 8 or more teachers (including the principal), or is assigned to conduct the summative evaluation of certified staff, is required to hold an administrator certificate.

  1. Certificate may be endorsed for service as a school principal, a superintendent, or a director of special education.

  2. Assistant superintendents are required to hold the Superintendent endorsement.

3. Assistant principals or vice principals are required to hold the School Principal endorsement.
4. Directors of special education are required to hold the Director of Special Education endorsement.
5. Possession of an administrator certificate does not entitle the holder to serve as a teacher at a grade level for which the educator is not qualified or certificated.
6. All administrator certificates require candidates to meet the Idaho Standards for School Principals.

B. School Principal Endorsement
1. Hold a master's degree from an accredited college or university
2. Have 4 years of full-time certificated experience working with PreK–12 students while under contract in an accredited school setting
3. Have completed an administrative internship in a state-approved program, or have 1 year of experience as an administrator in grades PreK–12
4. Provide verification of completion of a state-approved program of at least 30 semester credit hours or 45 quarter credit hours of graduate study in school administration for the preparation of school principals at an accredited college or university. This program shall include the competencies of the Idaho Standards for School Principals.
5. Obtain an institutional recommendation

C. Superintendent Endorsement
1. Hold an education specialist or doctorate degree or complete a comparable post-master's sixth-year program at an accredited college or university
2. Have 4 years of full-time certificated/licensed experience working with PreK–12 students while under contract in an accredited school setting
3. Have completed an administrative internship in a state-approved program for the superintendent endorsement or have 1 year of out-of-state experience as an assistant superintendent or superintendent in grades PreK–12
4. Provide verification of completion of an approved program of at least 30 semester credit hours or 45 quarter credit hours of post-master's degree graduate study for the preparation of school superintendents at an accredited college or university. This program in school administration and interdisciplinary supporting areas shall include the competencies in Superintendent Leadership in addition to the competencies in the Idaho Standards for School Principals
5. Obtain an institutional recommendation

D. Director of Special Education Endorsement (K–12)
1. Hold a master's degree from an accredited college or university
2. Complete 4 years of full-time certificated/licensed experience working with PreK–12 students while under contract in a school setting
3. Obtain college or university verification of demonstrated the competencies of the Director of Special Education in Idaho Standards for Initial Certification of Professional School Personnel
4. Obtain college or university verification of demonstrated competencies in the following areas, in addition to the competencies in the Idaho Standards for School Principals: Concepts of Least Restrictive Environment; Post-

School Outcomes and Services for Students with Disabilities Ages 3 to 21; Collaboration Skills for General Education Intervention; Instructional and Behavioral Strategies; Individual Education Programs (IEPs); Assistive and Adaptive Technology; Community-Based Instruction and Experiences; Data Analysis for Instructional Needs and Professional Training; Strategies to Increase Program Accessibility; Federal and State Laws and Regulations and School District Policies; Resource Advocacy; and Technology Skills for Referral Processes and Record Keeping

5. Complete an administrative internship/practicum in the area of administration of special education
6. Obtain an institutional recommendation

IX. Pupil Service Staff Certificate
   A. School counselors, school psychologists, speech-language pathologists, school social workers, school nurses, and school audiologists are required to hold the pupil service staff certificate, with the following endorsement(s) for which they qualify. Occupational therapists and physical therapists may be required, as determined by the local educational agency, to hold the certificate, with the endorsements for which they qualify.
      1. Standard Counselor Endorsement (K–12)
         a. Have a master's degree in school counseling
         b. Have completed 700 clock hours of supervised field experience, 75 percent of which must be in a K–12 school setting
         c. Obtain an institutional recommendation
      2. Speech-Language Pathologist Endorsement
         a. Have a master's degree in speech-language pathology
         b. Have completed a state-approved program in speech-language pathology
         c. Obtain an institutional recommendation
      3. Audiology Endorsement
         a. Have a master's degree in speech-language pathology
         b. Have completed a state-approved program in audiology
         c. Obtain an institutional recommendation
      4. School Social Worker Endorsement
         a. Have a master's degree in social work (MSW)
         b. Have completed a school social work practicum in a K–12 setting (post-MSW extensive experience working with children and families may be substituted)
         c. Obtain an institutional recommendation
      5. School Nurse Endorsement (valid 5 years; renewable)
         a. Hold a valid nursing (RN) license issued by the Idaho State Board of Nursing, and a baccalaureate degree in nursing, education, or a health-related field from an accredited institution
         b. Have completed 9 semester credit hours from a university or college in at least 3 of the following areas: health program management; child and adolescent development; counseling, psychology, or social work; or methods of instruction

        c.   Two years of full-time (or part-time equivalent) school nursing, community health nursing, or any area of pediatric, adolescent, or family nursing experience

        d.   Interim Endorsement—School Nurse. This endorsement will be granted to those who do not meet the educational and/or experience requirements but who hold a valid professional nursing (RN) license in Idaho. An Interim School Nurse Endorsement will be issued for 3 years while the applicant is meeting the educational or experience requirements, or both, and it is not renewable.

    6.   School Psychologist Endorsement

        a.   Have completed 60 graduate semester credit hours through 1 of the available options. See Idaho code 08.02.02.015.02.c at https://adminrules.idaho.gov/rules/current/08/080202.pdf for options.

        b.   Interim Endorsement—School Psychologist. This endorsement will be granted to those who do not meet the educational requirements but hold a master's degree in school psychology and are pursuing an educational specialist degree. This non-renewable endorsement will be issued for 3 years while the applicant is meeting the educational requirements.

    7.   Occupational Therapist Endorsement

        a.   Hold a current and valid Occupational Therapy license issued by the Occupational Therapy Licensure Board of Idaho

        b.   Candidate must maintain current and valid Occupational Therapy licensure for the endorsement to remain valid

    8.   Physical Therapist Endorsement

        a.   Hold a current and valid Physical Therapy license issued by the Physical Therapy Licensure Board of Idaho

        b.   Candidate must maintain current and valid Physical Therapy licensure for the endorsement to remain valid

X.   Postsecondary Specialist Certificate (valid 5 years; renewable by application accompanied by a new written recommendation from a representative of the postsecondary institution at the level of college dean or higher)

    A.   Granted to a current academic faculty member whose primary employment is with any accredited Idaho postsecondary institution

    B.   Used primarily for distance education, virtual classroom programs, and public and postsecondary partnerships

    C.   Candidates must:

        1.   Hold a master's degree or higher in the content area being taught

        2.   Be currently employed by the postsecondary institution in the content area to be taught

        3.   Supply a recommendation from the employing institution (i.e., the college dean)

XI. American Indian Language Certificate

    A.   Each Indian tribe shall provide to the State Department of Education the names of highly and uniquely qualified individuals who have been designated to teach the tribe's native language; these individuals may apply for this certificate.

    B.   The Office of Indian Education at the State Department of Education will process applications. Approved applications will be forwarded to the Office of Certification.

    C.   The Office of Certification will review the application and verify eligibility.

    D.   The State Department of Education will authorize eligible applicants to be American Indian Language teachers.

XII.   Junior Reserve Officer Training Corps (ROTC) Instructors

    A.   Each school district with a Junior ROTC program shall provide the State Department of Education with a list of names of those who have completed an official armed forces training program to qualify as high school Junior ROTC instructors.

    B.   Each school district with a Junior ROTC program shall provide the State Department of Education with a notarized copy of instructors' certificate(s) of completion.

Illinois

Requirements for Illinois Licenses with Endorsements

I. Licensure requirements for applicants completing Illinois-approved programs for teaching
   A. Those who seek to add a subsequent endorsement that requires a content area test must pass the applicable Illinois content area test. Out-of-state testing is not accepted.
   B. Passing score on the applicable content area test(s) prior to student teaching (or the last semester or term of internship if completing an approved program leading to an administrative or school service personnel endorsement)
      1. Content tests are valid indefinitely.
   C. Passing score on the teacher performance assessment (teaching endorsements only)
      1. Assessment of Professional Teaching (APT 188)* test for program completion if student teaching was completed prior to August 31, 2015
      2. Individuals completing student teaching September 1, 2015, or after will be required to pass the Education Teacher Performance Assessment (edTPA) instead of the APT 188.
      3. APT 188/edTPA scores are valid indefinitely.
     *Note: The APT test is no longer available as of August 31, 2020.
   D. Completion of an approved Illinois educator preparation program for the type of endorsement sought that includes course work addressing:
      1. Cross-categorical special education methods
        and
      2. Methods of reading and reading in the content area.
      3. Upon completion of the program, the Illinois institution will notify the Illinois State Board of Education (ISBE) via the Educator Licensure Information System (ELIS) that applicant qualifies for a license and/or endorsement.
   E. Educators who are completing an alternative preparation program can find the requirements for the alternative provisional educator and alternative provisional superintendent endorsement on an educator license with stipulations at https://www .isbe.net/Pages/Educator-License-with-Stipulations.aspx.
II. Professional Educator License (PEL) requirements for applicants trained out of state or out of the country (valid 5 fiscal years; renewable upon completion of professional development requirements. PEL Checklist is available at https://www.isbe.net/ Documents/PEL-Checklist-0817.pdf.)
   A. Option 1
      1. Bachelor's degree (master's degree if applicable) or higher from a regionally accredited institution of higher education
      2. A valid out-of-state license comparable to the Illinois PEL

B. Option 2
1. Bachelor's degree (master's degree if applicable) or higher from a regionally accredited institution of higher education
2. Illinois State Board of Education form 80–02 or 80–02S submitted to ISBE. Note: Form is available at http://www.isbe.net/Documents/80–02-standards-verification.pdf or https://www.isbe.net/Documents/PEL-Checklist-0817.pdf.
3. For teaching licenses, student teaching or 1 year experience on a valid teaching license
4. Completion of course work addressing methods of teaching exceptional children, reading methods, content area reading, and methods of teaching English-language learners. For details, consult http://www.isbe.net/Documents/pre-app-pel-coursework.pdf.
5. Licensure Tests: APT/edTPA content tests are all valid indefinitely for teaching licenses. Note: The APT 188 test is an option only for applicants who have completed student teaching before Fall 2015; for applicants relying on 1 year of valid teaching experience, the teaching experience must have been completed before Fall 2015. Those who seek to add a subsequent endorsement that requires a content area test must pass the applicable Illinois content area test. Out-of-state testing is not accepted.
6. For teaching licenses only, if the edTPA has not been passed at time of application, 1 of the below options may be utilized:
    a. Educator can enroll in student teaching portion of an educator preparation program and complete the edTPA during this time.
    b. Educator can provide evidence with application of having at least 1 year of full-time teaching experience and having achieved a "proficient" or higher (or equivalent) rating on most recent performance evaluation. Use form 80–01: Out-of-State Applicant Request to Waive edTPA.
C. Endorsements available are listed below; for more information on specific requirements for each, consult http://www.isbe.net/Pages/Subsequent-Teaching-Endorsements.aspx.
1. Teaching
    a. Early Childhood Education (Birth–grade 2)
    b. Elementary Education (1–6)
    c. Middle Grades (5–8)
    d. Secondary Education (9–12)
    e. Special Teaching (PreK–12) A specific content area endorsement should be selected if applicant applies for the Special Teaching (PreK–12) license.
    f. Special Education (K–age 21) For more information on the areas available, please consult https://www.isbe.net/Pages/Special-Education-Requirements.aspx.
2. Administrative
    a. Teacher Leader (PreK–12) (Note: at this time, through the entitlement process only from an Illinois institution upon completion)
    b. Principal (PreK–age 21)

       c.   Superintendent (PreK–age 21)

       d.   Chief School Business Official (PreK–age 21)

       e.   Director of Special Education (PreK–age 21)

   3.   School Support Personnel

       a.   School Social Worker (PreK–age 21)

       b.   School Counselor (PreK–age 21)

       c.   School Psychologist (PreK–age 21)

       d.   School Nurse (PreK–age 21)

       e.   Speech-Language Pathologist—nonteaching (PreK–age 21)

  D. Approvals: For more information, consult https://www.isbe.net/Pages/educator-licensure-approvals.aspx.

   1.   Short-term approvals are available for teachers at all grade levels who hold a PEL endorsed in teaching and seek to teach in other content areas or grades (excluding special education or safety and driver's education) with completion of 9 semester hours or applicable content test.

   2.   Short-term emergency approvals are available for educators who hold a PEL endorsed in teaching and seek to teach special education in grades K–age 21.

   3.   For information on other available approvals, consult https://www.isbe.net/Pages/educator-licensure-approvals.aspx.

III. Requirements for Educator License with Stipulations endorsements can be viewed in full at http://www.isbe.net/Pages/Educator-License-with-Stipulations.aspx and include:

  A. Alternative Provisional Educator

  B. Alternative Provisional Superintendent

  C. Career and Technical Educator

  D. Provisional Career and Technical Educator

  E. Part-Time Provisional Career and Technical Educator

  F. Chief School Business Official

  G. Transitional Bilingual Educator

  H. Paraprofessional Endorsement

IV. Substitute Teaching License (valid 5 years; may be renewed with a renewal application and the payment of registration fees)

  A. Hold a bachelor's degree from a regionally accredited institution of higher education

V. Content Area Endorsement Structure (teaching endorsements): Educators who hold a PEL endorsed in a teaching field may add additional content area endorsements. The PEL serves as a foundation to which any teaching endorsement can be added after applicable course work and testing are completed. Endorsements can be added at any grade level, even if the underlying teaching endorsement on the PEL is for a different grade range.

  A. Middle Grade Endorsements (5–8)

   1.   Eighteen semester hours of course work specific to or inclusive of middle grades, content-specific methods course work, and course work specific to the content area

   2.   Applicable content test. Refer to the requirements at https://www.isbe.net/Pages/Subsequent-Teaching-Endorsements.aspx.

  B. Senior High School Endorsements (9–12)

   1.   Eighteen semester hours of course work in the content area

  2. Applicable content test
  3. For a detailed list of endorsements and their requirements, refer to the
      Subsequent Teaching Endorsements page at http://www.isbe.net/Pages/
      Subsequent-Teaching-Endorsements.aspx.
C. For detailed requirements for Learning Behavior Specialist I (LBS I) and Learning
    Behavior Specialist II (LBS II), refer to the Special Education Requirements page at
    http://www.isbe.net/Pages/Special-Education-Requirements.aspx.

Indiana

Licensure Overview

For all license-specific details, consult REPA 3 Rule at http://www.in.gov/legislative/iac/20141217 -IR-511130399FRA.xml.pdf.

I. Levels of Licensure
   A. Initial Practitioner (valid 2 years; renewable under conditions). The first-level license for teaching, school services, and school administration
      1. Residency is the 2-year internship requirement which accompanies all Initial licenses and may include a school corporation-sponsored mentoring program.
      2. All license additions require successful completion of the required ETS Praxis content test if there is an approved test for the content area, as well as any course work requirements.
      3. An ETS Praxis content licensure test for candidates for initial licensure as school counselors is required.
      4. Out-of-state applicants with less than 3 years of teaching experience in an accredited institution (note: substitute teaching experience does not count) are eligible for this license if they:
         a. Have obtained an instructional license in another state by completing a state-approved educator preparation program or a state-approved alternative preparation program;
         b. Have passed a licensure test in their content area(s) and provide official documentation of passing scores;
         c. Possess a valid license from another state, which must be a full license (i.e., not temporary, emergency, substitute, or other);
            and
         d. Have completed an approved preparation program and passed a content test if they wish to receive license reciprocity in the 7 content areas listed in B3. directly below.
   B. Practitioner (valid 5 years; renewable for 5 years)
      1. For renewal, the second-level license requires 1 of the following:
         a. Completion of a Professional Growth Plan (PGP)
            or
         b. Six semester hours of specified course work
            or
         c. National Board Certification.
      2. All license additions require successful completion of the required ETS Praxis content test if there is an approved test for the content area, as well as any course work requirements.

3.   The 7 content areas that require both an approved program of course work and testing in order to be added to an existing license include:
     a.   Communication Disorders
     b.   Teachers of English Learners
     c.   Early Childhood Education
     d.   Elementary Generalists
     e.   Exceptional Needs (Mild Intervention, Intense Intervention, Blind and Low Vision, Deaf and Hard of Hearing)
     f.   Fine Arts content areas (Visual Arts, Vocal and General Music, Instrumental and General Music, and Theater Arts)
     g.   High Ability
4.   Out-of-state applicants with more than 3 years of teaching experience in an accredited institution are eligible for this license if they:
     a.   Have obtained an instructional license in another state by completing a state-approved educator preparation program or a state-approved alternative preparation program;
     b.   Have passed a licensure test in their content area(s) and provide official documentation of passing scores;
     c.   Possess a valid license from another state, which must be a full license (i.e., not temporary, emergency, substitute, or other);
          and
     d.   Have completed an approved preparation program and passed a content test if they wish to receive license reciprocity in the 7 content areas listed in B3. directly above.
C.   Accomplished Practitioner (valid 10 years; renewable for 10 years); requires a master's degree and at least 2 years of experience on a Practitioner license.
     1.   National Board Certification (NBTPS) can be used to obtain a 10-year Accomplished Practitioner license.
     2.   For renewal, the third-level license requires 1 of the following:
          a.   Completion of a PGP
               or
          b.   Six semester hours of specified course work
               or
          c.   National Board Certification.
     3.   Certain licenses have additional renewal requirements; for these and other license-specific details, consult REPA 3 Rule at http://www.in.gov/legislative/iac/20141217-IR-511130399FRA.xml.pdf.
D.   Reciprocal Permit
     1.   All persons who completed educator preparation in another US state, who have a valid license from that state, and who have satisfied the testing and degree requirements, are eligible for the Initial Practitioner license.
     2.   All persons who completed educator preparation in another US state, who have a valid license from that state, who have satisfied the testing and degree requirements, and who have 3 years of teaching in accredited schools from that state, are eligible for the Practitioner license.

E. Emergency Permit (renewable upon documentation of progress toward full licensure)
   1. Reserved for use by a school employer when it cannot locate a properly licensed educator for an assignment. (Note: After June 1, 2022, no emergency permits will be issued for special education areas.)
   2. The "continuing education" Emergency Permit is available under REPA, but it is not renewable.
F. Transition to Teaching (T2T) Permit (valid 3 years; nonrenewable)
   1. Many Indiana educator preparation institutions offer the Transition to Teaching option for the Initial teaching license for all of their approved programs.
      a. Applicants enrolled in the T2T program must already hold a bachelor's degree.
      b. The course of study of a Transition to Teaching program may be a part of a master's degree program, but a participant is not required to earn a master's degree to successfully complete the T2T program.
      c. Permit is available to a school corporation for a period of 3 years.
G. Advanced Degree License
   1. Applicant must have a master's degree or higher in the content area for which licensure is sought; must satisfy the test requirements for an Initial-level license in a content teaching area; and must have completed 1 year of teaching experience at the secondary or post-secondary level; advanced degree path licenses are only available in secondary content areas.
H. Career Specialist Permit
   1. Three eligibility options that use combinations of a bachelor's degree GPA, industry work experience, and testing. Issued for 2 years; renewable for 2-year periods. First renewal requires completion of a pedagogy component available online. Subsequent renewals require 40 hours of professional development.

Licensure Curriculum Requirements

I. Initial license for Elementary Generalist and Early Childhood Education: 3 routes available
   A. Completion of bachelor's degree from an institution of higher learning that includes a minor in a REPA content area, and a major with general education, professional education, and student teaching requirements;
      or
   B. Completion of a bachelor's degree from an institution of higher learning in a non-education area, *and either*:
      1. A minor in education that includes the essential pedagogy as described in the REPA,
         or
      2. A T2T program for career changers;
      or
   C. Completion of bachelor's degree from an institution of higher learning and a Master of Arts in Teaching (MAT) program approved by the Advisory Board.

D. All Indiana teacher preparation institutions must offer Option A (above) and must offer both the minor in education and the T2T program from Option B above.

II. Initial license for Secondary Education, Middle School Education, and P–12 Education: 3 routes available

A. Completion of an approved program for a REPA content area where the content area or major meets or exceeds the curriculum requirements of any other major offered by the institution for higher learning for that content area;
or

B. Completion of a bachelor's degree from an institution of higher learning that includes an appropriate major or content area, *and either*:
1. An education minor that includes the essential pedagogy as defined by the REPA,
or
2. Completion of a T2T program;
or

C. Completion of a bachelor's degree from an institution of higher learning and a Master of Arts in Teaching degree approved by the Advisory Board.

D. All Indiana teacher preparation institutions must offer Option A (above) and must offer both the minor in education and the T2T program from Option B above.

School Settings and License Content Areas

I. School Settings
A. Elementary (K–6)
B. Secondary (5–12)
C. Preschool through Grade 12 (P–12)
D. Early Childhood (P–3)
E. Middle School (5–9)

II. License Content Areas
A. Career and Technical Education: agriculture, business information and technology, marketing, family and consumer sciences, health science education, trade and industrial education
B. Business, computer education, early childhood education, elementary generalist, engineering and technology, exceptional needs, fine arts, high ability education, health, journalism, language arts, mathematics, physical education, reading, school librarian, science, social studies, teachers of English learners, virtual instruction, world languages
C. School Administration
1. Building-level administrator
2. District level: superintendent, director of career and technical education, director of curriculum and instruction, director of exceptional needs
3. Temporary superintendent
D. School services: communication disorders, school psychologist, school counselor, school nurse, school social worker

Iowa

Types of Licenses

I. Initial License (valid 2 years: renewable under prescribed conditions)
   A. Baccalaureate degree from a regionally accredited institution;
   B. Completion of an approved teacher preparation program;
   C. Completion of an approved human relations component;
   D. Completion of requirements for a teaching endorsement;
   E. Completion of the Iowa mandated tests (for applicants who graduated after January 1, 2013 and have less than 3 years' experience)
   F. Completion of the recency requirement of either 6 college credits or teaching experience within the last 5 years.
   G. These requirements must be completed for college semester-hour credit through a regionally accredited institution. Applicants who have completed a nontraditional program may or may not be eligible for Iowa licensure.

II. Standard License (valid 5 years; renewable under prescribed conditions)
   A. Completion of requirements for the initial license—see I, A–F, directly above; and
   B. Evidence of 2 years of successful teaching experience in a public school in Iowa, or of 3 years in any combination of public, private, or out-of-state schools.

III. Master Educator License (valid 5 years; renewable under prescribed conditions)
   A. Completion of requirements for the initial license—see I, A–F, directly above;
   B. Five years of teaching experience; and
   C. Master's degree in a recognized endorsement area or in curriculum, effective teaching, or a similar degree program which has a focus on school curriculum or instruction.

IV. Initial Administrator License (valid 1 year; renewable under prescribed conditions)
   A. Hold or be eligible for a standard license—see II, A and B, directly above;
   B. Three years of teaching experience;
   C. Does not have administrative experience;
   D. Completion of the requirements for an administrative endorsement; and
   E. Completion of a master's degree.

V. Professional Administrator License (valid 5 years; renewable under prescribed conditions)
   A. Standard license or eligibility for one (see II, A and B, directly above);
   B. Three years of teaching experience;
   C. Completion of the requirements for an administrative endorsement;
   D. Completion of the recency requirement listed under the 1-year conditional license; and
   E. Evidence of 1 year of successful administrative experience in a public school in Iowa, or of 2 years in any combination of public, private, or out-of-state schools.

VI. Exchange License (valid 2 years; nonrenewable)

    A.   Must complete a teacher preparation program from a state-approved and regionally accredited institution, then submit transcripts to verify;

    B.   Hold a baccalaureate degree from a regionally accredited institution;

    C.   Hold a valid or expired teaching license from another state;

    D.   Have no disciplinary action pending;

    E.   Have completed the Iowa mandated tests (for applicants who graduated after January 1, 2013 and have less than 3 years' experience); and

    F.   Have not completed all Iowa requirements for a teaching endorsement.

VII.   Initial Professional Service License (valid 2 years; renewable under prescribed conditions). May be issued to an applicant for licensure to serve as a school audiologist, school psychologist, school social worker, speech-language pathologist, supervisor of special education (support), director of special education of an area education agency, or school counselor who:

    A.   Has a master's degree in a recognized professional educational service area from a regionally accredited institution;

    B.   Has completed a state-approved program which meets the requirements for an endorsement in a professional educational service area;

    C.   Has completed the requirements for 1 of the professional educational service area endorsements; and

    D.   Meets the recency requirement.

        1.   For details, see 282—subrule 13.10(3) at http://www.boee.iowa.gov/agency _282.pdf.

VIII. Standard Professional Service License (valid 5 years; renewable under prescribed conditions)

    A.   Completes requirements listed for the initial professional service license; see VII, A–D directly above; and

    B.   Shows evidence of successful completion of a state-approved mentoring and induction program by

        1.   Meeting the Iowa standards as determined by a comprehensive evaluation; and

        2.   Completing 2 years of successful service experience in an Iowa public school.

        3.   In lieu of completion of a state-approved mentoring and induction program, the applicant must provide evidence of 3 years of successful service area experience in an Iowa nonpublic school or 3 years of successful service area experience in an out-of-state K–12 educational setting.

Teaching Endorsements

I. General requirements for the issuance of a license with an endorsement

    A.   Baccalaureate degree from a regionally accredited institution;

    B.   Completion of an approved human relations component;

    C.   Completion of the exceptional learner program, which must include preparation that contributes to the education of individuals with disabilities and the gifted and talented; and

    D.   Professional education core, with completed course work or evidence of competency in:

        1. Student learning: the practitioner understands how students learn and develop,

and provides learning opportunities that support intellectual, career, social, and personal development;

2. Diverse learners: the practitioner understands how students differ in their approaches to learning and creates instructional opportunities that are equitable and are adaptable to diverse learners;

3. Instructional planning: the practitioner plans instruction based upon knowledge of subject matter, students, the community, curriculum goals, and state curriculum models;

4. Instructional strategies: the practitioner understands and uses a variety of instructional strategies to encourage students' development of critical thinking, problem solving, and performance skills;

5. Learning environment/classroom management: the practitioner uses an understanding of individual and group motivation and behavior to create a learning environment that encourages positive social interaction, active engagement in learning, and self-motivation;

6. Communication: the practitioner uses knowledge of effective verbal, nonverbal, and media communication techniques, and other forms of symbolic representation, to foster active inquiry, collaboration, and support interaction in the classroom;

7. Assessment: the practitioner understands and uses formal and informal assessment strategies to evaluate the continuous intellectual, social, and physical development of the learner;

8. Foundations, reflection and professional development: the practitioner continually evaluates the effects of the practitioner's choices and actions on students, parents, and other professionals in the learning community, and actively seeks out opportunities to grow professionally;

9. Collaboration, ethics and relationships: the practitioner fosters relationships with parents, school colleagues, and organizations in the larger community to support students' learning and development;

10. Computer technology related to instruction;

11. Completion of pre−student teaching field-based experiences;

12. Methods of teaching, with an emphasis on the subject and grade level endorsement desired;

13. Student teaching in the subject area and grade level endorsement desired;

14. Preparation in reading programs, including reading recovery, and integration of reading strategies into content area methods course work; and

15. Content/subject matter specialization: the practitioner understands the central concepts, tools of inquiry, and structure of the discipline(s) the practitioner teaches and creates learning experiences that make these aspects of subject matter meaningful for students.

   a. This is evidenced by completion of a 30-semester-hour teaching major that must minimally include the requirements for at least 1 of the basic endorsement areas, special education teaching endorsements, or secondary level occupational endorsements.

b. For specific endorsement requirements, consult www.boee.iowa
.gov—endorsements.

Administrator Licenses

Applicants for the administrator license must first comply with the requirements for all Iowa prac-
titioners set out in 282—Chapter 13 (for details, consult https://www.legis.iowa.gov/docs/aco/
agency/282.pdf). Additionally, the requirements of rules 282—13.2(272) and 282—13.3(272)
and the license-specific requirements set forth under each license must be met before an applicant
is eligible for an administrator license.

I. Initial Administrator License (valid 1 year) may be issued to an applicant who:
A. Is the holder of or is eligible for a standard license;
B. Has 3 years of teaching experience;
C. Has completed a state-approved PK–12 principal and PK–12 supervisor of special
education program;
1. For details, see subrule 18.9(1) at https://www.legis.iowa.gov/docs/aco/agency/
282.pdf.
D. Is assuming a position as a PK–12 principal and PK–12 supervisor of special
education for the first time or has 1 year of out-of-state or nonpublic administrative
experience;
1. For details, see subrule 18.9(1) at https://www.legis.iowa.gov/docs/aco/agency/
282.pdf.
E. Has completed an approved human relations component;
F. Has completed an exceptional learner component; and
G. Has completed an evaluator approval program.
II. Superintendent/AEA Administrator. The holder of this endorsement is authorized
to serve as a superintendent for PK–12 or as an Area Education Agency (AEA)
administrator.
A. Program requirements
1. Specialist degree (or its equivalent: a master's degree plus at least 30 semester hours of planned graduate study in administration beyond the master's
degree);
2. Content: through completion of a sequence of courses and experiences
which may have been part of, or in addition to, the degree requirements, the
administrator has knowledge and understanding of:
a. Models, theories, and practices that provide the basis for leading
educational systems toward improving student performance;
b. Federal, state and local fiscal policies related to education;
c. Human resources management, including recruitment, personnel assistance
and development, evaluation and negotiations;
d. Current legal issues in general and special education;
e. Non-instructional support services management including but not limited
to transportation, nutrition and facilities; and

      f.   Practicum in PK–12 school administration in which, or in related course work, the administrator facilitates processes and engages in activities for:

          i.   Developing a shared vision of learning through articulation, implementation, and stewardship;

          ii.   Advocating, nurturing, and sustaining a school culture and instructional program conducive to student learning and staff professional growth;

          iii. Ensuring management of the organization, operations, and resources for a safe, efficient, and effective learning environment;

          iv. Collaborating with school staff, families, community members and boards of directors; responding to diverse community interests and needs; and mobilizing community resources;

          v.   Acting with integrity, fairness, and in an ethical manner; and

          vi. Understanding, responding to, and influencing the larger political, social, economic, legal, and cultural context.

B.   Administrative experience

    1.   The applicant must have had 3 years of experience as a building principal.

       a.   PK–12 or area education agency administrative experience is acceptable if the applicant acquires the 3 years of experience while holding a valid administrator license.

Kansas

Regardless of the type of license requested, any applicant for a first Kansas license must submit a fingerprint card and fee for the purpose of a Kansas Bureau of Investigation/Federal Bureau of Investigation background clearance.

License Types and Requirements

I. Initial Teaching License (valid 2 years; renewable)
   A. In-state applicants
      1. Bachelor's degree from a regionally accredited college or university
      2. Completion of a state-approved teacher preparation program
      3. Recency: have at least 8 credit hours or 1 year of accredited teaching experience completed within the last 6 years
      4. Passing scores on the content assessment in each of the endorsement areas on license
      5. Passing scores on the pedagogy assessment: Principles of Learning and Teaching (PLT)
   B. Out-of-state applicants
      1. See I, A, 1–3, directly above;
         and
      2. Passing scores on content and pedagogy tests: tests completed to achieve the out-of-state license may be acceptable;
         or
      3. May be issued a 2-year exchange license, if applicable;
         or
      4. May be issued a 1-year nonrenewable license;
         or
      5. May be issued a substitute license;
         or
      6. Meet experience requirements to come in at the professional license level.
II. Professional Teaching License (valid 5 years; renewable)
   A. In-state applicants
      1. Hold a currently valid Initial teaching license
      2. During its validity period, successfully complete the prescribed performance assessment
   B. Out-of-state applicants
      1. Bachelor's degree
      2. Completion of a state-approved preparation program in subject or field for which licensure is sought

3. Recency: at least 1 year of accredited teaching experience or 8 semester hours of college credit within the 6 year period immediately prior to application
4. Out-of-state professional license
5. Three years of recent accredited experience under a standard teaching license
   or
   Meet recency and verify at least 5 years of accredited experience under an initial or professional license
   or
   Passing scores on assessments in content and pedagogy, with an already completed performance assessment

III. Accomplished Teaching License (valid 10 years; renewable)
   A. Available only to teachers who have achieved National Board Certification from the National Board for Professional Teaching Standards (NBPTS) through completion of their advanced-level performance assessment process.
      1. Kansas-licensed teachers must also hold a currently valid Kansas professional-level teaching license as well as achieving National Board Certification.
      2. National Board–certified teachers coming from out-of-state may apply for this license as their initial Kansas license, as long as they also hold a currently valid professional-level teaching license in another state.
         a. Accomplished license will be valid for the validity length of National Board Certification.

IV. One-Year Nonrenewable Teaching License (valid only for current school year)
   A. Meet all requirements for an Initial license (see I, A, 1–5, directly above) except for all or part of the prelicensure tests
   B. Tests in which individual is deficient must be completed during the school year in order to upgrade to the Initial license.

V. Two-Year Exchange (Teaching or School Specialist) License (valid 2 years)
   A. Exchange Teaching
      1. Complete a state-approved teacher education program through college in home state
      2. Hold a standard valid license in that state
      3. Rectify all deficiencies in initial Kansas requirements during 2-year period
   B. Exchange School Specialist (school counselor, library media, reading specialist)
      1. Complete a state-approved school specialist program in home state
      2. Hold a standard valid school specialist license in that state
      3. Rectify all deficiencies in initial Kansas requirements during 2-year period
         a. Deficiencies may include completion of the content licensure examination; a 3.25 cumulative GPA in graduate course work; and/or recency credit.
      4. Hold a Kansas professional-level teaching license
      5. Neither leadership licenses nor alternative routes to licensure are eligible for exchange licensure.

VI. Substitute Licenses
   A. Standard Substitute License (valid 5 years; renewable)
      1. Hold a bachelor's degree
      2. Complete a teacher preparation program

3. Submit 1 fingerprint card for an FBI and Kansas Bureau of Investigation (KBI) background clearance report

   B. Emergency Substitute License (valid for current school year)

      1. Complete a minimum of 60 semester credit hours from regionally accredited college or university

      2. Submit 1 fingerprint card for an FBI and KBI background clearance report

VII. Provisional License (valid 2 years; renewable)

   A. Provisional Teaching Endorsement License

      1. Hold a valid Kansas license and have a plan of study for completing an approved program for a new teaching subject

      2. Fifty percent of the program for the new teaching area is complete

      3. A Kansas district must verify assignment of teacher in the provisional subject area at the appropriate level.

      4. To qualify for a second provisional, complete half the remaining course work deficiencies (have 75 percent of approved program completed).

      5. For Provisional Teaching Endorsement License in Special Education, see VII, A, 2, directly above.

         a. A valid license for general education is required.

         b. Course work in areas of methodology, characteristics, and a practicum is already completed.

         c. Kansas district must verify assignment of teacher in provisional special education area at the appropriate level.

   B. Provisional School Specialist License for school counselor, library media, or reading specialist

      1. Hold a valid 5-year professional teaching license

      2. Fifty percent of the school specialist program is completed

      3. Kansas district must verify assignment of applicant as a school specialist.

   C. Provisional license is not available for school leadership licenses.

VIII. Restricted Teaching License Alternative Pathway (valid 3 years while employed in school system)

   A. Meet all eligibility requirements:

      1. Hold a bachelor's degree or higher from a regionally accredited university

      2. Degree must be in a regular education content area in which applicant desires to teach or equivalent content course work must be completed.

      3. Most recent 60 semester credit hours of college course work show a cumulative GPA of 2.75.

      4. Passing score on the appropriate content assessment

   B. Request that the university hosting the alternative route program evaluate transcript to ensure that content requirements for subject matter teaching area are adequate

      1. Develop a plan of study with the alternative certification program staff; program length may vary depending on situation.

   C. Locate and apply for a teaching position, verifying that a restricted license is appropriate for it

   D. Apply for restricted license, coordinating application among individual, employing school district, and higher education institution providing the course work.

E. Once license is issued, applicant will teach full time while completing required professional education course work towards full licensure.

F. Submit a progress report every year verifying appropriate progress towards a full license; otherwise, restricted license will be cancelled

G. Apply for a full Kansas license with institutional recommendation once applicant successfully completes all course work and testing requirements on plan of study

H. Complete the PLT assessment

IX. School Specialist License

A. Initial School Specialist License

1. Graduate degree from a regionally accredited college

2. Complete graduate-level state-approved program

3. Cumulative GPA of 3.25 in graduate course work

4. Recency: have at least 8 credit hours or 1 year of accredited experience completed within the last 6 years

5. Currently valid Kansas professional teaching license (if applying for library media, reading specialist)

6. Successfully complete a school specialist content assessment

a. School counselor content test: complete Praxis II test number 0420—School Guidance and Counseling—with score of 600 or above

b. Library media specialist content test: complete Praxis II test number 0311—Library Media Specialist—with score of 630 or above

c. Reading specialist content test: complete Praxis II test number 0300—Reading Specialist—with score of 560 or above

B. Professional School Specialist License

1. In-state applicants

a. Hold a currently valid Initial School Specialist License (see IX, A, 1–6, directly above)

b. Complete the performance assessment while employed as a school specialist

2. Out-of-state applicants

a. See IX, A, 1–5, directly above; *and*

b. Successfully complete a school specialist content and performance assessment, *or*

Three years of recent accredited experience in a school specialist position while holding a valid standard school specialist license, *or*

Meet recency and at least 5 years of accredited school specialist experience under a standard school specialist license.

X. School Leadership Licenses: includes Program Leadership (supervisor/coordinator); Building Leadership (principal); District Leadership (superintendent)

A. Initial School Leadership License (valid 2 years)

1. Graduate degree from a regionally accredited college

2. Complete graduate-level state-approved program in school leadership
3. If applying for a district leadership license, completion of an approved building leadership program
4. Cumulative GPA of 3.25 in graduate course work
5. Recency: at least 8 credit hours or 1 year of accredited experience completed within the last 6 years
6. Minimum of 5 years of accredited experience under a valid standard license/certificate and having achieved the professional-level license
7. School leadership licensure assessment

B. Professional School Leadership license (valid 5 years)
1. Hold a currently valid Initial School Leadership License
2. Complete performance assessment while employed as an administrator

C. Out-of-state applicants
1. See X, A, 1–7, directly above;
   and
2. Successfully complete a school leadership content and performance assessment,
   or
   Three years of recent accredited experience in a school leadership position while holding a standard school leadership license,
   or
   Meet recency and at least 5 years of accredited school leadership experience under a standard school leadership license.

XI. New Licenses: Contact the Kansas State Department of Education (see Appendix 1) for full details
A. Transitional License (valid 1 year)
1. Provides immediate access to practice for:
   a. Out-of-state applicant without recent credit or experience
   b. Kansas educator with expired full license who is retired or out of practice

B. Interim Alternative License (valid 1 year; renewable for another year)
1. Guarantees license for immediate access to practice to out-of-state applicant whose preparation was through an alternative pathway

C. Restricted School Specialist License (for school counselor or library media)
1. Requires graduate degree and 3 years of professional experience in the counseling or library field
2. Must complete professional education during 3-year restricted license period while employed in school system

D. STEM License (valid for 1 school year; renewable for additional years)
1. Degree in life science, physical science, earth and space science, mathematics, engineering, computer technology, finance, or accounting
2. Five years of professional work experience in the subject matter for which the degree is held
3. District hire to teach only that subject matter based on the degree and experience

Endorsements by Levels

I. Early Childhood: Birth–Grade 3 or Birth–K
   A. Requires combined general education and special education curriculum: Early Childhood Unified
   B. Must be done with a general education license: Deaf or Hard of Hearing; Visually Impaired; School Psychologist

II. Early Childhood–Late Childhood: K–6
   A. Elementary
   B. Provisional is available for the following: Adaptive; Functional; Gifted; English for Speakers of Other Languages (ESOL).

III. Late Childhood–Early Adolescence: Grades 5–8
   A. Provisional is available for the following: History Comprehensive; Science; English Language Arts; Mathematics

IV. Early Adolescence–Late Adolescence/Adulthood: Grades 6–12
   A. Provisional is available for the following: English Language Arts; Mathematics; Agriculture; Biology; Business; Chemistry; Earth and Space Science; Family & Consumer Science; History and Government; Journalism; Physics; Psychology; Speech/Theatre; Technology Education; Communication Technology; Power, Energy, Transportation Technology; Production Technology; Adaptive; ESOL; Functional; Gifted

V. Early Childhood–Late Adolescence/Adulthood: PreK–12
   A. School Psychologist; Building Leadership; District Leadership; Program Leadership
   B. Provisional is available for the following: Deaf or Hard of Hearing; Visually Impaired; Adaptive, Functional; Gifted; ESOL; Library Media Specialist; Music; Instrumental Music; Vocal Music; Physical Education; Reading Specialist; School Counselor

VI. Grades 8–12
   A. STEM license

Kentucky

General Requirements

I. Recency of preparation
    A. Completed program of preparation within 5 years preceding date of receipt of certification application form
        or
        Completed 6 semester hours of additional graduate credit within preceding 5 years
        1. Applicants who have completed a 5th-year program and have 2 years of successful teaching experience within the last 10 years are exempt from the 6-hour requirement.
    B. Initial 1-year certification for special circumstances
        1. Those not meeting recency requirements in I, A, directly above, who have not previously held a regular Kentucky teaching certificate, but who otherwise qualify for certification shall be issued a 1-year initial certificate that
            a. Ends June 30 of next calendar year
            b. Is conditional on 6 semester hours of graduate credit applicable toward the usual renewal requirements being completed by September 1 of year of expiration
II. Duration of teaching certificates
    A. Issued for 5 years, with provisions for subsequent 5-year renewals, provided that by September 1 of the year of expiration, the applicant has completed
        1. Three years of successful teaching experience
            or
            At least 6 semester hours of graduate credit or the equivalent
    B. One-year certificates shall be issued for
        1. Beginning teacher internship*
            a. Upon successful completion of such internship as judged by majority vote of beginning teacher committee, 1-year certificate will be extended for remainder of the 5-year period.
        2. Initial certification for applicants not meeting recency requirements in I, A, directly above
            *This requirement is waived for the 2020–21 and 2021–22 school years.
III. Renewal of teaching certificates
    A. Requirements for subsequent 5-year renewals
        1. Completion by September 1 of the year of expiration of
            a. Three years of successful teaching experience
                or
                Six semester hours of graduate credit or the equivalent
        2. Credits for certificate renewal shall be earned after the issuance of the certificate.

        3.   Applicants holding a lapsed regular Kentucky teaching certificate shall not be required to take the written tests or to participate in the beginning teacher internship program.

  IV. Out-of-State Applicants

      A. Those who have completed 2 or more years of acceptable teaching experience outside of the Commonwealth of Kentucky and who otherwise qualify for certification shall not be required to take the written tests or to participate in the beginning teacher internship program.

   V. Requirements for 1-year certificate for beginning teacher internship*

      A. Completion of an approved program of preparation that corresponds to the certificate desired

      B. Passing scores on the Praxis II Subject Assessment appropriate for each content area in which certification is requested, in addition to the appropriate Principles of Learning and Teaching (PLT) test

          1.   All new teachers are required to take the PLT test in addition to the specialty(ies) test appropriate for the certification they are seeking. Contact the Education Professional Standards Board (see Appendix 1) for detailed information.

      C. Evidence of full-time employment in a Kentucky school as attested by the prospective employer

      *This requirement is waived for the 2020–21 and 2021–22 school years.

  VI. Upon successful completion of the approved program of preparation and upon completion of the designated tests with acceptable scores, the Education Professional Standards Board shall issue a statement of eligibility for employment that shall serve as evidence of eligibility for the 1-year certificate once a teaching position is secured. The statement of eligibility shall be valid for a 5-year period.

Approved Programs

The Commonwealth of Kentucky follows the "approved program" approach to certification. An individual should follow the program in effect at the college or university with the guidance of the college advisor and meet the General Requirements (see above). Applicants interested in certification should contact the Division of Certification (see Appendix 1) for the latest information.

    I. Interdisciplinary Early Childhood Education (Birth to Primary)

   II. Elementary School (Primary through Grade 5)

  III. Middle School (Grades 5 through 9)

      A. Preparation in 1 major or equivalent

         or

      B. Preparation in 2 teaching fields selected from the following: English and communications, mathematics, science, and social studies

          1.   Candidates who choose to prepare simultaneously for teaching in the middle school and for teaching exceptional children are required to complete only 1 middle school teaching field.

IV. Secondary School (Grades 8 through 12)
   A. Preparation includes 1 or more of the following specializations: English, mathematics, social studies, biological science, physics, chemistry, or earth science.
V. Middle/Secondary School (Grades 5 through 12)
   A. Preparation includes 1 or more of the following specializations: agriculture, business and marketing, family and consumer science, industrial education, technology education.
VI. Elementary/Middle/Secondary School (Primary through Grade 12)
   A. Preparation includes 1 or more of the following specializations: art, foreign language (Arabic, Chinese, French, German, Japanese, Latin, Russian, or Spanish), health, physical education, integrated music, vocal music, instrumental music, school media librarian.
VII. Exceptional Children (Primary through Grade 12, and for collaborating with teachers to design and deliver programs for pre-primary children)
   A. Preparation includes 1 or more of the following specializations: learning and behavior disorders; moderate and severe disabilities; hearing impaired or hearing impaired/sign proficiency; visually impaired; communication disorders (master's level); speech-language pathology assistant (bachelor's level).
VIII. Endorsements to Certificates (Primary through Grade 12)
   A. Computer science (8–12), English as a second language (P–12), gifted education (P–12), driver education (8–12), reading and writing (P–12), instructional computer technology (P–12), learning and behavior disorders (8–12), school nutrition (P–12), and school safety (P–12)
   B. Restricted Base Certificates: psychology (8–12), sociology (8–12), journalism (8–12), speech/media communications (8–12), theater (P–12), dance (P–12), computer information systems (P–12), English as a second language (P–12), school nurse (P–12), school social worker (P–12), Junior Reserve Officer Training Corps (8–12)
IX. Professional Certificate for Instructional Leadership
   A. Certification is offered for the following positions: Supervisor of Instruction, Level 1; Supervisor of Instruction, Level 2; Principal, All Grades, Level 1; Principal, All Grades, Level 2; Director of Special Education; Director of Pupil Personnel; School Psychologist; Guidance Counselor; and School Superintendent.

Principal, All Grades

I. Requirements for Principal, All Grades, Level 1
   A. As prerequisites for the Level 1 program of preparation for the initial Professional Certificate for Instructional Leadership, the candidate shall
     1. Have been admitted to the preparation program on the basis of criteria, developed by the teacher-education institution,
     2. Have completed 3 years of full-time teaching experience,
     3. Qualify for a Kentucky teaching certificate, and
     4. Successfully complete the School Leaders Licensure Assessment (SLLA) and the Kentucky specialty test of instructional and administrative practices. (Note: At press time, the state legislature was considering a bill to eliminate

the specialty test; please refer to http://www.epsb.ky.gov/ for the most current information.)

    a.   Applicants with out-of-state principal certification and 2 years of verified full-time principal experience are exempt from the SLLA.

  5. All applicants without 2 years of verified full-time principal experience must successfully complete a 1-year Kentucky principal internship program (KPIP)*. *KPIP is not currently funded by the state legislature and has been waived until it is funded.

B. The initial Professional Certificate for Instructional Leadership shall be issued for a period of 1 year upon successful completion of Level 1 preparation and the tests prescribed and upon obtaining employment for an internship position as principal or assistant principal. Upon proof of employment as a principal/assistant principal, the certificate shall be extended for 4 years.

C. The certificate shall be renewed subsequently for 5-year periods. The first renewal shall require the completion of the curriculum identified as the Level 2 program in the curriculum standards. Each 5-year renewal thereafter shall require the completion of 2 years of experience as a principal, or 3 semester hours of additional graduate credit related to the position of school principal, or 42 hours of approved training selected from programs approved for the Kentucky Effective Leadership Training Program.

D. If a lapse in certification occurs because of lack of completion of the Level 2 preparation, the certificate may be reissued for a 5-year period upon successful completion of the Level 2 preparation. If a certificate lapses with Level 2 preparation, but because of lack of the renewal requirements, the certificate may be reissued after the completion of an additional 6 semester hours of graduate study appropriate to the program.

E. Persons applying for the Professional Certificate for Instructional Leadership who satisfy the curriculum requirements and all other prerequisites and who have completed at least 2 years of successful full-time experience, including at least 140 days per year, as a school principal, within a 10-year period prior to making application will be exempt from the internship requirements for school principals but shall be required to pass the written examinations.

II. Standards for School Principal

  A. Individuals must meet the standards for principals outlined in the Professional Standards for Educational Leaders, available at https://education.ky.gov/teachers/PGES/Documents/Professional-Standards-for-Educational-Leaders.pdf.

Guidance Counselor

I. Provisional Certificate Requirements, Primary–Grade 12 (valid 5 years)

  A. Complete an approved master's level program in guidance counseling

  B. Renewable with proof of completion of at least 9 semester hours of graduate credit in areas of counseling or guidance counseling

II. Standard Certificate Requirements, Primary–Grade 12 (valid 5 years)

  A. Option 1

1. Successfully complete an approved master's level program in guidance counseling
2. Successfully complete additional 3 – 6 credit hours from an approved graduate-level counseling or guidance counseling program
3. One year of full-time employment as a provisionally certified guidance counselor in an accredited public or private school
4. Hold a valid Kentucky Professional teaching certificate
5. Complete at least 1 year of full-time classroom teaching experience

B. Option 2
1. See II, A, 1 and 2, directly above.
2. Complete at least 2 years of successful employment as a provisional full-time certified guidance counselor

C. Renewable upon completion of Effective Instructional Leadership Act (EILA) hours as specified by the Kentucky Department of Education by September 1 of the year of expiration

Library Media Specialist

I.   This standards- and performance-based credential is awarded for work with all grade levels after the following requirements have been met:
A. Transcript reflecting appropriate grades and courses,
B. Recommendation of the college or university,
C. Praxis II: Library Media Specialist test with satisfactory score, *and*
D. Internship.

II. For applicants with 2 years of experience as a Library Media Specialist, C and D, directly above, may be waived. Contact the Education Professional Standards Board (see Appendix 1) for more detailed information.

School Psychologist

I.   Provisional Certificate for School Psychologist
A. Requirements
1. Recommendation of the applicant's preparing institution
2. Successful completion of the institution's approved program of preparation
3. Passing score on the required assessment

B. Issued for a duration period of 1 year; may be renewed for an additional year if the individual is serving in the position of the school psychologist on at least a half-time basis.

C. Individual serves under the supervision of the preparing institution. During this first year of service, the employer of the Provisional Certificate shall permit the individual to engage in the preparing institution's internship component.

D. Internship may be served full-time during 1 school year or half-time during 2 consecutive years.

II. Standard Certificate for School Psychologist
    A. Option 1
        1. Completion of an approved program of preparation that corresponds to the certificate at a teacher-education institution that adheres to the National Association of School Psychologists Standards for Training Programs
        2. Completion of the appropriate assessment and a passing score as established in state regulations
    B. Option 2
        1. Possession of a valid certificate as a nationally certified school psychologist issued by the National School Psychology Certification System
    C. The Standard Certificate for School Psychologist shall be issued for a period of 5 years and may be renewed for subsequent 5-year periods with completion of 1 of the following:
        1. At least 3 years of experience as a school psychologist within each certification period and 72 hours of continuing professional development activities, *or*
        2. Six semester hours of graduate training related to school psychology.

Teacher for Gifted Education

I. Standards for Certificate Endorsement
    A. Classroom teaching certificate
    B. One year of teaching experience
    C. The completion of an approved graduate-level curriculum
        1. At least 9 semester hours of credit giving emphasis to the following content:
            a. Nature and needs of gifted education
            b. Assessment and/or counseling of the gifted
            c. Curriculum development for the gifted
            d. Strategies and materials for teaching the gifted
            e. Creative studies
        2. At least 3 semester hours of credit in a supervised practicum for gifted education; however, with 2 years of experience as a teacher for gifted, the practicum requirement may be waived.

Louisiana

I. Level 1 Professional Certificate (valid for 3 years)
   A. Eligibility requirements for Louisiana graduate
      1. Successfully complete state-approved traditional or alternate teacher preparation program;
      2. Hold minimum 2.50 GPA on a 4.00 scale. Applicants who do not meet this requirement may be certified if they meet the following requirements in an alternate teacher preparation program:
         a. Satisfactorily complete a personal interview by the program's admissions officer.
         b. If the program awards credit hours, the applicant shall achieve a minimum GPA of 3.00 in alternate teacher preparation program courses by the end of the first 12 credit hours and successfully complete the program.
         c. If the program does not award credit hours, the applicant shall demonstrate mastery of competencies as required by the program administrator and by the school system in which the applicant completes required clinical practice.
         d. Satisfactorily complete all program requirements as set forth by the Louisiana State Board of Elementary and Secondary Education (BESE), including any requirements for clinical practice, at graduation.
      3. Present appropriate scores on the National Teacher Examination (NTE) core battery (common exams) or the corresponding Praxis exams (core academic skills for educators in reading, writing, and mathematics); the Principles of Learning and Teaching (PLT) or other pedagogy exam required for the area(s) of certification; and the specialty area exam in the certification area in which the teacher preparation program was completed or in which the initial certificate was issued;
      and
      4. Be recommended by a state-approved university or private program provider for certification.
   B. Eligibility requirements for out-of-state graduate
      1. Possess a minimum of a bachelor's degree from a regionally accredited college or university;
      2. Successfully complete a teacher preparation program in another state;
      3. Hold a standard out-of-state teaching certificate; or if no certificate was issued, a letter from the State Department of Education in the state of origin verifying eligibility in that state for a certificate in the certification area(s);
      4. Pass all parts of Praxis exam(s) required for Louisiana certification:
         a. Present appropriate scores on the NTE core battery (common exams) or the corresponding Praxis exams (core academic skills for educators in reading, writing, and mathematics); the PLT or other pedagogy exam required for

the area(s) of certification; and the specialty area exam in the certification area in which the teacher preparation program was completed or in which the initial certificate was issued;
and

b. If applicant has obtained National Board Certification (NBC) in corresponding areas for which certification is being sought as well as certification/licensure in the state of origin, the examination required for NBC will be accepted to fulfill the testing requirements for certification;

5. Successfully complete student teaching, an internship, or 3 years of teaching experience in the candidate's area of certification;
and

6. Has not been out of teaching in the 5 years immediately preceding first employment or application for a Louisiana certificate.

a. A candidate who has not taught in 5 years may be issued a 1-year nonrenewable out-of-state (OS1) certificate while completing the 6 semester hours required for issuance of a 3-year nonrenewable (OS) certificate.

b. A candidate who is certified in another state can qualify for exclusion from the Praxis exam(s) required for Louisiana certification under the following criteria:

    i.   Meets all requirements for Louisiana certification except the Praxis exam requirements; has at least 3 years of successful teaching experience in another state, as verified by the out-of-state employing authority or state education agency (SEA); and teaches on an out-of-state certificate for 1 year in a Louisiana-approved public or an approved private school system.

    ii. The teacher's employing authority must verify that he/she has completed 1 year of successful teaching experience in a Louisiana-approved public or an approved private school and that he/she has been recommended for further employment.

    iii. The employing authority must request that the teacher be granted a valid Louisiana teaching certificate.

C. Eligibility requirements for Foreign Applicant—(OS) Certificate

1. Possess a bachelor's or higher degree verified by a regionally accredited institution in the United States

    a. If the institution is located in Louisiana, the dean of the College of Education must recommend the applicant for certification based upon Louisiana requirements.

    b. If the institution is located in another state/country, the guidelines prescribed for out-of-state applicants must be followed.
    or

    c. Credentials may be submitted for evaluation to a credentialing agency that follows the standards of the American Association of Collegiate Registrars and Admissions Officers (AACRAO). The original course-by-course evaluation must be submitted directly from the agency on "safe script" paper and must include a statement verifying the comparability of the baccalaureate degree in the field of education.

D. Eligibility requirements for Foreign Applicant—Level 1 Certificate

    1. Possess a bachelor's degree or higher verified by a regionally accredited institution in the United States;

        a. If the institution is located in Louisiana, the dean of the College of Education must recommend the applicant for certification based upon Louisiana requirements.

        b. If the institution is located in another state/country, the guidelines prescribed for out-of-state applicants must be followed.

        or

        c. Credentials may be submitted for evaluation to a credentialing agency that follows the standards of the AACRAO. The original course-by-course evaluation must be submitted directly from the agency on "safe script" paper and must include a statement verifying the comparability of the baccalaureate degree in the field of education.

    2. Present appropriate scores on the NTE core battery (common exams) or the corresponding Praxis exams (core academic skills for educators in reading, writing, and mathematics); the PLT or other pedagogy exam required for the area(s) of certification; and the specialty area exam(s) in the certification area(s) in which the teacher preparation program was completed or in which the initial certificate was issued.

II. Level 2 Professional Certificate (valid 5 years)

A. Eligibility requirements

    1. Hold or meet eligibility requirements for a Level 1 certificate; see Level 1 Professional Certificate, directly above;

    2. Either successfully meet the standards of effectiveness for 3 years pursuant to Bulletin 130 and mandated by Act 54 of the Louisiana 2010 Legislative Session

        or

        Receive a waiver of this provision from the Louisiana Department of Education, at the request of the employing local education agency (LEA), if the teacher was unable to meet the standards of effectiveness due to administrative error in the local implementation of the evaluation system any year prior to the 2015–2016 school year;

        and

    3. Accrue 3 years of experience in area(s) of certification in an approved educational setting.

    4. All out-of-state experience must be verified as successful by the out-of-state employing authority or SEA.

B. If the Level 2 certificate is the applicant's first certificate, a state-approved teacher preparation program provider must submit the request.

C. If the Level 1–certificated teacher qualifies for advancement to a Level 2 certificate, the request for the higher certificate must be submitted directly to the Louisiana Department of Education by the employing authority.

III. Level 3 Professional Certificate (valid 5 years)
    A. Eligibility requirements:
        1. Hold or meet eligibility requirements for Level 2 certificate; see Level 2 Professional Certificate, directly above;
        2. Hold a master's degree from a regionally accredited college or university; *and*
        3. Have 5 years of experience in area(s) of certification in an approved educational setting.
        4. All out-of-state experience must be verified as successful by the out-of-state employing authority or SEA.
    B. If the Level 3 certificate is applicant's first certificate, a state-approved teacher preparation program provider must submit the request.
    C. If the Level 2–certificated teacher qualifies for advancement to a Level 3 certificate, the request for the higher certificate must be submitted directly to the Louisiana Department of Education by the employing authority.

IV. Renewal/Extension Guidelines for Level 1, Level 2, and Level 3 certificates
    A. Level 1 certificate
        1. Valid for 3 years initially; may be extended thereafter for a period of 1 year at the request of a Louisiana employing authority (limited to 2 such extensions). Teachers must successfully meet the standards of effectiveness for the renewal of this certificate pursuant to state law and Bulletin 130, available at https://bese.louisiana.gov/policy.
    B. Level 2 and Level 3 Certificates:
        1. Valid for 5 years initially; may be renewed thereafter for a period of 5 years at the request of a Louisiana employing authority. For renewal, candidates must successfully meet the standards of effectiveness for at least 3 years during the 5-year initial or renewal period pursuant to state law and Bulletin 130.
        2. LEAs may request a one-time, 5-year renewal of the certificate if a teacher was unable to successfully meet the standards of effectiveness due to administrative error in the local implementation of the evaluation system in any year before the 2015–2016 school year.

V. Out-of-State (OS) Certificate (valid 3 years; nonrenewable)
    A. Issued to a teacher who has completed an out-of-state teacher preparation program and either holds or is eligible for a certificate in the state in which the program was completed. The teacher is not initially eligible for a Level 1, 2, or 3 Louisiana certificate but meets Louisiana certification requirements with the exception of the Praxis/National Teacher Exam requirements. It provides a transition period that permits the holder to be employed in Louisiana K–12 schools while he/she complies with Louisiana Praxis/NTE requirements or meets Praxis exclusion eligibility requirements. For continued employment as a teacher in a Louisiana school system after the 3-year period has elapsed, the OS certificate holder must fulfill guidelines for a Level 1 or higher certificate.
    B. Eligibility requirements:
        1. Hold a bachelor's degree from a regionally accredited college or university;
        2. Successfully complete a teacher preparation program in another state;

3. Hold a standard out-of-state teaching certificate, or if no certificate was issued, a letter from the State Department of Education or College of Education dean verifying eligibility in that state for a certificate in the certification area(s);

4. Successfully complete student teaching or internship in a certification area, or in lieu of student teaching or internship, have 3 years of successful teaching experience in a certification area;
   and

5. If applicant earned a degree 5 or more years prior to date of application, he/she must have been a regularly employed teacher for at least 1 semester, or 90 consecutive days, within the 5-year period immediately preceding first employment in Louisiana or application for a Louisiana certificate. Lacking this experience, he/she must earn 6 semester hours of credit in state-approved courses (see Chapter 12 of Bulletin 746 on website) during the 5-year period immediately preceding application. A candidate who has not taught in 5 years may be issued a 1-year nonrenewable (OS1) certificate while he/she completes 6 semester hours required for the issuance of a 3-year nonrenewable (OS) certificate.

6. Beginning January 1, 2017, the Louisiana Department of Education (LDE) will issue a letter of eligibility for an OS certificate to requesting teachers. The OS certificate will be issued at the request of the Louisiana employing authority.

VI. Advancing from OS to Professional Level 1, 2, or 3 Certificate
   A. Pass all parts of Praxis exam(s) required for Louisiana certification:
   1. Present appropriate scores on the NTE core battery (common exams) or the corresponding Praxis exams (core academic skills for educators in reading, writing, and mathematics); the PLT or other pedagogy exam required for the area(s) of certification; and the specialty area exam in the certification area in which the teacher preparation program was completed or in which the initial certificate was issued.
   2. If applicant has obtained NBC in corresponding areas for which certification is being sought as well as certification/licensure in the state of origin, the examination required for NBC will be accepted to fulfill the testing requirements for certification.
   3. A candidate who is certified in another state can qualify for exclusion from the Praxis exam(s) required for Louisiana certification under these criteria:
      a. He/she meets all requirements for Louisiana certification except the Praxis exam requirements; has at least 3 years of successful teaching experience in another state, as verified by the out-of-state employing authority or SEA; and teaches on an OS certificate for 1 year in a Louisiana-approved public or an approved private school system;
      b. The teacher's Louisiana employing authority verifies that he/she has completed 1 year of successful teaching experience in a Louisiana-approved public or an approved private school and that he/she has been recommended for further employment;
         and

c.   The employing authority requests that the teacher be granted a valid Louisiana teaching certificate.

VII.   Other Licenses and Certificates

Consult https://www.teachlouisiana.net/ for more details on the following credentials.

A.   World Language Certificate (WLC) PK–12 (valid 6 years). May be issued to a foreign associate teacher who participates in the LDE Foreign Associate Teacher Program, and who teaches world language and/or immersion in grades PK–12.

B.   Practitioner Licenses

1.   Practitioner Licenses 1 and 2 (issued for 1 school year, renewed annually, held a maximum of 3 years while the holder completes an alternate program). Upon completion of 3 years of employment on this certificate, the holder must fulfill guidelines for a Level 1 or higher certificate for continued employment in a Louisiana school system.

2.   Practitioner License 3 (issued for 1 school year, renewed annually, held a maximum of 4 years while the holder completes an alternate program). Upon completion of 4 years of employment on this certificate, the holder must fulfill guidelines for a Level 1 or higher certificate for continued employment in a Louisiana school system.

C.   Extended Endorsement License (EEL) (issued for 1 school year, renewable annually, held a maximum of 3 years while the holder pursues certification in the content area of the license)

D.   Standard Certificates for Teachers in Nonpublic Schools

1.   A standard certificate with an asterisk (*) following the certificate type is issued to a teacher in a nonpublic school. The asterisk (*) refers to a statement printed at the bottom of the certificate: "If this teacher enters a public/charter school system in Louisiana, he/she will be required to meet the standards of effectiveness pursuant to Bulletin 130 and mandated by Act 54 of the Louisiana 2010 Legislative Session for issuance of a Level 2 or Level 3 teaching certificate."

Educational Leadership Certificates

An individual who serves as an administrator and/or supervisor in Louisiana schools is required to obtain the appropriate credential for the area of assignment. A teacher already certified in Louisiana can have an educational leader certificate issued to provide administrative or supervisory services in a Louisiana school system.

I.   Educational Leader Certificate Level 1 (EDL 1) (valid 3 years initially; may be extended 1 year at request of an LEA; limited to 2 such extensions). For those who fill school and district educational leadership positions (e.g., assistant principal, principal, parish or city supervisor of instruction, supervisor of child welfare and attendance, special education supervisor, or comparable school/district leader positions).

A.   Master's Degree Pathway

1.   Hold or be eligible to hold a valid Louisiana Type B or Level 2 teaching certificate, or have a comparable level out-of-state teaching certificate;

2. Have 3 years of teaching experience in area of certification;

3. Completion of a competency-based graduate degree preparation program in the area of educational leadership from a regionally accredited institution of higher education;
    and

4. Have a passing score on the School Leaders Licensure Assessment (SLLA) in accordance with state requirements.

5. All out-of-state experience must be verified as successful by the out-of-state employing authority or SEA.

B. Alternate Pathway 1—For persons who already hold a master's degree:

1. Hold or be eligible to hold a valid Louisiana Type B or Level 2 teaching certificate, or have a comparable level out-of-state teaching certificate;

2. Have 3 years of teaching experience in area of certification;

3. Have earned a graduate degree from a regionally accredited institution of higher education;

4. Meet competency-based requirements, as demonstrated by completion of an individualized program of educational leadership from a regionally accredited institution of higher education. (An individualized program will be developed based on a screening of each candidate's competencies upon entering into the graduate alternative certification program);
    and

5. Have a passing score on the SLLA in accordance with state requirements.

6. All out-of-state experience must be verified as successful by the out-of-state employing authority or SEA.

C. Alternate Pathway 2—For persons who already hold a master's degree in education:

1. Hold or be eligible to hold a valid Louisiana Type B or Level 2 teaching certificate, or have a comparable level out-of-state teaching certificate;

2. Have 3 years of teaching experience in area of certification;

3. Have previously completed a graduate degree program in education from a regionally accredited institution of higher education;

4. Provide documented evidence of leadership experiences (240 clock hours or more) at the school and/or district level;
    and

5. Earn a passing score on the SLLA in accordance with state requirements.

6. All out-of-state experience must be verified as successful by the out-of-state employing authority or SEA.

D. Alternate Pathway 3—For persons who already hold a bachelor's degree from a regionally accredited institution of higher education and are seeking to add Educational Leader certification to a valid teaching certificate through a competency-based educational leader practitioner (residency) program:

1. Hold or be eligible to hold a valid Louisiana Type B or Level 2 teaching certificate, or have a comparable level out-of-state teaching certificate;

2. Have 3 years of teaching experience in area of certification;

3. Demonstrate strong knowledge of instruction through a rigorous screening process by an approved program provider;

4. Complete a competency-based educational leader practitioner/residency preparation program in the area of educational leadership from a state-approved private provider or a regionally accredited institution of higher education; *and*
5. Have a passing score on the SLLA in accordance with state requirements.
6. All out-of-state experience must be verified as successful by the out-of-state employing authority or SEA.

II. Educational Leader Certificate Level 2 (EDL 2) (valid 5 years initially; may be extended for 5 years at request of an LEA)

A. Hold a valid EDL 1 certificate, Louisiana provisional principal certification, or comparable level out-of-state educational leader certificate;
B. Have 3 years of teaching experience in area(s) of certification (if applicable, all out-of-state experience must be verified as successful by the out-of-state employing authority or SEA);
C. Participate in an education leader induction administered, if required by the LEA;
D. Either meet standards of effectiveness as an educational leader for 3 years pursuant to Bulletin 130 and R.S. 17:3902

   or

   Receive a waiver of this provision from the local department of education, at the request of the employing LEA, if the educational leader was unable to meet the standards of effectiveness any year prior to the 2015–2016 school year due to administrative error in the local implementation of the evaluation system; *and*
E. For individuals who are employed in a leadership capacity at the district level, earn "effective" ratings per local personnel evaluations for 3 years.

III. Educational Leader Certificate Level 3 (EDL 3) (valid 5 years initially; may be extended for 5 years at the request of an LEA). This certificate is required in order to serve as a school system superintendent or assistant superintendent.

A. Valid EDL 2 or 1 of the Louisiana administrative/supervisory certifications that preceded the educational leadership certification structure;
B. Five years of teaching experience in area of certification;
C. Five years of successful administrative or management experience in education at the level of assistant principal or above. The assistant principal experience would be limited to a maximum of 2 years of experience in that position; *and*
D. Passing score on the School Superintendent Assessment (SSA), in keeping with state requirements.
E. All out-of-state experience must be verified as successful by the out-of-state employing authority or SEA.

Counselor K–12

I. Counselor K–12 (Counselor in a School Setting)
A. Valid Louisiana teaching certificate (see E below)
B. Complete a standards-based master's degree program in school counseling from a

regionally accredited college or university approved by the Council for Accreditation of Counseling and Related Educational Program (CACREP).

    1. Candidates completing counseling programs that are not in the specialty area of school counseling must complete 6 credit hours of school counseling courses from a CACREP-accredited program.

C. Complete a practicum/internship from a CACREP-accredited program:

    1. Practicum in school counseling to include 100 contacts hours in a school setting *and*

    2. Internship in school counseling to include 600 contact hours in a school setting

D. Complete the PRAXIS examination in school guidance and counseling (0421 or 5421)

E. An Ancillary Counselor K–12 certificate can be issued if applicant is not a certified teacher but fulfills all other requirements listed above.

School Librarian

I. School Librarian

  A. Valid Louisiana elementary or secondary teaching certificate;

  B. Eighteen semester hours in library science, as follows:

    1. Elementary and/or secondary school library materials: 9 semester hours;

    2. Organization, administration, and interpretation of elementary and/or secondary school library service: 6 semester hours; *and*

    3. Elementary and/or secondary school library practice: 3 semester hours; *or*

    Three years of successful experience as a school librarian.

II. Ancillary School Librarian

  A. Master's degree in library science from a regionally accredited institution; *and*

  B. Passing score on Praxis Library Media Specialist examination (0311 or 5311).

Maine

Teacher and Educational Specialist Certificates

I. Conditional Certificate (valid 3 years, nonrenewable)
   A. Bachelor's degree from a regionally accredited college
   B. Completion of all content area (24 semester hours) course requirements (or, in the case of special education, 9 semester hours)
   C. Applicants who hold another professional certificate must have 6 semester hours in the content area for which they are applying. If the content area is designated a targeted need, the candidate must have 9 semester hours.
   D. Once a candidate qualifies, they must request issuance of the Conditional Certificate in writing.
II. Professional Certificate (valid 5 years; renewable)
   A. Meets all requirements for professional license as detailed in Chapter 115 in the Code of Maine Rules, available for download at https://www.maine.gov/sos/cec/rules/05/chaps05.htm.

Endorsements and Credentialing

PDFs detailing the most current requirements for each endorsement are available for download at http://www.maine.gov/doe/cert#. Please note that middle-level endorsements (for grades 5–8) are available only to applicants who already hold a teaching certificate.

I. Teacher Endorsements
   A. General Elementary Endorsement (K–8)
   B. Early Elementary Endorsement (K–3)
   C. Early Childhood Teacher (0 to age 5)
   D. English (5–8)
   E. English (7–12)
   F. Social Studies (5–8)
   G. Social Studies (7–12)
   H. Teacher of Students with Disabilities (0 to age 5)
   I. Teacher of Students with Disabilities (K–8)
   J. Teacher of Students with Disabilities (7–12)
   K. Teacher of Severely Impaired Students (K–12)
   L. Teacher of Blind or Visually Impaired (K–12)
   M. Teacher of Deaf or Hearing Impaired (K–12)
   N. Mathematics (5–8)
   O. Mathematics (7–12)
   P. Science (5–8)
   Q. Physical Science (7–12)

R.   Life Science (7–12)
S.   Physical Education (K–12)
T.   Adapted Physical Education (K–12)
U.   Dance (K–12)
V.   Health Education (K–12)
W.   Driver Education (7–12)
X.   Music (K–12)
Y.   Art (K–12)
Z.   Theater (K–12)
AA. Business Education
BB. English as a Second Language (K–12)
CC. Family and Consumer Science (K–12)
DD. Computer Technology (K–12)
EE. Gifted and Talented (K–12)
FF. Industrial Arts/Technology (K–12)
GG. Special Needs Teacher (9–12) Vocational Education
HH. Adult Education
II. Career and Technical Education (9–12)
JJ. World Language (K–12)

II. Administrator Endorsements
A.   Superintendent
B.   Assistant Superintendent
C.   Administrator of Special Education
D.   Assistant Administrator of Special Education
E.   Building Administrator
F.   Assistant Building Administrator
G.   Teaching Principal
H.   Adult and Community Education Director
I.   Assistant Adult and Community Education Director
J.   Curriculum Coordinator

III. Educational Specialist Endorsements
A.   Library/Media Specialist
B.   School Counselor
C.   Special Education Consultant
D.   Literacy Specialist
E.   Vocational Education Evaluator
F.   Athletic Director
G.   Speech and Hearing Clinician
H.   School Nurse (K–12)
I.   Cooperative Education Coordinator (9–12) CTE

IV. School Psychologist Endorsement

Maryland

Types of Certificates

I. Professional Eligibility Certificate (PEC). Valid for 5 years.
   A. Issued to an applicant who meets all certification requirements and is not currently employed in a Maryland local school system, state-operated school, or publicly funded nonpublic school.

II. Standard Professional Certificate I (SPC I). Valid for 5 years.
   A. Issued to an applicant who meets all certification requirements and is employed by a Maryland local school system, state-operated school, or publicly funded nonpublic school.

III. Standard Professional Certificate II (SPC II). Valid for 5 years.
   A. Issued to an applicant who completes the SPC I, is employed by a Maryland local school system, state-operated school, or publicly funded nonpublic school, has a professional development plan designed by the employee and employer, and submits the following:
      1. Verification of 3 years of satisfactory professional experience;
         and
      2. Six semester hours of acceptable credit.

IV. Advanced Professional Certificate (APC). Valid for 5 years.
   A. Issued to an applicant who meets all certification requirements and submits the following:
      1. Verification of 3 years of full-time professional school-related experience;
      2. Six semester hours of acceptable credit;
         and
      3. A master's degree
         or
         A minimum of 36 semester hours of post-baccalaureate course work, which must include at least 21 semester hours of graduate credit (the remaining 15 semester hours may include graduate or undergraduate course work and/or Maryland State Department of Education Continuing Professional Development [CPD] credits)
         or
         National Board Certification and a minimum of 12 semester hours of approved graduate course work after the conferral of the bachelor's or higher degree.

V. Resident Teacher Certificate (RTC). Valid for 2 years.
   A. Issued to an applicant who has been selected by a local school system to participate in an alternative teacher preparation program.

VI. Conditional Certificate (COND). Valid for 2 years.

    A.   Issued only at the request of a local school system superintendent to an applicant employed in a local school system who does not meet all professional certification requirements.

VII. Emergency Certificate (EC). Valid for 6 months after the state of emergency is lifted.

    A.   Issued during a state of emergency at the authorization of the State Superintendent of Schools.

    B.   Issued only to an applicant employed in a local school system or publicly funded nonpublic school who has met all coursework requirements but is still in need of assessments and/or a clinical internship.

Teacher Areas Overview

I.   Maryland issues certificates in the following teaching areas:

    A.   Early Childhood Education (PreK–3)

    B.   Elementary Education, grades 1–6

    C.   Mathematics Instructional Leader (PreK–6) (4–9) (endorsement only)

    D.   Instructional Leader: STEM, PreK–6 (endorsement only)

    E.   Middle School Areas: (4–9)

        1.   English Language Arts; Mathematics; Science; Social Studies; Mathematics Instructional Leader 4–9 (endorsement only)

    F.   Secondary Academic Areas: (7–12)

        1.   Agriculture/Agribusiness and Renewable Natural Resources; Biology; Business Education; Chemistry; Computer Science; Earth/Space Science; English; Environmental Science; Family and Consumer Sciences; Geography; History; Marketing; Mathematics; Physical Science; Physics; Political Science, Professional and Technical Education; Social Studies; Specialized Professional Areas; Speech Communication; Technology Education, Theater; Work-Based Learning Coordinator (endorsement only)

    G.   Special Education

        1.   Infant/primary (birth–grade 3); Elementary/middle (grades 1–8); Secondary/ adult (grades 6–adult); Severely and Profoundly Disabled

    H.   Specialty Areas (PreK–12)

        1.   American Sign Language; Art; Blind/Visually Impaired; Dance; Deaf and Hard of Hearing; English for Speakers of Other Languages; Environmental Education; Health; Music; Physical Education; World Languages

Testing

I.   All candidates applying for an initial teacher certificate are required to present qualifying scores on the Praxis CORE, ACT, SAT, or GRE if they do not have a minimum GPA of 3.0 on their most recently earned degree, and the appropriate content and pedagogy assessments where required (Praxis II, ACTFL, PPAT, edTPA).

    A.   The tests may be taken at any valid test site in the nation.

    B.   Applicants must meet testing requirements current at the time of application.

II. Out-of-state candidates who do not hold a professional certificate from their respective state must meet Maryland's testing requirements. Out-of-state candidates who hold a professional certificate may be eligible for a test exemption.

III. Applicants who have taken the teacher certification tests must submit their scores when applying for a Maryland certificate. Test scores must be sent to the Maryland State Department of Education in 1 of the following ways:

  A. Notation on an official college transcript;

  B. Photocopy of examinee's score report;
    or

  C. Verification from a state department of education.

Administrative or Supervisory Areas

Consult http://www.dsd.state.md.us/COMAR/SubtitleSearch.aspx?search=13A.12.04 for full regulations and for references to regulations, chapter, COMAR, and §B below.

I. Superintendent

  A. Superintendent I Certification

    1. Qualifies an individual to be assigned as a county deputy superintendent, assistant superintendent, or associate superintendent through either Traditional or Reciprocal Certification

    2. Education requirements for Traditional Certification

      a. Master's degree from an institute of higher education (IHE)

      b. Completion of 1 of the following:

        i. A Maryland State Department of Education (MSDE)–approved program that leads to certification as a superintendent
          or

        ii. A program offered by an IHE leading to certification as a superintendent in the state in which the institution is located
          or

        iii. Forty-five semester hours of graduate course work, including a minimum of 15 semester hours in education administration, taken at an IHE. Graduate course work earned under §A(3)(a) of this regulation may be applied toward the 45 required semester hours.

    3. Experience requirements for Traditional Certification

      a. Twenty-seven months of satisfactory teaching performance or satisfactory performance as a certified specialist as defined in COMAR 13A.12.03 in a PreK–12 setting
        and

      b. Twenty-four months of satisfactory administrative or supervisory experience in a PreK–12 setting

    4. Requirements for Reciprocal Certification

      a. A deputy, associate, or assistant superintendent who enters Maryland from another state may obtain a Superintendent I certification by:

        i.   Holding a valid professional state certificate in a like or comparable area;
           and

        ii.   Presenting verification of at least 36 months of satisfactory performance as a deputy, associate, or assistant superintendent during the past 7 years.

B.   Superintendent II Certification

   1.   Qualifies an individual to be a county superintendent through either Traditional or Reciprocal Certification

   2.   Education requirements for Traditional Certification

      a.   Master's degree from an IHE

      b.   Completion of 1 of the following:

        i.   An MSDE-approved program that leads to certification as a superintendent, to include course work covering public school administration, supervision, and methods of teaching
           or

        ii.   A program offered by an IHE leading to certification as a superintendent in the state in which the institution is located, to include course work covering public school administration, supervision, and methods of teaching
           or

       iii.   Sixty semester hours of graduate course work, including a minimum of 24 semester hours in education administration taken at an IHE, to include course work covering public school administration, supervision, and methods of teaching. Graduate course work earned under §B(3)(a) of this regulation may be applied toward the 60 required semester hours.

   3.   Experience requirements for Traditional Certification

      a.   Twenty-seven months of satisfactory teaching performance or satisfactory performance as a certified specialist as defined in COMAR 13A.12.03 in a PreK–12 setting
         and

      b.   Twenty-four months of satisfactory administrative or supervisory experience in a PreK–12 setting

   4.   Requirements for Reciprocal Certification

      a.   A superintendent who enters Maryland from another state may obtain Superintendent II certification by:

        i.   Holding a valid professional state certificate in a like or comparable area;

        ii.   Presenting verification of at least 36 months of satisfactory performance as a superintendent during the past 7 years;
           and

       iii.   Presenting verification of 2 years of graduate work at an IHE, to include course work covering public school administration, supervision, and methods of teaching.

II. Supervisors of Instruction, Assistant Principals, and Principals. For certification as an Administrator I or Administrator II:

A. Administrator I. To be assigned as a supervisor of instruction or assistant principal, candidates should

1. Have a master's degree from an IHE;

2. Have 27 months of satisfactory teaching performance or satisfactory performance on a professional certificate or satisfactory performance as a certified specialist;
    and

3. Complete 1 of the following:

    a. Department-approved program which leads to certification as a supervisor of instruction, assistant principal, or principal that includes the outcomes in the Maryland instructional leadership framework;
        or

    b. Approved program that leads to certification as a supervisor of instruction, assistant principal, or principal in accordance with the interstate agreement;
        or

    c. Eighteen semester hours of graduate course work taken at an IHE at the post-baccalaureate level to include a balance of content in the following categories: curriculum, instruction, and assessment; development, observation, and evaluation of staff; legal issues and ethical decision-making; school leadership, management and administration; special education (3 semester hours); and practicum, internship, or a collaboratively designed and supervised experience by the local school system and IHE to include department-approved instructional leadership outcomes with verification of this experience submitted by the applicant.

B. Administrator II. For an individual to be assigned as a school principal

1. The applicant, before initial appointment as principal, shall:

    a. Complete the requirements for Administrator I;
        and

    b. Present evidence of a qualifying score as established by the state board on a department-approved principal certification assessment.

2. A principal who enters Maryland from another state may obtain an Administrator II certificate if that principal held a valid professional state certificate and verifies at least 27 months of satisfactory performance as a principal during the past 7 years on the basis of which application is being made for a like or comparable Maryland certificate.

C. Special Provisions

1. An applicant who successfully completes the requirements under Regulation .05D of the chapter cited in the link above for the resident principal certificate may obtain an Administrator II certificate; consult the link above for full details.

2. A Standard Professional certificate or Advanced Professional certificate shall be considered valid for service as principal of an elementary school of not more than 6 teachers if the principal teaches at least 50 percent of the school day.

3. A person who holds the position of assistant principal on the date this regulation becomes effective shall meet the requirements of §B of the regulation cited in the link above not later than the end of the first full validity period after the renewal of the currently held certificate.

III. Library Media Administrator

A. The person designated by the local superintendent of schools as having responsibility for:

1. Administration and supervision of the library media program, including the supervision of the library media program in the individual schools; *and*

2. Development of policies, programs, budgets, and procedures for the library media services of the school system and its schools.

B. Education and Experience. To be certified as library media administrator, the applicant shall meet the requirements for certification as a library media specialist:

1. Have a master's degree from an IHE;

2. Have 3 years of satisfactory library media program experience; however, at the recommendation of the local school superintendent, 2 years of related satisfactory experience may be substituted for 2 years of library media program experience; *and*

3. Complete 1 of the options listed under Regulation .04B(3) of the chapter cited in the link above that would lead to certification as Administrator I.

C. Certificate Renewal. In addition to meeting the requirements of COMAR 13A.12.01.11B (see the link above), a library media administrator or a holder of a valid certificate for an education media administrator (Level III) shall satisfy the required reading course work contained in COMAR 13A.12.01.11A(5)(c) to renew the certificate.

IV. Supervisor of Guidance. For certification, the applicant shall:

A. Meet the requirements for certification as a guidance counselor;

B. Have 3 years of satisfactory performance as a guidance counselor; *and*

C. Have 12 semester hours of graduate credit from an IHE in any of the following areas, with at least 6 of those semester hours in school supervision or school administration: management; school supervision; school administration; program development; and program evaluation.

V. Supervisor of School Psychological Services. For certification, the applicant shall:

A. Meet the requirements for certification as a school psychologist under COMAR 13A.12.03.07 (see the link above);

B. Have a doctoral degree:

1. From a state or regionally credited school psychology program or National Association of School Psychologists (NCATE), or American Psychological Association–accredited school psychology program, *or*

2. In psychology or education or human development;

C. As part of or in addition to §B of the regulation cited in the link above, have

9 semester hours of graduate credits, including 3 semester hours in school law and 6 semester hours in supervision, management, or administration of schools; *and*

D. Have 3 years of experience as a school psychologist under COMAR 13A.12.03.07 (see the link above).

VI. Supervisor of Pupil Personnel. For certification, the applicant shall:
A. Meet the requirements for certification as a pupil personnel worker;
B. Have a master's degree from an IHE;
C. As part of or in addition to §B of the regulation cited in the link above, have a graduate course in the area of administration and supervision; *and*
D. Have 3 years of successful teaching experience. At the recommendation of the local superintendent of schools, 2 years of related experience may be counted for 2 years of teaching experience.

VII. Supervisor of Special Education
A. Principal (Handicapped Facility). For certification, the applicant shall:
1. Meet the requirements for certification in special education; *and*
2. Meet the requirements for certification as an Administrator II.
B. Supervisor of Special Education (Sole Assignment). For certification, the applicant shall:
1. Meet the requirements for certification in special education; *and*
2. Meet the requirements for certification as an Administrator I.
C. Special Provision. Supervisors with multiple area assignments shall meet the requirements set forth in Regulation .04 of the chapter cited in the link above.

VIII. Supervisor of Teachers of Hearing Impaired. The applicant shall:
A. Meet the requirements for certification as a teacher of the hearing impaired;
B. Have a master's degree from an IHE with at least 1 course in administrative and supervisory techniques and 1 course in curriculum development; *and*
C. Have experience which includes:
1. Three years of successful teaching experience with the hearing impaired, *or*
2. Four years of paid experience or its equivalent in a school setting, with 2 years of successful teaching experience with the hearing impaired.

Specialist Areas

For full requirements, consult http://www.dsd.state.md.us/COMAR/SubtitleSearch.aspx?search= 13A.12.03.

I. Gifted & Talented Specialist
II. School Counselor
III. Library Media Specialist

IV.   Pupil Personnel Worker
V.   Reading Specialist
VI.   Reading Teacher
VII. Psychometrist
VIII. School Psychologist
IX.   School Social Worker

Massachusetts

The following outlines general requirements. To identify specific requirements of the license you seek, please use the online Licensure Requirements Tool at https://gateway.edu.state.ma.us/elar/licensurehelp/LicenseRequirementsCriteriaPageControl.ser.

Teacher (PreK–12) Licenses

I. Provisional License (valid for 5 years of employment; nonrenewable; beginning July 1, 2019, an educator who holds 1 or more provisional licenses may be employed under said license[s] for no more than 5 years in total). Appropriate for an applicant who:
   A. Has a bachelor's degree
   B. Has a passing score on the Communication and Literacy Skills test
   C. Seeks a license as a core academic teacher and does not hold the Sheltered English Immersion Endorsements (SEI)
   D. Has passed all required Massachusetts Tests for Educator Licensure (MTEL)
      1. For licenses that do not have a subject matter knowledge MTEL (e.g., moderate special needs, instructional technology), applicants must complete a Competency Review (downloadable at http://www.doe.mass.edu/licensure/academic-prek12/teacher/license-types.html).

II. Initial License (valid for 5 years of employment; may be extended once for an additional 5 years). Appropriate for an applicant who:
   A. Has a bachelor's degree
   B. Has a passing score on the Communication and Literacy Skills test
   C. Has passed all required MTEL tests
   D. Holds the SEI endorsement (core academic teacher, principal/assistant principal, or supervisor/director only)
   E. Fulfills 1 of the following:
      1. Has completed an approved educator preparation program in Massachusetts
         or
      2. Has completed a state-approved educator preparation program in a state with which Massachusetts has signed the National Association of State Directors of Teacher Education and Certification (NASDTEC) Interstate Agreement or other agreement accepted by the Commissioner
         or
      3. Has completed an educator preparation program sponsored by a college or university outside Massachusetts that has been accredited by a national organization accepted by the Commissioner
         or
      4. Possesses the equivalent of at least an Initial license/certificate issued by a state

with which Massachusetts has signed the NASDTEC Interstate Agreement or other agreement accepted by the Commissioner

or

5. Has prepared outside of the United States and completed a Panel Review in accordance with Department guidelines.

III. Professional License (valid for 5 calendar years; renewable every 5 years thereafter). Appropriate for an applicant who:

A. Holds an Initial license in the same field as the Professional license sought

B. Has completed a 1-year induction program with a mentor and at least 50 hours of a mentored experience beyond the induction year

C. Has been employed under the Initial license for at least 3 years and has completed a 1-year induction program with a mentor and at least 50 hours of a mentored experience beyond the induction year

D. Has completed 1 of the following:

1. An approved licensure program for the Professional license sought as set forth in the Guidelines for Program Approval

or

2. A program leading to eligibility for master teacher status, such as those sponsored by the National Board for Professional Teaching Standards and others accepted by the Commissioner

or

3. A master's or higher degree or other advanced graduate program in an accredited college or university, including at least 12 credits of graduate-level courses in subject matter knowledge or pedagogy based on the subject matter knowledge of the professional license sought. These may include credits earned prior to application for the license.

IV. Temporary (valid for 1 year of employment; nonrenewable). Appropriate for an applicant who:

A. Has a bachelor's degree

B. Has been employed in another state under a valid license or certificate comparable to a Massachusetts Initial license for at least 3 years

C. Has not failed any part of the required MTEL tests

Administrator Licenses

I. Provisional License (Superintendent/Assistant Superintendent only; valid for 5 years of employment; cannot be extended or renewed; beginning July 1, 2019, an educator who holds 1 or more provisional licenses may be employed under said license[s] for no more than 5 years in total). Appropriate for an applicant who:

A. Has a bachelor's degree

B. Has completed at least 3 years of employment in an executive management/ leadership role or in a supervisory, teaching, or administrative role in a public/ charter school, private school, higher education, or other education setting accepted by the Department

C. Has passed the Communication and Literacy Skills test
II. Initial License (valid for 5 years; cannot be extended). Appropriate for an applicant who:
   A. Possesses an initial license in another educational role or a Provisional Superintendent/Assistant Superintendent license and has completed 3 years of employment in a district-wide educational setting
   B. Has passed the Communication and Literacy Skills test
   C. Has completed 1 of the following pathways:
      1. A state-approved educator preparation program
      2. An apprenticeship
      3. Panel Review
III. Professional License (valid for 5 calendar years; renewable every 5 years)
   A. Requirements for each administrator license at the Professional level are unique to each license field. Please use the online Licensure Requirements Tool to identify the appropriate pathway/requirement set.
IV. Temporary (valid for 1 year of employment; nonrenewable). Appropriate for an applicant who:
   A. Has a bachelor's degree
   B. Has been employed in another state under a valid license or certificate comparable to a Massachusetts Initial license for at least 3 years
   C. Has not passed or failed the Communication and Literacy Skills test

Professional Support Personnel Licenses

I. The Department issues the following professional support personnel licenses: School Counselor (PreK–8 and 5–12); School Nurse (all levels); School Psychologist (all levels); School Social Worker/School Adjustment Counselor (all levels). Requirements for each license are unique to each field; please use the online Licensure Requirements Tool to identify the appropriate pathway/requirement set.
   A. Initial License (valid for 5 years of employment; can be extended once for an additional 5 years of employment)
   B. Professional License (valid for 5 calendar years; renewable every 5 years)
   C. Temporary License (valid for 1 year of employment; nonrenewable). Appropriate for an applicant who:
      1. Is an experienced teacher from out of state
      2. Has a bachelor's degree
      3. Has been employed in another state under a valid license or certificate comparable to a Massachusetts Initial license for at least 3 years
      4. Has not passed or failed the Communication and Literacy Skills test

Michigan

Teaching Certificate Validity Levels

I. Elementary: An elementary certificate issued after September 1, 1988, is valid for teaching all subjects grades K–5, all subjects grades K–8 in a self-contained classroom, and subject area endorsements, as listed on the certificate.

II. Secondary: A secondary certificate issued after September 1, 1988, is valid for teaching in designated discipline areas in any grade or grade range from grades 6 to 12.

Types of Certificates

I. Michigan Standard Teaching Certificate (initial teaching license/credential; valid for 5 years)
   A. Applicants must provide proof of CPR/First Aid certification earned through a provider on the approved provider list at https://www.michigan.gov/lara/bureau-list/cclb/train/panel-main/cpr-and-first-aid-training in accordance with MCL 380.1531d.
   B. The Standard Teaching Certificate is issued upon successful completion of a state-approved teacher preparation program and a passing score on the appropriate Michigan Test for Teacher Certification (MTTC) exams.
      1. For information on Michigan-approved Educator Preparation Institutions (EPI) and programs, consult https://mdoe.state.mi.us/proprep/.
   C. Programs completed through colleges/universities outside of Michigan must be approved for the certification of teachers by another state; contact that state's education department for information. Upon completion of the out-of-state program, candidates must apply for a Michigan teacher certification, and their credentials must be evaluated by the Office of Educator Excellence (OEE).
   D. An applicant who has completed an alternative route teacher certification program in another state and holds a valid Standard Teaching Certificate based on completion of that program may apply to be evaluated for certification. This option is not available to applicants who have temporary, preliminary, or interim teaching certificates from other states.

II. Temporary Teaching Certificate (valid for 1 year; nonrenewable)
   A. The Temporary Teaching Certificate allows out-of-state candidates 1 year to pass the appropriate MTTC exam(s) after an OEE evaluation is conducted to determine they meet the following criteria:
      1. Hold a valid, acceptable teaching certificate from another state;
      2. Have never held a Michigan teaching certificate;
      3. Have applied for an initial Standard Teaching Certificate; *and*
      4. Meet all the requirements for the Standard Teaching Certificate, except for passing the MTTC exams.

B. Candidates do not apply for the Temporary Teaching Certificate; it is issued upon evaluation for initial certification.

C. Once a Temporary Teaching Certificate has been issued, the candidate must complete MTTC requirements in order to be issued a Michigan Standard Teaching Certificate.

III. Interim Teaching Certificate (ITC; valid for 5 years; nonrenewable). The ITC entitles the holder to teach full-time in a Michigan school as the teacher of record. Candidates are eligible for enrollment in an alternative route program if they meet the following criteria:

A. Hold at least a bachelor's degree from a regionally accredited college or university, with a grade point average of at least 3.0 on a 4.0 scale (or equivalent);

B. Pass the appropriate MTTC discipline area exam(s);

C. Provide proof of CPR/First Aid certification through a provider on the approved provider list at https://www.michigan.gov/documents/mde/Approved_First_Aid_and _CPR_Providers_397544_7.pdf.

D. To progress to the Standard Teaching Certificate while working under the ITC, or to add endorsements from an ITC to an existing certificate, the individual must:

1. Submit to and pass a criminal history check (see code R 390.1201), including FBI fingerprinting, in accordance with Michigan School Safety law, prior to employment by a local district or school;

2. Receive intensive observation and coaching;

3. Complete 3 years of satisfactory teaching experience under the ITC;

4. Be recommended by the approved alternative route provider for the Standard Teaching Certificate once all requirements have been met.

IV. Standard Teaching Certificate Renewal (each renewal valid for 5 years)

A. Completion of 1 of the following since the issuance of the Standard Teaching Certificate:

1. Six semester hours in an education-related professional learning program at an approved EPI;

    or

2. Six semester credit hours of academic credit appropriate to the grade level and content endorsement(s) of the certificate at any regionally accredited college or university;

    or

3. A total of 150 State Continuing Education Clock Hours (SCECHs) appropriate to the grade level and content endorsement(s) of the certificate held;

    or

4. A total of 150 annual District Provided Professional Development (DPPD) hours, in accordance with Michigan School Code Section 380.1527, through professional development programs that are appropriate to the grade level and content endorsement(s) of the certificate. Note: As of July 1, 2020, DPPD hours are awarded to educators by local area agencies as SCECHs through the Michigan Online Educator Certification System (MOECS).

    or

5. A combination of semester credit hours and SCECHs (25 SCECHs = 1 semester credit hour) totaling 150 hours.

B. A teacher who holds a Michigan Standard Teaching Certificate may be granted a one-time, 5-year renewal of the certificate based upon having earned an education-related master's degree or higher at any time.

C. A teacher who holds an expired Michigan Standard Teaching Certificate and holds a valid teaching certificate from another state is eligible for a one-time 5-year renewal of the Michigan Standard Teaching Certificate.

D. Educators who have been issued a School Counselor Endorsement (NT) on a Michigan Standard Teaching Certificate or a School Counselor License (SCL) are required to fulfill 50 hours of professional learning in accordance with MCL 380.1233 (6–8) prior to applying to renew. Hence, those credentialed as school counselors are not permitted to renew using a valid out-of-state credential or master's degree, nor any other advanced degree.

V. Professional Teaching Certificate (progressing from the Standard Teaching Certificate; valid for 5 years). Candidates must meet the following criteria:

A. Issued to applicants who already hold the Standard Teaching Certificate in the subject area(s) and grade levels for which he/she is seeking certification;

B. Three years of successful teaching experience since the issue date and within the content areas and grade level of the initial Standard Teaching Certificate;

C. Six semester credit hours of reading methods course work for elementary teachers and 3 semester credit hours for secondary certified teachers;

D. Three semester credit hours of reading diagnostics and remediation, which includes a field experience. This credit may be applied toward the professional learning requirement listed below in point E, assuming the credit was earned after the issue date of the most recent certificate or renewal.

E. Education-Related Professional Learning totaling 150 hours; or an education-related master's or higher degree earned at any time (even if previously utilized to renew the Standard Teaching Certificate) from a regionally accredited college or university;

F. Effectiveness ratings in accordance with MCL 380.1531j:

1. Consecutive: "effective" or "highly effective" ratings on annual year-end performance evaluations for the 3 consecutive school years immediately preceding application for a Professional Teaching Certificate;
    or

2. Nonconsecutive: "effective" or "highly effective" ratings on annual year-end performance evaluations for at least 3 nonconsecutive school years prior to applying for the Professional Teaching Certificate, including an Effective Educator Recommendation form completed by the chief school administrator of the school where applicant is currently employed.

G. Out-of-state applicants for the initial Professional Teaching Certificate must meet the requirements in V, A–C, above;
    and
    Have completed at least 18 semester hours in a planned program since the issuance of his/her initial Standard Teaching Certificate or have earned at any time an approved master's or higher degree

H. Candidates who hold a valid Standard Teaching Certificate from another state and meet all requirements at the time of application for the Professional Teaching

Certificate as noted in items V, A–C are exempt from the MTTC testing requirement.

VI. Temporary Professional Teaching Certificate (valid for 1 year; nonrenewable)
   A. Issued to out-of-state candidates who hold a valid, acceptable certificate from another state and
      1. Have never held a Michigan teaching certificate;
         and
      2. Meet all the requirements for the Professional Teaching Certificate, except for the reading methods course work.
   B. Candidates do not apply for this certificate; it is issued upon evaluation of an initial Professional Teaching Certificate.
      1. Once the Temporary Professional Teaching Certificate has been issued, the candidate must complete the reading methods requirement within 1 year of issuance in order to be issued a Michigan Professional Teaching Certificate.
      2. If the reading methods requirement is not met within 1 year after Temporary Professional Teaching Certificate issuance, the candidate must be evaluated for the Standard Teaching Certificate and pass the appropriate MTTC testing requirements.

VII. Professional Teaching Certificate Renewal (each renewal valid for 5 years)
   A valid out-of-state certificate, appropriate for K–12 education, may be used 1 time. Applicants may fulfill any combination of the following requirements since the issue date of the Professional Certificate Renewal, totaling 150 hours:
   A. Completion of 6 semester credit hours in an education-related professional learning program at an approved EPI, or 6 semester credit hours of academic credit appropriate to the grade level and content endorsement(s) of the certificate at any regionally accredited college or university;
      and/or
   B. Completion of 150 SCECHs appropriate to the grade level and content endorsement(s) of the certificate held;
      and/or
   C. Completion of 150 annual DPPD hours, in accordance with Michigan School Code Section 380.1527, through professional development programs appropriate to the grade level and content endorsement(s) of the certificate.
      1. SCECHs and/or DPPD hours must be earned since the issue date of the Standard Certificate.
      2. 25 SCECHs = 1 semester credit hour = 25 DPPD hours. Note: As of July 1, 2020, DPPD hours are awarded to educators by local area agencies as SCECHs through the Michigan Online Educator Certification System (MOECS).

VIII. Advanced Professional Teaching Certificate (progressing from the Professional Teaching Certificate; valid for 5 years; renewable)
   A. Applicants must hold a current or expired Professional Teaching Certificate
   B. Can be applied for any time after the Professional Teaching Certificate is received, or after that certificate expires, as long as requirements have been met
   C. Eligible candidates must meet all of the following criteria:

1. Hold a Professional Teaching Certificate;
2. Complete an approved Michigan Teacher Leader program or certification through the National Board for Professional Teaching Standards. (One of these designations must be evident on the Professional Teaching Certificate prior to submitting an application for an Advanced Professional Certificate.)
3. Have "highly effective" ratings for 3 out of the 5 most recent annual evaluations, with zero "ineffective" ratings within the last 5 evaluations per MCL 380.1249.

D. Advanced Certificate holders can apply for renewals after:
1. Maintaining the effectiveness ratings noted immediately above;
   and
2. Completing the required professional learning (including semester-hour credits, SCECHs, and/or DPPD hours) after the issue date of the most recent Advanced Certificate.

E. Holders of Permanent, Life, or Continuing Certificates may apply for the Advanced Certificate but are required to meet renewal criteria. Obtaining this certificate will put the holder on the renewal track requiring professional learning hours every 5 years.

IX. Standard Teaching Certificate Based on CTE Endorsements (initial certificate; valid for 5 years). Note: The Michigan Department of Education (MDE) no longer issues what was previously known as the Standard or Professional Career and Technical Education (CTE) Certificate. As of May 2021, the MDE transitioned to one teaching certificate for general and CTE endorsements. A Professional Teaching Certificate or Standard Teaching Certificate will be issued with CTE endorsements for eligible candidates.

A. To qualify for a Standard Teaching Certificate based on completion of an in-state CTE program, applicants must be recommended by the CTE educator preparation program and meet the following requirements:
1. Hold a bachelor's degree in any area with a major, minor, or emphasis in the field of specialization in which CTE certification is being requested;
2. Have documented work experience in the CTE area earned within the last 10 years, totaling a minimum of 2 years (4,000 hours);
   and
3. Have successfully completed a minimum of 6 semester credit hours of professional or CTE education credit.

B. Applicants who have completed an approved out-of-state CTE program must follow the guidelines provided on the Michigan Department of Education website at https://www.michigan.gov/documents/mde/Out_Of_State_Applicants_534635_7.pdf.

C. A Standard Teaching Certificate is valid for teaching courses in which instruction is limited to the occupation specified on the certificate in approved CTE programs.

X. Professional Teaching Certificate Based on CTE Endorsements (valid for 5 years; applicant must hold Standard Teaching Certificate)

A. Three years of successful teaching experience within the validity of the Standard Teaching Certificate;

B. The reading methods and reading diagnostic requirements outlined in Section 1531(4) at http://legislature.mi.gov/doc.aspx?mcl-380–1531.

C. To progress to the Professional Teaching Certificate Based on CTE Endorsements from the Standard Teaching Certificate Based on CTE Endorsements , an applicant must fulfill at least 1 of the following criteria:
1. Earn a master's degree or higher in an education-related area since the issue date of the most recent Standard Teaching Certificate or renewal;
2. Any combination of the following, totaling 150 hours (1 semester credit hour = 25 SCECHs or 25 DPPD hours) appropriate to the grade level and endorsement(s) of the certificate:
   a. Completion of 6 satisfactory semester credit hours earned at a regionally accredited college or university;
   b. Completion of 150 SCECHs via approved professional development activities;
   c. Completion of 150 DPPD hours via district-approved professional development programs.

XI. Preliminary School Psychologist Certificate (initial certificate; valid for 3 years). Applicants must:
A. Complete a minimum of 45 graduate semester credit hours in an approved school psychologist program;
B. Complete a supervised practicum of not less than 600 hours under the supervision of a certified school psychologist.
C. Possess a comparable valid out-of-state school psychologist certificate or license if the school psychologist credits were completed in another state.

XII. Preliminary School Psychologist Renewal (valid for 3 years; renewable 1 time). Applicants must:
A. Complete six semester credit hours in an approved school psychologist program from an approved Educator Preparation Institution (EPI) completed since the issue date of the Preliminary School Psychologist Certificate;
   or
B. Possess a valid out-of-state school psychologist certificate.

XIII. School Psychologist Certificate (valid for 5 years; renewable)
A. In-state applicants must:
1. Hold a current or expired Michigan Preliminary School Psychologist Certificate;
2. Complete a state-approved specialist-level degree or the equivalent (no fewer than 60 semester credit hours) in school psychology from an EPI with an approved school psychology program;
3. Complete an internship of no fewer than 1,200 clock hours.
B. Out-of-state applicants must:
1. Complete a specialist-level degree or the equivalent (no fewer than 60 semester credit hours) in school psychology with a 1,200-clock-hour internship from an out-of-state EPI;
2. Hold a valid Nationally Certified School Psychologist (NCSP) credential issued by the National Association of School Psychologists (NASP), or a valid, standard school psychologist certificate from the state where the program was completed.

XIV. School Psychologist Certificate Renewal (valid for 5 years). An applicant may renew using one of the following:
    A. Education Related Professional Learning relevant to the profession and practice of school psychologists earned after the issue date of the most recent certificate or renewal, including:
        1. One-hundred fifty clock hours of State Continuing Education Clock Hours (SCECHs);
           or
        2. One-hundred fifty clock hours of District Provided Professional Development (DPPD);
           or
        3. Six semester credit hours;
           or
        4. Any combination of SCECHs, DPPD hours, and credits equivalent to 150 clock hours (each semester credit counts for 25 clock hours)
      or
    B. A valid NCSP credential issued by the NASP;
        or
    C. A valid Michigan Professional Teaching Certificate
        or
    D. A valid school psychologist certificate from another state (can only be renewed once)

XV. Preliminary School Counselor Credential (PSCC; issued to in-state certification candidates only; valid for 3 years; nonrenewable). Applicants must:
    A. Complete a minimum of 30 semester credit hours of course work in a school counselor education program;
    B. Pass the school counselor subject area MTTC exam;
    C. Complete any outstanding courses that may include an internship/practicum during the 3-year validity period to be recommended by the in-state school counselor preparation institution for:
        1. The School Counselor Endorsement (NT) on a Michigan Teaching Certificate;
           or
        2. The School Counselor License (SCL).

XVI. Temporary School Counselor License (TSCL; valid for 1 year; issued to applicants who have completed all requirements for an out-of-state approved school counselor education program; nonrenewable)
    A. Candidates do not apply for this temporary license; it is issued upon evaluation of an initial application for a School Counselor License.
    B. To be issued the School Counselor Endorsement (NT) or the School Counselor License after being granted the TSCL, the candidate must meet Michigan testing requirements on the MTTC School Counselor (NT) exam within 1 year of the issuance of the TSCL.
    C. This temporary license may also be issued to applicants who:
        1. Hold at least a bachelor's degree;
        2. Complete successful experience serving in the role of a school counselor as

described in section 1233(2)(c)(i) of the revised school code, 1976 PA 451, MCL 380.1233;
and

3. Hold a valid out-of-state school counselor credential.

XVII. School Counselor License (SCL; valid for 5 years; effective February 6, 2020, renewable upon completion of requirements of MCL 380.1233[6−8])

A. Available to in-state and out-of-state applicants who have completed all requirements for an advanced degree or the equivalent of an approved school counselor education program.

B. In-state applicants must:
1. Complete a program through a Michigan-approved school counselor preparation institution;
2. Complete a minimum of 30 graduate-level semester credit hours in an approved school counselor preparation program, including an internship;
3. Complete a 600-clock-hour internship (with at least 300 of the clock hours in a school setting), based on an approved school counselor program under the supervision of a credentialed school counselor or a school counselor educator;
4. Pass the MTTC School Counselor (NT) exam.

C. Out-of-state applicants must:
1. Satisfy all of the following:
    a. Hold a school counselor credential issued by an out-of-state agency;
    b. Complete successful experience serving in the role of a school counselor as described in section 1233(2)(c)(i) of the revised school code, 1976 PA 451, MCL 380.1233;
    c. Hold a bachelor's degree from a regionally accredited out-of-state institution;
    d. Pass the MTTC School Counselor (NT) exam;
    or
2. Hold an advanced degree in school counseling;
    and
    Pass the MTTC School Counselor (NT) exam.

XVIII. School Counselor License Renewals (valid for 5 years; renewable upon completion of professional learning criteria)

A. As of February 6, 2020, school counselors issued a Michigan teaching certificate with the School Counselor (NT) Endorsement and/or the School Counselor License must meet professional development requirements as follows:
1. Per MCL 380.1233(6−8), school counselors must complete 50 specific professional development clock hours that align with MCL 380.1233(6−8).
    a. The 50 hours required per state law may count toward the total 150 hours needed for renewal.
    b. School counselors must complete 25 hours related to college preparation and selection and 25 hours related to career consultation (5 of which must include the exploration of military career options);
    and

    c. Any combination of the following earned since the issuance of the most recent School Counselor License or renewal may be used to accumulate the remaining 100 hours of professional learning hours:
        i.   Completion of 6 semester credit hours appropriate to the field of school counseling from a regionally accredited college or university; *or*
        ii. Six semester credit hours earned via an education-related professional learning program at an approved school counselor educator preparation institution; *or*
        iii. Completion of 150 SCECHs appropriate to the field of school counseling; *or*
        iv. Completion of 150 DPPD hours, in accordance with Michigan School Code Section 380.1527, completed through a district professional development program appropriate to the School Counselor License.

XIX. School Administrator Certificate (initial certificate; valid for 5 years). Administrators whose primary responsibility is administering instructional programs must hold a valid School Administrator Certificate.
   A. Two endorsements are available: Elementary/Secondary Administrator K–12 (ES) Building or Central Office (CO) District. Additionally, administrators in these positions prior to January 4, 2010, who have maintained their professional learning requirements are eligible for the Experience-Based Administrator Certificate (EZ).
   B. Certification requires completion of master's degree or higher from an approved program in educational leadership or administration offered by a regionally accredited college or university.
   C. A superintendent, principal, assistant principal, or other person whose primary responsibility is administering instructional programs:
      1. If employed as a school administrator after January 4, 2010, must hold a valid Administrator Certificate in accordance with SB 981.
      2. If employed as a school administrator on or before January 4, 2010, does not need to hold the Administrator Certificate for their current position, but must hold the Experience-Based School Administrator Certificate as defined by MCL 380.1246.
      3. A noncertified school administrator may be employed by a school district if enrolled in a program leading to certification as a school administrator not later than 6 months after date of employment.
         a. The school administrator has 3 years from the date of hire to meet the certification requirements.
         b. Districts that employ noncertified school administrators must obtain an annual School Administrator Permit and document the noncertified school administrator's progress toward obtaining a School Administrator Certificate prior to placing the administrator in the assignment. Failure to

meet ongoing requirements eliminate a school administrator's eligibility for the Permit.

XX. School Administrator Certificate Renewal (valid for 5 years)

A. A valid out-of-state certificate, appropriate for K–12 administration, may be used 1 time to renew a School Administrator Certificate.

B. A school administrator who holds a valid Michigan Professional Teaching Certificate meets the requirement for renewal of the School Administrator Certificate without completing additional professional learning.

C. Without a valid out-of-state certificate or Michigan Professional Teaching Certificate, certificate renewal requires any combination of the following, totaling 150 clock hours, completed since the issue date of the most recent School Administrator Certificate or renewal:

1. Completion of 6 semester credit hours in an education-related professional learning program appropriate to the School Administrator Certificate;
    or

2. Completion of 150 SCECHs appropriate to the content and grade level of the certificate and endorsement;
    or

3. Completion of 150 DPPD hours, in accordance with Michigan School Code Section 380.1527.

XXI. Previously Issued Certificates

A. Michigan no longer issues the following certificates; however, they are still valid for those who hold them:

1. Eighteen-Hour and 30-Hour Continuing Certificate

2. Permanent/Life Certificate

3. Full Vocational Authorization

Minnesota

Minnesota's 2017 Omnibus Education bill created a new system for the Professional Educator Licensing and Standards Board (PELSB) to issue educator licenses. Teaching licenses are now granted in one of 4 licensure tiers depending on the teacher's qualifications.

Tiered Licensure for Teachers

I. Requirements for all tiered licensure applicants:
   A. A bachelor's degree from a regionally accredited institution. The only exception is for those seeking a Career and Technical Education (CTE) or Career Pathway license, who must hold credentials in the relevant content area through one of the following:
      1. Associate's degree
      2. Professional certification
      3. Five years of work experience
   B. A criminal background check, including a fingerprint check. Note: PELSB must receive the results of the background check before a license can be issued. Fingerprint card information is available from PELSB (see Appendix 1).
II. Tier 1 (valid for up to 1 school year). Requirements include:
   A. Meet requirements for all tiered licensure applicants.
   B. A job offer with a Minnesota public school district or charter school. The district or charter school must advertise the position and attest that it could not find any qualified Tier 2, 3, or 4 candidates.
   C. For first renewal, Tier 1 teachers must attempt the Minnesota Teacher Licensure Examinations (MTLE) content tests aligned to their licensure area and participate in cultural competency training.
   D. License is renewable up to 3 times, unless the school district or charter school can verify good cause for additional renewals.
III. Tier 2 (valid for up to 2 school years). Requirements include:
   A. Meet requirements for all tiered licensure applicants.
   B. A job offer with a Minnesota public school district or charter school.
   C. Meet 1 of the following requirements:
      1. Enrollment in a Minnesota state-approved teacher preparation program aligned to the licensure area,
      2. A master's degree aligned to the licensure area,
         or
      3. Meet 2 of the following requirements:
         a. Completion of teacher preparation in the licensure area
         b. Eight upper-division credits in the licensure area
         c. Field-specific methods of training as part of teacher preparation

d.   Passing scores on the MTLE pedagogy and content tests aligned to the licensure area

e.   Two years of teaching experience in the licensure area

D.   For first renewal, the applicant must participate in cultural competency training.

E.   License is renewable up to 3 times, unless the school district or charter school can verify good cause for additional renewals.

IV.   Tier 3 (valid for 3 years). Requirements include:

A.   Meet requirements for all tiered licensure applicants.

B.   Pass the MTLE pedagogy and contents tests aligned to the licensure area.

C.   Meet 1 of the following requirements:

1.   Completion of a Minnesota state-approved teacher preparation program

2.   Completion of an out-of-state approved teacher preparation program with equivalent student teaching experience to that of a Minnesota teacher preparation program (currently 12 weeks)

a.   Certifying officer of the state-approved teacher preparation program must recommend the applicant for Minnesota licensure.

3.   Recommendation for licensure through the Licensure via Portfolio process

4.   Possession or past possession of a professional teaching license, in good standing, in another state and verification of 2 years of teaching experience in the licensure area

5.   Three years of teaching experience on a Tier 2 license in the licensure area with no placement on an improvement plan by the school district or charter school

D.   To renew, an applicant must have 75 clock hours and meet the mandatory components in place at the time of renewal.

E.   Tier 3 licensure can be renewed indefinitely.

V.   Tier 4 (valid for 5 years). Requirements include:

A.   Meet requirements for all tiered licensure applicants.

B.   Pass the Minnesota basic skills, pedagogy, and content exams aligned to the licensure area

C.   Meet 1 of the following requirements:

1.   Completion of a Minnesota state-approved teacher preparation program

2.   Completion of an out-of-state approved teacher preparation program with equivalent student teaching experience to that of a Minnesota teacher preparation program (currently 12 weeks)

D.   Verification of 3 years of teaching experience in Minnesota with no placement on an improvement plan by the school district

E.   To renew, an applicant must have 125 clock hours and meet the mandatory components in place at the time of renewal.

F.   Tier 4 licensure can be renewed indefinitely.

VI.   Testing Requirements for Teacher Licensure

A.   Minnesota accepts a variety of exam options for meeting the state's basic skills requirement. Please refer to PELSB's website at https://mn.gov/pelsb/aspiring-educators/requirements/ for full details.

B.   The Minnesota Teacher Licensure Examinations (MTLEs) are the means of assessing the pedagogical and content area knowledge of candidates for Minnesota licensure. MTLE information can be found at http://www.mtle.nesinc.com/.

VII. Teachers Prepared outside Minnesota
    A. Minnesota does not have licensure reciprocity with any other state.
    B. Applicants prepared out of state may be granted a Minnesota professional license when the following criteria are met:
        1. The teacher preparation institution is accredited by the regional association for the accreditation of colleges and secondary schools; consult http://www.ncahlc.org.
        2. The program leading to licensure, including alternative programs, has been recognized by the other state as qualifying the applicant completing the program for current licensure within that state.
        3. The program leading to licensure completed by the applicant is the same as, greater than, or not more than 2 years less than the grade-level range of the Minnesota licensure field for which application is made. A restricted teaching license may be issued where the out-of-state license is more limited in content or grade levels than a similar Minnesota license.
        4. The preparing institution verifies applicant completion of the approved licensure program and recommends the applicant for a license in the licensure field and at the licensure level.
        5. Program completion is verified by an official transcript or equivalent issued by the recommending institution or program.

VIII. Related Services Personnel
    A. Includes school counselors, school nurses, school psychologists, school social workers, and speech/language pathologists (see below for specific requirements).
    B. Related Services Personnel are not eligible for a Tier 1 license. In specific instances, school counselors, school psychologists, and speech language pathologists could qualify for a Tier 2 license. Contact PELSB for more information. Otherwise, related service licenses are granted at Tiers 3 and 4.
    C. Applications for school counselor (if the program completed is accredited by the Council for the Accreditation of Counseling and Related Educational Programs [CACREP]), school nurse, school psychologist, school social worker, and speech/language pathologists do not require a recommending signature.
    D. No testing is required for a related service license.

Administration

I. Licensure for superintendent, principal, or special education director. Requirements for all 3 positions include:
    A. Three years of successful teaching experience in any combination of the following:
        1. A public school classroom that required a state-issued teaching license
        2. A nonpublic school classroom that is accredited by an accrediting agency recognized by the state, a school directly recognized by the state, or a Bureau of Indian Education school

3. As a school psychologist, school social worker, school counselor, or speech language pathologist who holds the appropriate license to be in a school setting. Note: A special education director must verify 3 years of teaching experience as a special education teacher or as a school psychologist, school social worker, or speech language pathologist.

or

For applicants who do not have 3 years of teaching experience, they may meet the experience requirement by completing the alternative pathway for administrative licensure (see section III, below);

and

B. Completion of a specialist or doctoral program, or a program consisting of 60 semester credits beyond the bachelor's degree that includes a terminating graduate degree and topics preparatory for educational administration and specified Minnesota competencies.
   1. Each program must be approved by the Board of School Administrators and be offered at a regionally accredited Minnesota graduate school.
C. Additional position-specific requirements include:
   1. An applicant for licensure as a superintendent or principal must have field experience of at least 320 hours or 40 8-hour days to be completed within 12 continuous months in elementary, middle or junior high, and high schools as an administrative aide to a licensed and practicing school principal or superintendent, depending on the licensure sought.
      a. The field experience must include at least 40 hours or 1 week at each level not represented by the applicant's primary teaching experience.
         i. A person licensed as an elementary school principal must complete a field experience of at least 200 hours in secondary administration to qualify for licensure as a K–12 principal.
         ii. A person licensed as a secondary school principal must complete a field experience of at least 200 hours in elementary administration to qualify for licensure as a K–12 principal.
   2. An applicant for licensure as a director of special education must have a practicum or field experience that includes a minimum of 320 hours in an administrative position under the immediate supervision of a licensed and practicing director of special education.
      a. The field experience will include at least 40 hours or 1 week at a special education administrative unit other than the primary experience of the applicant.

II. Provisional License (valid 2 years; nonrenewable)
   A. Currently licensed elementary and secondary school principals seeking entry into a position as a K–12 principal may apply for a provisional license.
   B. Applicants who are coming from out of state who do not meet the necessary credits, field experience, and/or content requirement for a full Minnesota administrative license may qualify for a 2-year provisional license.
      1. Applicant must provide evidence of enrollment in an approved administrative licensure program prior to a provisional administrative license being issued.

III. Administrative Licensure without Teaching Experience for Superintendents, Principals, and Directors of Special Education. Requirements include:

A. Meet the degree requirement specified in I, B, directly above;

B. Satisfactorily complete a field experience in school administration as an intern in the license area sought:

1. In a school district setting appropriate for the license sought,

2. Under the supervision of educators from an approved college or university school administration program and a licensed practicing school administrator working in the area of the intern's field experience, *and*

3. The field experience must consist of at least 320 hours, of which at least 40 must be in each school level: elementary, middle grades, and high school, and is in addition to the teaching internship requirement below;

C. Demonstrate required basic teaching knowledge and skills by:

1. Presenting a portfolio or other appropriate presentation as determined by the approved school administration program demonstrating appropriate teaching knowledge and skills;

and

D. Fulfill teaching internship requirement ensuring that applicant shall have experience and knowledge in curriculum, school organization, philosophy of education, early childhood, elementary, junior high, middle school, and senior high schools through an internship that:

1. Includes 1 school year with a minimum hour equivalency of 1,050 hours of classroom experiences;

2. Is under the supervision of a licensed practicing school administrator;

3. Includes supervision provided by educators from an approved school administration program; *and*

4. Is based on a written agreement between the intern, the approved school administration preparation institution, and the school district in which the internship is completed.

IV. Licensure for Directors of Community Education. An applicant recommended for licensure as a director of community education shall:

A. Hold a bachelor's degree from a regionally accredited college or university; *and*

B. Satisfactorily complete a preparation program consisting of a minimum of 20 semester hours, or the equivalent, that provides a candidate recommended for licensure with the knowledge, skills, and dispositions in all of the subjects listed in Minnesota Rule 3512.0510, subparts 1 and 5.

C. The applicant must complete a field experience that includes at least 320 clock hours in an administrative position under the supervision of a licensed director of community education during which the candidate shall demonstrate the ability to apply the knowledge and skills listed in Minnesota Rule 3512.0510, subparts 1 and 5.

1. A person prepared in another state as director of community education may

substitute 1 year of experience as a district-wide director of community education in another state for the field experience.

School Counselor (K–12)

I. Requirements for Tier 3 License
   A. Hold a master's degree from a college or university that is regionally accredited by the association for the accreditation of colleges and secondary schools.
   B. Complete an approved preparation program leading to the licensure of school counselors or provide evidence of having completed a preparation program in school counseling accredited by the Council for the Accreditation of Counseling and Related Educational Programs; consult www.cacrep.org.

School Nurse (K–12)

I. Requirements for Tier 3 License
   A. Hold a bachelor's degree in nursing from a regionally accredited college or university.
   B. Be currently registered in Minnesota to practice as a licensed registered nurse under the Board of Nursing.
   C. Be currently registered in Minnesota as a public health nurse under the Board of Nursing.
II. Maintaining Board of Nursing Registration
   A. In order to retain school nurse license, current registration as a registered nurse and public health nurse must be maintained at all times since lapse in registration is grounds for revocation of school nurse license.

School Social Worker (K–12)

I. Requirements for Tier 3 License
   A. Hold a bachelor's or master's degree in social work.
   B. Be currently licensed in Minnesota to practice as a social worker under the Board of Social Work.
II. Maintaining Board of Social Work License
   A. In order to retain school social worker license, current Minnesota Board of Social Work license must be maintained at all times since lapse in license is grounds for revocation of school social worker license.

School Psychologist (K–12)

I. Requirements for Tier 3 License
   A. Complete an approved preparation program in school psychology accredited by the National Association of School Psychologists; consult http://www.nasponline.org/.
   or

B. Provide evidence of National Certification of School Psychologists through the National Association of School Psychologists.

Speech-Language Pathologist (K–12)

I. Requirements for Tier 3 License
   A. Complete an approved preparation program in speech-language pathology accredited by the Council on Academic Affairs of the American Speech-Language-Hearing Association; consult www.asha.org.
       or
   B. Provide evidence of a valid certificate of clinical competence from the American Speech-Language-Hearing Association.
       or
   C. Hold a speech-language pathology license granted by the Minnesota Department of Health.

Licensure Requirements, Levels, and Renewals

I. For the most accurate information on PELSB's approved programs for licensing in Minnesota, consult PELSB's website: https://mn.gov/pelsb/aspiring-educators/preparation-programs/approved-programs/
II. For a detailed listing of the 92 teacher licensure fields, 4 administrative licenses, and 5 related licenses, contact PELSB (see Appendix 1).
III. For information on how to renew a license, contact PELSB (see Appendix 1).

Mississippi

This information was current at press time. For the most current licensure guidelines, please visit the Mississippi Department of Education Office of Educator Licensure website at https://www.mdek12.0rg/OTL/OEL.

Standard Educator Licenses

I. Five-Year Educator License, Traditional Teacher Education Route
    A. Class A Five-Year Educator License (valid for 5 years; renewable)
        1. Bachelor's degree in teacher education from a state-approved or a National Council for Accreditation of Teacher Education (NCATE)/Council of the Accreditation of Educator Preparation (CAEP)–accredited program from a regionally/nationally accredited institution of higher learning
        2. Passing scores on Praxis II (Principles of Learning and Teaching Test)
        3. Passing scores on Praxis II (Specialty Area Test) in degree program (certain licensure areas may require more than 1 subject area assessment)
    B. Class AA Five-Year Educator License (valid for 5 years; renewable)
        1. See I, A, 1–3, directly above.
        2. Master's degree in the endorsement area in which license is requested
            or
            Master of Education degree
    C. Class AAA Five-Year Educator License (valid for 5 years; renewable)
        1. See I, A, 1–3, directly above.
        2. Specialist degree in the endorsement area in which license is requested
            or
            Specialist of Education degree
    D. Class AAAA Five-Year Educator License (valid for 5 years; renewable)
        1. See I, A, 1–3, directly above.
        2. Doctoral degree in the endorsement area in which license is requested
            or
            Doctor of Education degree
II. Five-Year Educator License, Alternate Route
    A. Class A Five-Year Educator License
        1. Route 1
            a. Bachelor's degree (non-education) from a regionally/nationally accredited institution of higher learning
            b. Passing scores on Core Academic Skills for Educators Test (Praxis Core), an ACT composite score of at least 21, or the equivalent SAT score
            c. Passing scores on Praxis II (Specialty Area Test) (certain licensure areas may require more than 1 subject area assessment)

    d.   Successful completion of a 1- or 3-year state-approved alternate route
         program (for details, consult https://www.mdek12.0rg/OTL/OEL/
         Alternate)
    e.   Application for a 5-year educator license
    or
2. Route 2
    a.   Hold a bachelor's degree with a minor or concentration in secondary
         education (7–12)
    b.   Passing scores on Praxis Core Academic Skills for Educators Test, an ACT
         composite score of at least 21, or the equivalent SAT score
    c.   Passing scores on Praxis II (Specialty Area Test) (certain licensure areas
         may require more than 1 subject area assessment)
    d.   Documentation of completion of student teaching from a state- or NCATE-
         approved program
B. Class AA, Class AAA, and/or Class AAAA Five-Year Educator License
    1. Meet the requirements for a Class A license
    2. Master's, specialist, or doctoral degree in the endorsement area in which license
        is requested
        or
        Master of Education degree or Specialist of Education degree
        or
        Doctor of Education degree
III. Reciprocity
    A. Class A Five-Year Educator Reciprocity License (valid 5 years; renewable)
        1. Granted to applicants who hold a valid standard out-of-state license (K–12)
            in an area in which Mississippi issues an endorsement if it meets minimum
            Mississippi license requirements or equivalent requirements
        2. Applicants must submit to the Office of Educator Licensure:
            a.   Original valid out-of-state license;
            b.   Sealed copy of all college transcripts;
                 and
            c.   Documentation showing a passing score on a core subject area assessment
                 required for certification by issuing state, or documentation that verifies
                 the out-of-state license was obtained in a manner equivalent with current
                 Mississippi license guidelines for that license.
    B. Class AA, AAA, or AAAA Five-Year Educator Reciprocity License
        1. Meet requirements for Class A Five-Year Educator Reciprocity License (see
            III, A, 1 and 2, directly above)
        2. Original valid out-of-state Standard Class AA (master's degree), Class AAA
            (specialist degree), or Class AAAA (doctoral degree) License in a Mississippi
            endorsement area
    C. Two-Year Reciprocity License (valid current teaching year plus 1 additional school
        year, to expire June 30; non-renewable)
        1. For applicant with a valid credential less than a standard license or certificate
            from another state. Applicant must submit to the Office of Educator Licensure:

a.   See III, A, 2, a and b, directly above.
2.   To convert this provisional license to a 5-year renewable license, the applicant must meet all requirements for a 5-year license in Mississippi.

IV.   Five-Year Educator License—Guidance and Counseling
    A.   Class AA Option One (valid 5 years; renewable)
       1.   Hold a Five-Year educator license
       2.   Complete a master's degree program in guidance and counseling
       3.   Passing score on Praxis II (Specialty Area for Guidance Counselor)
    B.   Class AA Option Two (valid 5 years; renewable)
       1.   Complete an approved master's degree program for guidance and counseling that includes a full year internship
       2.   Passing score on Praxis II (Specialty Area Test for Guidance Counseling)
    C.   Class AA Option Three (valid 5 years, renewable)
       1.   Hold National Certified School Counselor (NCSC) credential issued by National Board of Certified Counselors (NBCC)
    D.   Class AAA (valid 5 years; renewable)
       1.   Meet requirements for Class AA License (see IV, A–C, directly above)
       2.   Specialist degree in guidance and counseling
    E.   Class AAAA (valid 5 years; renewable)
       1.   Meet requirements for Class AA License (see IV, A–C, directly above)
       2.   Doctoral degree in guidance and counseling

V.   Five-Year Library/Media License (valid 5 years; renewable)
    A.   Class A Requirements (1 of the following):
       1.   Complete bachelor's degree program or higher in Library/Media, and attain passing scores on Praxis II (Principles of Learning and Teaching); and Praxis II (Specialty Area for Library/Media);
          or
       2.   Hold a Five-Year Educator license and complete an approved Library/Media program;
          or
       3.   Hold a Five-Year-Educator license and attain passing score on Praxis II (Specialty Area for Library/Media).
    B.   Class AA, AAA, or AAAA Requirements
       1.   Meet requirements for Class A license (see V, A, 1–3, directly above) and complete an approved master's (Class AA), specialist (Class AAA), or doctorate (Class AAAA) in library/media from a state-approved or regionally/nationally accredited institution of higher learning

VI.   Licenses Available
    A.   Mississippi Educator Teacher Education Route License
       1.   Five-Year Educator License
    B.   Alternate Route Licenses
       1.   MS Alternate Path to Quality Educators/Three-Year Alternate Route License
       2.   Teach MS Institute/Three-Year License
       3.   Master of Arts in Teaching/Three-Year License

      4.   American Board Certification/One-Year Alternate Route License

      5.   Five-Year Alternate Route License

  C. Special Subject Five-Year Educator Licenses

      1.   Audiologist, Child Development, Dyslexia Therapy, Early Oral Intervention Hearing Impaired B–K, Emotional Disability, Guidance and Counseling, Library Media, Performing Arts, Psychometrist, School Psychologist, Speech/ Language Clinician, Speech/Language Associate, Special Education Birth–Kindergarten, Special Education Mild/Moderate Disability K–12

  D. Career Technical Educator Licenses

      1.   Career Technical Non-Education Degree (Associate's Degree)/Three-Year License

      2.   Career Technical Non-Education Degree (Bachelor's Degree)/Three-Year License

      3.   Career Technical Educator License Non-Degree or Non-Education Degree/ Five-Year License

  E. Licenses by District Request Only

      1.   JROTC Non-practicing

      2.   One-Year License for Veteran Teachers Emergency Certificate

      3.   Expert Citizen License

      4.   Special, Non-Renewable License for Traditional Teacher Preparation Program Completers

      5.   Special, Non-Renewable License for Prospective Non-Traditional Teacher Preparation Program Completers

      6.   Special, Non-Renewable License for Adjunct Teachers

Administrator Licenses

I. Non-practicing Administrator License (Class AA, AAA, or AAAA; 5 years renewable): issued to an educator not currently employed in an administrative position

  A. Hold 5-year standard educator license

  B. Verification of 3 years of education experience

  C. Completion of an approved master's, specialist, or doctoral degree in educational administration/leadership from a state-approved or regionally/nationally accredited institution of higher learning

  D. Successful completion of School Leaders Licensure Assessment (SLLA), Educational Testing Service

  E. Institutional recommendation documenting completion of an approved planned program in educational leadership/supervision through a state-approved or regionally/nationally accredited institution of higher learning

  F. Validity is based upon validity of period of standard license currently held.

II. Entry-Level Administrator License (Class AA, AAA, or AAAA; valid 5 years; non-renewable): issued to an educator employed as a beginning administrator

  A. See I, A–E, directly above.

  B. Application for Entry-Level license upon obtaining first job as administrator (Orientation to School Leadership—OSL)

C. Letter from District stating the administrative position and date of administrative employment

III. Standard Career-Level Administrator License (Class AA, AAA, or AAAA; 5 years renewable)

   A. Complete School Executive Management Institute (SEMI) requirements

IV. Alternate Route Administrator License (Class AA, AAA, or AAAA)

   A. One-Year Alternate Route Administrator License (Class AA; valid 1 year; convertible to IV, B, directly below)

      1. Requirements
         a. Completion of Master of Education (MED) or higher education degree
         b. Passing score on Praxis Core Academic Skills for Educators Test or an ACT composite score of at least 21 and Praxis II (Principles of Learning and Teaching Test)
         c. Three years teaching experience for MED
         d. Successful completion of alternate route training
         e. Priority will be given to Superintendent/Board recommendation for admittance into an alternate route program.

      2. Conversion to Five-Year Entry-Level Alternate Route Administrator License
         a. Complete Alternate Route program
         b. See I, D, directly above.

   B. Five-Year Entry-Level Alternate Route Administrator License (Class AA; valid 5 years; non-renewable)

      1. Requirements
         a. See IV, A, 1, a–e, directly above.
         b. See I, D, directly above.

      2. Conversion to Standard Career-Level Alternate Route Administrator License within 5 years—see III, A, directly above.
         a. Completion of SEMI entry-level OSL requirements
         b. Completion of 6 hours of educational leadership course work from an approved educational leadership administrator program (courses must be in school law, school finance, instructional improvement or leadership, curriculum and instruction)

   C. Standard Career-Level Alternate Route Administrator License (Class AA, AAA, AAAA)

      1. Requirements
         a. See IV, A, 1, a–c, directly above.
         b. Completion of School Executive Management Institute (SEMI) entry-level requirements

   D. Five-Year Alternate Route Administrator License, Business Track (Class AA valid 5 years; non-renewable)

      1. Requirements:
         a. Complete 1 of the following: Master of Business Administration (MBA), or Master of Public Administration (MPA), or Master of Public Planning and Policy (MPP), or Doctor of Jurisprudence (JD);

      b.   Praxis Core Academic Skills for Educators or an ACT composite score of at least 21 and Praxis II (Principles of Learning and Teaching) Tests;

      c.   Five years of administrative/supervisory experience, meaning direct supervision of individuals and/or programs within a business, industry, and/or organization;

      d.   Successful completion of SLLA-Educational Testing Service; *and*

      e.   Successful completion of Alternate Route training.

      f.   Priority will be given to Superintendent/Board recommendation for admittance into an Alternate Route program.

   2.   Conversion to Career-Level Standard License within 5 years—see IV, B, 2, directly above.

E.   Other Administrative Licenses; for further information, consult http://www.sos.ms.gov/ACCode/00000398c.pdf.

   1.   Athletic Administrator

   2.   School District Business Administrator

Missouri

Educator Certification, Classification, and Renewals

I. General Qualifications for Certification
Identical for all teaching certificates, except for some areas of Vocational Education

  A. Baccalaureate degree from college/university with teacher education program approved by Missouri Department of Elementary and Secondary Education (DESE) or with teacher education program approved by state education agency in states other than Missouri

  1. No formal reciprocity for certification with other states; however, graduates from approved teacher-education programs within other states may obtain Missouri certificate based on meeting certain requirements.

  B. Recommendation for certification from designated official for teacher education in college/university where program was completed; not required with possession of a valid out-of-state certificate

  C. Professional education and content area GPA of 3.00 or higher on a 4.00 scale

  D. Successful completion of Missouri Content Assessment

  1. Consult DESE website (see Appendix 1) for list of the Missouri Specialty Area Tests and qualifying scores.

  E. Meet educational, professional, and subject area requirements as specified

  F. Applicants are required to complete a Missouri background check, including fingerprinting; for details, consult http://dese.mo.gov/eq/cert/index.html.

II. Classifications

  A. Initial Professional Certificate (valid 4 years)

  1. Assigned to new graduates of teacher-education programs and to individuals with less than 4 years of DESE-approved teaching experience who meet the minimum requirements and qualifications

  2. See I, A–E, directly above.

  3. To advance to next level, during valid dates of classification, the teacher must meet all of following requirements:

  a. Participate in district-provided and -approved mentoring program for 2 years

  b. Successfully complete 30 contact hours of professional development that may include college credits

  c. Participate in Beginning Teacher Assistance Program

  d. Successfully participate in a yearly performance-based teacher evaluation

  e. Complete 4 years of approved teaching experience

  B. Career Continuous Professional Certificate, or CCPC

  C. Administrative Classification

  1. School Leader K–12

  a. Initial Administrator Certificate (valid 4 years)

  i. Permanent or professional Missouri teaching certificate
    or

Baccalaureate degree and recommendation from state-approved teacher preparation program; and qualifying score on designated assessment for initial certification

ii. Minimum of 3 years of approved teaching experience (effective September 1, 2020)

iii. Complete designated building-level administrator's assessment

iv. Course in psychology and education of the exceptional child

v. Master's degree in educational leadership from approved college/university

vi. Recommendation for certification from approved college/university program

b. Transition Administrator Certificate—School Leader K–12 (valid 6 years)

i. Four years of state-approved administrator experience

ii. Two years of designated district-provided mentoring.

iii. Development, implementation, and completion of approved professional development plan

iv. Annual performance-based evaluation that meets or exceeds Missouri Performance-Based Principal's Evaluation

v. Completion of 8 semester hours towards advanced degree in educational leadership or 120 contact hours in professional development activities

c. Career Continuous Administrator Certificate—School Leader K–12

i. Educational specialist degree or higher in educational leadership, reading/literacy or curriculum/instruction.

ii. Performance-based principal evaluation

iii. Thirty contact hours of professional development annually

iv. Four years of state-approved administrator experience

2. Superintendent

a. Initial Administrator Certificate (valid 4 years)

i. EdS or EdD in educational administration/superintendency with recommendation from the degree-granting university

ii. Designated district-level administrator's assessment

iii. Minimum of 3 years of experience as a building- or district-level administrator at public or accredited nonpublic school

iv. See II, C, 1, a, i–vi, directly above.

b. Career Certificate Administrator

i. See II, C, 1, c, i–iv, directly above.

3. Special Education Administrator K–12

a. Initial Administrator Certificate—Special Education Director (valid 4 years)

i. Professional teaching certificate for an area of special education or student services

or

Baccalaureate degree and recommendation from state-approved teacher preparation program in an area of special education; and qualifying score on designated assessment

           ii.   Minimum of 3 years of approved special education or student services teaching experience (effective September 1, 2020)

           iii. See II, C, 1, a, i–vi, directly above.

      b.   Transition Administrator Certificate—Special Education Director (valid for 6 years)

           i.   See II, C, 1, b, i–v, directly above.

      c.   Career Administrator Certificate—Special Education Director

           i.   See II, C, 1, c, i–iv, directly above.

   4.   Career Education Director

      a.   Initial Administrator Certificate—Career Education Director (valid 4 years)

           i.   Permanent or professional or career education Missouri teaching certificate

               or

               Baccalaureate degree and recommendation from state-approved teacher preparation program; and qualifying score on designated assessment

           ii.   See II, C, 1, a, ii–vi, directly above.

      b.   Transition Administrator Certificate—Career Education Director (valid 6 years)

           i.   See II, C, 1, b, i–v, directly above.

      c.   Career Administrator Certificate—Career Education Director

           i.   See II, C, 1, c, i–iv, directly above.

D.   Student Services Classification

   1.   Counselor K–12 (valid 4 years)

      a.   Recommendation for certification from approved college/university with a school counseling program

      b.   Master's degree with major emphasis in school guidance and counseling from approved college/university based upon completion of approved program of at least 24 semester hours of approved graduate courses in guidance and counseling, with at least 12 semester hours focused upon guidance in elementary schools

      c.   Qualifying score on designated assessment

   2.   Career Student Services (valid 99 years)

      a.   Four years of state-approved school counseling experience

      b.   Participation in 2 years district-provided mentoring during the first 2 years of student services experience

      c.   Development, implementation, and completion of a professional development plan of at least 40 contact hours of professional development or 3 semester hours of graduate credit towards an advanced degree

      d.   Successful participation in an annual performance-based evaluation

   3.   For related certificates listed here, contact Educator Certification at Missouri's Department of Elementary and Secondary Education (http://dese.mo.gov/eq/cert/index.html).

      a.   Psychological Examiner K–12

      b.   School Psychologist K–12
- E. Classifications involving district application. For detailed information on these, contact Missouri Department of Elementary and Secondary Education (http://dese.mo.gov/divteachqual/teachcert/).
  1. Provisional (valid 2 years)
  2. Temporary Authorization Classification (valid 1 year)
- F. Career (Vocational) Classification Applicants may seek certificates below; for full details, contact Missouri Department of Elementary and Secondary Education (http://dese.mo.gov/eq/cert/index.html).
  1. Secondary Career Education Certificate
  2. Postsecondary/Adult Career Education Certificate
  3. Career Continuous Career Education (CCCE) Certificate

Areas and Types of Certification

I. Certification Levels
- A. Early Childhood (Birth–Grade 3)
- B. Elementary Education (1–6)
- C. Middle School (5–9)
  1. Language Arts
  2. Mathematics
  3. Science
  4. Social Studies
  5. Other Middle School Endorsements
- D. Secondary Education (9–12) (except as noted)
- E. Special Education (K–12)
- F. Student Services
- G. Administration
- H. Career Education (vocational)
- I. Other

II. Subject Areas

Agriculture; Art (K–12); Blind & Partially Sighted (B–12); Business Education; Career Education (Vocational) Director (7–12); Deaf and Hearing Impaired (B–12); Early Childhood Education (B–Grade 3); Early Childhood Special Education (B–Grade 3); English; English Language Learners (K–12); Family and Consumer Science (K–12); Foreign Languages (French [K–12]; German [K–12]; Spanish [K–12]); Gifted Education (K–12); Health (K–12); Library Media Specialist (K–12); Marketing Education; Mathematics; Mild/Moderate Cross-Categorical K–12; Music (Instrumental, Vocal) (K–12); Physical Education (K–12); School Counselor (K–12); School Leader (K–12); School Psychologist K–12; Science (Biology; Chemistry; Earth Science; Physics); Severely Developmentally Disabled (B–12); Social Science; Special Education Administrator; Special Reading (Remedial) (K–12); Speech/Theater; Superintendent, K–12; Technology and Engineering

Montana

Educator Licenses

For the most current information, please refer to the Montana Office of Public Instruction (OPI) website at http://opi.mt.gov/Educators/Licensure/Become-a-Licensed-Montana-Educator.

I. Class 2 Standard Teaching License (valid 5 years)
   A. To meet Montana's requirements for a Class 2 Standard Teaching License, applicants must meet one of the following criteria:
      1. Completion of an educator preparation program that is accredited by the National Council for Accreditation of Teacher Education (NCATE), Council for Accreditation of Educator Preparation (CAEP), or Montessori Accreditation Council for Teacher Education (MACTE), or that is a state-approved program from a regionally accredited college or university, and completion of student teaching or a supervised teaching experience through an educator preparation program;
         or
      2. Completion of National Board Certification program;
         or
      3. Completion of a non-traditional teaching program with 5 successful years of teaching experience, along with a current, standard, unrestricted out-of-state educator license.
   B. Applicant must submit verification of all of the following:
      1. If the educator preparation program completed by the applicant is not in Montana, the applicant must provide proof of a minimum score on the Montana-required Praxis test applicable to the requested endorsement area; and
      2. Completion of the free, online course, "An Introduction to Indian Education for All in Montana."
   C. Class 2 Standard Teaching License shall be renewable with verification of 60 renewal units earned during the 5 years of validity through August 31 of the year the license expires. Participation in renewal activities is equivalent to the following renewal units:
      1. One hour of attendance at a professional development activity = 1 renewal unit;
      2. One quarter college credit = 10 renewal units; and
      3. One semester college credit = 15 renewal units.
   D. A lapsed Class 2 Standard Teaching License may be reinstated by showing verification of 60 renewal units earned during the 5-year period preceding the application date of the new license.
II. Class 1 Professional Teaching License (valid 5 years)
   A. To meet Montana's requirements for a Class 1 Professional Teaching License, applicants must meet one of the following criteria:

1. Completion of an educator preparation program that is accredited by NCATE, CAEP, or MACTE, or that is a state-approved program from a regionally accredited college or university, and completion of student teaching or a supervised teaching experience through an educator preparation program; *or*
2. Completion of National Board Certification program; *or*
3. Completion of a non-traditional teaching program with 5 successful years of teaching experience, along with a current, standard, unrestricted out-of-state educator license.

B. Applicant must submit verification of all of the following:
1. A master's degree in education or endorsable teaching area(s) from a regionally accredited college or university, or certification by the National Board for Professional Teaching Standards;
2. If the educator preparation program completed by the applicant is not in Montana, the applicant must provide proof of a minimum score on the Montana-required Praxis test applicable to the requested endorsement area;
3. Completion of the free, online course, "An Introduction to Indian Education for All in Montana"; and
4. Verification of successful teaching experience while appropriately licensed and assigned: 3 years for applicants who completed a traditional educator preparation program and 5 years for applicants who completed a non-traditional educator preparation program.

C. Class 1 Professional Teaching License shall be renewable with verification of 60 renewal units earned during the 5 years of validity through August 31 of the year the license expires.
1. See I, Class 2 Standard Teaching License, C, 1–3, above, for renewal unit equivalencies.

D. A lapsed Class 1 Professional Teaching License may be reinstated by showing verification of 60 renewal units earned during the 5-year period preceding the application date of the new license.

Administrative Licenses

I. Class 3 Administrator's License (valid 5 years)
A. Appropriate administrative areas that may be approved for license endorsement are elementary principal, secondary principal, K–12 principal, K–12 superintendent, supervisor, and special education supervisor.
B. To obtain a Class 3 Administrator's License, an applicant must:
1. Be eligible for an appropriately endorsed Class 1, 2, or 5 license to teach in the school(s) in which the applicant would be an administrator or would supervise; *or*
2. Complete a non-traditional educator preparation program along with a current, standard, unrestricted out-of-state administrator license and verification of 5 years of successful administrative experience while appropriately licensed.

3. Complete required Montana coursework and the online course "Indian Education for All in Montana."

C. Class 3 Administrator's License shall be renewable with verification of 60 renewal units earned during the 5 years of validity through August 31 of the year the license expires.

1. See I, Class 2 Standard Teaching License, C, 1–3, above, for renewal unit equivalencies.

D. A lapsed Class 3 Administrator's License may be reinstated by showing verification of 60 renewal units earned during the 5-year period preceding the validation date of the new license.

II. Class 3 Administrator's License—Superintendent Endorsement

A. Applicant must provide verification of all of the following:

1. An education specialist, master's, or doctoral degree in education or education leadership;

2. Completion of an accredited professional educator preparation program for superintendents;

3. A minimum of 18 semester graduate credits in a school administrator preparation program, of which 12 must be beyond the master's degree in education leadership and include 3 credits in each of the following:

a. Montana school law,

b. Montana school finance,
   and

c. Montana collective bargaining and employment law;

4. A minimum of 3 years of teaching experience as an appropriately licensed teacher or specialist;

5. Licensure and endorsement as a P–12 principal;
   and

6. A minimum of 1 year of administrative experience as an appropriately licensed principal or 1 year of a supervised Board of Public Education–approved administrative internship as a superintendent.

B. Applicant must also submit a recommendation for the endorsement requested from the appropriate official from an accredited professional educator program.

III. Class 3 Administrator's License—Elementary Principal Endorsement

A. Applicant must provide verification of:

1. A minimum of 3 years of experience as an appropriately licensed and assigned Class 1 or 2 teacher at the elementary level;

2. A master's degree in educational leadership from an accredited professional educator preparation program or a master's degree related to education;

3. Completion of an accredited professional educator preparation program for elementary principals;

4. Completion of 3 semester credits of college coursework in Montana school law, including special education law;
   and

5. Recommendation for the endorsement from the appropriate official from an accredited professional educator program.

IV. Class 3 Administrator's License—Secondary Principal Endorsement
   A. Applicant must provide verification of:
   1. A minimum of 3 years of experience as an appropriately licensed and assigned Class 1 or 2 teacher at the secondary level;
   2. A master's degree in educational leadership from an accredited professional educator preparation program or a master's degree related to education;
   3. Completion of an accredited professional educator preparation program for secondary principals;
   4. Completion of 3 semester credits of college coursework in Montana school law, including special education law;
       and
   5. Recommendation for the endorsement from the appropriate official from an accredited professional educator program.

V. Class 3 Administrator's License—K–12 Principal Endorsement
   A. Applicant must provide verification of:
   1. A master's degree in educational leadership from an accredited professional educator preparation program as defined in Administrative Rules of Montana (ARM) 10.57.102 or a master's degree related to education;
   2. Completion of an accredited educator preparation program for K–12 principals;
   3. A minimum of 3 years of experience as an appropriately licensed and assigned Class 1 or 2 teacher;
   4. Completion of 3 semester credits of college coursework in Montana school law, including special education law;
       and
   5. Recommendation for the endorsement from the appropriate official from an accredited professional educator program.

VI. Class 3 Administrator's License—Supervisor Endorsement
   A. Issued in specific fields such as math, music, and school counseling, or in general areas such as elementary education, secondary education, and curriculum development.
   B. Applicants must submit verification of:
   1. Completion of a master's degree in the area requested for endorsement at a regionally accredited college or university;
   2. Meeting eligibility requirements for a Class 1 or Class 2 teaching license endorsed in the field of specialization;
   3. Three years of experience as an appropriately licensed and assigned teacher in a state-accredited P–K or K–12 setting;
   4. Completion of a supervised preparation program that is accredited by NCATE or CAEP, or that is a state-approved program from a regionally accredited college or university;
       and
   5. Recommendation for the endorsement from the appropriate official from an accredited professional educator program.

VII. Class 3 Administrator's License—Special Education Supervisor Endorsement

A. Issued in specific field of special education
B. Applicants must submit verification of:
   1. Completion of a supervisor preparation program that is accredited by NCATE or CAEP, or that is a state-approved program from a regionally accredited college or university in the following special education–related service fields: school psychologist, speech-language pathologist, audiologist, physical therapist, occupational therapist, registered nurse, clinical social worker, or clinical professional counselor;
   2. Meeting eligibility requirements for a Class 1 or Class 2 teaching license endorsed in the field of specialization;
   3. Completion of a master's degree in the area requested for endorsement (special education or related service area, school psychologist, speech-language pathologist, audiologist, physical therapist, occupational therapist, registered nurse, clinical social worker, or clinical professional counselor); *and*
   4. Three years of experience in an accredited school setting as an appropriately licensed and assigned teacher, or 5 years of experience in an accredited school setting as a fully licensed and assigned related services provider.

Additional Licenses

I. Class 4 Career and Technical Teaching License (valid 5 years)
   A. Three types of Class 4 licenses:
      1. Class 4A license issued to individuals holding a valid Montana teaching license, but without an appropriate career and technical education endorsement;
      2. Class 4B license issued to individuals with at least a bachelor's degree but who do not hold a valid Montana teaching license with the appropriate career and technical education endorsement; and
      3. Class 4C license issued to individuals who hold at least high school diploma or high school equivalency diploma and meet minimum requirements for endorsement.
   B. Class 4 license renewal requires 60 renewal units.
      1. Class 4A licenses shall be renewable by earning 60 renewal units. Endorsement-related technical studies may be accepted. The first renewal must show evidence of renewal units earned in the following content areas:
         a. Curriculum and instruction in career and technical education; *and*
         b. Safety and teacher liability.
      2. Class 4B or 4C licenses shall be renewable by earning 60 renewal units. The first renewal must show evidence of renewal units earned in the following content areas:
         a. Principles and/or philosophy of career and technical education;
         b. Curriculum and instruction in career and technical education;
         c. Learning styles/teaching styles; including serving students with special needs;

d. Safety and teacher liability;

e. Classroom management;

f. Teaching methods;

g. Career guidance in career and technical education; or

h. Endorsement-related technical studies, with prior OPI approval.

3. A lapsed Class 4 license may be reinstated by showing verification of 60 renewal units earned during the 5-year period preceding the validation date of the new license, including, for Class 4A licenses, renewal units in:

a. Curriculum and instruction in career and technical education;

b. Safety and teacher liability;
    and

c. Endorsement-related technical studies or industry-validated training.

C. Unless otherwise noted, to obtain an endorsement on a Class 4 license, an applicant must provide verification of a minimum of 10,000 hours of documented, relevant work experience, which may include apprenticeship training, documenting the knowledge and skills required in the specific trade in which they are to teach. Acceptable documentation of relevant work experience is determined by the Superintendent of Public Instruction and may include, but is not limited to:

1. Work experience completed and verified by previous employers, to include detailed description of duties performed during employment;

2. For self-employed individuals, examples of projects completed, letters of verification from clients or customers, profit and loss statements demonstrating viability of business or self-employment;

3. Verification of teaching experience in area requested for endorsement, accompanied by verification of substantial work experience in area requested for endorsement; or

4. Certificates of completion of appropriate technical programs or related college degrees and coursework, and industry certification (e.g., ASE, AWS).

D. Class 4A, 4B, or 4C Career and Technical Teaching License may be approved to teach traffic education if the license meets specific requirements; contact Montana Office of Public Instruction (OPI)—see Appendix 1—for full details.

II. Class 6 Specialist License (valid 5 years)

A. Class 6 Specialist Licenses may be issued with the following endorsements:

1. School psychologist
    or

2. School counselor

3. A Class 6 Specialist License may also be endorsed in traffic education if the licensee meets the requirements and is approved by the Superintendent of Public Instruction.

B. Class 6 Specialist License renewal requires verification of 60 renewal units earned during the 5 years of validity through August 31 of the year the license expires.

1. See I, Class 2 Standard Teaching License, C, 1–3, above, for renewal unit equivalencies.

III. Class 6 Specialist License—School Psychologist

    A. To obtain Class 6 Specialist License with school psychologist endorsement, applicant must provide verification of:

        1. A Nationally Certified School Psychologist (NCSP) credential from the National Association of School Psychologists (NASP);
            and

        2. Completion of a specialist-level degree from a NASP-accredited school psychologist program that included a 1,200-hour internship, of which 600 hours were in a school setting.

        3. For those applicants who did not earn at least a specialist-level school psychology degree from an NASP-accredited program:

            a. A master's degree or higher in school psychology or a related field from a regionally accredited college or university;
                and

            b. Recommendation from an NASP-accredited specialist program attesting to the applicant's qualifications being equivalent to NASP training standards, which included a 1,200-hour internship experience of which 600 hours were in a school setting.

IV. Class 6 Specialist License—School Counselor

    A. To obtain Class 6 Specialist License with a school counselor endorsement, applicant must provide verification of:

        1. A master's degree;
            and

        2. Completion of a Council for Accreditation of Counseling and Related Educational Programs (CACREP)–accredited school counselor program that included an internship in a school setting of 600 hours.

        3. For those applicants who did not earn a degree from a CACREP-accredited program:

            a. A master's degree in school counseling from a regionally accredited college or university;
                and

            b. Recommendation from an accredited specialist program that included an internship in a school setting of 600 hours.

V. Class 7 Native American Language and Culture Educator License (valid 5 years)

    A. The Superintendent of Public Instruction shall issue a Class 7 license based upon verification by the authorized representative of a tribal government that has a memorandum of understanding with the Superintendent of Public Instruction that the applicant has met tribal standards for competency and fluency as a requisite for teaching that language and culture.

    B. The Board will accept and place on file the criteria developed by each tribe for qualifying an individual as competent to be a specialist in its language and culture.

    C. A holder of a Class 7 Native American Language and Culture Teaching License may be approved to teach traffic education if the licensee meets the requirements and is approved by the Superintendent of Public Instruction.

    D. A school district may assign an individual licensed under this rule only to specialist services within the field of Native American language and culture under such supervision as the district may deem appropriate. No teaching license or endorsement is required for duties within this prescribed field.

VI. Class 8 Dual Credit Only Post-Secondary Faculty License (valid 5 years)

    A. Whenever a faculty member of a post-secondary institution is teaching a course for which 1 or more students will earn both high school and college credit, that faculty member is required to hold a Class 8 dual credit license, unless already licensed or eligible for licensure (as a Class 1, 2, or 4) and properly endorsed. Contact the Montana Office of Public Instruction for more details.

Nebraska

The term "certificate" will apply to Initial, Standard, and Professional (regular) Certificates. Other options formerly designated as certificates will now be designated as permits. The Nebraska Certification Office sends certificates electronically as email attachments, so all applicants must have a current email address.

Teaching Certificate Types

I. Initial Certificate (valid 5 years; renewable)
   A. Requires completion of:
      1. Bachelor's degree
         and
      2. An approved teacher education program with an endorsement recommendation from an approved institution.
         a. Six semester hours must be completed within the past 5 years.
   B. Renewable with 6 semester hours or 1 year of documented experience teaching in the past 5 years in an approved school.
II. Standard Certificate (valid 5 years; renewable)
   A. Requirements include holding a valid Initial Certificate and at least 2 consecutive years of teaching experience.
   B. Renewable with 6 semester hours or 1 year of teaching experience within the past 5 years.
III. Professional Certificate (valid 10 years; renewable)
   A. Issued with completion of master's degree in curriculum and instruction, special education, educational technology, or the applicant's content field.
   B. Renewable with 6 approved semester hours or 1 year of teaching experience within the past 5 years.

Requirements for Teaching Certificates

I. Professional, Standard, and Initial Certificates. Requirements for all include:
   A. Bachelor's degree;
      1. Originals of all college transcripts are required.
   B. Recommendation and endorsement by college for teacher training program completed;
   C. At least 6 hours of college coursework in the past 5 years or 1 year work experience as a contracted teacher half-time or more, within the past immediate 5 years;
   D. Praxis Core Academic Skills for Educators;
   E. Praxis Subject Assessment(s) for the area(s) of endorsement the person wants to add to the certificate;

F.   Human relations training—an approved human relations course addressing the 6 competencies found in statute;

G.   Special education training—an approved special education course addressing the exceptional child in the classroom;
     and

H.   Fingerprinting required for applicants who have not lived in Nebraska for 5 consecutive years prior to the date of application.

  1.   Applicant must have no felony convictions.

II.   Standard and Professional Certificates Additional Requirements:

  A.   Both require 2 years of teaching experience during the previous 5 years.

  B.   Professional Certificate also requires a master's degree in curriculum and instruction, educational technology, or in the person's content area.

III.   Permits with deficiencies. For more detailed information, consult the website at https://www.education.ne.gov/TCERT/.

  A.   Provisional Teaching Permits

  1.   Provisional Teaching Permit (valid 2 years; not renewable)

    a.   Issued to persons reentering the profession who do not have recent teaching experience and need to complete course hours

    b.   Need to complete Praxis Core Academic Skills for Educators and Praxis Subject Assessment or special education training requirement

  B.   Alternative Program Teaching Permit

  1.   Issued at the request of a school district to employ a person who has completed a bachelor's degree plus 50 percent of their pre–student teaching requirements and 75 percent of their content courses to take a difficult-to-fill position

  2.   Issued to applicants with a completed bachelor's degree, an alternative certification pathway, an offer of employment from a Nebraska school, teaching employment and certification in another state, and an approved plan for addressing deficiencies

  C.   Substitute Teaching Permit

  1.   State Substitute Permit (valid 5 years)

    a.   Issued to applicants with a bachelor's degree who have completed a teacher education program

    b.   Allows holder unlimited days per year to substitute in Nebraska schools

  2.   Local Substitute Permit (valid 3 years)

    a.   Issued to applicants with at least 60 college hours including 1 education class

    b.   Allows holder to substitute only in 1 district for no more than 90 days per year

  D.   Temporary Teaching Certificate (valid 6 months)

  1.   Issued to those persons who have not completed the human relations training but have met all other requirements for a regular certificate

  E.   Conditional Teaching Permit (valid for up to 1 year)

  1.   Allows teaching while fingerprints are being processed or at the direction of the Commissioner when existing deficiencies prevent the issuance of a regular certificate in a timely manner

F. Transitional Teaching Permit (valid 1 year in 1 district only) for those enrolled in the Transitional Certification Program

G. Career Education Permit (valid 3 years)
   1. Issued to a person with a particular area of expertise who is offering a career education program to students in 1 Nebraska school district

H. Postsecondary Teaching Permit (valid 3 years)
   1. Issued to college employees who are teaching dual credit courses for both college and high school credit
   2. Human relations training requirement
   3. Postsecondary Permit Verification form

I. Military Teaching Permit (valid 3 years)
   1. Issued to military spouses or retired military who do not meet all Nebraska teaching requirements. Applicants must show evidence of current service by applicant or spouse, hold a teaching certificate in another state, and show 2 years of teaching experience.
   2. Human relations training requirement
   3. Fingerprinting required for applicants who have not lived in Nebraska for 5 consecutive years prior to the date of application
   4. Nebraska district employment verification letter

Administrative Certificates

I. Professional Administrative Certificate (valid 10 years). Requirements include:
   A. Two years of teaching experience;
   B. Completion of a specialist degree or more than 60 hours in educational administration;
   C. Six semester hours of graduate work in educational administration within 5 years of the date of application,
   or
   Have been serving as a school administrator for 2 or more years within the past 5;
   and
   D. Successful completion of Praxis Core Academic Skills for Educators, Praxis Subject Assessment, human relations and special education (SPED) training.

II. Standard Administrative Certificate (valid 5 years). Requirements include:
   A. Two years of teaching experience;
   B. Completion of a master's degree in educational administration;
   C. Six semester hours of graduate work in educational administration within 5 years of the date of application,
   or
   Have been serving as a school administrator for 2 or more years within the past 5;
   and
   D. Human relations, Praxis Core Academic Skills for Educators, Praxis Subject Assessment, and SPED training completed.

III. Provisional Administrative Permit (valid 2 years; not renewable)

A. Candidate must have at least 75 percent of a superintendent's program completed or 50 percent of a principal's program completed.
B. Candidate must have employment offered by a Nebraska district.
IV. Temporary Administrative Certificate (valid 6 months)
    A. Issued to applicant to complete human relations training

Support Services Certificates/Permits

I. School Nurse and Educational Audiologist
  A. Standard Special Services Certificate (valid 5 years). Requirements include:
    1. Human relations training;
    2. Additional subject-specific required training or coursework;
    3. Completion of an approved program in candidate's specialty; *and*
    4. Six hours of college credit within the past 5 years or 1 year of valid experience.
  B. Provisional Special Services Permit (valid 1 year) for Speech-Language Technician only. Requirements include:
    1. Human relations training
    2. Bachelor's degree in Communication Disorders
    3. Letter offering employment as a Speech-Language Technician in a Nebraska district
  C. Special Services Permit for Coaching
    1. Human relations training
    2. Courses in First Aid and Principles of Coaching completed
  D. Temporary Special Services Certificate (valid 6 months)
    1. Issued to applicants who have met all other requirements for a Special Services Certificate to complete human relations training

Nevada

Fingerprinting is required for all initial licenses and licensure renewals.

Teaching Certificates and Requirements

I. Standard License (valid 5 years)
    A. Bachelor's degree from a regionally accredited college/university, completion of a teacher education program that meets state-approved program standards, and completion of competency and state-mandated testing in the area applied for.
    B. Renewal is based on completion of at least 1 semester credit of college/university coursework or 15 hours of professional development, which must be related to the licensee's area of endorsement or to the profession of education, during each year of validity of the license.

II. Provisional License (valid 3 years)
    A. Same requirements as the Standard License except with provisions for state-mandated testing and/or up to 6 credits of coursework.
    B. All provisions must be met prior to the expiration date. Once all provisions are satisfied prior to expiration date, license may be changed to Standard or Professional.

III. Professional License (valid 6 years)
    A. Meet requirements for the renewable license, submit master's degree from a regionally accredited college/university, and verify 3 years of successful teaching experience at the K–12 grade level.
    B. Renewal is based on completion of at least 1 semester credit of college/university coursework or 15 hours of professional development, which must be related to the licensee's area of endorsement or to the profession of education, during each year of validity of the license.

IV. Professional License (valid 8 years)
    A. Meet requirements for the renewable license, complete an educational specialist degree program from a regionally accredited college/university, and verify 3 years of successful teaching experience at the appropriate K–12 grade level. Renewal requirement is completion of at least 1 semester credit of college/university coursework or 15 hours of professional development, which must be related to the licensee's area of endorsement or to the profession of education, during each year of validity of the license.

V. Professional License (valid 10 years)
    A. Meet requirements for the renewable license, complete a doctoral degree program from a regionally accredited college/university, and verify 3 years of successful teaching experience at the appropriate K–12 grade level. Renewal requirement is completion of at least 1 semester credit of college/university coursework or 15 hours of professional development, which must be related to the licensee's area

of endorsement or to the profession of education, during each year of validity of the license.

Basic Qualifications for Licensure

I. Degree(s) and credits for courses must have been earned from a regionally accredited college or university.
II. Foreign transcripts must be accompanied by a course-by-course and degree equivalency evaluation done by an approved evaluator service (list available on website; see Appendix 1) before applicant applies for licensure.
III. A license is issued based on the evaluation of the applicant's official transcript(s).

Elementary School (Kindergarten–8th Grade)

I. Standard Elementary License Requirements
  A. Bachelor's degree from accredited college or university and completion of a Commission on Professional Standards in Education–approved program of preparation for teaching in elementary grades
  B. Completion of the following:
    1. Elementary professional education, semester hours 65
      a. Supervised student teaching 8
      b. Teaching methods of teaching basic elementary subjects, including, but not limited to, mathematics, science, and social studies 9
      c. Teaching of literacy or language arts 9
      d. Three semester hours of credit in the following: classroom and behavior management, including without limitation, social, emotional, and academic development; multicultural education and culturally relevant pedagogy; multi-tiered systems of support; strategies for working with children with disabilities; child development and learning......................... 9
      e. Six semester hours of credit each in mathematics, science, and social studies 18
      f. Professional education coursework* 3
    *This must include the parental involvement/family engagement course.
  C. Completion of required competency testing as specified on website (see Appendix 1)
II. Professional Elementary License Requirements
  A. Meet all requirements for Elementary License
  B. Hold a master's degree or higher in education
  C. Have 3 years of verifiable elementary teaching experience in state-approved schools

Middle School (7th–9th Grades)

I. Requirements to teach in designated middle school or junior high school
  A. Hold bachelor's or higher degree from accredited college or university, and
    1. Complete Commission-approved preparation program for teaching at this level
      or

Complete professional education coursework, semester hours 24
Hours to include:

a. Supervised student teaching in designated middle or junior high school, semester hours 8

b. A course in methods and materials for teaching major or minor field of specialization at middle school, junior high school, or secondary grade level, or a middle or junior high school level integrated methods course

c. Course of study regarding education or curricular adaptation for pupils with disabilities and/or a course or study regarding educational foundations or methods in teaching English-language learners, semester hours ... 3

d. Coursework in at least 2 of the following areas: middle school foundations, history, theory or philosophy; middle school curriculum, pedagogy, or assessment; adolescent growth and development; nature and needs of the adolescent including social, emotional, and cultural concerns; classroom management strategies; school/family/community collaboration; or supervision and evaluation of programs and pupils in a middle school, semester hours 6
   and

e. Coursework in any of the following subjects: English as a second language/bilingualism or biculturalism; educational technology; tests and measurement; educational psychology; education of the exceptional child; multicultural education; or educational research, semester hours 6
   and

2. Credits in a major field of endorsement or area of concentration, semester hours. 24

B. Subsequent minor fields of endorsement may be added to the license upon verification of 14 semester hours of credit, or by passing a subject-matter exam in the area of endorsement.

C. Complete required competency testing as specified on the Department of Education website (see Appendix 1)

II. Endorsement areas: art; English/language arts; foreign language (see Department of Education website in Appendix 1 for specifics); mathematics; music; science; and social science

A. Mathematics endorsement requires completion of 3 semester credits, to include a course in college algebra or concepts of calculus, including an introduction to limits, derivatives and integrals, precalculus, or differential calculus.

B. Major or minor fields of endorsement or area of concentration shall be deemed to be met if applicant holds bachelor's degree or a higher degree with a major, minor, or area of concentration identified on official transcript of record conferred by regionally accredited college or university.

III. A person who holds a valid Nevada license to teach elementary education, early childhood education, special education, or secondary education may obtain a license to teach middle school by passing a subject-matter exam in the area of endorsement the applicant wishes to teach. In such a case, the applicant would not be required to complete additional pedagogy coursework.

Secondary School

I. Authorization
   A. A license endorsed in a recognized teaching field is required for teaching in departmentalized seventh and eighth grades, junior high schools, senior high schools, and designated and approved middle schools. Endorsements are dependent upon the applicant's field of specialization or concentration, usually designated as majors or minors or areas of concentration.

II. Standard Secondary License Requirements
   A. Bachelor's degree and completion of a Commission-approved program of preparation for secondary school teaching,
     or
   B. Bachelor's degree and completion of the following:
     1. A teaching field major from a regionally accredited institution
     2. Secondary professional education, total semester hours as detailed below...... 22
        a. Supervised teaching and/or teaching internship... 8
        b. A course in methods and materials of teaching in field of specialization.
        c. A course of study regarding education or curricular adaptation for pupils with disabilities.. 3
        d. A course of study regarding parental involvement/family engagement 3
        e. Additional secondary pedagogy courses 8
        f. Check with Department of Education (see Appendix 1) for specific requirements in occupational education.
     or
   C. A person who holds a valid Nevada license to teach elementary education, early childhood education, special education, or secondary education may obtain a license to teach secondary school by passing a subject-matter exam in the area of endorsement the applicant wishes to teach. In such a case, the applicant would not be required to complete additional pedagogy coursework.

III. Professional Secondary License Requirements
   A. Meet all requirements for Standard Secondary License
   B. Hold a master's degree or higher
   C. Have 3 years of verified teaching experience in state-approved secondary schools

IV. Available Secondary Teaching Endorsements
   A. Academic endorsements (comprehensive major/minor): art, biological science, English, general science, instrumental and vocal music, instrumental music, mathematics, physical education, physical education and health, physical science, recreational physical education, social studies, speech and drama, vocal music
   B. Secondary business and industry endorsements: accounting and finance; administrative services; aerospace engineering; agricultural business systems; agricultural leadership; communication and policy; agricultural mechanics technology; animal science; animation; architectural and civil engineering; architectural design; automation technology; automotive service technician; automotive technology; aviation maintenance technician; aviation technology; baking and pastry; biomedical sciences; biotechnology; business management; collision repair technology;

community health science; computer science; construction technology; cosmetology; criminal justice; culinary arts; cybersecurity; dance performance; dental science; diesel technology; digital game development; drafting and design; early childhood education; electrical engineering; electronic technology; emergency medical technician; emergency telecommunication; energy technologies; entrepreneurship; environmental engineering; environmental management; ethnic dance; ethnic music; family and consumer sciences; fashion, textiles and design; fire science; floriculture design and management; food science technology; foods and nutrition; forensic science; furniture and cabinetmaking; graphic design; health information management; hospitality and tourism; human development; information technology for networking; information technology for service and support; interior design; landscape design and management; law enforcement; manufacturing technologies; marketing; mechanical engineering; mechanical technology; medical assisting; metalworking; military science/JROTC; natural resources and wildlife management; nursing assistant; ornamental horticulture and greenhouse management; pharmacy practice; photography; radio production; respiratory science; sports and entertainment marketing; sports medicine; teaching and training; theatre technology; veterinary science; video production; web design and development; welding technology

C. All comprehensive fields of concentration require the following:

1. Majors, semester hours 36
2. Minors, semester hours 24

See the Department of Education website (see Appendix 1) for specific coursework requirements for each listed comprehensive major/minor area of endorsement.

D. Single-subject academic endorsements: anthropology, biology, botany, chemistry, composition and rhetoric, computer science, dance, dramatic or theatrical arts, earth science, economics, English or American literature, environmental science, geography, geology, health education, history of the US and world, journalism and communication, linguistics, physics, physiology, political science, psychology, reading, sociology, speech, world languages, zoology

E. Secondary career and technical education endorsements: accounting and finance; administrative services; aerospace engineering; agricultural business systems; agricultural leadership, communication, and policy; agricultural mechanics technology; animal science; animation; architectural and civil engineering; architectural design; automation technology; automotive service technician; automotive technology; aviation maintenance technician; aviation technology; baking and pastry; biomedical sciences; biotechnology; business management; collision repair technology; community health science; computer science; construction technology; cosmetology; criminal justice; culinary arts; cybersecurity; dance performance; dental science; diesel technology; digital game development; drafting and design; early childhood education; electrical engineering; electronic technology; emergency medical technician; emergency telecommunication; energy technologies; entrepreneurship; environmental engineering; environmental management; ethnic dance; ethnic music; family and consumer sciences; fashion, textiles and design; fire science; floriculture design and management; food science technology; foods and nutrition; forensic science; furniture and cabinetmaking;

graphic design; health information management; hospitality and tourism; human development; information technology for networking; information technology for service and support; interior design; landscape design and management; law enforcement; manufacturing technologies; marketing; mechanical engineering; mechanical technology; medical assisting; metalworking; military science/ JROTC; natural resources and wildlife management; nursing assistant; ornamental horticulture and greenhouse management; pharmacy practice; photography; radio production; respiratory science; sports and entertainment marketing; sports medicine; teaching and training; theatre technology; veterinary science; video production; web design and development; welding technology

F.   All single-subject majors and minors require the following:
1.   Majors, semester hours 30
2.   Minors, semester hours 16

While there are no specific coursework requirements for single-subject endorsements, all coursework taken must be relevant to the endorsement being sought.

Early Childhood Education (Birth–Grade 2)

I.   Standard Early Childhood License Requirements
A.   Bachelor's degree from accredited college or university and completion of a Commission-approved program of preparation for teaching children from birth through grade 2;
or
B.   Bachelor's degree from accredited college or university and completion of the following:
1.   Coursework in early childhood education, semester hours 35
a.   Eight semester hours of supervised student teaching in a program of early childhood education involving children from birth through grade 2. In lieu of completing 8 semester credits of student teaching, an applicant may have 1 year of verifiable experience teaching pupils in a program of early childhood education conducted by a public school, a public agency, or a licensed private school. 8
b.   Twenty-seven hours of coursework in early childhood education for children who are developing typically and atypically, consisting of 3 credits in each of the following, with instruction in assessment and evaluation embedded in all required courses:............................. 27
i.   Child development and learning
ii.   Language and literacy
iii. Mathematics
iv.   Science
v.   Social studies
vi.   Strategies for working with children with disabilities
vii. Classroom management, which must include, without limitation, positive discipline and guidance and social, emotional, and academic development

                  viii. Culturally and linguistically responsive pedagogy
                  viv. Play theory and creativity
        or

C. Hold a current, valid, non-alternative license to teach elementary
    1.   Experience teaching pupils under 6 years of age, consisting of
        a.   Eight semester hours of student teaching;
            or
        b. One year of verifiable experience teaching pupils in a program of early childhood education for a public school, public agency, or licensed private school;
            or
        c.   Equivalent field experience;
            or
        d. A practicum conducted by an accredited college or university;
            and
            At least 6 semester hours of coursework in early childhood education, consisting of courses in any of the following: early childhood curriculum; emergent language and literacy; play theory and creativity;
            and
            At least 6 semester hours of coursework in any of the courses listed directly above, or in any of the following: child development and learning; culturally and linguistically responsive pedagogy; classroom management, which must include, without limitation, positive discipline and guidance and social, emotional, and academic development.

D. Completion of required competency testing as specified on website (see Appendix 1).

II. Professional Early Childhood Education License Requirements
    A. Meet all requirements for Standard Early Childhood Education License
    B. Hold a master's degree or higher
    C. Have 3 years of verifiable teaching experience in state-approved schools

Special Education

Available endorsements on a Special Education License include adaptive physical education, alternative education, autism, early childhood developmentally delayed, generalist, gifted and talented, hearing impairments, intellectual disabilities, orientation and mobility, speech and language impairments, and visual impairments. Contact the Department of Education (see Appendix 1) for more detailed information in this area.

Administration

I. Authorization
    A. An Administrator of a School endorsement is required for the following: superintendent, associate superintendent, assistant superintendent, principal,

vice principal, supervisor, administrative assistant, and program supervisor or coordinator.

    B.   An Administrator of a Program endorsement is required for an individual who supervises or coordinates a program of nursing, school psychology, speech therapy, physical therapy, occupational therapy, or any other program area unless that person holds an Administrator of a School endorsement.

II.   Professional Administrator of a School Endorsement: Must meet requirements A or B below.

    A.   Complete the following:

        1.   Master's degree

        2.   Five years of verified/licensed teaching experience at the K–12 level, or in an early childhood education program, in state-approved schools

        3.   At least 36 semester hours of graduate courses in school administration, to include administration and organization of schools; supervision and evaluation of instruction; development of personnel; school finance; school law; curriculum; educational research; internship or field experience in school administration; and other courses considered to be part of an administrative program for educators

    or

    B.   Hold a master's degree or higher in educational administration from an accredited institution, and have 5 years of verified/licensed teaching experience as per section II, A, above.

III.   Professional Administrator of a Program Endorsement

    A.   Hold a master's degree

    B.   Hold a valid license in program for which endorsement is requested

    C.   Have and submit to Department evidence of 5 years of experience as a licensed employee in early childhood education, kindergarten, or grades 1–12

    D.   Have completed at least 27 semester hours in administration courses (which may not be taken as independent study), to include:

        1.   Administration and organization of a school or the role of a program administrator in the applicant's endorsement area

        2.   General principles of supervision of personnel or supervision of personnel for a program in the applicant's endorsement area

        3.   Finances of a school or finances of a program in the applicant's endorsement area

        4.   The laws that apply to schools

        5.   The evaluation and development of personnel for a school or for a program in the applicant's endorsement area

Other Licensed School Personnel

    I.   Available endorsements: music therapist, reading specialist, school counselor, school library media specialist, school mental health professional, school nurse, school psychologist, school social worker

II.   All endorsements for licensed school personnel are valid for grades K–12. For a list of specific coursework/degree and professional licensure or certification requirements, refer to the Department of Education website (see Appendix 1).

Special Endorsements

I. Available special endorsements: American Sign Language; art; audiological services; bilingual education; computer applications; computer literacy; computer programming; cultural competency; dance; drivers' education; English language acquisition and development (ELAD); foreign language; Great Basin language; JROTC; music; Navajo language and government of the Navajo nation; physical education; reading; social, emotional and academic development (SEAD)

II. For specific coursework/degree requirements for each listed endorsement, refer to the Department of Education website (see Appendix 1).

III. Some special endorsements are valid for grades K–12; others are specific to the level of the applicant's base teaching license. Refer to the Department of Education website for specific information on each endorsement (see Appendix 1).

New Hampshire

Pathways for Licensure for Teachers, Educational and Instructional Specialists, and Administrators

I. Approved Educator Preparation Program (New Hampshire)—approved professional preparation programs in New Hampshire
    A. The New Hampshire State Board of Education approves programs of professional preparation in education and the chairperson of the Education Department of each institution recommends licensure to Credentialing (recommendations valid for 3 years).

II. Approved Educator Preparation Program (Out of State)—for out-of-state graduates of approved professional educator preparation programs or experienced out-of-state educators. Applicant must have:
    A. Graduated from an approved educator preparation program in another state or jurisdiction (recommendations valid for 3 years). Note: If the program was completed more than 3 years prior to application, the applicant must provide documentation of licensure in the endorsement that is within 3 years of its expiration date from the same state in which the program is located.

III. Demonstrated Competencies: Portfolio/Oral Board—This rigorous portfolio and oral examination process is for candidates who have gained the necessary competencies, skills, and knowledge required for licensure in a specific subject area and/or educator role (e.g., teacher, administrator, or specialist) through a means other than the completion of an approved educator preparation program.
    A. To qualify a candidate shall:
        1. Hold at least a bachelor's degree (additional endorsement-specific degrees may be required),
        2. Have met specific prerequisite licensure testing requirements, *and*
        3. Have at least 4 months of full-time continuous educator experience in the area of endorsement for which licensure is being requested (additional endorsement-specific experience may be required).
            a. Educator experience does not have to be acquired in a public school; experience in a private school is acceptable.

IV. Demonstrated Competencies: National or Regional—national/regional licensures, National Board for Professional Teaching Standards, National Association of School Psychologists, or US Department of Defense

V. Demonstrated Competencies: Transcript Analysis—course-by-course transcript review; available only for administrative endorsements

VI. Demonstrated Competencies: Experience—full, valid educator credential based on a bachelor's or higher degree from a state or jurisdiction other than New Hampshire and employment verification as a licensed, full-time, regular teacher for at least 3 out of the last 7 years

VII. Site-Based Licensing Plan—A New Hampshire school employer may hire a candidate who meets eligibility requirements. The employer should submit the candidate's Individualized Professional Development Plan (meeting all the required competencies for licensure) for full licensure.

VIII. Additional endorsement-specific requirements include:
   A. Superintendent
      1. Post-master's degree in educational administration,
         and
      2. Three years of experience as an education administrator in the K–12 setting,
         and
      3. Three letters of recommendation (addressing leadership)
   B. Principal
      1. Master's degree in educational leadership or education,
         and
      2. Five years of full-time experience as an educator,
         and
      3. Three letters of recommendation (addressing leadership)
   C. School Counselor
      1. Master's degree in school counseling, counseling, mental health, psychology, or social work
   D. Special Education Categorical Area
      1. Licensure as special education teacher or early childhood special education teacher
   E. Reading and Writing Specialist
      1. Master's degree in literacy or a related field,
         and
      2. Three years of experience as a classroom teacher
   F. Reading and Writing Teacher
      1. Two years of experience as a classroom teacher
   G. Elementary Education Mathematics Specialist
      1. Master's degree in math, education, or related field,
         and
      2. Three years of classroom teaching experience in mathematics at the K–6 level
   H. Curriculum Administrator
      1. Master's degree in curriculum and instruction or education,
         and
      2. Five years as a classroom teacher
   I. Special Education Administrator
      (Related areas/roles include: special education teacher, speech-language pathologist or specialist, school psychologist, blind and vision impairment, deaf and hard of hearing, specific learning disabilities, intellectual and developmental disabilities, physical and health disabilities, and emotional and behavioral disabilities.)

      1.   Master's degree in special education or related area,
           and

      2.   Five years in special education or related area,
           and

      3.   Three letters of recommendation (addressing leadership)

J.   Career and Technical Education (CTE) Director

      1.   Master's degree in educational leadership or education,
           and

      2.   Three years of experience as a CTE educator,
           and

      3.   Three letters of recommendation (addressing leadership)

IX.   Other endorsement-specific requirements can be found on the New Hampshire Department of Education website.

Licensure rules are subject to revision. To monitor the status of any pending changes, please visit the New Hampshire Department of Education website.

New Jersey

Applicants are strongly advised to consult the New Jersey Licensing Code, available at http://www.state.nj.us/education/code/current/title6a/chap9b.pdf, for specific eligibility requirements for obtaining certificates.

Certification Overview

I. New Jersey certificates are issued under 3 categories; for detailed listings of the many certificates and specific requirements for them, go to https://www.nj.gov/education/license/.
   A. Instructional certificates for classroom teachers, including career and technical education
   B. Administrative certificates for school administrator, principal, supervisor, and school business administrator
   C. Educational services certificates for such positions as school social worker, school psychologist, learning disabilities teacher-consultant, student assistance coordinator, etc.
   D. In addition, the following certificates may be issued when the appropriate requirements have been satisfied:
      1. Emergency certificate: a substandard 1-year license issued only in limited fields of educational services
      2. County substitute credential: a temporary certificate issued by the county office which allows the holder to temporarily perform the duties of a fully licensed and regularly employed teacher when none is available
II. Endorsements
   A. An endorsement is an area of certification with distinct grade-level and subject matter authorizations in which a certificate holder is authorized to serve.
III. Certification Process for Novice Educators
   A. Certificate of Eligibility (CE): for applicants who did not complete a teacher preparation program. Requirements:
      1. Hold a bachelor's or advanced degree from a regionally accredited college or university.
      2. Meet all minimum requirements in N.J.A.C. 6A:9B-5, including, but not limited to, citizenship, minimum age, and examination in physiology, hygiene, and substance abuse requirements.
      3. Achieve cumulative minimum GPA of 3.00 (when 4.00 GPA equals an A grade) in baccalaureate, higher degree, or state-approved post-baccalaureate certification program with at least 13 semester-hour credits.
         a. For students graduating before September 1, 2016, same requirements apply except minimum GPA is 2.75.

      b.   A candidate graduating on or after September 1, 2016, with a GPA that is below 3.00, but at least 2.75, and achieves a score on the appropriate state test of subject matter knowledge that exceeds the passing score by 10 percent or more may be deemed to meet the requirements. For a summary of GPA and score flexibility, visit https://www.nj.gov/education/license/gpa.htm.

      c.   A candidate graduating on or after September 1, 2016, with a GPA that is below 3.00, but at least 2.75, and is sponsored by a provisional training program may be deemed to meet the requirements.

   4.   Satisfy the endorsement requirements and exceptions pursuant to N.J.A.C. 6A:9B-9–11, including, but not limited to, passing the appropriate state test(s) of subject matter knowledge and completing the required subject area course requirements.

   5.   After September 1, 2015, achieve a minimum score on a Commissioner-approved assessment of basic reading, writing, and mathematics skills;

      or

      Achieve a minimum score on the SAT, ACT, or GRE. All minimum scores are established by the New Jersey Department of Education and are available on its website at https://www.nj.gov/education/license/req/Teacher%20Candidate%20Basic%20Skills%20Requirement%20Final%2010.13.21.pdf.

B.   Certificate of Eligibility with Advanced Standing (CEAS): for applicants who did complete a teacher preparation program. Requirements:

   1.   The candidate shall meet the requirements in III, A, 1–5, directly above, and complete 1 of the following programs of teacher preparation:

      a.   A New Jersey college program, graduate or undergraduate, approved by the Department for the preparation of teachers;

      b.   A college preparation program included in the interstate certification reciprocity system of the National Association of State Directors of Teacher Education and Certification (NASDTEC);

      c.   An out-of-state educator preparation program approved by the National Council for the Accreditation of Teacher Education (NCATE), Teacher Education Accreditation Council (TEAC), or any other national professional education accreditation body recognized by the Council on Higher Education Accreditation approved by the Commissioner;

      d.   An educator preparation program approved for certification by the Department in a state party to the NASDTEC Interstate Contract, provided the program was completed on or after January 1, 1964, and the state in which the program is located would issue the candidate a comparable endorsement;

         or

      e.   An out-of-state college teacher education program approved by the state department of education in which the program is located.

   2.   The teacher preparation programs listed in III, B, 1, a–e, directly above, must culminate in college supervised student teaching.

   3.   A candidate who graduates on or after September 1, 2016, will meet the

requirements in III, B, 1, a–e, directly above, if they fall within the parameters in 3, a and b, directly below. For details, consult https://nj.gov/education/license/praxis/GPA%20Flexibility%20Table%20Final.pdf.

    a.   A GPA that is below 3.00, but at least 2.75, and a score in the appropriate state test of subject matter knowledge exceeding the passing score by 10 percent or more;

        or

    b.   A GPA that is 3.50 or higher, and a score in the appropriate state test of subject matter knowledge falling below the passing score by no more than 5 percent;

  4.   Pass a Commissioner-approved performance-based assessment of teaching if graduation date was on or after September 1, 2017.

C.   Standard Certificate Requirements:

  1.   Possess a provisional certificate;

      and

  2.   Successfully complete a state-approved district training program while employed provisionally in a position requiring the appropriate instructional certificate.

  3.   CE holders must also:

    a.   Pass the performance assessment if they did not pass it prior to earning a CE (effective for candidates who begin teaching academic year 2017–2018);

       and

    b.   Complete a CE educator preparation program pursuant to N.J.A.C. 6A:9A–5, unless exempt under the reciprocity rule at N.J.A.C. 6A:9B–8.8.

  4.   Further eligibilities and their restrictions are available at https://www.nj.gov/education/license/.

  5   A candidate who holds National Board of Professional Teacher Standards (NBPTS) Certification and the corresponding out-of-state license or out-of-state certificate shall be eligible for the standard certificate in the NBPTS certificate field without additional requirements.

IV. Provisional Certificate

A.   School-based training and evaluation program provided to all novice teachers during first year of New Jersey teaching. See N.J.A.C. 6A:9B-8.4 for full details.

B.   Building principal recommends standard certification at completion of program requirements.

C.   Both alternatively and traditionally prepared teacher candidates participate and receive support by veteran teachers in their school. Contact Department of Education (see Appendix 1) for full details.

D.   Alternate route candidates complete 400 hours of formal instruction in professional education aligned with New Jersey Professional Standards for Teachers.

E.   Effective academic year 2017–2018, provisional teachers holding a CE with a Preschool–Grade 3 endorsement must complete 400 hours of formal instruction or 24 semester-hour credits pursuant to N.J.A.C. 6A:9A-5.4(a)1.

V. Interstate Reciprocity

A. Through reciprocity, the Certification and Induction Office shall issue an instructional CEAS to candidates who:
   1. Have a valid CEAS issued by another state in a subject area or grade level also offered by the Department, following the completion of a CEAS educator preparation program that includes clinical practice and endorsement in a subject that is also issued in New Jersey;
   2. Passed a subject matter test to receive their out-of-state endorsement or passed the appropriate New Jersey subject matter test;
      and
   3. For candidates who graduated September 1, 2017, and later, passed a performance assessment that is approved by the state in which the certificate was issued, unless the candidate holds National Board for Professional Teacher Standards (NBPTS) or the Meritorious New Teacher Candidate (MNTC) designation.
B. A candidate who meets all requirements in A1 and A2 above but did not take a state-approved performance assessment because it was not required for educator preparation program completion and/or for certification in that state shall be issued a CE.
   1. The candidate shall meet all requirements for provisional and standard certification pursuant to N.J.A.C. 6A:9B-8.4 and 8.7, respectively, but shall be exempt from:
      a. CE certification requirements pursuant to N.J.A.C. 6A:9B-8.3(a);
      b. The provisional certification requirement to be enrolled in a CE educator preparation program pursuant to N.J.A.C. 6A:9B-8.4(a)4;
      c. The renewal of provisional certification requirement to be enrolled in or to have completed a CE educator preparation program pursuant to N.J.A.C. 6A:9B-8.5(b)4;
         and
      d. The standard certification requirement to complete a CE educator preparation program pursuant to N.J.A.C. 6A:9B-8.7(a)4ii.
C. Through reciprocity, the Certification and Induction Office shall issue a standard certificate to candidates who:
   1. Hold valid standard certificate issued by another state;
      and
      demonstrate at least 2 effective years of teaching within 3 consecutive years of the last 4 calendar years, as documented by letter from applicant's supervisor or appropriate district representative;
      or
   2. Hold National Board of Professional Teaching Standards certificate.

Educational Services Certification

For a full listing of available endorsements, authorizations, and related requirements, see the New Jersey Department of Education website at https://nj.gov/cgi-bin/education/license/endorsement.pl?string=Educational%20Services%20Certificates&maxhits=1000&field=1&type=es.

Administrator Certification

I. The requirements for administrative certification for school administrators, principals, supervisors, and school business administrators are defined in N.J.A.C. 6A:9B-12.1–12.8.

II. For more detailed information on available administrative endorsements, authorizations, and related requirements, see the New Jersey Department of Education website at https://nj.gov/cgi-bin/education/license/endorsement.pl?string=Administrative Certificates&maxhits=1000&field=1&type=sl.

New Mexico

Note: As of September 1, 2020, applicants for licensure who need to meet the testing requirements must obtain passing scores on the required Praxis tests. For more information regarding the transition to Praxis, the required tests for each license, and passing scores, consult https://webnew.ped .state.nm.us/bureaus/licensure/.

Routes to Initial Teacher Licensure

I. Option 1—Approved Program
   A. Possess a bachelor's and/or master's degree from a regionally accredited college or university;
   B. Complete an approved educator preparation program that includes student teaching; *and*
   C. Pass the Praxis tests required or possess a valid certificate issued by the National Board for Professional Teaching Standards (NBPTS).

II. Option 2—Reciprocity
   A. Possess a bachelor's and/or a master's degree from a regionally accredited college or university;
   B. Possess a current valid and standard certificate/license from another state or country, or possess a valid certificate issued by the NBPTS.
   C. Provide proof of having completed an approved teacher education program (if the program is not contained on a transcript, provide documented evidence of the program completed);
   D. Provide copies of test scores for exams required to receive an out-of-state or out-of-country license; *and*
   E. Provide evidence of having satisfactorily taught under the out-of-state certificate or license from the school and/or supervisor where taught.

III. Option 3—Alternative Licensure
   A. Possess a bachelor's degree, including 30 semester hours in a particular field, *or*
      Possess a master's degree, including 12 graduate semester hours in a particular field, *or*
      Possess a doctorate degree in a particular field;
   B. Pass the Praxis tests required; *and*
   C. Complete an approved alternative program through an accredited New Mexico college or university; *or*
      Complete the Online Portfolio (OPAL).

Endorsements for Teaching License

I. An endorsement is a teaching field on a teaching license.

II. Endorsements available are visual arts; technology education; health; physical education; library media; gifted; psychology; social studies; language arts; reading; Teachers of English to Speakers of Other Languages (TESOL); science; information technology coordinator; business education; mathematics; modern, classical, and native language; bilingual education; family and consumer science; agriculture; and performing arts.

III. General endorsement requirements: submit an endorsement application with transcripts reflecting:

    A. A minimum of 24 semester hours of credit in the endorsement area, plus the exam for beginning teachers (teaching field):

        1. An elementary license requires 6 hours in upper division, while a special education license requires 12 hours in upper division;
            or

        2. Provide proof of having passed a content knowledge assessment in the endorsement area (the teaching field).

        3. Core subject areas—language arts, social studies, science, and mathematics—are available as endorsements if middle-level content exam(s) are passed.

IV. Detailed requirements for adding each endorsement to a teacher license are available at https://webnew.ped.state.nm.us/bureaus/licensure/adding-endorsements/.

Licenses

I. Level 1 Elementary License (valid 5 years)

    A. Requirements

        1. Bachelor's degree from a regionally accredited college or university;

        2. Minimum of 30–36 semester hours in an elementary education program including student teaching;

        3. Six semester hours of credit in the teaching of reading for those who first entered any college or university on or after August 1, 2001;

        4. Minimum of 24 semester hours in 1 teaching field, such as mathematics, science, language arts, etc.;
            and

        5. Passage of the Praxis tests:

            a. Core Academic Skills for Educators: Reading, Writing, and Mathematics;

            b. Principles of Learning and Teaching: Grades K–6;

            c. Elementary Education: Curriculum, Instruction, and Assessment; and

            d. Teaching Reading: Elementary;
            or

        Possess a certificate issued by the National Board for Professional Teaching Standards.

II. Level 1 Middle Level Education, Grades 5–9 (valid 5 years)

    A. This license authorizes individuals to teach in a departmentalized setting.

        1.   Individuals must be endorsed in the subject they are teaching.

    B.   Requirements for Option I:

        1.   Bachelor's degree from a regionally accredited college or university;

        2.   Minimum of 30–36 semester hours in a middle level education program, including student teaching;

        3.   Three semester hours of credit in teaching reading for those who first entered any college or university on or after August 1, 2001;

        4.   Minimum of 24 semester hours in at least 1 teaching field such as mathematics, science, language arts, etc., with 12 of those hours earned at the upper-division level (300 and above);
           and

        5.   Passage of the Praxis tests:

           a.   Core Academic Skills for Educators: Reading, Writing, and Mathematics;

           b.   Principles of Learning and Teaching: Grades K–6, or Principles of Learning and Teaching: Grades 7–12; and

           c.   One of the Content Assessments for first endorsement on the license (plus coursework).

    C.   Requirements for Option II:

        1.   Possess a New Mexico elementary, secondary, PreK–12 specialty, or special education license;

        2.   Provide verification of 5 years of successful teaching experience at the middle school level;

        3.   Complete a minimum of 24 semester hours of credit in each subject the teacher teaches, 6 of which must be upper-division credit;
           and

        4.   Pass the Praxis test in each subject the teacher teaches;
           or
           Possess a certificate issued by the National Board for Professional Teaching Standards.

III.   Level 1 Secondary Education, Grades 6–12 (valid 5 years)

    A.   This license authorizes individuals to teach in a departmentalized setting.

        1.   Individuals must be endorsed in the subject they are teaching.

    B.   Requirements

        1.   Bachelor's degree from a regionally accredited college or university;

        2.   Minimum of 24 semester hours in a secondary education program, to include student teaching;

        3.   Three semester hours of credit in teaching reading for those who first entered any college or university on or after August 1, 2001;

        4.   Minimum of 24 semester hours in at least 1 teaching field, such as mathematics, science, language arts, etc., with 12 of those hours earned at the upper division level (300 and above);
           and

        5.   Passage of the Praxis tests:

           a.   Core Academic Skills for Educators: Reading, Writing, and Mathematics;

           b.   Principles of Learning and Teaching: Grades 7–12; and

      c.   One of the Content Assessments for first endorsement on the license (plus coursework);

or

Possess a certificate issued by the National Board for Professional Teaching Standards.

IV.   Educational Administration, PreK–12 Program

    A.   Bachelor's and master's degree from a regionally accredited college or university;

    B.   Minimum of 18 semester hours of graduate credit in an educational administration program;

    C.   Completion of an administrative apprenticeship/internship at a college/university or under the supervision of a local superintendent;

    D.   Hold a Level 2 or 3A New Mexico teaching license;

and

    E.   Pass the content knowledge assessment in educational administration.

V.   Approved licenses. For comprehensive requirements for each license not detailed above, consult https://webnew.ped.state.nm.us/bureaus/licensure/how-to-apply/.

    A.   Administrators

       1.   Education administration, PreK–12

    B.   Teachers

       1.   Blind and visually impaired, birth–12; birth–3 early childhood; birth–PreK; PreK–3; elementary, K–8; middle level, 5–9; PreK–12 specialty; secondary, 6–12; secondary vocational-technical, 7–12; special education, PreK–12

    C.   Instructional support providers (PreK–12 unless otherwise noted)

       1.   Alcohol, drug, and substance abuse counselor; certified occupational therapy assistant; educational diagnostician; interpreter for the deaf; licensed practical nurse; occupational therapist; orientation and mobility specialist; physical therapist; physical therapist assistant; recreational therapist; rehabilitation counselor; school counselor; school nurse; school psychologist; school social worker; speech-language pathologist; speech-language pathologist fellow; speech-language pathologist apprentice; audiologist

    D.   Support providers (PreK–12 unless otherwise noted)

       1.   Athletic coaching, 7–12; educational assistant; health assistant; substitute teacher

VI.   Alternative licenses. For comprehensive requirements, consult https://webnew.ped.state.nm.us/bureaus/licensure/.

VII.   Three-Tiered Licensure Systems

    A.   Three-tiered licensure system is designed to attach base salaries to each level of teaching licenses, and it includes annual evaluation and licensure advancement.

    B.   The Professional Development Dossier (PDD) is the cornerstone of advancement for teachers in the 3-Tiered Licensure System.

       1.   Teachers must complete the PDD in order to advance from Level 1 to Level 2 and to advance from Level 2 to Level 3. To complete the dossier, teachers must register (and obtain guided instruction) at TeachNM at https://webnew.ped.state.nm.us/bureaus/licensure/dossier-and-opal/educator-resources-for-completing-the-dossier-or-opal/.

          a.   They must have the approval of their district.

New York

Types of Certificates

I. Initial Certificate (valid 5 years)
   A. Entry-level certificate issued in specific subject areas and grade levels for classroom teaching and educational leadership
   B. A Conditional Initial Certificate (valid 1 year; nonrenewable; leads to Initial Certificate) may be issued to applicants who hold a valid teaching certificate from another US state or territory in the subject area of the New York State certificate title sought, have completed an out-of-state teacher preparation program comparable with a New York State teacher preparation program, and have completed all Initial Certificate requirements except for the edTPA.
II. Internship Certificate (valid up to 2 years; nonrenewable while applicant is matriculated in a teacher education, school leadership, or school counseling program and completing the internship requirement)
   A. Issued to a student at least halfway through a New York State–registered and approved graduate teacher education, school leadership, or school counseling program
III. Professional Certificate (valid continuously)
   A. Certificate holders must register and successfully complete 100 clock hours of acceptable Continuing Teacher and Leader Education (CTLE) during each 5-year registration period.
   B. Advanced-level certificate issued in specific subject areas and grade levels for classroom teaching and educational leadership
IV. A full listing of other certificates, including Supplementary Certificates and Transitional Certificates, is available at http://www.highered.nysed.gov/tcert/certificate/typesofcerts .html.

Certification Pathways

Links to detailed requirements for each certification pathway are available at http://eservices.nysed .gov/teach/certhelp/CertRequirementHelp.do.

I. Approved Teacher Preparation Program—for high school and college graduates:
   A. Complete a New York State–registered teacher preparation program;
   B. Pass the appropriate New York State certification exams—see Testing, below; *and*
   C. Complete appropriate workshop requirements.
II. Individual Evaluation—for career changers, persons educated outside of the United States, and persons not graduated from a teacher preparation program that leads to state certification:

A. Earn a bachelor's degree with a GPA of at least 2.5;

B. Satisfy semester-hour requirements in liberal arts and sciences general core, content core, and pedagogical core competencies for the area of the certificate title sought;

C. Pass the appropriate New York State certification exams—see Testing, below;

D. Student teach or gain paid teaching experience for at least 40 days in the area of the certificate title sought;
   and

E. Complete appropriate workshop requirements.

III. Alternative Teacher Preparation Program ("Transitional B" Program)—for career changers, college graduates:

A. Possess a bachelor's degree (minimum 3.0 GPA) with an academic major, or 30 semester hours, in the subject area of the certificate title sought, of which 12 semester hours can be in a related subject area;

B. Enroll in a New York State–registered Transitional B program;

C. Complete appropriate workshop requirements;

D. Pass the appropriate New York State certification exams—see Testing, below;
   and

E. For the Initial Certificate, complete the Transitional B program, hold the Transitional B Certificate, and pass the edTPA in the area of the certificate title sought.

IV. National Board Certification—for teachers certified by the National Board for Professional Teaching Standards (NBPTS):

A. Hold a valid NBPTS certificate in the area of the certificate title sought;
   and

B. Complete appropriate workshop requirements.

V. Interstate Reciprocity—for certified teachers from other states who meet requirements in either A or B. For list of acceptable out-of-state certificates, see http://www.highered .nysed.gov/tcert/certificate/levelcert.html.

A. Initial Certificate

1. College Teacher Education Program (outside New York)

   a. Complete a comparable, approved teacher preparation program, in the subject area of the certificate title sought, at a college in another US state or territory, that leads to an institutional recommendation for certification in the state in which the college is located;

   b. Possess a bachelor's or higher degree with a 2.5 cumulative GPA;

   c. Pass the appropriate New York State certification exams—see Testing, below;
      and

   d. Complete appropriate workshop requirements.
   or

2. Endorsement of Certificate

   a. Possess a valid, comparable US state or territory certificate in the subject area of the certificate title sought;

   b. Have 3 years of teaching experience out of the last 7 years, completed in a public school while holding a valid certificate in the subject area of the certificate title sought;

       c.   Have evaluation ratings of Effective or Highly Effective for the teaching experience;

       d.   Possess a bachelor's or higher degree with a 2.5 cumulative GPA; *and*

       e.   Complete appropriate workshop requirements.

   B.   Conditional Initial Certificate (valid 1 year, during which time applicant must complete the appropriate edTPA; see Testing, below)

       1.   Meet the requirements for A1, above, with the exception of the edTPA, enabling individuals to complete the edTPA during the 1-year certificate validity period; *and*

       2.   Possess a valid, comparable US state or territory certificate in the subject area of the certificate title sought.

VI.   Additional Certificate—for New York State–certified teachers seeking additional certificates:

   A.   Possess a valid New York State classroom teaching certificate;

   B.   Satisfy the content core requirements and the pedagogical coursework for the certificate title sought;

   C.   Pass the appropriate New York State Content Specialty Test(s) (CSTs); *and*

   D.   Complete appropriate workshop requirements.

VII.   Supplementary Certificate—for New York State–certified teachers seeking to teach another subject area while completing requirements for the Initial Certificate in that subject area:

   A.   Possess a valid New York State classroom teaching certificate;

   B.   Satisfy the 9 or 12 semester-hour content core requirements, depending on the certificate title sought;

   C.   Obtain a recommendation from the employing school district; *and*

   D.   Pass the appropriate New York State Content Specialty Test(s) (CSTs).

VIII.   New York State Initial Certificate—for New York State–licensed speech-language pathologists:

   A.   Hold a New York State speech-language pathology license and be registered in the profession; *and*

   B.   Complete appropriate workshop requirements.

IX.   Transitional G Certificate—for college professors with appropriate credentials and experience:

   A.   Possess a master's or higher degree in the subject area of the certificate title sought;

   B.   Have completed 2 years of satisfactory teaching experience at the college level in the subject area of the certificate title sought within the past 10 years;

   C.   Obtain a recommendation from the employing school district; *and*

   D.   For the Initial Certificate, pass the Educating All Students Test and complete the pedagogical core (6 undergraduate semester hours, 4 graduate semester hours, or 2 years' experience under the Transitional G Certificate).

Testing

For full details of required examinations, see http://www.highered.nysed.gov/tcert/certificate/certexam.html.

I. Individuals seeking a teaching certificate must achieve qualifying scores on a set of assessments determined by the certificate title.
    A. Candidates who are certified by the NBPTS in the area of the certificate title sought are not required to take any certification exams.
    B. Candidates who meet the requirements for the Endorsement of a Certificate pathway are not required to take any certification exams.

North Carolina

Licensure Categories

I. Initial Professional License (intended for teachers with 0–2 years of teaching experience; valid 3 years). Applicant must have:
  - A. Completed an approved educator preparation program (EPP) from a regionally or nationally accredited college or university;
    or
    Completed another state's approved alternative route to licensure;
    and
  - B. Earned at least a bachelor's degree from a regionally or nationally accredited college or university.

II. Continuing Professional License (intended for teachers with 3 or more years of teaching experience; valid 5 years). Issued to teachers who:
  - A. Have 3 or more years of teaching experience;
    or
  - B. Have 3 or more years of experience in another state and are fully licensed in another state,
    and
    1. Meet North Carolina's State Board of Education (NCSBE)–required licensure exam(s) (consult https://www.dpi.nc.gov/educators/educators-licensure)
       or
    2. Have passed, at a satisfactory level, another state's licensure exam that the North Carolina Department of Public Instruction has determined is comparable to North Carolina's assessment
       or
    3. Have certification from the National Board for Professional Teaching Standards (NBPTS),
       and
    4. Demonstrate evidence of effectiveness by evaluation data, including student growth (where applicable), from the state in which the current license is held.

III. Residency License—replaces the Lateral Entry License per NC GS 115C-270.20(a)(5). This alternative pathway license is issued for 1 year in a teaching area, with the option to renew twice, within no longer than a 3-year period. All requirements to convert a Residency License to either an Initial Professional License or Continuing Professional License must be completed before the expiration of the second renewal of the Residency License.
  - A. Issued at the request of an employing school system to applicant who meets the following:
    1. Holds at least a bachelor's degree;
    2. Has either completed 24 hours of coursework in the requested licensure area

or passed the NCSBE-required content area examination(s) for the requested licensure area; ·

3. Is enrolled in a recognized EPP with a minimum GPA of 2.7 (see exceptions for GPA requirement in NCSBE Policy TCED-009);
   and

4. Meets all other requirements established by the NCSBE, including completing pre-service requirements prior to teaching.

B. To renew a Residency License for the second or the third year, the local education agency (LEA) must verify that the license holder:

1. Taught at least 6 calendar months, as defined in Section 1.20 of NCSBE Policy LICN-001, during the prior school year;

2. Continued enrollment with an EPP;

3. Remained employed as a teacher in an LEA;
   and

4. Completed 10 days of required professional development (in the first year of the Residency License).

C. Individuals must complete all requirements, pass NCSBE-required licensure testing requirements, and receive the recommendation of an EPP to convert the Residency License to the Initial or Continuing Professional License within 3 years of the effective date of the Residency License.

IV. Emergency License—a 1-year, nonrenewable license issued to an individual who:

A. Holds a bachelor's degree with 18 hours of coursework relevant to the requested license area, but has not completed a recognized educator preparation program,
   and

B. Does not qualify for the Residency License.

C. All other NCSBE requirements must be met, including pre-service teacher training.

Licensure Renewal

I. Continuing Professional License must be renewed every 5 years.

II. Requirements to renew the Continuing Professional License:

A. NBPTS Certification

1. Eight credits for completion; 2 credits for renewal

B. Renewal Credits: Credits required for renewal differ based on the date of the license expiration. For the most accurate information, consult NCSBE Policy LICN-005.

C. Definition and equivalencies

1. One unit of renewal credit is equivalent to 1 quarter hour, or 1 in-service credit from a North Carolina public school system, or 10 contact/clock hours of professional development.

2. One semester hour is equivalent to 1.5 units of renewal credit.

D. Exclusions and restrictions

1. For a professional educator's license to remain current, all credit must be earned by the expiration date of the existing professional educator's license.

    2.   To renew an expired professional educator's license, 8 units of renewal credit must be earned within the most recent 5-year period.

III. Activities accepted for renewal credit:
- A. College or university courses
  - 1. Official transcripts are required as documentation; grade reports and unofficial transcripts are not accepted.
- B. Local in-service courses or workshops
  - 1. The administrative unit certifies credits.
- C. Classes and workshops approved by the school system
  - 1. Documentation of completion is provided by the agency sponsoring the activity.

IV. Credits required for licenses expiring on or after June 30, 2019:
- A. Grades K–5: 3 subject area; 3 literacy; 2 digital learning competencies
- B. Grades 6–12: 3 subject area; 2 digital learning competencies; 3 general
- C. Student Services Personnel: 3 professional discipline area; 2 digital learning competencies; 3 general
- D. Administrators: 3 executive's role; 2 digital learning competencies; 3 general
- E. As a condition of employment per NCSBE Policy LICN-005, LEAs reserve the right to assign literacy requirements for any educator.

Administrators/Special Service Personnel

I. Requirements for administrators, special service, and instructional support personnel
- A. Obtain a valid Continuing Professional License
- B. Student services personnel who have completed an approved EPP
  and
  - 1. Have satisfied NCSBE-approved testing requirements are issued a Continuing Professional License.
  - 2. Have not satisfied NCSBE-approved testing requirements are issued an Initial Professional License.
    - a. Special service personnel who are issued the Initial Professional License must attempt their NCSBE-required licensure exams in the first year of the license and pass the exam before or during the third year of the license.
    - b. When North Carolina's testing requirements are satisfied, the license is converted to a Continuing Professional License.
- C. Student services personnel who are fully licensed in another state and have 3 or more years of student services school experience in another state will be issued the Continuing Professional License when they:
  - 1. Meet NCSBE-required licensure exams,
    or
  - 2. Earn National Board Certification,
    or
  - 3. Provide evidence of successfully passing a comparable state-approved licensure exam(s) in the state where they completed their EPP.

License Areas and Requirements

I. School Administrator—Superintendent
    A. Must hold both the North Carolina principal's license (master's level or above) *and*
    B. Superintendent's license at the advanced graduate level (6th-year degree or doctorate) issued under the authority of the NCSBE.

II. School Administrator—Principal
    A. Completion of an approved program in school administration at the master's level or above
    B. No provisional principal license is issued for service as a principal.

III. School Administrator—Assistant Principal
    A. Completion of an approved program in school administration at the master's level or above
    B. Provisional principal license is issued for service as an assistant principal if the local board determines there is a shortage of individuals with principal licensure.
    C. Affiliation with a master's school administrator program must occur before the expiration of the provisional license. Provisional principal licenses shall be issued for 3 school years, during which time program requirements must be completed.

IV. Curriculum Instructional Specialist
    A. Completion of an approved program for a curriculum instructional specialist at the master's level or above
    B. NTE/Praxis Educational Leadership: Administrative and Supervision required score

V. Career-Technical Education Director
    A. Completion of an approved program for a career-technical education director at the master's level or above

VI. Exceptional Children Program Administrator (licensure is a supervisory classification)
    A. Master's degree in an exceptional children area or an advanced (6th-year) degree in school psychology;
        and
        Three graduate semester hours of credit in each of the following:
        1. Administration,
        2. Curriculum development, and
        3. Supervision;
        and
        NTE/Praxis Educational Leadership: Administrative and Supervision required score.
        or
    B. A master's degree in administration and/or curriculum instruction,
        and
        Nine semester hours of coursework in exceptional children,
        and
        NTE/Praxis Educational Leadership: Administrative and Supervision required score.

VII. Instructional Technology Specialist—Computers
    A. Completion of an approved college or university program in instructional technology specialist (computers) at the master's level or above

VIII. Instructional Technology Specialist—Telecommunications
    A. Completion of an approved college or university program in instructional technology specialist telecommunications at the master's level or above
  IX. Media Supervisor
    A. Master's degree in school media
    B. Three graduate semester hours in each of the following:
      1. Administration
      2. Curriculum development
      3. Supervision
    C. Required testing: NTE/Praxis Educational Leadership: Administrative and Supervision (for details, consult http://www.ets.org/praxis/nc)
  X. Media Coordinator
    A. One of the following:
      1. Completion of an approved program for a media coordinator at the master's level or above
        or
      2. Completion of an approved program after July 1, 1984, allows a provisional license upon employment with requirement to update to master's level
        or
      3. Obtain a provisional media coordinator license (for details, consult https://www.dpi.nc.gov/educators/educators-licensure/licensure-administrators-and-student-services)
    B. Required testing: NTE/Praxis Library Media Specialist (for details, consult http://www.ets.org/praxis/nc)
  XI. School Counselor
    A. Completion of an approved program in school counseling at the master's level or above
    B. NTE/Praxis Professional School Counselor test required score
  XII. School Social Worker
    A. Completion of an approved program in school social work at the bachelor's level or above
XIII. School Psychologist
    A. Completion of an approved program in school psychology at the 6th-year level or above
    B. NTE/Praxis School Psychology required score
XIV. School Speech-Language Pathologist
    A. Current valid North Carolina Board of Examiners for Speech and Language Pathologists and Audiologists (NCBOESLPA) license
  XV. School Audiologist—currently under review for NCSBE policy revisions.

North Dakota

North Dakota teachers are licensed by the state Education Standards and Practices Board (ESPB), while administrators and other school personnel are licensed by the state Department of Public Instruction (DPI).

Types of Licenses

I. North Dakota Century Code Authority
   A. Individual must hold valid North Dakota license issued by the North Dakota ESPB in order to be permitted or employed to teach in any state public school.
   B. Nonpublic schools must employ licensed teachers to be approved and in compliance with compulsory attendance laws.

II. Licensure Level
   A. Level I indicates that individual still has educational or employment requirements to meet before receiving regular Level II license, or that they are not currently maintaining contracted employment.
   B. Level II indicates that individual has met all basic requirements for regular North Dakota Educators' Professional License.
   C. Level III indicates that individual has earned advanced degrees beyond bachelor's level (master's, specialist, or doctoral) or National Board for Professional Teaching Standards (NBPTS) advanced licensure.

III. Types of Educator's Licenses and Procedures
   A. Forty-Day Provisional: Issued to applicants who have been offered a job and have completed entire application process with exception of background investigation. Letter from school administrator indicating desire to issue contract without background investigation being complete and letter from applicant indicating any criminal background history are needed by ESPB prior to issuing this license.
   B. Initial License (valid 2 years): Issued to first-time applicants who have met all state requirements for licensure
   C. Regular (valid 5 years): Issued to individuals who have met all requirements for a state Educator's Professional License and have successfully taught for 18 months (full-time equivalent) in state
   D. Alternate License (valid 1 year): Issued in documented shortage area. License is initiated by letter from local school administrator indicating search for qualified applicant and desire for this license to be issued. Requirements include:
      1. School's request letter and successful background check
      2. Bachelor's degree in appropriate content area
      3. Plan of study from college of education where applicant will complete 8 semester hours each year toward teaching degree

E. Out-of-State Reciprocal (valid 2 years, can be renewed once): Issued to individuals who do not hold valid license from another state and have not met this state's standards and rules. Plan of study is developed for each individual indicating coursework needed. Individual has 4 years to complete all requirements.

F. Other State Educator's License (OSEL; valid 2 years or 5 years): Issued to individuals who hold a valid license from another state, have met that state's testing requirements, and have completed a traditional teacher education program.

G. Additional types of educator's licenses and procedures. For full details, consult http://www.nd.gov/espb/licensure/license-information/types-licenses.
    1. Two-Year Renewal
    2. Interim/Substitute (2 years)
    3. Re-Entry (2 years)
    4. Probationary (2 years)
    5. Minor Equivalency Endorsement
    6. Kindergarten Endorsement
    7. Major Equivalency Praxis Endorsement
    8. Thirty-Year Life License

Elementary School

I. North Dakota Educator's Professional License
    A. Bachelor's degree from an accredited college approved to offer teacher education
    B. Professional requirements, credits in professional education, including student teaching, overall grade point average of 2.5, 34 semester hours
    C. Valid for 2 years for teaching in the level of preparation
    D. A 5-year renewal may be issued with 2 years of successful full-time teaching experience in the state. Each renewal of the 5-year license requires 6 semester hours of work.
    E. Submission of PPST/Praxis I/Core Academic Skills for Educators scores in reading, writing, and mathematics that meet or exceed North Dakota cut scores
    F. Submission of Praxis II content and pedagogy test scores that meet or exceed North Dakota cut scores
    G. Background investigation, including Bureau of Criminal Investigation and the FBI

Secondary School

I. North Dakota Educator's Professional License
    A. Same as Elementary School, I, A–G
    B. Thirty-two semester hours

Superintendent (Regulated by State DPI)

I. Provisional Credential
    A. Valid until the end of the second school year following the year in which the provisional credential is issued; not renewable

B.   Issued as the initial credential to an individual who does not meet the qualifications for a professional credential
C.   Issued to those who have a Level I principal's credential but lack the superintendent coursework, the experience, or both that are necessary for the superintendent professional credential
D.   Applicant must fulfill all the following standards:
   1.   Hold a valid North Dakota teaching license during the life of the credential
   2.   Have at least 3 years of teaching experience, verified in a letter of recommendation by a supervisor or employer who has firsthand knowledge of the individual's professional work
   3.   Have at least 2 years of administrative experience comprising at least half-time as an elementary or secondary principal, a central office administrator, or an administrator of an approved school with a 12-year program. This experience is to be verified by a supervisor or employer who has firsthand knowledge of the individual's professional work.
   4.   Complete the requirements for the Level I elementary or secondary principal credential and 8 additional hours of designated coursework specific to the superintendency (see state DPI, Appendix 1)
II.   Professional Credential
A.   Issued to coincide with the period for which the individual is licensed to teach by the ESPB and may be renewed. An individual holding a lifetime Educator's Professional License must renew the credential every 5 years.
   and
B.   Issued upon satisfying credential standards; see I, D, 1–4, directly above.
III.   Renewal Requirements
A.   Applicant must fulfill 1 of the following:
   1.   Provide a copy of official transcripts showing satisfactory completion of at least 8 semester hours of graduate work in education, of which 4 semester hours are in the area of educational administration;
      or
   2.   Provide a copy of official transcripts showing satisfactory completion of at least 4 semester hours of graduate work and verification of attendance or participation in at least 6 administrative educational conferences or workshops from a state-approved list with specific verification.

Secondary Principal (Regulated by State DPI)

I.   Provisional Credential
A.   Issued as the initial credential to an individual who does not meet the qualifications for a Level I professional credential; valid until the end of the third school year following the year in which the provisional credential is issued; the provisional credential can be renewed once for 2 additional school years, provided that the individual has completed 20 credits of their master's degree program and, if employed as a principal, has participated in the principal mentoring program.

B. Issued to a person enrolled in a state-approved program in educational leadership who has submitted 3 letters of recommendation, 1 of which must come from a supervisor, stating that the individual has demonstrated leadership competency.

C. Issued upon satisfying the following credentials standards with specific verification of each:

1. Valid North Dakota Educator's Professional License issued by the ESPB
2. At least 3 years of teaching or administrative experience (as defined by DPI Administrative Rules) or a combination thereof in grades 5–12:
   a. Equal to full-time equivalency as defined by the North Dakota Century Code.
   b. Positions must have been stated on a professional contract.

II. Level I Professional Credential

A. Issued to coincide with the period for which the individual is licensed to teach by the ESPB and may be renewed at the end of that period. An individual holding a lifetime Educator's Professional License must renew their credential every 5 years.
   and

B. Issued upon satisfying the following credentials standards:

1. See I, C, 1 and 2, directly above.
2. The Level I credential requires 1 of the following:
   a. Master's degree in educational administration from a state-approved program, including an internship specific to grades 5–12;
      or
   b. Master's degree with a major certifiable by the ESPB in addition to 20 semester hours of credit that include designated courses specific to the secondary level contained within a master's degree in educational administration from a state-approved program, including an internship specific to grades 5–12.

III. Renewal Requirements

A. To renew the Level I professional credential, an individual shall submit 1 of the following:

1. A copy of official transcripts of 8 semester hours of graduate work in education acquired after the date of the original credentialing or last renewal, of which 4 semester hours are in the area of educational administration;
   or
2. A copy of official transcripts of 6 semester hours of graduate work in education acquired after the date of the original credentialing or last renewal and verification of attendance or participation in at least 6 educational conferences or workshops from a designated list with specific verification.

Elementary Principal (Regulated by State DPI)

I. Provisional Credential

A. Issued as the initial credential to an individual who does not meet the qualifications for a Level I professional credential; valid until the end of the third school year following the year in which the provisional credential is issued; the provisional credential can be renewed once time for 2 additional school years, provided that the individual has completed 20 credits of their master's degree program and, if employed as a principal, has participated in the principal mentoring program.

B. Issued to a person enrolled in a state-approved program in educational leadership who submitted 3 letters of recommendation, 1 of which must come from a supervisor, stating that the individual has demonstrated leadership competency.

C. Issued upon satisfying the following credentials standards with specific verification of each:
1. A valid North Dakota teaching license issued by the ESPB
2. At least 3 years of teaching or administrative experience (as defined by DPI Administrative Rules) or a combination thereof in grades K–8:
   a. Equal to full-time equivalency as defined by the North Dakota Century Code.
   b. Positions must have been stated on a professional contract.

II. Level I Professional Credential

A. Issued to coincide with the period for which the individual is licensed to teach by the ESPB. An individual holding a lifetime Educator's Professional License must renew their credential every 5 years.
and

B. Issued upon satisfying the following credential standards:
1. See I, C, 1 and 2, directly above.
2. The Level I credential requires 1 of the following:
   a. Master's degree in educational administration that includes designated coursework specific to the elementary level from a state-approved program, including an internship specific to grades K–8,
   or
   b. Master's degree with a major certifiable by the ESPB in addition to 20 semester hours of credit that includes designated courses specific to the elementary level contained within a master's degree in educational administration from a state-approved program, including an internship specific to grades K–8.

III. Renewal Requirements

A. To renew the Level I professional credential, an individual must submit 1 of the following:
1. A copy of official transcripts of 8 semester hours of graduate work in education acquired after the date of the original credentialing or last renewal, of which 4 semester hours are in the area of educational administration;
   or
2. A copy of official transcripts of 6 semester hours of graduate work in education acquired after the date of the original credentialing or last renewal and verification of attendance or participation in at least 6 educational conferences or workshops from a designated list with specific verification.

K–12 Principal Credential (Regulated by State DPI)

The K–12 principal credential is issued to any individual who meets the requirements of both the elementary and secondary principal credentials. These individuals must complete an internship at both the elementary and secondary level. Individuals who hold the K–12 principal credential may serve as principal for any combination of grades K–12.

School Counselor (Regulated by State DPI)

I. School Counselor Credentials
    A.   Credential designations: SC03 for grades PreK–12
    B.   Credential is valid only while the individual holds a North Dakota Educator's Professional License or a professional school counseling restricted license.
        1.   A credential must be renewed each time the individual's Educator's Professional License is renewed.
        2.   Holders of a lifetime North Dakota Educator's Professional License must renew the credential every 5 years.
        3.   To renew the credential, submit a copy of college transcripts documenting 4 semester hours of graduate coursework in education, of which 2 semester hours must be in counseling.
            a.   Two semester hours of required counseling coursework may be replaced by 30 clock hours of continuing education hours in counseling with a signed verification of attendance or participation by the conference or workshop sponsor, the employer, or a school district business manager.
    C.   SC03 credential standards—counselor must:
        1.   Hold a valid Educator's Professional License from the state Education Standards and Practices Board;
            and
        2.   Have a master's degree in counseling, education, or a related human service field and the following graduate core counseling coursework content from a state-approved school counseling program:
            a.   Elementary school counseling;
            b.   Secondary school counseling;
            c.   Supervised school counseling internship consisting of a minimum of 450 contact hours, of which at least 150 are at both the elementary and secondary level;
            d.   Counseling program management;
            e.   Counseling theories;
            f.   Assessment techniques;
            g.   Group counseling;
            h.   Career counseling and assessment;
            i.   Social and multicultural counseling;
            j.   Ethics and law;
             and

      k.   Counseling techniques.

  D. If a school is unable to employ a credentialed counselor, the school may employ a licensed teacher to serve as the counselor on a plan of study. Contact DPI for details at 701–328–2244.

Library Media (Regulated by State DPI)

Contact the Department of Public Instruction (see Appendix 1) for a detailed listing of required coursework, official application forms, and instructions.

  I. Librarian (LM03)
    A. Valid North Dakota Educator's Professional License
    B. Complete coursework in library media from a state-approved program as detailed in Subsection 1 of Section 67–11–04–05, 15 semester hours*
    C. Validity Length
      1. Valid only while the individual holds a valid North Dakota Educator's Professional License
      2. Must be renewed each time professional license is renewed; 2 graduate semester hours in library media and information science from a state-approved program
        a. Individual holding a lifetime North Dakota Educator's Professional License must renew the credential every 5 years.

  II. Library Media Specialist (LM02)
    A. Valid North Dakota Educator's Professional License
    B. Complete coursework in library media from a state-approved program as detailed in Subsection 1 of Section 67–11–04–05, 15 semester hours*
      Subsection 2 of Section 67–11–04–05, 9 semester hours*
    C. See I, C, directly above.

  III. Library Media Director (LM01)
    A. Master's degree in library science, media education, education, or educational administration from a state-approved program
    B. Valid North Dakota Educator's Professional License (based on bachelor's degree with a licensable major or minor or an endorsement in elementary, middle-level, or secondary education)
    C. Complete coursework in library media from a state-approved program as detailed in Subsection 1 of Section 67–11–04–05, 15 semester hours*
      Subsection 2 of Section 67–11–04–05, 9 semester hours*
      Subsection 3 of Section 67–11–04–05, 6 semester hours (graduate in school library or school administration)

  IV. Plan of Study Option to qualify for library media director, library media specialist, or librarian credentials
    A. If a school is unable to employ a credentialed librarian, the school may employ a licensed teacher to serve as librarian if the licensed teacher has completed at least 6 semester hours in library media coursework and has submitted a written plan of study showing at least 6 graduate or undergraduate semester hours in library media coursework to be completed annually until credential is earned.

    B.   Once plan is approved, the licensed teacher must document a minimum of 6 semester hours of library media coursework each year until qualified for required credential

V.   Renewal Requirements (LM03, LM02, LM01): All are renewed by submitting application form and documenting completion of 2 semester hours of graduate credit in library media and information science.

*graduate or undergraduate

Ohio

Ohio's standards are performance-based and lead to licensing based on assessments (administered under the authority of the State Board of Education) of the performance of teachers during their participation in the Ohio Resident Educator Program. Applicants for any license or permit must complete both an Ohio and an FBI criminal background check, conducted by the Bureau of Criminal Identification and Investigation. For full details, consult Educator Licenses at education .ohio.gov.

Resident Educator

I. Resident Educator License (valid 4 years)—for applicants seeking initial teaching license:
   A. A degree required by license
   B. Evidence of good moral character
   C. Successful completion of an approved program of preparation
   D. Recommendation by dean or head of teacher education at institution approved to prepare teachers
   E. Successful completion of Ohio Assessments for Educators (OAE) examination in content and professional knowledge, or equivalent out-of-state licensure exam for out-of-state applicants
      1. For world languages, the American Council on the Teaching of Foreign Languages (ACTFL) Oral Proficiency Interview and Writing Proficiency Test are also required.
   F. Completed coursework in teaching of reading, 12 semester hours
      1. For early childhood, primary, middle childhood, and intervention specialist licenses, at least 1 separate 3-semester-hour course in teaching of phonics is required.
      2. For multi-age and adolescence to young adult licenses, 3 semester hours in teaching of reading are required.
   G. Individuals who have completed licensure programs at colleges/universities outside of the state of Ohio apply to the Ohio Office of Educator Licensure (see Appendix 1).
   H. Beginning March 1, 2020, applicants seeking a new 4- or 5-year teaching license in 1 of the following areas must pass the Ohio Assessment for Educators Foundations of Reading (OAE 090) test:
      1. Early childhood education (grades PreK–3)
      2. Primary (PreK–5)
      3. Primary Intervention Specialist (PreK–5)
      4. Middle childhood education (grades 4–9)

5. Intervention specialist: mild/moderate, moderate/intensive, hearing impaired, visually impaired, or gifted

6. More information can be found at http://education.ohio.gov/Topics/Teaching/Licensure/Prepare-for-Certificate-License/FAQs-about-Foundations-of-Reading-Test-Requirement.

II. Alternative Resident Educator License (valid 4 years)—provides an accelerated pathway to classroom teaching. To enroll in an approved Alternative Resident Licensure Program, candidates must:

A. Request an alternative resident educator evaluation;

B. Hold a bachelor's degree with a GPA of 2.5 or higher or a master's degree with a GPA of 3.0 or higher from an accredited institution of higher education;

C. Successfully complete the OAE examination in content;

   1. For world languages, the American Council on the Teaching of Foreign Languages (ACTFL) Oral Proficiency Interview and Writing Proficiency Test are also required.

D. Successfully complete the Intensive Pedagogical Training Institute (IPTI) or an Alternative Resident Educator Institute (AREI) approved by the Chancellor of the Ohio Department of Higher Education.
   and

E. Complete mandatory background checks by the FBI and the Ohio Bureau of Criminal Identification and Investigation.

F. To advance to a 5-year professional license, applicants must:

   1. Complete 4 years of successful teaching experience under the alternative educator license;

   2. Complete 12 semester hours of specific professional education coursework from a college or university approved in teacher preparation
      or
      Complete a Professional Development Institute approved by the Ohio Department of Higher Education;

   3. Complete a 3-semester-hour course in the teaching of reading in the content area for all subject areas *except* integrated language arts and intervention specialist licensure areas, which require successful completion of at least 6 semester hours in the teaching of reading, including at least 1 separate 3-semester-hour teaching of phonics course (*please note* that the reading coursework requirement is separate from the professional education requirement listed above);

   4. Successfully complete the OAE examination in content and professional knowledge;
      and

   5. Complete all components of the Ohio Resident Educator Program.

Professional Licenses

I. Professional Teacher License (valid 5 years)—for applicants who already hold an Ohio teaching license but wish to seek licensure in a new area. For more information and a list

of license areas, visit http://education.ohio.gov/Topics/Teaching/Licensure/Apply-for
-Certificate-License/Educator-License-Types-and-Descriptions.

    A. Baccalaureate degree

    B. See I, Resident Educator License, B, C, and E, above.

Professional Pupil Services Licenses

I. Professional Pupil Services License (valid 5 years)

    A. Evidence of good moral character

    B. Completion of an approved program of preparation for orientation and mobility specialist, school audiologist, school counselor, school nurse, school psychologist, school social worker, or school speech-language pathologist

    C. Recommendation by dean or head of teacher education

    D. Completion of examination prescribed by the State Board of Education, if applicable

    E. Other professional pupil personnel license areas include occupational therapist and physical therapist. Please consult Educator Licenses at education.ohio.gov for details.

Professional Administrator Licenses

I. Professional Administrator License

    A. Evidence of good moral character

    B. Master's degree

    C. Recommendation by dean or head of teacher education at institution approved to prepare teachers

    D. Successful completion of an educational leadership examination prescribed by the State Board of Education

II. License Areas

    A. Principal License

        1. Successful completion of an approved preparation program for principal licensure.

        2. Valid for working with

            a. Ages 3–12 and grades PreK–6

            b. Ages 8–14 and grades 4–9

            c. Ages 10–21 and grades 5–12

        3. A principal must have 2 years of successful teaching experience with students of the ages and grade levels for which the principal license is sought.

        4. Alternative Principal License—Ohio offers various alternative pathways to licensure for principals, detailed here: http://education.ohio.gov/Topics/Teaching/Licensure/Resident-License-Options/Alternative-Principal-License.

    B. Administrative Specialist License

        1. Valid for working in central office or supervisory capacity

        2. Prior to issuance, applicant must have completed 2 years of successful teaching experience under professional teacher's license and must have successfully completed approved program of preparation.

3. Alternative Administrative Specialist License—Ohio offers various alternative pathways to licensure for administrative specialists, detailed here: http://education.ohio.gov/Topics/Teaching/Licensure/Resident-License-Options/Alternative-Administrative-Specialist-License.

C. Superintendent License
1. Prior to issuance, applicant must have completed 3 years of successful experience in position requiring principal or administrative specialist license and must have successfully completed approved preparation program for superintendents.
2. Alternative Superintendent License—Ohio offers various alternative pathways to licensure for superintendents, detailed here: http://education.ohio.gov/Topics/Teaching/Licensure/Resident-License-Options/Alternative-Principal-License.

Oklahoma

For the most current certification information, refer to the Oklahoma State Department of Education (OSDE) website at https://sde.ok.gov/teacher-certification.

Traditional Licensure and Certification

I. Standard Teaching License (valid 5 years, renewable)
    A. Requirements for licensure
        1. Graduate from an accredited institution of higher education that has an approved teacher education program for the certification area sought
        2. Successfully complete a higher education teacher education program approved by the Office of Educational Quality and Accountability (OEQA) or a state-approved program from a non-Oklahoma college (signed form required)
        3. Meet all other requirements as established by the Oklahoma State Board of Education (OSBE)
        4. Successfully complete the 3 required competency examinations:
            a. Oklahoma General Education Test (OGET)
            b. Oklahoma Subject Area Test(s) (OSAT)
            c. Praxis Professional Assessment (PPAT)
        5. Have on file with the OSBE current fingerprint-based criminal history record searches from both the Oklahoma State Bureau of Investigation (OSBI) and Federal Bureau of Investigation (FBI)
        6. Apply for certification and pay the appropriate processing fee
    B. Requirements for applicants who hold a full teaching credential from another state
        1. Apply for certification and pay the appropriate processing fee
        2. Provide official transcripts of highest degree earned
        3. Submit the Proof of Teaching form and copies of all out-of-state teaching certificates (not required for obtaining certification, but submission is encouraged)
        4. Applicants with a full teaching credential from another state who meet the above requirements are eligible for certification in Oklahoma in subject areas equivalent to the out-of-state credential they hold.
II. Standard Teaching Certificate (valid 5 years, renewable)
    A. Additional subjects may be added to the certificate by testing: contact Teacher Certification for details (see Appendix 1).
        1. As of November 1, 2009, traditionally certified early childhood, elementary, and special education teachers and teachers alternatively certified through the Troops to Teachers program may add special education areas by testing only. All other applicants must complete a full university program, receive a

recommendation from the certification officer at the university, and pass the appropriate subject area test.

2. Applicants for specialist certification (library media specialist, school counselor, school psychometrist, school psychologist, speech-language pathologist, and reading specialist) must complete a full university program, receive a recommendation from the certification officer at the university, and pass the appropriate subject area test.

III. Administrator Certificate
  A. Principal Standard Certificate (valid 5 years, renewable)
    1. Hold a standard master's degree
    2. Complete an Oklahoma-approved building-level leadership skills program in education administration
    3. Achieve a passing score on the Principal Comprehensive Assessment
    4. Complete 2 years of successful teaching experience in an OSBE-accredited Oklahoma public or private school
  B. Superintendent Standard Certificate (valid 5 years, renewable)
    1. Hold principal certification or completion of a building-level leadership skills program in education administration that is state approved and includes a standard master's degree
    2. Achieve a passing score on the Superintendent Comprehensive Assessment
    3. Complete an Oklahoma-approved district-level leadership skills program in educational administration
    or
    Have completed an Oklahoma-approved master's degree program in education administration between July 1, 2005, and August 25, 2012
    4. Complete 2 years of successful administrative experience in an OSBE-accredited Oklahoma public or private school
  C. Alternative Administrator Credential for Principal or Superintendent (valid 3 years, nonrenewable)
    1. Hold a standard master's degree
    2. Complete 2 years of relevant work experience in a supervisory or administrative capacity
    3. Achieve passing scores on the required administrator assessment
    4. Have on file with the director of teacher education at an Oklahoma-accredited institution of higher education (IHE) a declaration of intent to earn standard certification through completion of an approved alternative administrative preparation program within 3 years.
      a. OSDE will issue a standard certificate upon successful completion of the alternative administrative preparation program.

Alternative Routes to Teaching

I. Alternative Placement Program
  A. Provides an opportunity for individuals with nonteaching degrees to teach in Oklahoma-accredited schools.

B. Eligibility requirements
   1. Baccalaureate degree from an accredited college/university recognized by the Oklahoma State Regents for Higher Education (OSRHE) and a retention GPA of 2.5 or higher
      or
      Baccalaureate degree from an accredited college/university recognized by the OSRHE plus 2 years of postbaccalaureate work experience relevant to the desired certification area
      or
      Terminal degree (PhD, EdD, MD, DO JD, etc.) recognized by the United States Department of Education
   2. A master's degree is required to be licensed as a school counselor, reading specialist, or library media specialist.
C. Applicants must demonstrate competency in a field that corresponds to the area of specialization they seek. See the Oklahoma Alternative Placement Program Education Application for a list of eligible certification areas. Competency is demonstrated by providing documentation of 1 of the following:
   1. Academic major in a field that corresponds to a certification area (30 or more relevant credit hours on a higher education transcript)
   2. Academic minor (15 or more relevant credit hours on a higher education transcript) plus at least 1 year of qualified work or volunteer experience verified by a reference relative to the minor or 15 credit hours
   3. At least 3 years of relevant work or volunteer experience, plus a written recommendation from an employer or volunteer coordinator
   4. Publication of a relevant article in a peer-reviewed academic or trade journal
   5. Other documentable means of demonstrating competency, subject to approval of the OSDE
D. Once approved to seek an alternative license, applicant must:
   1. Complete the OGET and OSATs required for the area of approval
   2. Have on file with the OSBE current approved OSBI and FBI criminal history fingerprint checks
E. Once the OSDE issues an Alternative Initial License, applicant must within 3 years pass the PPAT and complete a professional education component.
   1. The professional education component is determined at the time of review. However, all applicants must complete a college course addressing classroom management and a college course addressing pedagogy. Once requirements have been met, a standard teaching certificate may be applied for with the appropriate application and fee.
II. Additional Alternative Certificates
   A. Oklahoma also offers alternative certificates in the following programs; contact the OSDE (see Appendix 1) for full details.
      1. CareerTech Instructor Certification
      2. Troops to Teachers
      3. Four-Year-Olds and Younger Certificate

4. Oklahoma Title I Paraprofessional Teaching Credential (Teaching Assistant)
5. Career Development Program for Paraprofessionals
6. Non-Traditional Special Education Certification Program
7. American Board for Certification of Teacher Excellence (ABCTE)
8. Teach for America

Oregon

In July 2015, Oregon began a phased-in approach to a complete redesign of licensure terminology and requirements. That redesign is complete for teaching and administrator licenses and the work on personnel services licenses was completed during 2021 and implemented in January of 2022. Please contact the Oregon Teacher Standards and Practices Commission (TSPC) (see Appendix 1) for the most current information, which is also available at https://www.oregon.gov/tspc.

Teaching Licenses

I. Preliminary Teaching License (valid 3 years), issued to new teachers who have completed a Commission-approved teacher preparation program. Note: If you completed an out-of-state teacher preparation program, you must first apply for the Reciprocal Teaching License. Applicants for the Preliminary Teaching License must:
    A. Be at least 18 years old
    B. Hold a bachelor's degree or higher from a regionally accredited institution or a foreign equivalent
    C. Complete a Commission-approved teacher preparation program (official verification of completion is required)
    D. Pass a subject matter test for the applicant's teaching content area(s) if necessary
    E. Pass the required Protecting Student and Civil Rights in the Educational Environment exam*
    F. Pass a criminal background clearance, including fingerprints, if necessary
II. Professional Teaching License (valid 5 years), issued to experienced teachers who have successfully demonstrated an advanced level of educator knowledge, skills and dispositions. Applicants for this license must:
    A. Hold an Oregon Preliminary, Reciprocal, Basic, Initial or Initial II Teaching License
    B. Have 4 full years or more of full-time teaching experience or 6 full years of teaching experience in a .50 FTE or greater teaching assignment
    C. Pass a criminal background clearance, including fingerprints, if necessary
    D. Complete 1 of the following advanced professional education programs. Exceptions: Applicants who currently hold an Initial II, Continuing, Standard or Basic Teaching License do *not* need to complete an advanced professional education program.
        1. Advanced Professional Development Program: New teachers work with their school districts to design a program to complete at least 150 Professional Development Units (PDUs) of advanced professional development specifically tailored to their performance goals as novice teachers.
        2. Advanced Degree Program: Complete any advanced degree program reasonably related to improving an educator's teaching skills (e.g., a master's degree in the applicant's content area)
        3. Endorsement Program: Complete a Commission-approved program to add new

subject matter areas (e.g., English for Speakers of Other Languages [ESOL], Elementary Education, Music, etc.)

4. Specialization Programs: Complete a program to add new specialized areas (e.g., Bilingual, TAG, Dual Language, Autism, American Sign Language, etc.)
5. Advanced Licensure Program: Teacher Leader, School Counselor, School Psychology, School Social Worker, Administrator, or Professional Teaching licensure programs
6. National Board of Professional Teaching Standards Certification

III. Reciprocal Teaching License (valid 1 year; nonrenewable), issued to teachers who have completed an educator preparation program and hold an active and valid nonprovisional teaching license from another state. Applicants for this license must:

A. Hold a valid and active nonprovisional teaching license from another state
B. Never have held an Oregon educator license or charter school registration nor have completed an Oregon educator preparation program
C. Hold a bachelor's degree or higher from a regionally accredited institution or foreign equivalent
D. Have completed an approved out-of-state teacher preparation program (official verification of completion required)
E. Pass a criminal background clearance, including fingerprints, if necessary
F. Prior to the expiration of the Reciprocal License, apply for and meet the requirements for a Preliminary or Professional Teaching License, including:
   1. Qualifying for an Oregon endorsement by receiving a passing score on Oregon-approved subject matter tests (unless applicant qualifies for reciprocity or waiver of subject matter tests as provided in OAR 584–220–0015)
   2. Passing the required Protecting Student and Civil Rights in the Educational Environment exam*

IV. Restricted Teaching License (valid 1 year; renewable twice), issued to qualified individuals who have at least a bachelor's degree and who have substantial preparation in the subject matter in their teaching area, but have not completed a teacher preparation program. Note: Applicants who have failed to complete an Oregon teacher preparation program are not eligible. Applicants for this license must:

A. Have a letter of sponsorship provided by the employing school district directly to the Teacher Standards and Practices Commission
B. Be at least 18 years old
C. Never have previously held a Restricted Teaching License
D. Hold a bachelor's degree or higher from a regionally accredited institution or foreign equivalent
E. Provide evidence of substantial preparation or work experience in the requested teaching area
F. Pass the required Protecting Student and Civil Rights in the Educational Environment exam*
G. Pass a criminal background clearance, including fingerprints, if necessary

V. Substitute Teaching License (valid 3 years), issued to educators who have completed a teacher preparation program but do not hold a regular Oregon teaching license. Applicants for this license must:

A. Hold a bachelor's degree or higher from a regionally accredited institution or foreign equivalent

B. Have a valid and active nonprovisional teaching license from another state
or
Have completed an Oregon teacher preparation program that resulted in eligibility for a nonprovisional Oregon teaching license

C. Pass the required Protecting Student and Civil Rights in the Educational Environment exam (not required for applicants who have ever held an Oregon Basic or Standard Teaching License or have ever successfully taken and passed the exam)*

D. Pass a criminal background clearance, including fingerprints, if necessary

VI. Other teaching licenses and registrations available in Oregon include American Indian Languages Teaching License; Career and Technical Education Licenses (Restricted CTE, Preliminary CTE, Professional CTE); Charter School Teacher Registration; Emergency Teaching License; International Visiting Teacher License; Legacy Teaching License; License for Conditional Assignment; Limited Teaching License; Restricted Substitute Teaching License; and Teacher Leader License. For information on the requirements for obtaining these licenses, contact TSPC (see Appendix 1).

Teaching Authorizations

All licenses are authorized in grades PreK–12. Limits on what licensees can teach are controlled by the endorsement(s) held and the National Center for Education Statistics (NCES) course codes associated with the endorsement(s).

Subject Matter Endorsements

I. Teachers must receive the currently specified passing score on each of 1 or more tests of subject mastery for license endorsement.

A. Oregon Educator Licensure Assessments (ORELA) exams in advanced mathematics, art, biology, general business, chemistry, Chinese, , elementary education, English, English for Speakers of Other Languages (ESOL), family and consumer sciences, foundational English language arts for middle grades, foundational mathematics for middle grades, foundational science for middle grades, foundational social studies for middle grades, French, German, health, integrated science, library media, music, physical education, physics, social studies, Spanish, special education

B. Praxis/ETS exams in agriculture, early intervention, hearing impaired, marketing, reading, speech communication, technology education, vision impaired

C. Since there are no Praxis exams in drama, Latin, Russian, and Japanese, contact TSPC (see Appendix 1) for requirements.

Personnel Licenses

I. School Counselor License (valid 3 years), issued to educators who have completed a school counselor preparation program and hold a master's degree. Applicants for this license must:

A. Hold a bachelor's degree or higher from a regionally accredited institution or foreign equivalent
B. Hold a master's or higher degree in counseling, education, or related behavioral sciences from a regionally accredited institution or foreign equivalent
C. Have completed an initial program in school counseling as part of the master's degree or separately in an approved school counseling program
D. Pass the required Protecting Student and Civil Rights in the Educational Environment exam*
E. Pass a criminal background clearance, including fingerprints, if necessary

II. Professional School Counselor License (valid 5 years), issued to school counselors who possess advanced school counseling preparation and experience. Applicants for this license must:
A. Meet all requirements for the Preliminary School Counselor License
B. Hold a master's or higher degree in the behavioral sciences or their derivative therapeutic professions from a regionally accredited institution or foreign equivalent
C. Have completed an initial graduate program in school counseling
D. Have 5 years of school counseling experience at least half-time or more on any nonprovisional license appropriate for the assignment
E. Pass a criminal background clearance, including fingerprints, if necessary
F. Demonstrate minimum school counselor competencies by completing 1 of the following:
    1. An advanced program in counseling competencies in a Commission-approved professional school counselor program
    2. Validation of all advanced counseling competencies through assessment by a Commission-approved professional development program offered by an institution, an employer, or the two working together
        or
        A doctoral degree in educational, vocational, or clinical counseling; or in clinical or counseling psychology from a regionally accredited institution or foreign equivalent

III. Reciprocal School Counselor License (valid 1 year; nonrenewable), issued to qualified applicants who have held an out-of-state school counselor license or who have completed an out-of-state program in school counseling. Applicants for this license must:
A. Hold a nonprovisional school counselor license from another state
B. Never have held an Oregon educator license or charter school registration nor have completed an Oregon educator preparation program
C. Hold 1 of the following: a master's or higher degree in counseling, education, or related behavioral sciences from a regionally accredited institution or foreign equivalent
D. Pass a criminal background clearance, including fingerprints, if necessary
E. Apply for and meet the requirements for a Preliminary School Counselor License before the Reciprocal School Counselor License expires

IV. Restricted School Counselor License (valid 1 year; renewable 4 times), issued to qualified individuals who have a bachelor's degree and are admitted to a school counselor preparation program. Applicants for this license must:

    A.   Have a letter of sponsorship from the employing school district, provided by the sponsoring district directly to TSPC

    B.   Hold a bachelor's degree or higher from a regionally accredited institution or foreign equivalent

    C.   Never have held a Restricted School Counselor License

    D.   Meet 1 of the following qualifications:

        1.   Be enrolled in a school counselor program approved for school counseling licensure by any state

        2.   Have been a full-time certified child development specialist (CDS) for at least 3 academic years

           or

           Have a master's degree in a counseling-related field

        3.   Pass the required Protecting Student and Civil Rights in the Educational Environment exam*

        4.   Pass a criminal background clearance, including fingerprints, if necessary

V.   Other personnel licenses and certificates available in Oregon include: Emergency School Counselor License; Emergency School Nurse; Emergency School Social Worker; Limited Student Service; School Psychologist; School Social Worker; Professional School Nurse; Professional School Psychologist; Professional School Social Worker; Reciprocal School Psychologist; Reciprocal School Social Worker; and Restricted School Social Worker. For information on the requirements for obtaining these licenses, contact TSPC (see Appendix 1).

Administrative Licenses

I.   Principal License (valid 3 years), issued to educators who have completed a principal preparation program and hold a master's degree. It is valid for work as a building-level administrator. Applicants for this license must:

    A.   Have 3 full years of full-time or 6 full years of half-time or more experience as a full-time licensed educator

    B.   Hold a master's or higher degree in the arts and sciences or an advanced degree in the profession from a regionally accredited institution or a foreign equivalent

    C.   Complete, as part of the master's degree or separately, an initial graduate program in school administration at an institution approved for administrator education

    D.   Complete course on Oregon school law and finance or demonstrate equivalent competency (Oregon program completers automatically meet this requirement, as the course is embedded into all approved Oregon administrator programs.)

    E.   Pass the required Protecting Student and Civil Rights in the Educational Environment exam*

    F.   Pass a criminal background clearance, including fingerprints, if necessary

II.   Professional Administrator License (valid 5 years), issued to educators who have completed an initial administrator preparation program and have advanced preparation beyond a master's degree. The license is required for work as a district-wide administrator. Applicants for this license must:

A. Hold a master's or higher degree in the arts and sciences or an advanced degree in the profession from a regionally accredited institution or a foreign equivalent

B. Have 3 full years of full-time or 6 full years of half-time or more experience on any administrator license appropriate for the assignment in a public or accredited private school setting

C. Complete, beyond the master's degree, an advanced program in administrative competencies consisting of at least 18 semester hours or 27 quarter hours of graduate credit or the equivalent in school administration or educational leadership.

D. Pass a criminal background clearance, including fingerprints, if necessary

III. Reciprocal Administrator License (valid 18 months; nonrenewable), issued to educators who have completed an out-of-state administrator preparation program and are licensed as a school administrator in another state. Applicants for this license must:

A. Hold a valid and active nonprovisional license for school administration from another state

B. Never have held an Oregon educator license or charter school registration nor have completed an Oregon educator preparation program

C. Hold a master's or higher degree in the arts and sciences or an advanced degree in the profession from a regionally accredited institution or foreign equivalent

D. Pass a criminal background clearance, including fingerprints, if necessary

E. Apply for and meet the requirements for a Preliminary or Professional Administrator License before the Reciprocal Administrator License expires, including the following:
   1. Complete an Oregon school law and finance course
   2. Pass the required Protecting Student and Civil Rights in the Educational Environment exam*

IV. Restricted Administrator License (valid 1 year; renewable twice), issued to qualified individuals who have at least a master's degree and who have substantial administrative preparation but have not completed an administrator preparation program. Applicants for this license must:

A. Have a letter of sponsorship from the employing school district, provided by the district directly to TSPC

B. Hold a master's or higher degree in the arts and sciences or an advanced degree in the profession from a regionally accredited institution or a foreign equivalent

C. Never have held a Restricted Administrator License

D. Pass the required Protecting Student and Civil Rights in the Educational Environment exam*

E. Provide official transcripts and other evidence of substantial completion of academic preparation or substantial work experience in administration

F. Pass a criminal background clearance, including fingerprints, if necessary

V. Other administrative licenses and registrations available in Oregon include Charter School Administrator Registration and Emergency Administrator License. For information on the requirements for obtaining these licenses, contact TSPC (see Appendix 1).

*Note: At the beginning of the COVID-19 pandemic, the Protecting Student and Civil Rights in the Educational Environment exam was suspended due to limited availability of testing centers. As of January 1, 2022, the requirement remains suspended, eliminating the need for the Reciprocal License in some instances.

By law, applicants must demonstrate knowledge of Title VI of the Civil Rights Act of 1964, Title IX of the Education Amendments of 1972, and other relevant federal and state statutes prohibiting discrimination, as well as ethical standards of professional conduct for licensees. The Commission is working to create a new assessment to assure that each applicant has met this statutory requirement and expects to reinstate the requirement during 2022.

Pennsylvania

Level I Certification

I. Instructional and Educational Specialist I (valid 6 years of service; nonrenewable)
    A. Hold a bachelor's degree and complete an approved education preparation program in the area requested with a cumulative grade point average of 3.0 on a 4.0 scale.
    B. Receive the recommendation of the preparing entity.
    C. Meet all Pennsylvania testing requirements.
        1. All applicants must take the Pennsylvania tests required for certification unless they hold National Board for Professional Teaching Standards Certification.
        2. Applicant should consult the www.education.pa.gov website for testing information (see Appendix 1).
    D. Meet citizenship and good moral character requirements.
II. Career and Technical Instructional I (valid 8 years of service; nonrenewable)
    A. Minimum of 2 years of wage-earning experience in addition to the learning period required to establish competency in the occupation to be taught.
    B. Successful completion of the occupational competency examination or evaluation of credentials for occupations where examinations do not exist.
    C. Eighteen credit hours in an approved program of career and technical teacher education.
        1. For Career and Technical I certificates issued on or after January 1, 2013, the 18 credit hours must include the equivalent of at least 3 credits in accommodations and adaptations for diverse learners in an inclusive setting.
    D. Receive the recommendation of the preparing entity.
    E. Present evidence of satisfactory achievement on the assessment of basic skills. Consult the www.education.pa.gov website for testing information (see Appendix 1).
    F. Meet citizenship and good moral character requirements.
III. Administrative I: Principal PK–12 (valid 5 years of service; nonrenewable) or Administrative: Career and Technical Director (valid 99 years)
    A. Hold a bachelor's degree.
    B. Complete 3 years of professional experience in an educational setting related to the instructional process.
    C. Complete an approved graduate-level education preparation program including an internship in the area requested with a cumulative grade point average of 3.0 on a 4.0 scale.
    D. Receive the recommendation of the preparing entity.
    E. Meet testing requirements listed on the www.education.pa.gov website (see Appendix 1).
    F. Meet citizenship and good moral character requirements.
IV. Administrative Provisional (valid 5 years of service; nonrenewable)
    A. Hold a bachelor's degree.

    B.   Complete 3 years of professional experience in an educational setting related to the instructional process.

    C.   Verification of an employment offer from a Pennsylvania public school, specifically for a position as a principal, vice principal, assistant principal, or vocational administrative director.

    D.   Meet citizenship and good moral character requirements.

    E.   Must complete additional education and testing requirements within the first 2 years of employment.

V. Supervisory (valid 99 years)

    A.   Hold a bachelor's degree.

    B.   Complete 5 years of satisfactory service relevant to the area for which the Supervisory certificate is sought.

        1.   Supervisor Pupil Personnel Services requires certified education specialist service.

        2.   Supervisor Curriculum & Instruction requires certified instructional service.

    C.   Complete an approved education preparation program including an internship in the area requested with a cumulative grade point average of 3.0 on a 4.0 scale.

    D.   Receive the recommendation of the preparing entity.

    E.   Meet testing requirements listed on the www.education.pa.gov website (see Appendix 1).

    F.   Meet citizenship and good moral character requirements.

VI. Career and Technical Supervisor (valid 99 years)

    A.   Complete 3 years of satisfactory certified vocational teaching experience.

    B.   Complete an approved graduate-level education preparation program including an internship in the area requested with a cumulative grade point average of 3.0 on a 4.0 scale.

    C.   Receive the recommendation of the preparing entity.

    D.   Meet testing requirements listed on the www.education.pa.gov website (see Appendix 1).

    E.   Meet citizenship and good moral character requirements.

Level II Certification

I. Instructional Certificates

    A.   Complete 3 years of satisfactory service on a Level I certificate.

    B.   Complete a Pennsylvania Department of Education–approved induction program for educators initially certified on or after June 1987.

    C.   Meet credit requirements:

        1.   Educators must provide evidence of 24 semester-hour post-baccalaureate credits.

        2.   Effective September 1, 2011, educators issued a Level I certificate after September 22, 2007, must earn at least 6 post-baccalaureate credits of collegiate study in the area(s) of certification and/or designed to improve professional practice as part of the 24 post-baccalaureate credits requirement. See CSPG No. 7 on the www.education.pa.gov website (see Appendix 1) for details.

D. All instructional areas of certification simultaneously convert to a Level II certificate.

II. Education Specialist Certificates
A. Educators must provide evidence of 24 semester-hour post-baccalaureate credits.
B. Complete 3 years of satisfactory service on the Level I certificate.
C. Complete a Pennsylvania Department of Education–approved induction program for certificates issued on or after September 1, 2001.
D. Most educational specialist areas of certification must be independently converted to a Level II certificate when all requirements are met.

III. Career and Technical Instructional Certificates
A. Effective July 1, 2018, educators holding a Career and Technical Instructional Level I certificate may be recommended for Level II certification by their Pennsylvania-approved preparatory entity after completing a total of 42 semester-hour credits earned in Career and Technical I programs, including:
1. At least 6 credits, or 180 hours, or an equivalent combination thereof, regarding accommodations and adaptations for students with disabilities in an inclusive setting; and
2. At least 3 credits, or 90 hours, or an equivalent combination thereof, in teaching English-language learners.
B. Requires a minimum of 3 years of satisfactory service in Pennsylvania in any occupational competency area(s) for which the certificate was issued.
C. Requires completion of a Pennsylvania Department of Education–approved induction program.
D. Meet testing requirements listed on the www.education.pa.gov website (see Appendix 1).
E. All career and technical areas of certification will simultaneously convert to a Level II certificate provided all requirements are met.

IV. Administrative and Supervisory Certificates
A. Educational requirements
1. The holders of Administrative certificates issued in accordance with regulations established prior to September 1999 and who have served in the capacity of principal, assistant principal, or vice principal in a Pennsylvania public school prior to January 1, 2008, have no additional educational requirements for Level II.
2. Educators granted Administrative certificates prior to January 1, 2008, but who are employed for the first time in a position of principal, assistant principal, or vice principal in a Pennsylvania public school on or after January 1, 2008, must complete the Principal's Induction Program within 5 years of service to retain the certificate.
3. An Administrative (principal) certificate issued on or after January 1, 2008, requires the completion of an approved Principal's Induction Program. No individual may serve as principal, vice principal, or assistant principal on an Administrative I certificate for more than 5 service years in Pennsylvania public schools.
4. Supervisory certificates have no additional educational requirements.

    B.   Service requirements
        1.   Administrative I and Supervisory I certificates issued in accordance with regulations established prior to September 1, 1999, are made permanent by completion of 3 years of satisfactory service in Pennsylvania in each Administrative/Supervisory certificate area.
        2.   Administrative and Supervisory certificates issued in accordance with September 1, 1999, regulations are valid for 99 years.
        3.   Administrative I certificates issued in accordance with Act 45 of 2007 require 3 years of satisfactory Administrative I service in Pennsylvania.

V.   Program Specialist Certificate
    A.   Program Specialist certificates do not have a Level II. Their validity is tied to a Pennsylvania Instructional certificate.
        1.   Service on a Program Specialist certificate is creditable toward the experience requirements for Level II Instructional certification. This service is charged against the period of validity of the Level I Instructional certificate.
        2.   Once an educator has completed 3 years of combined satisfactory service on the Instructional certificate and/or Program Specialist certificate and has satisfied all educational requirements for Level II certification, the educator may convert the prerequisite Level I Instructional certificate to a Level II certificate.
    B.   Program Specialist certificates issued to candidates completing an out-of-state program that is not tied to a Level I Instructional certificate are valid for 99 years.

Types of Certificates

I.   Instructional Certificates
    A.   Elementary: Grades PK–4; Grades 4–8 with a concentration in English, mathematics, science and/or social studies.
    B.   Secondary Grades 7–12: Citizenship Education; Communication; Computer Science; Cooperative Education; English; Marketing (Distributive) Education; Mathematics; Safety/Driver Education; Biology; Chemistry; Earth and Space; General Science; Physics; Social Studies.
    C.   Grades PK–12 certificates: Agriculture; American Sign Language; Arabic; Art Education; Business, Computer and Information Technology; Chinese; Environmental Education; Family and Consumer Science; French; German; Greek; Health Education; Health and Physical Education; Hebrew; Hindi; Italian; Japanese; Latin; Library Science; Marketing (Distributive) Education; Music Education; Portuguese; Reading Specialist; Russian; Spanish; Special Education: Hearing Impaired; Special Education: PK–12; Special Education: Speech/Language Impaired; Special Education: Visually Impaired; Technology Education.

II.   Educational Specialist certificates (PK–12): Dental Hygienist; Elementary and Secondary School Counselor; Home and School Visitor; Instructional Technology Specialist; School Nurse; School Psychologist; School Social Worker; School Speech-Language Pathologist.

III.   Supervisory certificates (PK–12 unless otherwise indicated): Curriculum and Instruction;

Pupil Personnel Services; Career and Technical Education (7–12); Single Instructional Area and Pupil Service Areas.

IV.   Administrative certificate: Principal (PK–12); Career and Technical Administrative Director (7–12); Administrative Provisional I (PK–12).

V.   Letter of Eligibility (PK–12): Superintendent; Intermediate Unit Executive Director.

VI.   Career and Technical certificate (7–12): See www.education.pa.gov for a complete list of subjects.

Rhode Island

I. A three-tiered certification system provides multiyear certificates that demonstrate the educator has met all Rhode Island requirements for certification. This applies to educators who have worked all years of their certification cycle.
   A. Initial Educator Certificate (valid 3 years; renewable). Held by all educators when they are certified for the first time in Rhode Island.
   B. Professional Educator Certificate (valid 5 years; renewable). Awarded to holders of Initial Educator Certificates after completing required professional learning units while working under their certificate.
   C. Advanced Educator Certificate (valid 7 years; renewable). Held by educators who meet 1 aspirational benchmark identified by RIDE (Rhode Island Department of Education) and complete required professional learning units while working under a Professional Educator Certificate.
   D. Certificate renewal and advancement is contingent upon completion of professional learning units (PLUs). The ongoing professional learning requirements are to be phased in incrementally between 2020 and 2030. For details, consult the Regulations Governing the Certification of Educators in Rhode Island available at https://www.ride.ri.gov/InsideRIDE/LegalSupport/Regulations.aspx.
II. Preliminary Educator Certificates allow educators who are not fully certified to serve as educators of record while pursuing certification.
   A. Alternate Route Preliminary Certificate (valid 1 year; may be renewed once)
      1. For prospective educators who are enrolled in a Rhode Island–approved alternate route preparation program
   B. Career and Technical Education (CTE) Preliminary Certificate (valid 3 years; may be renewed once to add 4 years)
      1. For prospective educators who have met certificate area requirements related to education, licensing, work experience, and testing. For a detailed list of area-specific requirements, consult the RIDE certification website (see Appendix 1).
   C. Emergency Preliminary Certificate (valid 1 year; renewable up to 3 times)
      1. For prospective educators at the request of an employing agency when a fully certified, qualified educator who meets the criteria for the position cannot be secured
   D. Expert Residency Preliminary Certificate (valid 1 year; renewable up to 3 times)
      1. For prospective educators who have a bachelor's degree, demonstrate subject matter proficiency through content examinations, and have met coursework or experience requirements relevant to the desired certification area
         a. Certified educators seeking to add new certification areas may also use this certificate as part of a route to certification in that area.
   E. Expert Residency Shortages Preliminary Certificate (valid 3 years; may be renewed once to add 4 years)

1. For prospective educators who have a bachelor's degree and demonstrate subject matter proficiency in the shortage area
F. Fast-Track Principal Expert Residency Preliminary Certificate (valid 1 year, renewable up to 3 times)
    1. For individuals who hold a master's degree or higher with extensive experience (10 years) and who meet eligibility requirements and coursework or assessment requirements
G. Temporary Initial Educator Preliminary Certificate (valid 1 year; nonrenewable)
    1. For prospective educators who seek certification through reciprocity and meet all requirements for the Rhode Island Initial Educator Certificate except for the Rhode Island certification testing requirements
H. Visiting Lecturer Preliminary Certificate (valid 1 year; renewable)
    1. Issued at the request of an employing agency for individuals who have distinctive qualifications and therefore a unique capacity to enhance educational programs in districts
    2. This certificate is not a route to full certification.
I. Preliminary School Nurse Teacher Certificate (valid 1 year; renewable 5 times)
III. Certificates Available
For the specific requirements of each of the certificates listed below, consult the Regulations Governing the Certification of Educators in Rhode Island available at https://www.ride.ri.gov/InsideRIDE/LegalSupport/Regulations.aspx.
A. Teacher Certificates
    1. Early Childhood Certificates (PK–2, unless otherwise specified)
        a. Early Childhood Education; Early Childhood Special Education (Birth–Grade 2); Early Childhood Bilingual and Dual Language Education (PK–2); Early Childhood English to Speakers of Other Languages (PK–2)
    2. Elementary Certificates (Grades 1–6)
        a. Elementary Education; Elementary Special Education; Elementary Bilingual and Dual Language Education; Elementary English to Speakers of Other Languages
    3. Middle Grades Teacher Certificates (Grades 5–8)
        a. English; Mathematics; Middle Grades Bilingual and Dual Language Education; Middle Grades English to Speakers of Other Languages; Middle Grades Special Education Teacher; Science; Social Studies
        b. Educators can attain middle grades certification in the following ways:
            i. Option 1: Earn a Middle Grades English, Mathematics, Science, or Social Studies Certificate independent of any other certificate
            ii. Option 2: Extend an Elementary Education Teacher Certificate
            iii. Option 3: Extend a Secondary Grades Biology, Chemistry, English, General Science, Mathematics, Physics, or Social Studies certificate
    4. Secondary Grades Teacher Certificates (Grades 7–12)
        a. Agriculture; Biology; Business Education; Career and Technical Education; Chemistry; English; General Science; Mathematics; Physics; Social Studies; Secondary Grades Bilingual and Dual Language Education;

Secondary Grades English to Speakers of Other Languages; Secondary Grades Special Education Teacher

    5.   All Grades Teacher Certificates (PK–12)

        a.   All Grades Bilingual and Dual Language Education; All Grades English as a Second Language; All Grades Special Education—Deaf and Hard of Hearing—American Sign Language; All Grades Special Education—Deaf and Hard of Hearing—Oral/Aural Communication; All Grades Special Education—Severe Intellectual Disability; All Grades Special Education—Visually Impaired Adapted Physical Education; Art; Dance; Family and Consumer Science; Health; Library Media; Music; Physical Education; Registered School Nurse; School Nurse Teacher; Technology Education; Theatre; World Language

B.   Administrator Certificates

    1.   Building-Level Administrator (PK–12); Building Level Administrator PK–12 Fast-Track; District Level Administrator—Curriculum, Instruction, and Assessment; District Level Administrator—Special Education; School Business Administrator; Superintendent of Schools

C.   Support Professional Certificates

    1.   English as a Second Language Specialist/Consultant; Instructional Leader; Mathematics Specialist/Consultant; Reading Specialist/Consultant; School Counselor; School Psychologist; School Social Worker; Speech and Language Pathologist

South Carolina

Steps to Certification

To access step-by-step instructions for required materials, specific forms, and information on how to submit them for each of the categories below, consult https://ed.sc.gov/educators/certification/.

I. Uncertified Applicants. For those who have completed an approved teacher education program but have not yet been certified:
    A. Submit an official transcript from each college or university attended, as well as a college recommendation form signed by designated college official; and
    B. Submit the required teaching content area examination score(s) and the required score on the examination of general professional knowledge (pedagogy) as adopted by the South Carolina Board of Education for purposes of certification.

II. Reciprocal Applicants
    A. Applicants with a valid standard certificate issued by another state, a United States territory, or the Department of Defense Dependents Schools (DODDS) may be eligible for certification through South Carolina's reciprocity agreement.
        1. Interstate reciprocity does not apply to Career and Technology Education Work-Based, Temporary, or Alternative certification.
    B. To evaluate the status of existing credentials, review on the website South Carolina's current reciprocity agreement with the states, territories, and countries (see Appendix 1).
    C. Individuals with certification from the National Board for Professional Teaching Standards (NBPTS), upon application and presentation of a valid, standard out-of-state certificate, will receive a professional certificate in their field.
    D. Reciprocal Certificate Types
        1. Reciprocal Initial Certificate (valid for 3 academic school years)
            a. Certificate is for those with less than 3 years of teaching experience or those who do not have 27 months of full-time school teaching experience in the last 7 years on that valid standard certificate.
            b. Requirements
                i.   Must present valid standard out-of-state certificate.
                ii. Subject(s) shown on the certificate must be considered comparable to the subject(s) issued in South Carolina.
                iii. All certification areas issued in that state will also be issued on the South Carolina certificate provided the areas are initially requested on the application. Areas not requested initially would have to meet South Carolina's add-on requirements at the date of the request.
                iv. The appropriate level of Principles of Learning and Teaching (PLT) and successful summative evaluation on the state-approved teacher

evaluation model must be presented during the life of the initial certificate and before the professional certificate is issued.

2. Reciprocal Professional Certificate (valid for 5 academic school years)
    a. Must present verification of 27 months of full-time PreK–12 school teaching experience in the last 7 years on that valid standard certificate.
    b. See 1, Reciprocal Initial Certificate, b, directly above.
3. NBPTS certificates are not eligible for reciprocity but are taken into consideration when issuing a South Carolina certificate based on reciprocity with an eligible state. Applicants holding NBPTS certification should submit a copy of the NBPTS certificate along with their eligible out-of-state certificate. The NBPTS certificate qualifies the educator for immediate advancement to the professional certificate type (regardless of experience qualifications) and may extend the validity period of the certificate. The expiration date of the NBPTS certificate is used as the end date of the professional certificate.
    Note: Holding NBPTS certification in a field does not qualify an educator to add the field to their South Carolina certificate.

Required Credentials

For complete requirements for each position, consult the website (see Appendix 1).

I. District professional staff, including district administrators and district consultants, curriculum specialists, and coordinators
    A. Master's degree and certification in the area of primary responsibility
II. School administrators and professional support staff
    A. Master's degree and certification in the area of primary responsibility
III. Teachers of special education
    A. Acceptable certification, determined by the area of disability in which all or the majority of the teacher's students are classified.
        1. Acceptable certification for a resource or itinerant special education teacher is determined by the area of disability in which the majority of the teacher's students (i.e., caseload) are classified.
IV. Teachers of PreK–Grade 6; Grades 7–8; Grades 9–12
    A. Acceptable certification and all mandatory attendant training
    B. Teachers of credit-bearing courses in grades 7 and 8 must hold either middle-level certification in the content area or secondary certification in the content area.
        1. Additionally, these teachers must have passed either the middle-level or secondary Praxis II exam in the content area or the National Teacher's Examination in the content area.
    C. Teachers of Career and Technology Education must have acceptable certification and all mandatory attendant training.

South Dakota

Teacher Certification

Information about South Dakota educator certification rules can be found at https://doe.sd.gov/certification/.

I. Initial Certification (valid 5 years)
   A. Licensure candidates require the following:
      1. Bachelor's degree or higher from a regionally accredited institution of higher education,
      2. Passing score on state-designated pedagogy test,
      3. Completion of a 3-credit South Dakota Indian Studies course, *and*
      4. Written verification of completed teacher education program from a regionally accredited institution of higher education.
         a. Applicants from a foreign country must provide a transcript evaluation completed by an approved agency.
   B. Preparation types for initial licensure include Early Childhood (birth–grade 3), Elementary (K–grade 8), Secondary (grades 5–12), Career and Technical Education (grades 7–12), K–12 (music, art, health, etc.), Early Childhood Special Education (birth–grade 3), and K–12 Special Education.
II. Alternative Certification
   A. An alternative preliminary certificate (2-year; renewable) is required for applicants applying for alternative certification through the following programs:
      1. General Education alternative certification
      2. Teach for America alternative certification
      3. Career and Technical Education (CTE) alternative certification
      4. Administrator alternative certification (if applicant does not have an educator certificate)
      More information is available at https://doe.sd.gov/certification/AltCert.aspx.
   B. Once an individual meets the requirements for an alternative certification program, they receive a 5-year standard educator certificate.
   C. General Education Alternative Certification
      1. Applicant may teach grades 5–8, secondary, and K–12 general education areas while pursuing alternative certification. Requirements include:
         a. A valid alternative preliminary certificate,
         b. An offer of employment from a public school or South Dakota Department of Education–accredited school, *and*
         c. Bachelor's degree or higher.

    d.   Applicant must add subject-area endorsements based on the requirements for each endorsement.

    e.   Certificate holder may not teach grades or content areas beyond the endorsements listed on certificate.

2. Applicant receives a 1-year certificate that can be renewed twice; after 3 years the certificate is invalid if all requirements have not been completed.

3. Requirements to move to a teaching certificate include:

    a.   Complete 15 transcripted credits in classroom management, teaching methods and differentiated instruction, adolescent psychology, and South Dakota Indian Studies;
      and

    b.   Pass a state-designated pedagogy test.

D. Career and Technical Education Alternative Certification

1. Applicant may teach grades 7–12 CTE endorsement areas while pursuing alternative certification. Requirements include:

    a.   A valid alternative preliminary certificate,

    b.   An offer of employment from a public school or Department-accredited school,
      and

    c.   An associate of applied science degree or higher in a relate CTE field, 4,000 hours of work in a related CTE field, or national certification in a related CTE field.

    d.   Certificate holder may not teach grades or content areas beyond the endorsements listed on the certificate.

2. Applicant receives a 1-year certificate that can be renewed twice; after 3 years the certificate is invalid if all requirements have not been completed.

3. Requirements to move to a teaching certificate include:

    a.   Complete 9 transcripted credits with a grade of "C" or higher in Mentored Internship, CTE Methods, and Adolescent Psychology;

    b.   Complete a 3-credit South Dakota Indian Studies course;

    c.   Pass a state-designated pedagogy test;

    d.   Adhere to the South Dakota Code of Professional Ethics;
      and

    e.   Receive sign-off from the employing district.

Note: Mentored Internship and CTE Methods must include the topics of classroom management, student assessment, and differentiated instruction.

E. Teach for America Alternative Certification

1. Applicant may teach as an elementary teacher, secondary teacher, or K–12 teacher while pursuing alternative certification. Requirements include:

    a.   A valid alternative preliminary certificate,

    b.   An offer of employment from a public school or Department-accredited school,

    c.   Bachelor's degree or higher,
      and

        d.   Participation in the Teach for America program.

        e.   Certificate holder may not teach grades or content areas beyond the endorsements listed on the certificate.

2.   Applicant receives a 1-year certificate that can be renewed twice; after 3 years the certificate is invalid if all requirements have not been completed.

3.   Requirements to move to a teaching certificate include:

        a.   Complete 15 transcripted credits in classroom management, teaching methods and differentiated instruction, adolescent psychology, and South Dakota Indian Studies;
            and

        b.   Pass a state-designated pedagogy test.

F.   Special Education Alternative Certification

1.   Provides general education teachers an alternative pathway to receive the special education endorsement. Applicant must teach Early Childhood Special Education or K–12 Special Education while pursuing the alternative certificate. Requirements include:

        a.   A valid teaching certificate,

        b.   Minimum 3 years of teaching experience in the past 5 years,
            and

        c.   Verification of employment by the qualifying district.

2.   Applicant receives a 1-year certificate that can be renewed twice; after 3 years the endorsement is removed from the certificate if all requirements are not completed.

3.   Requirements to move to a teaching certificate include:

        a.   Complete a 6-credit, year-long practicum,

        b.   Complete 9 credits of coursework in special education law, assessment, and a special education–related course,

        c.   Pass a state-designated pedagogy test if required,

        d.   Pass a state-designated content test,
            and

        e.   Receive sign-off from the applicant's employing school.

Note: All coursework used to meet the requirements must be completed within 10 years prior to the application.

Endorsements

I.   To be certified to teach an assignment or act as an administrator or education specialist, certified educators must have the appropriate endorsement that meets state certification (see table 1).

II.   An educator must request an endorsement to be added to a certificate. Endorsements will not be added automatically after passing the state-designated test or completing the requirements of the endorsement.

III.   As of July 1, 2019, South Dakota will adhere to the following philosophy for adding endorsements:

A. Individuals with early childhood preparation may add endorsement for early childhood–grade 12 and K–12 endorsements (music, health, etc.) by demonstrating content and pedagogical knowledge.

B. Individuals with elementary preparation may add endorsement for early childhood–grade 12 and K–12 endorsements by demonstrating content and pedagogical knowledge.

C. Individuals with secondary preparation may add endorsement for grades 5–12 and K–12 by demonstrating content and pedagogical knowledge.

D. Individuals with K–12 preparation may add endorsement for grades 5–12 and K–12 endorsements by demonstrating content and pedagogical knowledge.

E. Individuals with early childhood special education (SPED) preparation may add endorsement for early childhood–grade 12 and K–12 endorsements by demonstrating content and pedagogical knowledge. The K–12 special education endorsement may be added by demonstrating content and pedagogical knowledge.

F. Individuals with K–12 SPED may add endorsements for grades 5–12 and K–12 endorsements by demonstrating content knowledge. The early childhood special education endorsement may be added by demonstrating content and pedagogical knowledge.

Administration

I. Initial Certification Requirements (valid 5 years)

    A. As of July 1, 2019, superintendent, assistant superintendent, principal, or assistant principal applicants require all of the following:

        1. Bachelor's degree or higher from a regionally accredited institution of higher education,

        2. Completion of a school superintendent or principal program from a regionally accredited institution of higher learning,

        3. Completion of a 3-credit South Dakota Indian Studies course, *and*

        4. Written recommendation from a regionally accredited institution of higher education verifying completion of the approved program.

           a. Applicants from a foreign country must provide a transcript evaluation completed by an approved agency.

    B. Preparation types

        1. School superintendent is eligible to be a school superintendent or assistant superintendent in an educational setting from early childhood through grade 12.

        2. K–12 principal is eligible to be a principal or assistant principal in an educational setting from early childhood through grade 12.

II. Administrator Alternative Certification—Principal

    A. Allows applicant to perform the duties as a principal completing the administrator alternative certification. Requirements include:

        1. Alternative preliminary administrator certificate (if the applicant does not have an educator certificate),

        2. Employment by a qualifying district,

Table 1: Pedagogy Endorsement Requirements

Adding an Endorsement to an Existing Preparation

Beginning July 1, 2019, Pedagogy Test Required to Add an Endorsement

I have ↓ I want →	EC Endorsement	Elementary Endorsements		Secondary Endorsements (5–12)	K–12 Endorsements		CTE Endorsements		EC SPED Endorsement	K–12 SPED Endorsement
		K–4	5–8		Elementary	Secondary	Methods	PLT		
Early Childhood Preparation	None	None	K–6 or 7–12 PLT	7–12 PLT	K–6 PLT	7–12 PLT	Yes	7–12 PLT*	None	7–12 PLT
Elementary Preparation	None	None	None	7–12 PLT	None	7–12 PLT	Yes	7–12 PLT	None	7–12 PLT
Secondary Preparation	Prep Required	Prep Required	None	None	K–6 PLT	None	Yes	None	Prep Required	K–6 PLT
K–12 Preparation	Prep Required	Prep Required	None	None	None	None	Yes	None	Prep Required	None
Career and Technical Education Preparation	Prep Required	Prep Required	None	None	K–6 PLT	None	None	None	Prep Required	K–6 PLT
Early Childhood SPED Preparation	None	None	K–6 or 7–12 PLT	7–12 PLT	K–6 PLT	7–12 PLT	Yes	7–12 PLT*	None	7–12 PLT
K–12 SPED Preparation	Prep Required	Prep Required	None	None	None	None	Yes	None	None	None

(EC, Early Childhood; CTE, Career and Technical Education; SPED, Special Education; PLT, Principle of Learning and Teaching)

*Not required for Early Childhood Development Career Pathway

K–6 PLT	5622 Principle of Learning and Teaching	Cut Score 160
7–12 PLT	5624 Principle of Learning and Teaching	Cut Score 157
Waiver of PLT	The PLT test may be waived if verification of two or more years of state-certified teaching experience in the grade span of the endorsement is documented.	K–6 PLT = Experience in K–8 grade span
		7–12 PLT = Experience in 5–12 grade span

3. Bachelor's degree or higher,
4. Completion of a state-approved teacher education program or alternative certification program,
5. Three or more years of teaching experience, *and*
6. Passing score on the state-designed school leadership assessment.

B. Applicant receives a 1-year certificate that can be renewed 4 times; after 5 years the certificate is invalid if all requirements have not been completed.
C. Requirements to move to a standard administrator certificate with a principal endorsement include completion of 18 transcripted credits with a grade of "C" or higher in instructional leadership, ethical and inclusive leadership, cognitive coaching and facilitation skills, creating a safe and inclusive school environment, process management, systems management, educational law and policy, and a 3-credit South Dakota Indian Studies course.

III. Administrator Alternative Certification—Superintendent

A. Allows applicant to perform the duties as a superintendent completing the administrator alternative certification. Requirements include:
1. Alternative preliminary administrator certificate (if the applicant does not have an educator certificate),
2. Employment by a qualifying district,
3. Master's degree or higher,
4. Three or more years of experience in a management role in a business or district, or as a teacher with a leadership role, *and*
5. Passing score on the state-designed school superintendent assessment.

B. Applicant receives a 1-year certificate that can be renewed 4 times; after 5 years the certificate is invalid if all requirements have not been completed.
C. Requirements to move to a standard administrator certificate with a superintendent endorsement include completion of 21 transcripted credits with a grade of "C" or higher in leadership and district culture, organizational management, values and ethics of leadership, educational policy and law, communication, community relations, curriculum planning and development, school finance, instructional management, and a 3-credit South Dakota Indian Studies course.

Certificate Renewal

I. Individuals who wish to renew a current South Dakota teaching certificate or update a lapsed certificate need specific items to complete an online application; for more information, visit https://doe.sd.gov/certification/renewal.aspx.

A. All certificates are valid until the expiration date of the certificate.
B. Educator certificates are valid from the date of issuance until June 30 of the year of expiration.
C. If renewal requirements are not completed by July 1, the certificate is expired.
D. A certificate becomes invalid if all renewal requirements are not met before October 1 of that year.

E. State statute requires all applicants for any initial certificate or renewal to meet a minimum of 1 clock hour of suicide awareness and prevention training.

F. All renewal applicants must complete and document 6 credits, which can be a combination of continuing education contact hours and university credits.

Reciprocity

I. South Dakota offers reciprocity based on the following conditions:

A. Approved Educator Program license-holder applicants must:

1. Hold a teacher, administrator, or educator specialist license from an approved program at a regionally accredited university;

2. Provide verification of a successful student teaching, internship, or field experience;
    and

3. Provide verification from licensing state that there are no ethics violations or disciplinary action.

B. Alternative Certification license-holder applicants must:

1. Have completed the alternative certification process in another state,

2. Provide verification of 3 years of teaching within the past 5 years,

3. Provide verification of a valid educator's license from the issuing state,
    and

4. Provide verification from licensing state that there are no ethics violations or disciplinary action.

II. All reciprocity applicants must provide a sign-off from the university from which they obtained their degree along with supporting transcript documentation.

III. All reciprocity applicants must complete a 3-credit South Dakota Indian Studies course and 1 clock hour of suicide awareness and prevention training.

IV. Applicants may request a 1-year provisional certificate, during which time they may complete the South Dakota Indian Studies course. This certificate may be renewed 1 time.

V. Applicants who have an active certificate in another state may receive endorsements based on a review of the out-of-state certificate and the equivalent South Dakota endorsements. Unless otherwise stipulated, no additional content or pedagogy requirements apply.

VI. Information about reciprocity based on completion of an approved education program can be found at https://doe.sd.gov/certification/documents/RECIPROCITY-%20ED.pdf. Information about reciprocity based on completion of an alternative certification program can be found at https://doe.sd.gov/certification/documents/RECIPROCITY-ALT.pdf.

Tennessee

For full details on current licensure requirements, consult https://www.tn.gov/education/licensing.

License Requirements for Teachers and School Service Personnel

I. Practitioner Teacher License (valid 3 years; renewable once)
   A. Initial license issued to applicant who meets the following criteria:
      1. Is at least 18 years old
      2. Holds a bachelor's degree from a regionally accredited college or university
      3. Is enrolled in or has completed a state-approved educator preparation program and is recommended for licensure by the program provider
      4. Submits qualifying scores that are no more than 5 years old on all required assessments as defined in the Professional Assessments for Tennessee Educators Policy 5.105 (for specifics, visit https://www.tn.gov/sbe/rules—policies-and-guidance/policies.html and https://www.ets.org/praxis/tn/requirements/)
      5. Meets requirements in at least 1 endorsement area
      6. Provides official transcripts of all credits earned through an institution of higher education
   B. To renew or advance the practitioner teacher license, all educators must complete an approved education preparation program and pass all required assessments.
II. Professional Teacher License (valid 6 years; renewable)
   A. In order to advance from a practitioner license to a professional license, an educator shall meet the following requirements:
      1. Complete an approved educator preparation program and submit qualifying scores on all State Board–required assessments as defined in the Professional Assessments for Tennessee Educators Policy prior to the end of the validity period of the first issuance of the practitioner license
      2. Obtain 3 years of qualifying experience as an educator as defined by the Department
      3. Earn 30 professional development points
   B. License is renewed based on the submission of 60 documented PDPs.
III. Practitioner Occupational License (valid 3 years; renewable once)
   A. Initial license issued to applicant who meets the following criteria:
      1. Holds a high school diploma or higher
      2. Is enrolled in or has completed a state-approved occupational educator preparation program
      3. Is recommended by a state-approved occupational educator preparation program
      4. Has a minimum of 5 years of relevant work experience, completed within the last 10 years, in the area of endorsement or equivalent education attainment as defined by the Department

5. Holds an active industry license or credential for the area of endorsement as defined by the Department, if applicable

B. To renew or advance the practitioner occupational license, all educators must complete an approved occupational educator preparation program.

IV. Professional Occupational License (valid 6 years; renewable)

A. In order to advance from a practitioner occupational teacher license to a professional occupational teacher license, an educator shall meet the following requirements:

1. Complete 3 years of qualifying experience as an educator as defined by the Department

2. Complete a State Board–approved educator preparation program

3. Earn 30 professional development points, a minimum of 20 of which shall come from new teacher training provided by the Department as indicated by SBE Educator Licensure Rule Chapter 0520–02–03

4. Hold an active industry license or credential for the area of endorsement as defined by the Department, if applicable

5. For educators who received the practitioner occupational teacher license on or after July 1, 2018, submit qualifying scores on all required assessments as defined in the Professional Assessments for Tennessee Educators Policy.

B. In order to renew the professional occupational teacher license educators must meet the following requirements:

1. Earn 60 professional development points as indicated by SBE Educator Licensure Rule Chapter 0520–02–03

2. Provide verification of an active industry license or credential for the area of endorsement as defined by the Department, if applicable

V. Additional Requirements for Out-of-State Applicants

A. Educators applying from out of state will apply for a practitioner license (valid 3 years; renewable once) and must meet the following criteria:

1. Hold a bachelor's degree from a regionally accredited college or university

    or

    Submit a recommendation from the out-of-state provider where the educator completed an approved program (all out-of-state educator preparation programs must meet conditions stipulated in Tennessee State Board Rule 0520–02–03)

2. Submit qualifying scores that are no more than 5 years old on all required assessments as defined in the Professional Assessments for Tennessee Educators Policy 5.105

VI. Additional Requirements for School Service Personnel

A. The Bible teacher, driver education teacher, school food service supervisor, superintendent, JROTC, and supervisor of attendance endorsements have additional requirements.

B. School service personnel in the roles of school audiologist, school counselor, school educational interpreter, school food service supervisor, school psychologist, school social worker, and school speech-language pathologist have additional requirements.

C. For details concerning A and B, consult the Tennessee Board of Education's Educator Licensure Rule 5 Chapter 0520–02–03. Rule documents are available online at https://publications.tnsosfiles.com/rules/0520/0520.htm.

License Requirements for Administrators

I.   Instructional Leader License—Aspiring (valid 3 years; not renewable)
   A.   Issued to applicant who will serve as assistant principal and meets the following criteria:
      1.   Has at least 3 years of qualifying experience as an educator as defined by the Department
      2.   Is enrolled in a State Board–approved instructional leader preparation program
      3.   Is recommended by the State Board–approved instructional leader preparation provider

II. Instructional Leader License (ILL; valid 3 years; renewable)
   A.   Issued to applicant who meets the following criteria:
      1.   Holds an advanced degree from a regionally accredited college or university
      2.   Has at least 3 years of qualifying experience as an educator as defined by the Department
      3.   Has completed a State Board–approved instructional leader preparation program
      4.   Is recommended by the State Board–approved instructional leader preparation provider
      5.   Submits qualifying scores that are no more than 5 years old on all required assessments as defined in the Professional Assessments for Tennessee Educators Policy
   B.   Educators holding the ILL may renew the license through 1 of the following pathways:
      1.   Serve in a Tennessee Academy for School Leaders (TASL)–mandated position for at least 2 years of the validity period of the license and be current in all TASL requirements
            or
      2.   Successfully complete a Department-approved instructional leadership training

III. Instructional Leader License—Professional (ILL-P; valid 6 years; renewable)
   A.   Educators currently holding the ILL may seek advancement to the ILL-P through 1 of the following advancement pathways:
      1.   Tennessee Academy for School Leaders (TASL) Pathway. Educators seeking advancement through the TASL pathway shall meet the following requirements:
            a.   Be recommended by the TASL director
            b.   Successfully complete the Beginning Principals Academy or the Beginning Supervisors Academy
            c.   Be recommended by the educator's director of schools, verifying the educator has a minimum of 2 years of successful experience as a principal, assistant principal, or instructional supervisor as demonstrated by an overall evaluation rating of "at expectations" or higher on a state-approved administrator evaluation model during the most recent validity period of the ILL
      2.   Individual Professional Learning Plan (IPLP). Educators seeking advancement through the IPLP pathway shall meet the following requirements:

      a. Be recommended by the TASL director

      b. Successfully complete an IPLP in coordination with an approved instructional leader preparation program

      c. Be recommended by the educator's director of schools, verifying the educator has a minimum of 2 years of successful experience as a principal, assistant principal, or instructional supervisor as demonstrated by an overall evaluation rating of "at expectations" or higher on a state-approved administrator evaluation model during the most recent validity period of the ILL

B. Educators may renew the ILL-P through 1 of the following pathways:

  1. TASL Pathway. Educators who currently serve in a TASL-mandated position shall meet the following renewal requirements:

      a. Have served as an instructional leader in a TASL-mandated position for at least 4 years of the validity period of the ILL-P

      b. Meet all TASL requirements

  2. Instructional Leadership Training Pathway. Educators seeking renewal who do not currently serve in a TASL-mandated position shall successfully complete a Department-approved instructional leadership training.

Endorsements Issued

For a complete list of active endorsements, consult the Tennessee Board of Education's Educator Licensure Policy 5.502. Policy documents are available online at https://www.tn.gov/sbe/rules—policies-and-guidance/policies.html.

Texas

The rules adopted by the State Board for Educator Certification (SBEC) are part of a larger body of state agency rules that are collected and published as the Texas Administrative Code. The SBEC may adopt new rules or amendments to or repeals of existing rules at any time. Visit the Texas Education Agency website at http://www.tea.texas.gov for the most recent rule changes.

Certification Overview

I. General certification requirements
   A. Hold bachelor's degree from institution of higher education that at the time was accredited or otherwise approved by an accrediting organization recognized by the Texas Higher Education Coordinating Board.
      1. Exceptions to the bachelor's degree requirement are allowed for the following certificate areas:
         a. Health Science: Grades 6–12
         b. Trade and Industrial Education: Grades 6–12
         c. Trade and Industrial Workforce Training: Grades 6–12
   B. Complete teacher training through an approved program, offered through colleges and universities, school districts, regional service centers, community colleges, and other entities.
   C. Successfully complete appropriate teacher certification tests for subject and grade level. Specific Texas Examinations of Educator Standards (TExES) and other tests are required, depending on applicant's background and certification sought; contact the Texas Education Agency (TEA) at http://www.tea.texas.gov for a list of certification tests and information on which tests are required.
      1. Teachers certified in another state or country must submit an application for a review of credentials to initiate the certification process.
II. Routes to educator certification
   A. Traditional undergraduate programs where the certificate is earned as part of a bachelor's degree program
   B. Post-baccalaureate programs designed to prepare baccalaureate degree holders seeking educator certification in conjunction with an additional degree
   C. Alternative certification programs for educator preparation designed to prepare degree holders seeking educator certification without an additional degree
      NOTE: SBEC-approved alternative certification programs are available at some institutions of higher education, regional education service centers, large school districts, and private entities.
   D. Additional certification based on examination: for teachers holding a classroom teaching certificate and bachelor's degree

1. Such teachers may add classroom certification areas by successfully completing appropriate certification examination(s) for area(s) sought.
2. Certification by examination not available for:
   a. Initial certification
   b. Teacher of Students with Visual Impairments Supplemental: Early Childhood–Grade 12 certificate
   c. Early Childhood: Prekindergarten–Grade 3 certificate
   d. Certification other than classroom teacher (e.g., school counselor, principal, superintendent, school librarian, educational diagnostician, reading specialist)
   e. Certificate for which no certification examination has been developed
E. Certification based on credentials from another jurisdiction
   1. Applicants holding an acceptable certificate or credential from another state, US territory, or country may apply for a Texas certificate. Credential must be equivalent to a certificate issued by TEA and must not have been revoked or suspended or be pending such action.
   2. One-Year certificate in 1 or more subject areas may be issued to applicant who holds a standard credential issued by a jurisdiction outside Texas and who meets specified requirements as determined by TEA credentials review. Applicants certified outside the state may apply for exemption of Texas tests by submitting the required documentation and following the process outlined at https://tea .texas.gov/Texas_Educators/Certification/Out-of-State_Certification/Out-of -State_Test_Exemptions/.

Certificate Types, Classes, and Renewal

I. Types of certificates: designates period of validity, personnel, and requirements for each certificate (CPE stands for continuing professional education)
   A. Standard (valid 5 years; renewable with 150 CPE hours)
      1. Replaced Lifetime Provisional and Professional certificates, and educators holding Lifetime certificates have been exempted from renewal process.
         a. Lifetime certificates were issued through September 1, 1999. Individuals are now issued Standard certificates that must be renewed every 5 years. Many Texas educators may hold both Lifetime and Standard certificates.
      2. Standard teacher certificate requirements
         a. See Certification Overview, I and II, above.
   B. One-Year (nonrenewable)
      1. Issued for out-of-state or out-of-country candidates.
   C. Intern (valid 1 year)
      1. Issued to an individual enrolled in an educator preparation program and serving in a supervised internship to satisfy clinical experience requirements of the certificate.
         a. Holder must be employed by accredited Texas public or private school in a position appropriate for the certificate sought.

       b.   Holder must pass all appropriate content pedagogy exams for the certificate category.

       c.   Holders of intern certificates for classes other than "teacher" must meet all qualifications and requirements for the class of certification sought.

   D.   Probationary (valid 1 year; renewable for 1 renewal year)

       1.   Issued to an individual enrolled in an educator preparation program and serving in an additional supervised internship to satisfy field experience or coursework requirements of the certificate.

          a.   Holder must be employed by accredited Texas public or private school in a position appropriate for the certificate sought.

          b.   Holder must pass all appropriate content pedagogy exams and pedagogy and professional responsibilities exams for the certificate category.

          c.   Holders of intern certificates for classes other than "teacher" must meet all qualifications and requirements for the class of certification sought.

       2.   Renewal contingent on enrollment of applicant in educator preparation program and employment in appropriate position, with mentoring and supervision throughout validity period.

   E.   Emergency permit (valid for 1 school year, with options for reissuance for Junior Reserve Officer Training Corps [JROTC] instructors and options for renewal limited to individuals serving as teachers of students with visual impairments)

       1.   Issued to degreed individual who does not have any appropriate certificate required for assignment.

   F.   Non-Renewable permit (valid for 1 year only)

       1.   Issued to degreed individual who has completed educator preparation program but has not yet passed TExES test(s).

II. Classes of certificates

   A.   Superintendent (valid 5 years; renewable with 200 CPE hours)

   B.   Principal (valid 5 years; renewable with 200 CPE hours)

   C.   Classroom teacher (valid 5 years; renewable with 150 CPE hours)

   D.   Reading specialist (valid 5 years; renewable with 200 CPE hours)

   E.   School librarian (valid 5 years; renewable with 200 CPE hours)

   F.   School counselor (valid 5 years; renewable with 200 CPE hours)

   G.   Educational diagnostician (valid 5 years; renewable with 200 CPE hours)

III. Certificate renewal

   A.   Standard requirements

       1.   Hold a valid Standard certificate that has not been, nor is in the process of being, sanctioned by TEA,

       2.   Successfully complete a criminal history review,

       3.   Not be in arrears of child support,

       4.   Complete the required number of CPE clock hours, *and*

       5.   Submit online application to TEA with appropriate renewal fee.

Administrator Certification

I. Principal as Instructional Leader certificate and endorsement (valid 5 years; renewable with 200 CPE hours)
    A. Requirements for certificate
        1. Successfully complete a TEA-approved principal preparation program and be recommended for certification by that program.
        2. Successfully pass TExES Principal as Instructional Leader certification exam and Performance Assessment for School Leaders (PASL).
        3. Successfully pass the PASL to add the Principal as Instructional Leader endorsement to an existing Texas certificate valid to serve in the role of principal.
        4. Hold master's degree from institution of higher education that at the time was accredited or otherwise approved by an accrediting organization recognized by the Texas Higher Education Coordinating Board.
        5. Hold a valid classroom teaching certificate.
        6. Have 2 years of creditable teaching experience as classroom teacher.
        NOTE: The Principal as Instructional Leader certificate became eligible for issuance on December 1, 2018, and the Principal as Instructional Leader endorsement became eligible for issuance on September 1, 2019.
II. Superintendent certificate (valid 5 years; renewable with 200 CPE hours)
    A. Requirements for certificate
        1. Satisfactorily pass TExES Superintendent certification exam.
        2. Successfully complete a TEA-approved superintendent preparation program and be recommended for certification by that program.
        3. Hold at a minimum a master's degree from an accredited institution of higher education that at the time was accredited or otherwise approved by an accrediting organization recognized by the Texas Higher Education Coordinating Board.
        4. Hold a principal certificate or the equivalent issued under this title by another state or country,
            or
            Have at least 3 credible years of managerial experience in a public school district, which must include responsibility for:
            a. Supervising or appraising faculty or staff;
            b. Conducting district-level planning and coordination of programs, activities, or initiatives;
                and
            c. Creating or maintaining a budget.
        5. Candidate must submit an application to TEA staff for the substitution of managerial experience as defined above. TEA staff will review the application and will notify the applicant, in writing, of approval or denial within 60 calendar days from date of receipt.
    B. Induction for new superintendents
        1. One-year mentorship for first-time superintendents (including those new to state)

        a.   Include at least 36 clock hours of professional development directly related to identified standards.

    2.   Mentorship program must be completed within the first 18 months of employment as superintendent.

Utah

As of November 1, 2019, changes to the Utah Administrative Code went into effect initiating an overhaul of the educator licensing structure (see Rule R277–301).

As of July 1, 2020, all current Utah educator Academic Pathway to Teaching (APT) and Alternative Routes to Licensure (ARL) licenses converted to the Associate Educator License (see below).

As of July 1, 2020, all current Utah educator Standard Level 1, 2, or 3 licenses converted to the Professional Educator License (see below).

Holders of the Associate Educator License must work with a state-approved university or local education agency (LEA) alternate educator preparation program in order to advance to the Professional Educator License.

Anyone pursuing an alternate pathway to licensure must obtain an Associate Educator License, be hired at an LEA in Utah with an approved alternate educator preparation program, and complete all requirements associated with the Professional Educator License.

For the most current licensing information, consult the Educator Licensing website at https://www.schools.utah.gov/curr/licensing.

License Levels

I. Associate Educator License (valid 2 years)
   A. Requirements
      1. Pass a fingerprint-based background check initiated online through the Utah State Board of Education (USBE)
      2. Obtain a Comprehensive Administration of Credentials for Teachers in Utah Schools (CACTUS) number by registering an account with the Utah Education Network
      3. Hold a bachelor's degree or higher from a regionally accredited institution
         or
         Be currently enrolled in a university-based, USBE-approved educator preparation program that will result in a bachelor's degree or higher from a regionally accredited institution
         or
         Hold skill certification in a specific Career and Technical Education (CTE) area
      4. Complete the required professional learning modules
         a. Educator Ethics (including the Educator Ethics Review)
         b. Special Education Law and Instruction
         c. Classroom Management and Instruction
         d. Utah Effective Teaching Standards

5. Meet content knowledge assessment requirements
   a. For an elementary license area, pass an approved elementary knowledge test measuring content in mathematics, reading/language arts, social studies, and science
   b. For a secondary or CTE license area:
      i. Pass an approved content knowledge test
         or
         Hold a bachelor's degree or higher with a major in the content area (or be enrolled in a program that will result in such)
         or
         Hold appropriate CTE certification in the area of expertise
6. Be currently enrolled in a USBE-approved, university or LEA educator preparation program

II. Professional Educator License (valid 5 years)
   A. Requirements
      1. Meet all requirements of the Associate Educator License
      2. Hold a bachelor's degree or higher from a regionally accredited institution
         or
         Hold skill certification in a specific CTE area
      3. Have the recommendation of a USBE-approved educator preparation program
         or
         Hold a current standard educator license in the area sought issued by a licensing jurisdiction outside of Utah
      4. Meet content knowledge and pedagogical requirements

Licensure Areas of Concentration

A license area of concentration designates the specific education setting or role in which the license holder is qualified. Available license areas include Early Childhood, Elementary, Secondary, Educational Leadership, Career and Technical Education (CTE), School Counselor, School Psychologist, Special Education, Preschool Special Education, Deaf Education, Speech-Language Pathologist, Speech-Language Technician, School Social Worker, and Communication Disorders. Educators with a current license may attach additional license areas to their Utah educator license by meeting eligibility requirements for each area. Consult R277–504, R277–505, and R277–506 of the Utah Administrative Code for area-specific eligibility requirements.

Vermont

Those applying for an initial educator license who hold a current educator license in a state that has signed the National Association of State Directors of Teacher Education and Certification (NASDTEC) Interstate Agreement are waived of meeting Vermont testing requirements. All educators approved for initial licensure are issued a comparable Level I Vermont Educator License, provided that they meet jurisdictional requirements.

Vermont no longer accepts paper applications. To apply for licensure, educators must use the Vermont Online Licensing System for Educators found at https://alis.edlicensing.vermont.gov/login .aspx. Finally, the Rules Governing the Licensure of Educators and the Preparation of Educational Professionals were revised in the summer of 2021. To access the current rules, go to the Vermont Agency of Education website at https://education.vermont.gov/documents/vsbpe-rules-governing -the-licensing-of-educators-and-preparation-of-educational-professionals-6–11–2021.

Pathways to Initial Licensure

I. Initial Licensure
- A. An applicant who is not licensed and has successfully completed a state-approved program or a program accredited by a nationally recognized accrediting entity in a state that has signed the NASDTEC Interstate Agreement will be considered for licensure.
  1. The applicant will be subject to the same requirements for initial licenses awarded in Vermont, including criminal background checks, affirmations, and Vermont's Jurisdiction Specific Requirements.
  NOTE: Jurisdiction Specific Requirements are additional requirements for licensure beyond performance and knowledge standards, including requirements concerning degrees, years of experience, testing, practicum or internship, and professional licensure or credentials. These are determined by Vermont Statute or the Vermont Standards Board for Professional Educators (VSBPE). For the latest such requirements, consult Rule 5440 (Licensing Endorsements) in the Rules Governing the Licensure of Educators.
  2. The applicant shall meet requirements for updated knowledge and skills as established by VSBPE policy when there is a time lapse of 10 or more years between the time of recommendation for licensure and application for licensure.
- B. An applicant who is not licensed and has successfully completed a state-approved program or a program approved by a nationally recognized accrediting entity in a state that has not signed the NASDTEC Interstate Agreement may apply for licensure though transcript review. An applicant who meets the requirements and Jurisdiction Specific Requirements shall be issued a comparable license and/or endorsement(s) according to the Rules Governing the Licensure of Educators.

1. The applicant shall meet requirements for updated knowledge and skills as established by VSBPE policy when there is a time lapse of 10 or more years between the time of recommendation for licensure and application for licensure.

C. An applicant for initial licensure in Vermont who holds a professional license in another state that has signed the NASDTEC Interstate Agreement, and holds the degree required for the endorsement, and meets the Jurisdiction Specific Requirements shall be issued a Level I Professional Educator's License with a comparable endorsement(s) according to the provisions of the Rules Governing the Licensure of Educators.

D. An applicant for Vermont licensure who holds a professional license in a state that has not signed the NASDTEC Interstate Agreement, or an applicant whose category of licensure is not covered by the agreement, shall be evaluated by the Vermont Agency of Education Licensing Office on an individual basis by transcript review to establish whether the applicant meets the competency requirements.

   1. Only coursework that appears for credit on an official transcript and for which the applicant received a grade of B or better may be counted toward the requirements for initial licensure through transcript review.

   2. The applicant shall meet requirements for updated knowledge and skills as established by VSBPE policy.

E. An applicant for Vermont licensure who is certified by the National Board for Professional Teaching Standards shall be issued a license in the comparable endorsement area, provided the applicant meets all jurisdictional requirements.

F. Alternative Routes to Licensure

   1. Peer Review (Vermont's non-higher-education-based, approved Alternative Licensure Program) for individuals seeking licensure as a teacher or administrator

      a. An individual who holds at least a bachelor's degree from a regionally or nationally accredited or state-approved institution and who has successfully completed a major, or its equivalent, in the liberal arts and sciences, or in the content area of the endorsement sought, may be licensed by completing an alternate preparation process, Peer Review, approved by the VSBPE.

      b. For endorsement areas requiring an advanced degree, the individual must hold the specified advanced degree in order to be deemed eligible to proceed through peer review.

   2. Transcript Review for individual seeking licensure as a teacher or administrator

      a. For endorsements for which Vermont does not have an approved preparation program, an applicant for a Vermont license who has not completed an approved preparation program may be evaluated by the VSBPE, or its designee, on an individual basis by transcript review of coursework appearing on an official transcript for which the applicant received credit to establish whether the applicant meets the competency requirements according to the Rules Governing the Licensure of Educators.

      b. An applicant seeking initial licensure in an endorsement area for which Vermont has an approved preparation program may choose to seek a recommendation for initial licensure through Vermont's Peer Review Alternative Licensure program.

    c.   Administrator candidates must also meet the degree, supervised field experience, examination, and requirements for updated knowledge and skills as established by the VSBPE.

    d.   An applicant for Vermont licensure who is certified by the National Board for Professional Teaching Standards shall be issued a license in the comparable endorsement area.

II.   General Requirements for All Licensure Candidates

   A.   The applicant must hold a baccalaureate degree from a nationally or regionally accredited or Vermont-approved institution and must have successfully completed a major, or its equivalent, in the liberal arts and sciences or in the content area of the endorsement sought.

      1.   Exceptions include an applicant for a Career Technical Education endorsement or an educator who holds a Career Technical Education endorsement; however, an applicant who currently holds a Career Technical Education endorsement and would like to add a sub-endorsement must provide documentation of work experience in the sub-endorsement area. Documented work experience of 6 years (12,000 hours) in the career cluster is required if the educator holds a high school diploma or the equivalent, or of 4 years (8,000 hours) if the educator holds an associate degree or the equivalent.

      2.   Applicants for the Junior ROTC Instructor endorsement must have current certification as a Junior Reserve Officer Training Corps Instructor by the United States Department of Defense.

      3.   Candidates for a School Nurse endorsement must hold a Vermont Clinical RN License and a baccalaureate degree from a nationally accredited 4-year nursing program.

         a.   Candidates for an Associate School Nurse endorsement must hold a Vermont Clinical RN License and an associate degree.

   B.   Documentation of the specified content knowledge, performance standards, and additional requirements, if any, for the endorsement(s) being sought

   C.   Documentation of required student teaching or administrative internship experience

      1.   Student teaching: evidence of at least 13 consecutive weeks of supervised, concentrated field experience required for initial licensure, including an internship, or other concentrated field experience in which the candidate shall gradually assume the full professional roles and responsibilities of an educator in the initial endorsement area sought.

      2.   Administrator supervised field experience: a minimum of 300 hours of supervised, substantive field experience in 2 or more types of school settings.

   D.   The educator has knowledge and skills in the content of his or her endorsement(s) at a level that enables students to meet or exceed the standards represented in both the fields of knowledge and the vital results of Vermont's Common Core Standards, Core Teaching Standards, and Next Generation Science Standards (for science teachers).

   E.   The educator fulfills general competencies in teaching, Vermont's Core Teaching Standards, and, if an administrator, the Core Leadership Standards.

F.   Testing requirements
   1.   Praxis Core Academic Skills Test is required for all educators for initial licenses, excluding the endorsement areas of Junior ROTC Instructor, School Nurse, Associate School Nurse, Social Worker, Driver and Traffic Safety Education (In-Vehicle only), and Work-Based Learning Coordinator.
      a.   Meet scores on 3 individual core tests (reading, 156; writing, 162; and mathematics, 150)
   2.   Praxis II for applicants seeking initial license or additional endorsement in any of the following areas:
      a.   Mathematics, Social Studies, English, Science, Early Childhood Education (PreK–3 grade span only), Elementary Education, Art, Music, Physical Education, Modern or Classical Languages, English Language Learner (ELL), School Psychologist, and American Sign Language (ASL).
      b.   Requirements for speech language pathologists: clinical licensure as a speech language pathologist in Vermont, and a minimum of a practicum in an educational setting in the diagnosis and management of individuals with communication delays and disorders under the supervision of a licensed educational speech language pathologist or ASHA-certified speech language pathologist.
      c.   For middle grades: English, Mathematics, Science, or History/Social Science
      d.   The School Leaders Licensure Assessment (SLLA) is required for all Educators seeking any administrator endorsement unless they have completed a post-Baccalaureate degree in educational leadership, completed a ROPA-approved teacher leadership program, or hold a current administrator endorsement.
   3.   Exemptions from Praxis II testing requirements are available only if applicant is currently licensed from a state that has signed the NASDTEC Interstate Agreement.

Licensure Levels and Types with Renewal Requirements

I.   Level I: Professional Educator License (valid 3 years; renewable)
   A.   Issued to an applicant who has satisfactorily met all requirements for licensure
      1.   See II, General Requirements for All Licensure Candidates, A–F, above.
   B.   To renew a Level I license an educator must complete 45 hours of professional learning, including a minimum of 15 hours of new learning specific to the endorsement being renewed per the Rules Governing the Licensure of Educators. (See VI, Renewal Requirements, below.)
II.   Level II: Professional Educator License (valid 5 years; renewable)
   A.   Issued to an educator, upon recommendation of a local or regional standards board, or the Vermont Agency of Education Licensing Office if the educator is not served by a local or regional standards board, who has:
      1.   Successfully practiced in the endorsement area in Vermont for 3 years under a valid Level I license,

and

2. Provided documentation from a supervising administrator demonstrating that the educator is performing at a professional level in relation to the Core Teaching Standards or the Core Leadership Standards.

B. To renew a Level II license, an educator must complete 90 hours of professional learning if renewing a Level II license that was held for 5 years, including a minimum of 30 hours of new learning specific to the endorsement being renewed. (See VI, Renewal Requirements, below.)

III. Apprenticeship License: for individuals seeking Career Technical Education endorsements (valid 4 years; renewable for 1 additional year under extenuating circumstances). An Apprenticeship license is not a Professional Educator license.

IV. Provisional License or Endorsement (valid 2 school years)

A. A superintendent, director, headmaster of an independent school, career technical director, or entities receiving state-appropriated grants for statewide hearing-impaired, dead/hard-of-hearing, or intensive-needs special education may apply to the Vermont Agency of Education for a Provisional license or endorsement when the local district is unable to find an appropriately licensed and/or endorsed applicant after making all reasonable efforts to do so.

B. The application for a Provisional license or endorsement shall include a plan for obtaining a Level I license or endorsement and an explanation of how the applicant will be mentored and supervised during the 2-year period of the Provisional license.

C. Qualifications

1. Possess a baccalaureate degree (except for those seeking the Associate School Nurse license, which requires an associate degree, and the Junior ROTC license, for which applicant must hold Department of Defense certification as a Junior ROTC Instructor) and meet at least 1 of the following criteria:

a. Possess any valid educator license from Vermont or another state,

or

Possess any expired Vermont educator license or any expired license from another state, provided the license expired no fewer than 2 years and no longer than 10 years ago,

or

Have a major or the equivalent in the content area of the provisional endorsement sought,

or

Have successfully completed the Praxis II licensure content assessment for the provisional endorsement sought.

D. If extenuating circumstances prevented an individual from completing the approved plan for Level I licensure, a new 1-year Provisional license (formally known as an extension) may be granted.

V. Emergency Licenses and Endorsements (valid for the school year for which it was issued and only for the assignment for which it was issued; cannot be extended for a second year, nor can an individual be issued an Emergency license for any endorsement more than once)

A. See IV, A, directly above, except for Emergency license.

B. Emergency licenses shall be issued only to individuals who hold a baccalaureate degree (except Career Technical Education) but do not meet the qualifications for a Provisional license (see IV, C, directly above).

C. The application for an Emergency license shall include an explanation of how the applicant will be mentored and supervised.

D. No Emergency endorsements will be issued for the following: Assistant Director for Adult Education, Career Technical Center Director, Career Technical Education School Counseling Coordinator, Career Technical Education Special Needs Coordinator, Director of Curriculum, Director of Special Education, Driver and Traffic Safety Education, Early Childhood Special Educator, Educational Speech Language Pathologist, Intensive Special Education Teacher, Junior ROTC Instructor, Principal, School Nurse, Associate School Nurse, School Counselor, School Psychologist, School Social Worker, Special Educator, Special Education Consulting Teacher, Superintendent, Teacher of the Deaf and Hard of Hearing, and Teacher of the Visually Impaired.

VI. Renewal Requirements

A. Level I renewal

1. To receive a 3-year renewal, the educator shall show professional growth through completion of a minimum of 3 credits or 45 hours of professional learning in the endorsement area.

2. Level I endorsement holders who have practiced in Vermont in the endorsement area after 3 years shall seek a recommendation from their local or regional standards board, or the Vermont Agency of Education Licensing Office if educator is not served by a local or regional standards board, for a Level II endorsement.

   a. An educator who does not receive a recommendation for a Level II endorsement upon initial application shall renew the Level I endorsement after 3 years of professional practice and reapply for a Level II license prior to the expiration of the renewal.

   b. Level I endorsement of an educator who does not receive a recommendation for a Level II endorsement after another 3 years of professional practice shall become lapsed and may be reinstated.

   c. Level I license holders employed as educators in Vermont but who have not practiced in a particular endorsement area for 3 years shall seek a recommendation for renewal of that Level I endorsement through their local or regional standards board, or the Vermont Agency of Education Licensing Office if the educator is not served by a local or regional standards board.

   d. Educators may renew Level I endorsements under which they are not currently teaching by completing 3 credits or 45 hours of professional learning per endorsement. There is no limit to the number of times these endorsements may be renewed.

   e. An educator shall present evidence of any required additional licenses or credentials specific to a particular endorsement.

B. Level II renewal

1. Level II license holders shall seek a recommendation for renewal of their Level

II license and endorsement(s) from their local or regional standards board, or the Vermont Agency of Education Licensing Office if not employed in a Vermont school served by a local or regional standards board.

2. The local or regional standards board, or the Vermont Agency of Education Licensing Office if educator is not served by a local or regional standards board, shall recommend renewal of a Level II endorsement if the applicant presents:

    a. Documentation of a minimum of 9 credits or 135 hours of professional learning, at least 3 credits or 45 hours of which must address the specific content knowledge and performance standards of each endorsement recommended for renewal if renewing a Level II license that was held for 7 years,

        or

        Documentation of a minimum of 6 credits or 90 hours of professional learning, at least 2 credits or 30 hours of which must address the specific content knowledge and performance standards of each endorsement recommended for renewal if renewing a Level II license that was held for 5 years.

    b. Evidence of any required additional licenses or credentials specific to a particular endorsement.

Endorsements

I. In order to be valid, each professional educator's license shall have 1 or more endorsements.

II. The holder of any license who wishes to qualify for an additional endorsement via Transcript Review shall present evidence of meeting the content knowledge and performance standards of the endorsement.

    A. Depending on the endorsement, a minimum of a major, or the equivalent, or 18 credit hours in the endorsement field is required.

III. Endorsements may be obtained in the following areas:

    A. Administrator endorsements
        1. Assistant Director for Adult Education
        2. Career Technical Center Director
        3. Director of Special Education
        4. Principal
        5. Superintendent
        6. Director of Curriculum

    B. Art (Grades PreK–8, 5–12, or PreK–12); Associate School Nurse (Grades PreK–12); Bilingual Education (Grades PreK–12); Business Education (Grades 5–12); Career Technical Education School Counseling Coordinator (Grades 7–12); Computer Science (Grades 7–12); Dance (Grades PreK–6, 7–12, PreK–12); Design and Technology Education (Grades 5–12); Driver and Traffic Safety Education (Grades 9–12); Early Childhood Education (Birth to PreK, Grades PreK–3, Birth–Age 3); Educational Technology Specialist (Grades PreK–12); Elementary Education (Grades K–6); English (Grades 7–12); English Language Learner

(ELL) (Grades PreK–6, 7–12, or PreK–12); Family and Consumer Sciences (Grades 5–12); Health Education (Grades PreK–8, 5–12, or PreK–12); Junior Reserve Officer Training Corps (ROTC) Instructor (Grades 9–12); Mathematics (Grades 7–12); Middle Grades (with 1 or more of the required content areas of Mathematics, English/Language Arts, Science, and Social Studies) (Grades 5–9); Modern and Classical Languages (Grades PreK–6, 7–12, or PreK–12); Music; Physical Education (Grades PreK–8, 5–12, or PreK–12); School Counselor (Grades PreK–12); School Librarian (Grades PreK–12); School Nurse (Grades PreK–12); School Psychologist (Grades PreK–12); School Social Worker (Grades PreK–12); Science (Grades 7–12); Social Studies (Grades 7–12); Specialized Literacy Professional (for holder of endorsement in either Early Childhood, Elementary Education, Middle Grades, or Special Education; Grades PreK–12); Theatre Arts (Grades PreK–8, 5–12, and PreK–12); Work-Based Learning Coordinator (Grades 9–12); Career Technical Special Needs Coordinator (Grade 8–Age 21); Early Childhood Special Educator (Birth–Age 6); Intensive Special Education Teacher (Ages 3–21); Special Educator (Grades K–8, Grade 7–Age 21, or K–Age 21); Educational Speech Language Pathologist (Ages 3–21); Teacher of the Visually Impaired (Ages 3–21); Teacher of the Deaf and Hard of Hearing (Ages 3–21); Online Teaching Specialist (Grades PreK–12).

Virginia

General Requirements for Licensure

I. Applicants for licensure must:
   A. Be at least 18 years of age
   B. Pay the appropriate fees as determined by the Virginia Board of Education and complete the application process
   C. Have earned a baccalaureate degree (with the exception of the Technical Professional License) from a regionally accredited college or university and meet requirements for the license sought. Persons seeking initial licensure through approved programs from Virginia institutions of higher education shall only be licensed as instructional personnel if the education endorsement programs are approved by the Virginia Board of Education.
      1. Individuals who have earned a degree from an institution in another country shall hold the equivalent of a regionally accredited college or university degree in the United States, as verified by a Virginia Department of Education–approved credential evaluation agency for the degree required for the license.
   D. Possess good moral character and be free of conditions outlined in Part VII of 8VAC20–23–720 et seq., available at https://law.lis.virginia.gov/admincode/title8/agency20/chapter23/section720/.
II. All candidates who hold at least a baccalaureate degree from a regionally accredited college or university and who seek an initial Virginia teaching license shall obtain passing scores on professional teacher's assessments prescribed by the Virginia Board of Education.
   A. With the exception of the career switcher program, which requires assessments as prerequisites, individuals shall complete the professional teacher's assessments within the 3-year validity of the initial provisional license.
   B. Candidates seeking a Technical Professional License, the International License, the School Manager License, or the Pupil Personnel Services License are not required to take the professional teacher's assessments.
   C. Individuals who hold a valid out-of-state license (full credential with no deficiencies) that shall be in force at the time the application for a Virginia license is made are exempt from the professional teacher's assessment requirements. Documentation must be submitted to verify the school's status as a public or accredited nonpublic school.
III. All individuals seeking an initial endorsement in early/primary education PreK–3, elementary education PreK–6, special education—general curriculum, special education—deaf and hard of hearing, special education—blindness and visual impairments, and individuals seeking an endorsement as a reading specialist must obtain passing scores on a reading instructional assessment prescribed by the Virginia Board of Education.

IV. Licensure by reciprocity is set forth in 8VAC20–22–100. A school leader's assessment prescribed by the Virginia Board of Education must be met for all individuals who are seeking an initial endorsement authorizing them to serve as principals and assistant principals in the public schools.

V. Individuals seeking an initial administration and supervision endorsement who are interested in serving as central office instructional personnel are not required to take and pass the school leader's licensure assessment prescribed by the Virginia Board of Education.

VI. Individuals seeking initial licensure must:

A. Demonstrate proficiency in the use of educational technology for instruction, complete study in child abuse recognition and intervention in accordance with curriculum guidelines developed by the Virginia Board of Education in consultation with the Virginia Department of Social Services, and receive professional development in instructional methods tailored to promote student academic progress and effective preparation for the Virginia Standards of Learning end-of-course and end-of-grade assessments.

B. Provide evidence of completion of certification or training in emergency first aid, cardiopulmonary resuscitation (CPR), and the use of automated external defibrillators (AED). The certification or training program shall be based on the current national evidence-based emergency cardiovascular care guidelines for CPR and the use of an AED, such as a program developed by the American Heart Association or the American Red Cross, and include the hands-on practice of the skills necessary to perform CPR. The Virginia Board of Education shall provide a waiver of this requirement for any person with a disability whose disability prohibits such person from completing the certification or training.

C. Receive instruction or training, as described in subsection D of 23.1–902 of the Code of Virginia, on positive behavior interventions and supports; crisis prevention and de-escalation; the use of physical restraint and seclusion, consistent with regulations of the Board of Education; and appropriate alternative methods to reduce and prevent the need for the use of physical restraint and seclusion.

D. The teacher of record for verified credit courses for high school graduation must hold a Virginia license with the appropriate content endorsement.

E. Every teacher seeking an initial license in the Commonwealth with an endorsement in the area of career and technical education shall have an industry certification credential, as defined in 8VAC20–22–10, in the area in which the teacher seeks endorsement. If a teacher seeking an initial license in the Commonwealth has not attained an industry certification credential in the area in which the teacher seeks endorsement, the Virginia Board of Education may, upon request of the employing school division or educational agency, issue the teacher a provisional license to allow time for the teacher to attain such credential.

F. Effective July 1, 2017, every person seeking renewal of a license must provide evidence of completion of dyslexia awareness training, provided by the Virginia Department of Education, on the indicators of dyslexia as defined by the Virginia Board of Education pursuant to regulations and the evidence-based interventions and accommodations for dyslexia.

Types of Licenses

Unless otherwise indicated, licenses are valid for 10 years and renewable. For full information on the licenses listed below, refer to the Virginia Licensure Regulations for School Personnel (8VAC20−23) at https://law.lis.virginia.gov/admincode/title8/agency20/chapter23/.

I. Provisional License (valid up to 3 years; nonrenewable). Requirements include:
   A. A baccalaureate degree or higher from a regionally accredited college or university, *and*
   B. Completion of the requirements for a regular 10-year license within the validity period of the provisional license.

II. Collegiate Professional License (valid 10 years; renewable). Requirements include:
   A. A baccalaureate degree or higher from a regionally accredited college or university, *and*
   B. Satisfactory completion of the professional teacher's assessments prescribed by the Virginia Board of Education.

III. Postgraduate Professional License (valid 10 years; renewable). Requirements include:
   A. Completion of all requirements for the Collegiate Professional License, *and*
   B. Graduate degree or higher from a regionally accredited college or university.

IV. Technical Professional License (valid 10 years; renewable). This license can be issued in Career and Technical Education, Education Technology, and Military Science. Requirements include:
   A. Diploma from an accredited high school or Virginia Board of Education–approved high school equivalency credential;
   B. Academic proficiency, skills in literacy, communication, technical competency, and occupational experience;
   C. Demonstrated competency in the endorsement area sought;
   D. Completion of 9 semester hours of specialized professional studies credit from a regionally accredited college or university (must include 3 semester hours of human development, 3 semester hours of curriculum and instruction, and 3 semester hours of instructional technology or classroom and behavior management);
   E. Successful completion of a 1-year, full-time teaching experience in a public school or accredited nonpublic school in the area of endorsement;
   F. Individuals seeking an endorsement to teach military science must have the appropriate credentials issued by the US military; *and*
   G. A license issued by the appropriate Virginia board for those program areas requiring a license and a minimum of 2 years of satisfactory experience at the journeyman level or an equivalent, *or*
   Completion of a registered apprenticeship program and 2 years of satisfactory experience at the journeyman level or an equivalent level in the trade, *or*
   Four years of work experience at the management or supervisory level or equivalent,

or a combination of 4 years of training and work experience at the management or supervisory level or equivalent.

V. School Manager License (valid 10 years; renewable). Requirements include:
   A. A baccalaureate degree from a regionally accredited college or university,
   B. Three years of successful managerial experience,
      and
   C. Recommendation for the license by a Virginia school division superintendent.

VI. Pupil Personnel Services License (valid 10 years; renewable). Requirements include:
   A. An appropriate graduate degree from a regionally accredited college or university,
      and
   B. An endorsement for guidance counselor, school psychologist, school social worker, or vocational evaluator.
   C. This license does not require teaching experience unless otherwise outlined under the specific endorsement's requirements.

VII. Division Superintendent License (valid 10 years; renewable). Requirements include:
   A. A graduate degree from a regionally accredited college or university that meets the requirements specified in 8VAC20–22–630.
   B. The individual's name must be listed on the Virginia Board of Education's list of eligible division superintendents.

VIII. International Educator License (valid up to 5 consecutive years; nonrenewable). This license provides a cultural exchange opportunity for Virginia students and international teachers. Applicants must:
   A. Be employed by a Virginia public or accredited nonpublic school;
   B. Hold non-US citizenship and be a nonpermanent resident;
   C. Serve as an exchange teacher for a time period not to exceed 5 consecutive years;
      and
   D. Meet the following requirements as verified by a state-approved, federally designated exchange visitor program:
      1. Be proficient in written and spoken English,
      2. Demonstrate competence in the appropriate academic subject areas by meeting credential requirements for a qualified teacher in the exchange country,
      3. Hold the US equivalent of a baccalaureate degree or higher as determined by an approved credential evaluation agency,
      4. Hold US or foreign educator credentials and have completed at least 1 year of successful teaching experience that enables the educator to fulfill a similar requirement in their home country,
         and
      5. Meet requirements as verified by a state-approved, federally designated Exchange Visitor Program (22 CFR Part 62).

IX. Teach For America License (valid 2 years; nonrenewable). Requirements include:
   A. A baccalaureate degree or higher from a regionally accredited college or university;
   B. Meets requirements prescribed by the Virginia Board of Education for all endorsements sought, or has met the qualifying scores on the content area assessment prescribed by the Board for the endorsements sought;

C. Possesses good moral character according to criteria developed by the Virginia Board of Education;

D. Has been offered and has accepted placement in Teach For America;

E. Has successfully completed preservice training and is participating in the professional development requirements of Teach For America, including teaching frameworks, curricula, lesson planning, instructional delivery, classroom management, assessment and evaluation of student progress, classroom diversity, and literacy development;

F. Has an offer of employment from a local school board to teach in a public elementary or secondary school in the Commonwealth or in a preschool program that receives state funds pursuant to subsection C of 22.1–199.1 of the Code of Virginia;
    and

G. Receives a recommendation from the employing school division for a Teach For America License in the endorsement area in which the individual seeks to be licensed.

H. The Virginia Board of Education may extend a Teach For America license for 1 additional year upon request of the employing school division; no Teach For America license shall exceed a total of 3 years in length.

I. Upon completion of at least 2 years of full-time teaching in a public elementary or secondary school, an individual holding a Teach For America license shall be eligible to receive a renewable license if the applicant has:
    1. Achieved satisfactory scores on all professional teacher's assessments required by the Virginia Board of Education,
       and
    2. Received a satisfactory evaluation at the end of each year of employment.

X. Online Teacher License (valid 10 years; renewable). Valid only for teaching online courses. Teachers who hold a 10-year renewable license issued by the Virginia Board of Education may teach online courses for which they are properly endorsed and do not have to seek this license. Requirements include:

A. Meet requirements for endorsement in a content area and achieve the qualifying scores on the content area assessment prescribed by the Virginia Board of Education,
    and

B. Complete a 3-semester-hour course in online instructional methods.
Note: Online teaching experience is not acceptable to meet the full-time teaching requirements for other license types.

Alternate Routes to Licensure

I. Career switcher alternate route to licensure for career professions:
    A. Available to career switchers who seek teaching endorsements PreK–12 with the exception of special education.
    B. An individual seeking a Provisional License through the career switcher program must meet the following prerequisite requirements:

1. Completed application;
2. A baccalaureate degree from a regionally accredited college or university;
3. Completion of requirements for an endorsement in a teaching area or the equivalent through verifiable experience or academic study;
4. A minimum of 3 years of full-time work experience or its equivalent; *and*
5. Qualifying scores on the professional teacher's assessments as prescribed by the Virginia Board of Education.

C. The Provisional Career Switcher License is awarded at the end of Level I preparation, is valid for 1 year, and may be issued for a period not to exceed 3 years. The candidate must complete all components of the career switcher alternate route for career professions.

D. Level I requirements must be completed during the course of a single year and may be offered through a variety of delivery systems, including distance learning programs. Career switcher programs must be certified by the Virginia Department of Education. If an employing agency recommends extending the Provisional License for a second year, the candidate will enter Level III of the program.
   1. Level I preparation includes:
      a. Minimum of 180 clock hours of instruction, including field experience
   2. Level II preparation during first year of employment includes:
      a. Seeking employment in Virginia with the 1-year Provisional Career Switcher License
      b. Continued Level II preparation during the first year of employment with a minimum of 5 seminars that will include a minimum of 20 cumulative instructional hours
      c. One year of successful, full-time teaching experience in a Virginia public or accredited nonpublic school under a 1-year Provisional License, under the direction of a trained mentor
      d. Upon completion of Levels I and II of the career switcher alternate route to licensure program and submission of a recommendation from the Virginia educational employing agency, the candidate will be eligible to apply for a 5-year renewable license.
   3. Level III preparation, if required, includes:
      a. Postpreparation, if required, to be conducted by the Virginia employing educational agency to address the areas where improvement is needed as identified in the candidate's professional improvement plan
      b. Upon completion of Levels I, II, and III of the career switcher alternate route to licensure program and submission of a recommendation from the Virginia educational employing agency, the candidate will be eligible to receive a 10-year renewable license.

E. Verification of program completion will be documented by the certified program provider and the division superintendent or designee.

F. Certified providers implementing a career switcher program may charge a fee for participation in the program.

II. Other alternate routes to licensure are available to those seeking a teaching endorsement in PreK–12, experiential learning, special education, and other areas. For more information, refer to section 8VAC20–23–90 of the Virginia Licensure Regulations for School Personnel at https://law.lis.virginia.gov/admincode/title8/agency20/chapter23/.

Requirements

I. General requirements:
   A. Completion of an approved program, including:
      1. A degree from a regionally accredited college or university in the liberal arts and sciences (or equivalent);
      2. Professional teacher's assessments as prescribed by the Virginia Board of Education;
      3. Specific endorsement requirements; and
      4. Professional studies requirements, including supervised classroom experience in the endorsement area.

      or

   B. If employed by a Virginia public or nonpublic school, completion of the alternate route to licensure.

II. Professional studies requirements—which may be met through integrated coursework or modules—total 18 semester hours for adult education, PreK–12 endorsements, and secondary grades 6–12 endorsements; for early/primary PreK–3, elementary education PreK–6, and special education, the total is 21 semester hours.
   A. Human growth and development and learning (birth through adolescence): 3 semester hours
   B. Curriculum and instruction: 3 semester hours
   C. Classroom and behavior management: 3 semester hours
   D. Assessment of and for learning: 3 semester hours
   E. Foundations of education and the teaching profession: 3 semester hours
   F. Language and literacy:
      1. Early/primary PreK–3 and elementary education PreK–6, language acquisition, and reading and writing: 6 semester hours
      2. Middle education, language acquisition and reading development: 3 semester hours; and literacy in the content area: 3 semester hours
      3. Special education, language acquisition, and reading and writing: 6 semester hours
      4. Secondary education, literacy in the content area: 3 semester hours
   G. Supervised classroom experience:
      1. Supervised clinical experience shall be comprised of early field experience and a minimum of 10 weeks of successful student teaching in the endorsement area sought.
      2. Full-time classroom experience for a minimum of 300 clock hours (including pre- and postclinical experiences) with at least 150 clock hours spent supervised in direct teaching activities at the level of endorsement

3. One year of successful full-time teaching experience in the endorsement area in a public or accredited nonpublic school may be accepted in lieu of the supervised teaching experience.

Endorsements for Early/Primary Education, Elementary Education, and Middle Education

The alternate route requirements apply to individuals seeking licensure outside of state-approved programs and through the alternate route to licensure. Institutions of higher education (IHEs) with approved programs in Virginia are not subject to specific semester-hour requirements since they incorporate state competencies into their programs.

I. Early/primary education PreK–3 endorsement requirements:
    A. Graduation from an approved teacher preparation program in early/primary education PreK–3
        or
    B. A degree from a regionally accredited college or university in the liberal arts and sciences (or equivalent) and completed coursework that covers the early/primary education PreK–3 competencies and fulfills the following 48 semester-hour requirements: English (must include composition, oral communication, and literature): 12 semester hours; mathematics: 9 semester hours; science (including a laboratory course): 12 semester hours in at least 2 science disciplines; history (must include American history and world history): 6 semester hours; social science (must include geography and economics): 6 semester hours; and arts and humanities: 6 semester hours

II. Elementary education PreK–6 endorsement requirements:
    A. Graduation from an approved teacher preparation program in elementary education PreK–6
        or
    B. A baccalaureate degree or higher from a regionally accredited college or university in the liberal arts and sciences (or equivalent) and fulfilling the following semester-hour requirements: English (must include composition, oral communication, and literature): 12 semester hours; mathematics: 15 semester hours; science (including a laboratory course): 15 semester hours in at least 2 science disciplines; history (must include American history and world history): 6 semester hours; social science (must include geography and economics): 6 semester hours; and arts and humanities: 3 semester hours

III. Middle education 6–8 endorsement requirements:
    A. Graduation from an approved teacher preparation discipline-specific program in middle education 6–8 with at least 1 area of academic preparation from the areas of English, mathematics, science, and history and social sciences
        or
    B. A degree from a regionally accredited college or university in the liberal arts and sciences (or equivalent), completion of a minimum of 21 semester hours in at least 1 area of academic preparation (concentration) that will be listed on the license, and completion of the minimum requirements for those areas in which the individual is

not seeking an area of academic preparation. Areas: English (21 semester hours), mathematics (24 semester hours), science (21 semester hours), history and social sciences (21 semester hours). The requirements for each subject area are detailed in the Virginia Licensure Regulations for School Personnel.

Endorsements for PreK–12 and Secondary Grades 6–12, Special Education, and Adult Education

The alternate route requirements apply to individuals seeking licensure outside of state-approved programs and through the alternate route to licensure. IHEs with approved programs in Virginia are not subject to specific semester-hour requirements since they incorporate state competencies into their programs.

I. Individuals seeking licensure with PreK–12 endorsements, special education, secondary grades 6–12 endorsements, and adult education may meet requirements through the completion of an approved program or, if employed by a Virginia public or nonpublic school, through the alternate route to licensure. Components of the licensure program include a degree in the liberal arts and sciences (or equivalent), professional teacher's assessments as prescribed by the Virginia Board of Education, specific endorsement requirements, and professional studies requirements. For endorsement-specific requirements, refer to the Virginia Licensure Regulations for School Personnel.

Washington

General Certificate Information

I. The teacher certificate authorizes service in the primary role of teacher.

II. The administrator certificate authorizes service in the primary role of building-level administration (principal), program administration (program administrator), or district-wide general administration (superintendent).

III. The educational staff associate (ESA) certificate authorizes service as school psychologist, counselor, social worker, school nurse, physical therapist, occupational therapist, or speech-language pathologist or audiologist.

IV. The paraeducator certificate is a state initiative to provide standards-based training and a professional growth track for paraeducators. Beyond the general certificate, paraeducators may obtain subject matter certificates—English language learner (ELL) and special education—and an advanced certificate. See the Paraeducator Certification section below for more information.

V. Levels of Certificates available to first-time applicants
   A. Teaching Certificates
      1. Residency Teaching Certificate
      2. Professional Teaching Certificate
      3. Career and Technical Educator (CTE) Teaching Certificate
   B. Administrator Certificates
      1. Residency Administrator Certificate—Principal and Program Administrator
      2. Professional Administrator Certificate—Principal and Program Administrator
      3. Initial Administrator Certificate—Superintendent Only
   C. Educational Staff Associate Certificates
      1. Residency ESA Certificate—School Counselor and School Psychologist
      2. Professional ESA Certificate—School Counselor and School Psychologist
      3. Initial ESA Certificate—School Nurse, Occupational Therapy, Physical Therapy, School Speech-Language Pathologist or Audiologist, Social Worker, School Behavioral Analyst
      4. Continuing ESA Certificate—School Nurse, Occupational Therapy, Physical Therapy, School Speech-Language Pathologist or Audiologist, Social Worker, School Psychologist, Counselor, School Behavioral Analyst

VI. Candidates for all professional, continuing, and first 5-year residency renewal certificates must complete coursework in issues of abuse, which must include information related to:
   A. Identification of physical, emotional, sexual, and substance abuse;
   B. The impact on learning and behavior;
   C. The responsibilities of a teacher, administrator, or ESA to report abuse or to provide assistance to victimized children;
   and

D. Methods of teaching about abuse and its prevention.
E. School nurses, counselors, psychologists, and social workers must also complete a suicide prevention training every 5 years.

Teaching Certificates

I. Residency Teaching Certificate
   A. Baccalaureate degree or higher from an accredited institution
   B. Completion of a state-approved teacher education program or alternate route program
      or
      Three years of out-of-state P–12 teaching experience and a regular out-of-state teaching certificate
   C. Completion of the WEST-B (Washington Educator Skills Test-Basic, a test of basic skills in reading, writing, and math), or approved alternative, and a WEST-E/NES (Washington Educator Skills Test-Endorsements/National Evaluation Series) content test in each endorsement area or approved alternative.
      1. For a list of all approved alternatives, visit the department website (see Appendix 1).
      2. The passing score requirement on the WEST-B or approved alternate basic skills testing has been removed. Content area testing such as the WEST-E/NES or an approved alternative still requires obtaining a passing score.
   D. Residency Teacher (First Issue) Certificate is issued without a defined expiration date. Once certificate holders are employed and reported as teachers by a Washington school district on the Washington State personnel report (S-275) with 1.5 full-time equivalent experience, their certificate will expire on the following June 30. Those teachers will need to submit a residency reissuance application to have a new certificate issued with a 5-year expiration date. Until this takes place, the certificate is valid without a defined expiration date.
   E. Certificate Endorsements
      1. Endorsements indicate the content area(s) and/or specializations for which the teacher is prepared.
      2. Teachers may obtain endorsements on their Washington certificate in several ways:
         a. Program + Test. Complete a college/university program approved to offer the endorsement. This can be in-state or out-of-state.
         b. National Board for Professional Teaching Standards. Earn National Board Certification in a Washington endorsement area. (A list of NBPTS-eligible endorsements can be found here: https://www.pesb.wa.gov/workforce/developing-current-educators/endorsements/.)
         c. Testing. Pass WEST-E/NES or an approved alternative test for a qualifying endorsement. (Test-only endorsements and an overview of how to add an endorsement can be found here: https://www.k12.wa.us/certification/teacher-certificate/already-washington-certified-educators/adding-endorsement.)

    d.   Migration Chart. Certain endorsements may be added by means of migration to align previously issued endorsements with current standards.

II.   Professional Teacher Certificate (valid for 5 years; renewable)

    A.   As of September 1, 2011, to earn a professional certificate, teachers must:

        1.   Have 1.5 years of teaching experience

        2.   Hold a certificate from the NBPTS

           a.   For full details about the portfolio of evidence requirements, visit www .pesb.wa.gov.

        3.   Complete an issues of abuse course

    B.   Existing professional certificates will remain valid until the expiration date stated on the certificate.

        1.   Renewal requires 100 clock hours, credits, Professional Growth Plans (PGPs), a renewed National Board Certificate, or a combination of these options every 5 years.

Administrator Certificates

I.   Residency Administrator Certificate—Principal and Program Administrator (valid until completion of 2 years of service in the role in Washington)

    A.   Master's degree from an accredited institution

    B.   Completion of an administrator preparation program in the administrative role or 3 years of successful experience in another state in the administrative role while holding a regular certificate in the role issued by another state

    C.   For Principal only:

        1.   Hold or have held a regular Teaching Certificate, CTE Certificate, or ESA Certificate

        2.   Verification of 3 years of successful school-based instructional experience in an educational setting

II.   Professional Administrator Certificate—Principal and Program Administrator

    A.   Completion of an approved professional certification program for either the principal or program administrator role or completion of a Continuing Administrator License (CAL) program in Oregon

III.   Initial Administrator Certificate—Superintendent Only (valid 7 years)

    A.   Master's degree from an accredited institution

    B.   Completion of an administrator preparation program for superintendent or 3 years of successful experience as a superintendent, deputy superintendent, or assistant superintendent while holding a superintendent certificate issued by another state

    C.   Valid regular Teaching, ESA, or Administrator (Principal or Program Administrator) Certificate

IV.   Continuing Administrator Certificate—Superintendent Only (valid for 5-year periods; renewed upon completion of 100 clock hours, credits, PGPs, or a combination of these options)

    A.   Completion of all requirements for the Initial Administrator Certificate—Superintendent

    B.   Master's degree plus 60 quarter hours (40 semester hours) of graduate-level coursework in education completed after the baccalaureate degree, or a doctorate in education

C. Completion of 180 days of service as a superintendent, deputy superintendent, or assistant superintendent, 30 days of which must have been in the same school district

Educational Staff Associate Certification

I. Residency Educational Staff Associate (ESA) Certificate for school counselor and school psychologist
   A. Completion of master's degree with major in the appropriate specialization
   B. Completion of state-approved program for certification in the appropriate ESA role
      or
      If no program, must have completed 3 years of out-of-state K–12 experience in the ESA role under that certificate
      1. For school psychologist only: must hold Nationally Certified School Psychologist (NCSP) Certificate issued after December 31, 1991, by the National School Psychology Certification Board; if the other state didn't require a certificate, must have 3 years of out-of-state experience in that role.
   C. Completion of a comprehensive examination required in the master's degree program. If a candidate has been awarded a master's degree without a comprehensive examination, the candidate, as a condition for certification, must arrange to take such an examination with any accredited college or university and provide the superintendent of public instruction with an affidavit from the chair of the department of the academic field that he or she has successfully completed this comprehensive examination.
      1. School Counselor
         a. Successful completion of a proctored, comprehensive examination of the knowledge included in the coursework for the required master's degree, given by an accredited institution of higher education
            or
         b. Passing score on the Praxis II Professional School Counselor examination administered by Educational Testing Service (ETS)
      2. School Psychologist
         a. Successful completion of a proctored, comprehensive examination of the knowledge included in the coursework for the required master's degree, given by an accredited institution of higher education
            or
         b. Passing score on the Praxis II School Psychologist examination administered by ETS

II. Professional ESA Certificate for school counselor and school psychologist (valid minimum of 5 years). Requirements:
   A. Hold a certificate from the NBPTS if a school counselor (a Professional ESA Certificate for school counselor issued on the basis of holding a valid NBPTS school counselor certificate will have a validity of 5 years or the validity of the NBPTS certificate, whichever is greater)

or

Hold a valid certificate from the National Association of School Psychologists (NASP) if a school psychologist

B. Course on issues of abuse (see III, A, 5, immediately below, for full description of required course content)

C. Completion of an approved suicide prevention course (see III, A, 6, immediately below, for full description of required course content)

III. Continuing ESA Certificate

A. For school psychologist

1. Candidate must have completed 180 days of experience in the role (or the equivalent of 180 days of full-time service), of which 30 days must be in the same district.

2. Candidate must hold a master's degree with a major or specialization in school psychology and must have completed at least 10 quarter (7 semester) credit hours of graduate work offered by a college or university with a state-approved school psychologist program (totaling 100 clock hours equivalent),
    or
    100 clock hours of study, which meet the state continuing education clock-hour criteria pursuant to Washington Administrative Code (WAC) 181–85,
    or
    A combination of credits and clock hours equivalent to the above.

3. The above academic study shall be:
    a. Based on the school psychologist performance domains included in WAC 181–78A-270(5)(a);
    b. Taken subsequent to the issuance of the Initial or Residency Certificate for school psychologist;
        and
    c. Determined in consultation with and approved by the candidate's employer or the administrator of a state-approved school psychologist preparation program.

4. Candidate must have completed a comprehensive exam relevant to the field of specialization. For those who did not complete such an exam as part of a master's degree program, there are acceptable alternatives; for more information, visit https://www.k12.wa.us/certification/educational-staff-associate-certificates/esa-first-time-applicant/school-psychologist-first-time.

5. Candidates must have taken coursework in issues of abuse, which must include information related to identification of physical, emotional, sexual, and substance abuse; the impact on learning and behavior; the responsibilities of an ESA to report abuse or to provide assistance to victimized children; and methods of teaching about abuse and its prevention.

6. Effective July 1, 2015, candidates shall attest to the completion of a Professional Educator Standards Board–approved suicide prevention training within the previous 5 years, per Revised Code of Washington (RCW) 28A.410.226.

B. For school nurse, school occupational therapist, school physical therapist, school social worker and school speech-language pathologist or audiologist

1. The Continuing ESA Certificate is the advanced-level regular certificate available for these positions. For full details, see https://www.k12.wa.us/certification/educational-staff-associate-certificates/esa-reissue-renewal-conversion-and-upgrade/upgrade-initial-continuing-esa.

IV. Initial ESA Certificate for school counselor, school psychologist, school social worker, school nurse, school occupational therapist, school physical therapist, and school speech-language pathologist or audiologist

A. The Initial ESA Certificate is the first-level regular certificate for these positions. For full details, see https://www.k12.wa.us/certification/educational-staff-associate-certificates/esa-first-time-applicant#content.

Career and Technical Educator Certification

I. Initial Career and Technical Educator (CTE) Certificate

A. Route 1 (University/Full Teacher Program)

1. Hold a bachelor's degree, which includes 45 quarter hours in specialty study
2. Complete a state-approved CTE plan in one of the 4 broad endorsement areas: Agricultural, Business and Marketing, Family and Consumer Sciences, Technology Education
3. Complete an approved content knowledge test (e.g., WEST-B, WEST-E/NES)
4. Complete an issues of abuse course (part of the program if in-state)
5. Have 1 year of occupational experience (2,000 hours)
    a. If all or part of this experience is more than 10 years old, 300 hours must be recent. Volunteer hours may be used for the 300 recent hours only.
    b. Only for Family and Consumer Sciences, the 2,000 hours may be teaching experience.
6. Must also apply for the Residency Teacher Certificate (or apply to add endorsement to the Residency Teacher Certificate)

B. Route 2 (Business and Industry Route/Specialty Program Areas)

1. This will not net one of the 4 broad endorsement areas (see I, A, 2, immediately above).
2. Complete a Professional Educator Standards Board–approved program for the Business and Industry (B&I) route or any other out-of-state approved B&I route program.
    a. To view the B&I routes list for Washington follow the Business and Industry route PDF link at https://www.k12.wa.us/certification/teacher-certificate/career-and-technical-education-applicants/initial-career-and-technical-educator-cte-certificate.
3. Complete an issues of abuse course
4. Take the WEST-B test
5. Have 6,000 hours (3 years) of occupational experience in the last 10 years, including 1 year of non-teaching occupational experience.
    a. Up to 4,000 hours can be teaching.
        i. Biomedical Science and Health Science Biotechnology applicants may have all 6,000 hours in teaching biology.

        ii.   STEM applicants may have all 6,000 hours in teaching experience in science, technology, engineering, and/or math.

II.   Out-of-State Applicants

    A.   Copy of out-of-state CTE (or vocational) certificate and 3 years of teaching grades (7–12) in the subject area

       or

       Verification of CTE program completion from out of state

    B.   Verification of 2,000 hours (1 full year) of non-teaching industry experience in the last 10 years

       1.   For the 4 broad endorsement areas (see I, A, 2, above), applicant must also apply for Residency Teacher Certificate.

       2.   For other specialty areas, applicant must meet the experience requirements outlined above (see I, A, 5, and I, B, 5).

III.   CTE Conditional Certificate (issued for up to 2 school years)

    A.   CTE Conditional Certificates are initiated by the school district or skills center within the E-Certification account of the individual requested. The district completing the district request must have the correct available role of E-Certification District Personnel Administrator in order to complete the district request within E-Certification. Please visit the following link for information on how to complete this process: http://k12.wa.us/Certification/e-Cert/default.aspx. On the right-hand side of the page are the E-Certification User Guides.

    B.   Applicant must have fingerprints on file.

    C.   The certificate is subject to specific limitations, and the applicant must complete a written training plan developed in coordination with the CTE administrator and the CTE advisory committee.

    D.   If the applicant needs Worksite Learning or Career Choices or a combination of both, the applicant must be enrolled in a CTE program and have already completed the Worksite Learning coursework.

Paraeducator Certification

I.   General Paraeducator Certificate (valid for lifetime)

    A.   Complete the Fundamental Course of Study

    B.   Earn 70 clock hours or equivalents

II.   Subject Matter Certificate (valid for 5 years; renewable)

    A.   English Language Learners

       1.   Complete the Fundamental Course of Study

       2.   Earn 20 clock hours or equivalents in ELL subject matter

    B.   Special Education

       1.   Complete the Fundamental Course of Study

       2.   Earn 20 clock hours or equivalents in Special Education subject matter

III.   Advanced Paraeducator Certificate (valid for 5 years; renewable)

    A.   Hold a General Paraeducator Certificate

    B.   Earn 75 additional clock hours or equivalents related to the duties of an advanced paraeducator

West Virginia

West Virginia educator certification rules were in the process of review at press time. The most current information can be found in West Virginia State Board (WVSB) Policy 5202 at http://wvde.state.wv.us/policies/.

General Information and Requirements

I. West Virginia licenses include:
   A. Professional Certificate
   B. Provisional Alternative Teaching Certificate
   C. Temporary Certificate
   D. Provisional Teaching Certificate (nonrenewable)
   E. Provisional Teaching Certificate (renewable)
   F. Career/Technical Education Certificate
   G. Temporary Career/Technical Education Certificate
   H. First-Class/Full-Time Permit (Professional and CTE)
   I. Adult Permit
   J. Authorization
   K. Paraprofessional Certificate (granted to service personnel)
   L. Advanced Credential

II. Valid grade levels
   A. Preschool Education (PreK)
   B. Preschool to Adult (PreK–Adult)
   C. Kindergarten to Grade 12 (K–12)
   D. Early Education (PreK–K)
   E. Early Childhood (K–4)
   F. Elementary Education (K–6)
   G. Middle Childhood (5–9)
   H. Adolescent (9–Adult)
   I. Adult (Adult)
   J. Middle to Adult (5–Adult)
   K. Select Authorizations (K–5), (5–10)

Licenses for Professional Educators

I. General requirements for all applicants for certificates detailed in this section:
   A. Applicant must be of good moral character; physically, mentally, and emotionally qualified to perform the duties of a teacher; and 18 years old.
   B. FBI background check for initial certificates
   C. State background check for initial certificates

II.   Provisional Alternative Teaching Certificate (valid 1 year)

    A.   This certificate may be issued to an individual who currently possesses a valid West Virginia Statement of Eligibility; meets prescribed experience and/or academic and professional standards from an out-of-state institution of higher education (IHE), as described in WVSB Policy 5202, or holds a valid Alternative Teaching Certificate; is employed full-time in a West Virginia public school system; and meets the requirements of WVSB Policy 5202. This certificate is issued for 1 year, may be renewed twice, and is not eligible for additional endorsement based on passing content proficiency exams described in WVSB Policy 5202.

III.   Provisional Teaching Certificate

    A.   Applicant must be of good moral character; physically, mentally, and emotionally qualified to perform the duties of a teacher; and 18 years old.

    B.   FBI background check for initial certificates

    C.   State background check for initial certificates

    D.   Minimum proficiency levels in WVSB-approved tests:

        1.   Basic skills: Praxis (CORE)—Pre-Professional Skills in Reading, Writing, and Mathematics or proof of eligible exemption as stated in the WVBE Licensure and Testing Directory located on the WVDE website (wvde.us)

        2.   Content specialization(s): appropriate Praxis II test(s)

        3.   Professional knowledge: Praxis II test that includes at least a portion of the grade levels indicated on license sought or an approved Teacher Performance Assessment (TPA) as indicated in WVSB Policy 5100

    E.   Successful completion of a regionally accredited IHE's state-approved program and the recommendation of the designated official at the college or university through which the program was completed

    F.   Out-of-state applicants must meet the following criteria:

        1.   Applicant must be of good moral character; physically, mentally, and emotionally qualified to perform the duties of a teacher; and 18 years old.

        2.   FBI background check for initial certificates

        3.   State background check for initial certificates

        4.   Bachelor's degree or master's degree from an accredited IHE or an equivalent degree from an IHE in a foreign country (must be evaluated as per G, 2, immediately below)

    G.   Out-of-state applicants must submit proof of:

        1.   Successful completion of an out-of-state approved teacher education program from an accredited IHE

            or

            Verification of successful completion of a state's Alternative Certification Program

            or

            Evaluated foreign academic credentials

            or

            Valid out-of-state certificate

            and

        2.   All West Virginia–required licensure exams

IV. Initial Professional Teaching Certificate (valid 3 years)

A. A valid out-of-state professional certificate (no tests are required under this option)
or
Successful completion of a state-approved alternative delivery program that incorporates the pre-professional skills, content, and professional education standards approved by the state board, including a student teaching experience or documentation of an "in lieu" experience
and

B. Successful completion of a Beginning Educator Internship/Induction (W. Va. Code §18A-3C-3) for classroom teachers or qualifies for exemption as stated in section 9.5
and

C. Successful completion of a nationally-normed, WVBE-approved, scientifically valid and reliable TPA
or
Applicants admitted into a WVBE-approved EPP prior to September 1, 2021, who have been continuously enrolled may use passing scores on the Principles of Learning and Teaching (PLT) to convert the Provisional Teaching Certificate
and

D. Six semester hours of appropriate college/university coursework reflecting a 3.0 GPA, or WVDE e-Learning coursework within the last 5 years related to the public school program as defined in section 9.10.g and completed subsequent to the issuance of the Provisional Teaching Certificate to be converted
or
Hold a minimum of a master's degree plus 30 Salary Classification based on the awarding of a master's degree
or
Have reached 60 years of age and present a copy of the birth certificate or official government-issued documentation
and

E. Complete one of the following:

1. Three years of full-time teaching experience under the Provisional Teaching Certificate and in 1 or more area(s) of endorsement on such certificate in West Virginia
and
Successful evaluations for each year taught under the Provisional Teaching Certificate within the West Virginia Educator Evaluation System with an earned performance rating of Emerging or above; and recommendation of the employing county superintendent, multi-county CTE administrator, or WVDE West Virginia Schools of Diversion and Transition (WVSDT) Superintendent or designee
or

2. Hold a valid out-of-state license and have completed a minimum of 5 years of successful teaching experience in a public school within the last 7 years in the area for which licensure is being sought and in the state where the license was issued

V. Professional Five-Year Teaching Certificate (valid 5 years)

    A. Successful completion of the Beginning Educator Internship for classroom, unless the applicant holds a valid out-of-state certificate and has 5 years of teaching experience in another state, or received the Initial West Virginia Teaching Certificate prior to January 1, 1992

    B. Six semester hours of appropriate college/university coursework reflecting a 3.0 GPA and related to the public school program, or 2 WVDE e-Learning courses, unless the applicant holds a minimum of a master's degree plus 30 Salary Classification based on the awarding of a master's degree

    C. Two years of experience, 1 year of which must be completed in West Virginia, within 1 endorsement, or a combination of the endorsements, on the Initial Professional Teaching Certificate

    D. Recommendation of the superintendent in the county in which the educator teaches, or if the educator has not been employed within the past 12 months in a West Virginia public school system, a character recommendation form completed by a non-relative

VI. Permanent Professional Teaching Certificate (valid unless surrendered, suspended, or revoked)

    A. Hold or be eligible for the Five-Year Professional Teaching Certificate
       and
       Master's degree related to the public school
       and
       Five years of educational experience, including 2 within the specialization(s) for which the permanent certificate is requested
       or

    B. Hold a valid Professional Five-Year Teaching Certificate
       and
       Renew the Professional Five-Year Teaching Certificate once based on:

       1. Six semester hours of appropriate renewal credit reflecting a 3.0 GPA or 2 WVDE e-Learning courses
          or

       2. Minimum of a master's degree plus 30 Salary Classification based on the awarding of a master's degree
          or

       3. Age 60
       or
       Hold certification through the National Board for Professional Teaching Standards (NBPTS)

VII. Requirements for renewal of any Professional Teaching Certificate:

       1. Six semester hours of appropriate college/university coursework reflecting a minimum 3.0 GPA and related to the public school program, or 2 West Virginia Department of Education (WVDE) e-Learning courses, unless the applicant holds a master's degree plus 30 Salary Classification or has reached age 60 and presents a photocopy of his or her birth certificate

          a. The 6 semester hours must meet 1 of the following criteria:

          i.   Courses relevant to a master's degree in a curriculum related to the public school program
              or
          ii.   Courses related to improvement of instruction and the applicant's current endorsement area
              or
         iii. Courses needed to qualify for an additional endorsement
              or
         iv. Credit prescribed by the county as a result of an applicant's evaluation
     b.   If the applicant only has 3 hours of coursework or 1 WVDE e-Learning course, a 1-year certificate may be requested.
   2.   Recommendation of the employing county's superintendent

VIII. Individuals who hold a valid out-of-state teaching certificate, have completed a state-approved educator preparation program, and hold a bachelor's degree from a regionally accredited IHE should visit http://wvde.state.wv.us/certification for specific information.

Specializations

I. Recognized Programmatic Level

   A. Preschool Education (PreK–PreK), Early Education (PreK–K), Early Childhood (K–4), Middle Childhood (5–9), Adolescent (9–12), Adult (Adult)

II. Grade-Level Options for General Education Specializations Current Programs:

   A. Agriculture (5–Adult); Algebra I (5–Adult); Algebra II (5–Adult); American Sign Language (PreK–Adult, 5–Adult); any Modern Foreign Language (PreK–Adult, 5–Adult); Art (PreK–Adult, 5–Adult, 5–9); Biology (9–Adult); Business Education (5–Adult, 9–Adult); Chemistry (9–Adult); Chemistry/Physics (9–Adult); Chinese (PreK–Adult, 5–Adult); Computer Science Education (PreK–Adult); Dance (PreK–Adult, 5–Adult); Driver Education (9–Adult); Earth and Space Science (5–Adult); Early Childhood Education (K–4); Early Education (PreK–K); Elementary Education (K–6); Elementary Math Education (K–6); Elementary Math Specialist (K–6); English (5–Adult, 5–9); English as a Second Language (PreK–Adult); Family & Consumer Science (5–Adult); French (PreK–Adult, 5–Adult); General Math through Algebra I (5–9); General Science (5–Adult, 5–9); Geometry (5–Adult); German (PreK–Adult, 5–Adult); Health (PreK–Adult, 5–Adult); Instructional Technology (PreK–Adult); Japanese (PreK–Adult, 5–Adult); Journalism (5–Adult, 9–Adult); Latin (PreK–Adult, 5–Adult); Marketing (9–Adult); Mathematics Comprehensive (5–Adult); Music (PreK–Adult); Oral Communications (5–Adult, 9–Adult); Physical Education (PreK–Adult, 5–Adult, 5–9); Physics (9–Adult); Preschool Education (PreK–PreK); Reading (PreK–K, K–6, 5–Adult); Reading Specialist* (PreK–Adult); Russian (PreK–Adult, 5–Adult); School Library/Media (PreK–Adult); Social Studies (5–Adult, 5–9); Spanish (PreK–Adult, 5–Adult); Technology Education (5–Adult); Theater (PreK–Adult); Wellness (Health–Physical Education) (PreK–Adult)

III. Grade-Level Options for Special Education Specializations:
    A. Autism (PreK–PreK, K–6, 5–Adult); Emotional/Behavior Disorders (K–6, 5–Adult); Gifted (1–12); Deaf and Hard of Hearing (PreK–Adult); Intellectual Disabilities (K–6, 5–Adult); Multi-Categorical (E/BD, MI, SLD) (K–6, 5–Adult); Preschool Special Needs (PreK–K); Severe Disabilities (K–Adult); Specific Learning Disabilities (K–6, 5–Adult); Visually Impaired (PreK–Adult)
IV. Grade-Level Options for Student Support Specializations (all are PreK–Adult):
    A. Counselor,* School Nurse, School Psychologist,* Social Services and Attendance, Speech-Language Pathologist,* Speech Assistant
V. Grade-Level Options for Administrative Specializations (all are PreK–Adult):
    A. General Supervisor,* Principal,* Superintendent*

*Master's degree required

Administrative Certificates

I. Provisional Administrative Certificate (valid for 5 years)
    A. Persons applying for the Administrative Certificate endorsed for school principal, supervisor of instruction, and/or superintendent based on completion of an accredited educational leadership program, or a valid out-of-state administrative certificate, and a minimum of 3 years of management-level or teaching experience will be granted a renewable Provisional Administrative Certificate valid for 5 years.
    B. Individuals holding a Provisional Administrative Certificate may be employed as an administrator in a West Virginia school system but are unable to perform evaluation until they hold an Initial Administrative Certificate with the completion of the Evaluation Leadership Institute (ELI).
II. Professional Administrative Certificate (valid for 5 years)
    A. Upon employment as an administrator in a West Virginia school system and completion of the ELI as required by W. Va. Code §18A-3A-3, the applicant will be issued a Professional Administrative Certificate valid for 5 years.
III. Permanent Professional Administrative Certificate (remains valid unless surrendered, suspended, or revoked)
    A. Requirements for converting the Initial Professional Administrative Certificate to the Permanent Professional Administrative Certificate:
      1. Six semester hours of appropriate renewal credit related to the public school program or 2 WVDE e-Learning courses
         or
         Master's degree plus 30 Salary Classification
      2. Five years of educational experience
        a. Two years of experience must be in any, or a combination of, the specializations reflected on the Professional Administration Certificate.
        b. One year of experience must be completed in West Virginia.
      3. Recommendation of superintendent

Student Support Certificates

I. School Counselor
  A. Temporary Professional Student Support Certificate for out-of-state applicants (valid 1 year, nonrenewable)
    1. Issued to applicant who meets requirements for a Provisional Student Support Certificate (see Licenses for Professional Educators, II, above) and the following criteria:
      a. Master's degree in counseling from a regionally accredited IHE in a state other than West Virginia
      b. Successful completion of an accredited school counseling program
      c. GPA of 3.0
  B. Initial Professional Student Support Certificate (valid 3 years)
    1. Issued to applicant who meets the following criteria:
      a. Master's degree in counseling from an accredited IHE
      b. Successful completion of an accredited school counseling program
      c. West Virginia–required Praxis exam
  C. Professional Student Support Certificate (valid 5 years)
    1. Issued to applicant who meets the requirements for a Professional Five-Year Student Support Certificate:
      a. Two years of work experience (1 year of which must be completed within West Virginia) as a school counselor
        and
      b. Six semester hours of college coursework relating to public education or 2 WVDE e-Learning courses
        or
        Master's degree plus 30 Salary Classification
        or
        Has reached 60 years of age
  D. Permanent Professional Student Support Certificate
    1. Issued to an applicant who meets the requirements for a Permanent Professional Teaching Certificate:
      a. Five years of educational work experience in the area(s) for which certification is held, including 2 years' work as a school counselor (1 year must be completed within West Virginia)
        and
      b. Six semester hours of college coursework relating to public education or 2 WVDE e-Learning courses
        or
        Master's degree plus 30 Salary Classification
        or
        Has reached 60 years of age
II. School Psychologist
  A. Temporary Professional Student Support Certificate

1. Issued to applicant who meets requirements for a Provisional Student Support Certificate
2. See I, School Counselor, A, directly above.
   B. Initial Professional Student Support Certificate (valid 3 years)
     1. Issued to applicant who completes master's degree in a field related to education from an accredited institution of higher education as defined in WVSB Policy 5202
     2. See I, School Counselor, B, directly above.
   C. Professional Student Support Certificate (valid 5 years)
     1. See I, School Counselor, C, directly above.
   D. Permanent Professional Student Support Certificate
     1. See I, School Counselor, D, directly above.

III. Speech-Language Pathologist
   A. Temporary Student Support Certificate
     1. Issued to applicant who meets requirements for a Provisional Student Support Certificate
     2. See I, School Counselor, A, directly above.
   B. Initial Professional Student Support Certificate
     1. Issued to applicant who earns a master's degree in an approved program in speech-language pathology from a regionally accredited IHE
   C. See I, School Counselor, C and D, directly above.

IV. Renewal of the Professional Student Support Certificate
   A. Application for renewal of the Professional Student Support Certificate for School Counselor, School Psychologist, and Speech-Language Pathologist must be submitted after January 1 of the year in which the license expires.
   B. The applicant for licensure must submit evidence of satisfying the following:
     1. Completed 6 semester hours of appropriate college/university coursework related to the public school program with a minimum 3.0 GPA or 2 WVDE e-Learning courses
       a. If the applicant only has 3 hours of coursework or 1 WVDE e-Learning course, a 1-year certificate may be requested.
     2. See Licenses for Professional Educators, VII, B, above, except that requirements must be met in the 5-year period immediately preceding the date of application.

V. Professional Five-Year Student Support Certificate
   A. Six semester hours of appropriate college/university coursework reflecting a 3.0 GPA and related to the public school program or 2 WVDE e-Learning courses
     or
     Minimum of a master's plus 30 Salary Classification
   B. Two years of experience within 1 endorsement, or a combination of endorsements, on the Initial Professional Student Support Certificate
   C. Recommendation of superintendent

VI. Permanent Professional Student Support Certificate
   A. Complete the following:
     1. Five years of educational experience in areas for which certification is held (1 year must be completed in West Virginia)

and

2. Master's degree related to the public school program
    or
    Professional Five-Year Student Support Certificate
    and

3. Six semester hours of appropriate renewal credit reflecting a 3.0 GPA or
    2 WVDE e-Learning courses
    or
    Minimum of a master's degree plus 30 Salary Classification
    or
    Has reached 60 years of age

    or

B. Hold NBPTS Certification

Wisconsin

Educator Standards

I. Teacher Standards: To receive a license to teach in Wisconsin, an applicant shall complete an approved program and demonstrate proficient performance in the knowledge, skills, and dispositions under all of the following standards:

  A. Pupil Development. The teacher understands how pupils grow and develop, recognizing that patterns of learning and development vary individually within and across the cognitive, linguistic, social, emotional, and physical areas. The teacher designs and implements developmentally appropriate and challenging learning experiences for pupils.

  B. Learning Differences. The teacher uses his or her understanding of individual pupil differences and diverse cultures and communities to ensure inclusive learning environments that enable each pupil to meet high standards.

  C. Learning Environments. The teacher works with others to create environments that support individual and collaborative learning, and that encourage positive social interaction, active engagement in learning, and self-motivation.

  D. Content Knowledge. The teacher understands the central concepts, tools of inquiry, and structures of each discipline he or she teaches. The teacher creates learning experiences that make the discipline accessible and meaningful for pupils to assure mastery of the content.

  E. Application of Content. The teacher understands how to connect concepts and use differing perspectives to engage pupils in critical thinking, creativity, and collaborative problem solving related to authentic local and global issues.

  F. Assessment. The teacher understands and uses multiple methods of assessment to engage pupils in their own growth, to monitor pupil progress, and to guide the teacher's and pupil's decision making.

  G. Planning for Instruction. The teacher plans instruction that supports every pupil in meeting rigorous learning goals by drawing upon knowledge of content areas, curriculum, cross-disciplinary skills, pedagogy, pupils, and pupils' communities.

  H. Instructional Strategies. The teacher understands and uses a variety of instructional strategies to encourage pupils to develop a deep understanding of content areas and their connections, and to develop skills to apply knowledge in a meaningful way.

  I. Professional Learning and Ethical Practice. The teacher engages in ongoing professional learning. The teacher uses evidence to continuously evaluate the teacher's own practice, including the effects of the teacher's choices and actions on pupils, their families, other educators, and the community. The teacher adapts the teacher's own practice to meet the needs of each pupil.

  J. Leadership and Collaboration. The teacher seeks appropriate leadership roles and opportunity in order to take responsibility for pupil learning, to collaborate with pupils, their families, educators, and the community, and to advance the profession.

II. Administrator Standards: To receive a license in a school administrator category, an applicant shall complete an approved program in school administration and demonstrate proficient performance in the knowledge, skills, and dispositions under all of the following standards:

  A. Mission, Vision, and Core Values. Effective educational leaders develop, advocate, and enact a shared mission, vision, and core values of high-quality education, academic success, and well-being of each pupil.

  B. Ethics and Professional Norms. Effective educational leaders act ethically and according to professional norms to promote each pupil's academic success and well-being.

  C. Equity and Cultural Responsiveness. Effective educational leaders strive for equity of educational opportunity and culturally responsive practices to promote each pupil's academic success and well-being.

  D. Curriculum, Instruction, and Assessment. Effective educational leaders develop and support intellectually rigorous and coherent systems of curriculum, instruction, and assessment to promote each pupil's academic success and well-being.

  E. Care and Support. Effective educational leaders cultivate an inclusive, caring, and supportive school community to promote each pupil's academic success and well-being.

  F. Professional Capacity of School Personnel. Effective educational leaders develop the professional capacity and practice of school personnel to promote each pupil's academic success and well-being.

  G. Professional Community. Effective educational leaders foster a professional community of teachers and other professional staff to promote each pupil's academic success and well-being.

  H. Meaningful Engagement. Effective educational leaders engage families and the community in meaningful, reciprocal, and mutually beneficial ways to promote each pupil's academic success and well-being.

  I. Operations and Management. Effective educational leaders effectively manage school operations and resources to promote each pupil's academic success and well-being.

  J. School Improvement. Effective educational leaders act as agents of continuous school improvement to promote each pupil's academic success and well-being.

  K. Teacher Standards. Effective educational leaders understand and demonstrate competence in the teacher standards under Wisconsin Administrative Code PI 34.002.

III. Pupil Services Standards: To receive a license in a pupil services category (school counselors, school social workers, school psychologists, and school nurses), an applicant shall complete an approved program and demonstrate proficient performance in the knowledge, skills, and dispositions under all of the following standards:

  A. The pupil services professional understands the Ten Teacher Standards.

  B. The pupil services professional understands the complexities of learning and has knowledge of comprehensive, coordinated practice strategies that support pupil learning, health, safety, and development.

C. The pupil services professional has the ability to use research, research methods, and knowledge about issues and trends to improve practice in schools and classrooms.

D. The pupil services professional understands and represents professional ethics and social behaviors appropriate for school and community.

E. The pupil services professional understands the organization, development, management, and content of collaborative and mutually supportive pupil services programs within educational settings.

F. The pupil services professional is able to address comprehensively the wide range of social, emotional, behavioral, and physical issues and circumstances that may limit pupils' abilities to achieve positive learning outcomes through development, implementation, and evaluation of system-wide interventions and strategies.

G. The pupil services professional interacts successfully with pupils, parents, professional educators, employers, and community support systems such as juvenile justice, public health, human services, and adult education.

License Stages for Teachers, Administrators, and Pupil Services

I. Provisional Educator License (valid 3 years; renewable)
   A. Issued to an applicant who completes 1 of the following approved pathways
       1. Approved Program
           a. Hold a bachelor's degree or higher
           b. Complete state-approved educator preparation program
               i.   Officer of the institution's state-approved educator preparation program must endorse applicant.
               ii. Additional requirements/experience may be required for specific license areas.
               iii. Meet applicable Wisconsin statutory and testing requirements
       2. License Based on Reciprocity
           a. Hold a valid teacher or administrator license in another state
           b. Have 1 year of successful experience under that license or under a license or permit in Wisconsin
       3. Online Alternative Program
           a. Complete an alternative teacher certification program operated by an alternative preparation program provider that is a nonprofit organization under section 501(c)(3) of the Internal Revenue Code
               i. The program must operate in at least 5 states, have been in operation for at least 10 years, and require the candidate to pass both a subject area and pedagogy test known as the Professional Teaching Knowledge exam to receive a certificate.
       and
   B. Applicant must also complete a satisfactory background check
II. Lifetime Educator License
   A. Issued to an applicant who has held a provisional license; submits verification of

6 semesters of successful teaching, pupil services, or administrative experience in a school district; meets all statutory requirements; and has satisfactory background checks.

III. Master Educator License
    A. Mastery of Wisconsin standards evidenced by
        1. Portfolio assessment through the Wisconsin Master Educator Assessment Process (WMEAP) requiring:
            a. Related master's degree
            b. Demonstrated improvement in pupil learning
            c. Assessment by Department of Public Instruction (DPI)–trained WMEAP Team
            d. Professional contributions
            or
        2. National Board of Professional Teaching Standards Certification
    B. Satisfactory background check

Testing Requirements

I. Content knowledge proficiency is demonstrated by
    A. A passing score on a standardized test (e.g., Praxis II or American Council for the Teaching of Foreign Languages [ACTFL] World Language tests),
    B. A GPA of 3.0 or higher in content area,
        or
    C. A content portfolio developed by the educator preparation program.

II. Foundations of Reading Test
    A. A passing score of 240 or higher is required for any applicant seeking initial licensure as an elementary teacher, special education teacher, reading teacher, or reading specialist.
    B. Special education teacher candidates can complete a Department-approved course of study that satisfies all of the following:
        1. The course of study provides rigorous instruction in the teaching of phonemic awareness, phonics, vocabulary, reading comprehension, and fluency.
        2. A student in the course of study receives feedback and coaching from an individual who is an expert in reading instruction.
        3. A student in the course of study demonstrates competence in phonemic awareness, phonics, vocabulary, reading comprehension, and fluency by providing a portfolio of work.

III. Contact the Teacher Education, Professional Development, and Licensing team at the Wisconsin Department of Public Instruction (see Appendix 1) or visit https://dpi.wi.gov/licensing/epp/testing-epp for more information.

Wyoming

General Licensure Information

I. All teachers and administrators employed in a Wyoming school district must be licensed in accordance with state law. The Wyoming Professional Teaching Standards Board (PTSB) requires all Wyoming educators to have completed an approved teacher preparation program from an accredited institution of higher education (IHE) in order to become licensed to teach in a Wyoming school district.

II. There are 2 routes to teacher licensure in Wyoming.
   A. Licensure through program completion requires the completion of an educator preparation program from an accredited college or university.
   B. Licensure through out-of-state work experience requires that the applicant has taught 3 out of the last 6 years in the state of licensure, including verification of full-time teaching, administrative, or other school experience, signed by the respective school administrators. Please note that student teaching is not accepted as experience in this regard.

Requirements for Initial Licensure

I. To obtain initial, first-time licensure, applicants must meet all the following requirements:
   A. Complete an approved educator preparation program at an accredited college or university. The program must:
      1. Include student teaching;
      2. Lead to an institutional recommendation for licensure;
         and
      3. Lead to licensure in the state where the program is located.
   B. Submit an institutional recommendation for licensure, signed by an authorized official, recommending the applicant for licensure in the applicable endorsement area(s)
   C. Submit official college transcripts documenting completion of teacher preparation program
   D. Undergo fingerprinting and complete a background check
   E. Demonstrate knowledge of the US and Wyoming Constitutions either through coursework or by successfully passing an exam
   F. Pass approved Praxis II exams in 2 teaching areas:
      1. Elementary Education—a passing score on Praxis II exam 5001 by passing the included tests with the following scores or better: 5002, 157; 5003, 157; 5004, 155; and 5005, 159
      2. Social Studies Composite—a passing score of 158 or better on Praxis II exam 5081/0081 Social Studies: Content Knowledge for grades 6–12, and 5089/0089 Middle School Social Studies for grades 5–8

     G.   Submit a complete application packet and pay appropriate fees

II.   Out-of-state applicants

     A.   All out-of-state applicants are required to submit the documentation listed below in addition to their complete application packet, fingerprint cards, institutional recommendation (if applicable), and US and Wyoming Constitutions requirements.

         1.   Verification of work history for the past 6 years, signed by each of the applicant's school administrators or board chairs during that time period

         2.   Copy of the applicant's current, valid teaching certificate or license from the state in which he or she taught

         3.   Copy of the applicant's test scores from Praxis II exam(s) or an equivalent exam from his or her state

         4.   In accordance with the National Association of State Directors of Teacher Education and Certification (NASDTEC) Interstate Agreement, PTSB may require an out-of-state applicant to complete additional requirements to obtain a Wyoming teaching license.

Endorsements by Grade/Age Level

Endorsement(s) for which an applicant qualifies will appear on the standard license. As determined by program approval standards, the endorsement(s) will allow teachers to provide instruction in the classroom or the school personnel to provide services in the areas identified on the license. Teaching endorsements are valid at the grade level for which they are issued.

    I.   Birth to Age 5: Early Childhood/Special Education

   II.   Birth to Age 8 (or Grade 3): Early Childhood

  III.   Birth to Age 5: Preschool Early Childhood (excluding Kindergarten)

  IV.   Elementary Level K–6: art; elementary teacher; English as a second language; music; music instrumental; music vocal; reading; physical education; adapted physical education; institutional teacher, world languages

   V.   Middle Level 5–8: art; English as a second language; health; language arts; mathematics; music; music instrumental; music vocal; reading; physical education; adapted physical education; science; social studies; world languages

  VI.   Secondary level 6–12: agriculture; anthropology; art; biology; business; chemistry; computer science; drama; driver's education; earth science; economics; English; English as a second language; family consumer science; geography; health; history; journalism; mathematics; music; music instrumental; music vocal; physical education; adapted physical education; physical science; physics; political science; psychology; reading; social studies comprehensive; sociology; speech; trade and technical; at-risk/alternative teacher; institutional teacher; world language (Chinese, Japanese, French, Latin, German, Russian, Italian, Spanish)

 VII.   K–12: art; audiology; educational diagnostician; English as a second language; health; gifted and talented; music; music instrumental; music vocal; physical education; adapted physical education; reading; institutional teacher; school nurse; world languages

VIII.   Special Education K–6/5–8/6–12/K–12: exceptional generalist; exceptional specialist—behavioral & emotional disabilities; exceptional specialist—cognitive disability; exceptional specialist—deaf and hard of hearing; exceptional specialist—learning disability; exceptional specialist—physical and health disability; exceptional specialist—visual disability

Additional School Personnel

I. School Administrator (valid 5 years)
   A. An individual who holds a standard Wyoming educator license may apply to add a school administrator endorsement to his or her license.
   B. This endorsement allows individuals to serve as an administrator or superintendent in any Wyoming school in accordance with his or her grade level of preparation.
   C. The following school administrator endorsements are offered by PTSB:
      1. District superintendent
      2. School principal
      3. Program director
   D. Requirements:
      1. Hold Wyoming licensure in a teaching or related services field
      2. Have completed an educational leadership program, from an accredited college/university, that leads to an institutional recommendation in educational leadership, school principal, educational administrator, or other equivalent endorsement areas
   E. Educators who are applying concurrently for initial licensure and a school administrator endorsement must submit a complete application for initial, first-time licensure and have at least 3 years of K–12 teaching or related service experience.
II. School Librarian (valid 5 years)
   A. An individual with this endorsement is eligible to serve as a school librarian in a Wyoming K–12 school.
   B. Endorsement requires completion of a program in school library science, K–12.
III. School Counselor (valid 5 years)
   A. Endorsement requires an institutional recommendation indicating completion of a master's or higher degree in school counseling.
IV. School Psychologist (valid 5 years)
   A. Endorsement requires an institutional recommendation indicating completion of a master's or higher degree in school psychology.
V. School Social Worker (valid 5 years)
   A. Endorsement requires an institutional recommendation indicating completion of a master's or higher degree in school social work.

Appendix 1

How to Contact State Offices of Certification

Alabama
Educator Certification Section
Office of Teaching and Leading
Alabama State Department of
    Education
5215 Gordon Persons Building
P.O. Box 302101
Montgomery, AL 36130–2101
334–694–4557 (7:30–5:00)
www.alabamaachieves.org/teacher
    -center/teacher-certification

Alaska
Alaska Department of Education
    and Early Development

Mailing Address:
Attn: Teacher Certification
PO Box 110500
Juneau, AK 99811–0500

Physical Address:
801 West 10th Street, Suite 200
Juneau, AK 99801–1878
907–465–2831
907–465–2441 (fax)
education.alaska.gov/
    TeacherCertification
tcwebmail@alaska.gov

Arizona
Arizona Department of Education
    Educator Certification

Mailing Address:
Arizona Department of
    Education—Certification Unit
P.O. Box 6490
Phoenix, AZ 85005–6490

Physical Address:
Arizona Department of Education
1535 West Jefferson Street
Phoenix, AZ 85007
602–542–4367 (8:30–4:30)
www.azed.gov/educator
    -certification/educator
    -certification-career
certification@azed.gov

Arkansas
Office of Educator Licensure
State Department of Education
Four Capitol Mall, Room 106-B
Little Rock, AR 72201
501–682–4342 (8:00–4:30)
501–682–4898 (fax)
ArkansasEd.gov
Melissa.Jacks@arkansas.gov

California
Commission on Teacher
    Credentialing
1900 Capitol Avenue
Sacramento, CA 95811–4213
916–322–4974 (12:00–4:00)
Live online chat at www.ctc.ca
    .gov/commission/contact-the
    -commission/CERT-contact
www.ctc.ca.gov
credentials@ctc.ca.gov

Colorado
Department of Education
Educator Talent Division
6000 East Evans Avenue, #2100
Denver, CO 80222
303–866–6628 (7:30–12:30)
866–522–4284 (fax)
www.cde.state.co.us/cdeprof
cdelicensing@cde.state.co.us

Connecticut
Bureau of Educator Standards and
    Certification
State Department of Education
P.O. Box 150471
Hartford, CT 06115–0471
860–713–6969
860–713–7017 (fax)
www.sde.ct.gov/sde/cert
teacher.cert@ct.gov

Delaware
Educator Licensure and Certification
Delaware Department of Education
Collette Education Resource Center
35 Commerce Way, Suite 1
Dover, DE 19904
302–857–3388 (8:00–4:30)
www.doe.k12.de.us
deeds@doe.k12.de.us

District of Columbia
Office of the State Superintendent of
    Education
Educator Quality and Effectiveness
Teaching & Learning Unit
1050 First Street, NE
Washington, DC 20002
202–727–6436
osse.dc.gov/ed-credentials
osse.asklicensure@dc.gov

Florida
Bureau of Educator Certification
Florida Department of Education
Room 201, Turlington Building
325 West Gaines Street
Tallahassee, FL 32399–0400
800–445–6739 (in US)
850–245–5049 (outside US)
www.fldoe.org/teaching/
   certification
Submit email on website

Georgia
Professional Standards Commission
Educator Certification Division
200 Piedmont Avenue SE
Suite 1712, West Tower
Atlanta, GA 30334–9032
404–232–2500 (metro Atlanta and
   outside Georgia)
800–869–7775 (in-state, outside
   metro Atlanta)
www.gapsc.com
mail@gapsc.com

Hawaii
Hawaii Teacher Standards Board
Licensing Section
650 Iwilei Road, Suite 268
Honolulu, HI 96817
808–586–2600
808–586–2606 (fax)
hawaiiteacherstandardsboard.org
htsb@hawaii.gov

Idaho
Certification/Professional Standards
   Commission
State Department of Education
650 West State Street, P.O. Box
   83720
Boise, ID 83720–0027
208–332–6882
www.sde.idaho.gov/cert-psc/cert/
certification@sde.idaho.gov

Illinois
ISBE Educator Effectiveness
   Department
100 North First Street
Springfield, IL 62777–0001
217–557–6763
217–524–1289 (fax)
www.isbe.net/Pages/Educator
   -Licensure.aspx
licensure@isbe.net

Indiana
Office of Educator Licensing
Indiana Department of Education
115 West Washington Street
South Tower, Suite 600
Indianapolis, IN 46204
317–232–9010
www.doe.in.gov/licensing
licensinghelp@doe.in.gov
Email documents: transcript@doe
   .in.gov

Iowa
Iowa Board of Educational
   Examiners
701 East Court Avenue, Suite A
Des Moines, IA 50309–4941
515–281–3245
515–281–7669 (fax)
boee.iowa.gov

Kansas
Teacher Licensure and Accreditation
Kansas State Department of
   Education
Landon State Office Building
900 SW Jackson Street
Topeka, KS 66612
785–296–2288
785–296–7933 (fax)
www.ksde.org/Agency/Division
   -of-Learning-Services/Teacher
   -Licensure-and-Accreditation

Kentucky
Kentucky Department of Education
Office of Educator Licensure and
   Effectiveness
Division of Educator Licensure and
   Quality
300 Sower Boulevard
Frankfort, KY 40601
502–564–4606
888–598–7667
502–564–7080 (fax)
www.epsb.ky.gov
KDElicensure@education.ky.gov

Louisiana
Louisiana Department of Education
Division of Educator Licensure
www.teachlouisiana.net
Submit email at ldoe.force.com/s/
   ask-certification

Maine
Certification Office
Maine Department of Education
23 State House Station
Augusta, ME 04333–0023
207–624–6603
207–624–6604 (fax)
www.maine.gov/doe/cert
cert.doe@maine.gov

Maryland
Maryland State Department of
   Education
Certification
200 West Baltimore Street
Baltimore, MD 21201–2595
410–767–0385
certinfo.msde@maryland.gov
www.mdcert.org

Massachusetts
Department of Elementary and
   Secondary Education (ESE)
Office of Educator Licensure
75 Pleasant Street
Malden, MA 02148–4906
781–338–3000 (24/7 automated)
800–439–2370 (TTY)
www.doe.mass.edu/licensure/

Michigan
Office of Educator Excellence
Michigan Department of Education
608 West Allegan Street
P.O. Box 30008
Lansing, MI 48909
517–241–5000
www.michigan.gov/moecs
MDE-EducatorHelp@michigan.gov

Minnesota
Professional Educator Licensing and
    Standards Board
1021 Bandana Boulevard East, Suite
    222
St. Paul, MN 55108–5111
651–539–4200
mn.gov/pelsb
pelsb@state.mn.us

Mississippi
Office of Educator Licensure
Mississippi Department of
    Education
P.O. Box 771
Jackson, MS 39205–0771
601–359–3483
www.mdek12.0rg/OTL/OEL
teachersupport@mde.k12.ms.us

Missouri
Educator Certification
P.O. Box 480
Jefferson City, MO 65102–0480
573–751–0051
dese.mo.gov/educator-quality/
    certification
certification@dese.mo.gov

Montana
Educator Licensure
Office of Public Instruction
P.O. Box 202501
Helena, MT 59620–2501
406–444–3150
opi.mt.gov/Educators
cert@mt.gov

Nebraska
Teacher Certification
Nebraska Department of Education
301 Centennial Mall South
P.O. Box 94987
Lincoln, NE 68509–4987
402–471–0739
www.education.ne.gov/tcert
nde.tcertweb@nebraska.gov

Nevada
Nevada Department of Education
www.doe.nv.gov/educatorlicensure/
license@doe.nv.gov

Office of Educator Licensure–
    Southern Nevada
2080 East Flamingo Road, Suite 210
Las Vegas, NV 89119
702–486–6458
702–486–6450 (fax)

Office of Educator Licensure–
    Northern Nevada
700 East Fifth Street
Carson City, NV 89701
775–687–9115

New Hampshire
New Hampshire Department of
    Education
Division of Educator Support and
    Higher Education
Bureau of Credentialing
101 Pleasant Street
Concord, NH 03301–3852
603–271–2409
www.education.nh.gov
cert.info@doe.nh.gov

New Jersey
New Jersey Department of
    Education
Office of Recruitment, Preparation,
    and Certification
P.O. Box 500
Trenton, NJ 08625–0500
609–292–2070
www. nj.gov/education/license/
licensing.requests@doe.nj.gov

New Mexico
New Mexico Public Education
    Department
Attn: Licensure
300 Don Gaspar
Santa Fe, NM 87501
505–827–5821
505–827–5820 (fax)
webnew.ped.state.nm.us/bureaus/
    licensure/
licensureunit@state.nm.us

New York
Office of Teaching Initiatives
New York State Education
    Department
89 Washington Avenue, 5N EB
Albany, NY 12234
518–474–3901
www.highered.nysed.gov/tcert
tcert@nysed.gov

North Carolina
Department of Public Instruction
6301 Mail Service Center
Raleigh, NC 27699–6301
919–807–3310 (out of state)
800–577–7994 (in-state only)
www.dpi.nc.gov/educators/educators
    -licensure
asklicensure@dpi.nc.gov

North Dakota
Education Standards and Practices
    Board
Teacher Licensure
2718 Gateway Avenue, Suite 204
Bismarck, ND 58503–0585
701–328–9641
701–328–9647 (fax)
www.nd.gov/espb/licensure
espbinfo@nd.gov

Department of Public Instruction
600 East Boulevard Avenue,
    Department 201
Bismarck, ND 58505–0440
701–328–2260
701–328–4770 (fax)
www.nd.gov/dpi/educators/
dpischoolapproval@nd.gov

Ohio
Office of Educator Licensure
Ohio Department of Education
25 South Front Street, Mail Stop 504
Columbus, OH 43215–4183
614–466–3593
877–644–6338 (toll-free)
614–752–8406 (fax)
education.ohio.gov/Topics/
    Teaching/Licensure
educator.licensure@education.ohio
    .gov

Oklahoma
Teacher Certification
Oklahoma State Department of
    Education
2500 North Lincoln Boulevard,
    Room 212
Oklahoma City, OK 73105–4599
405–521–3337
405–522–1520 (fax)
www.ok.gov/sde/teacher
    -certification
certification@sde.ok.gov

Oregon
Teacher Standards and Practices
    Commission
250 Division Street NE
Salem, OR 97301
503–378–3586
503–378–4448 (fax)
www.oregon.gov/tspc
contact.tspc@oregon.gov

Pennsylvania
Pennsylvania Department of
    Education
Bureau of School Leadership and
    Teacher Quality
333 Market Street, 12th Floor
Harrisburg, PA 17126–0333
717–728–3224
717–787–3356
717–783–6736 (fax)
www.education.pa.gov/Educators/
    Certification
ra-edcertquestions@pa.gov

Rhode Island
Office of Educator Excellence and
    Certification Services
Rhode Island Department of
    Education
255 Westminster Street
Providence, RI 02903–3400
401–222–8893
www.ride.ri.gov/
    TeachersAdministrators/
    EducatorCertification.aspx
EQAC@ride.ri.gov

South Carolina
Office of Educator Services
8301 Parklane Road
Columbia, SC 29223
803–896–0325
803–896–0368 (fax)
ed.sc.gov/educators/certification
certification@ed.sc.gov
transcripts@ed.sc.gov (for emailing
    transcripts)

South Dakota
South Dakota Department of
    Education
Office of Educator Certification
800 Governors Drive
Pierre, SD 57501
605–773–3426
doe.sd.gov/certification/
certification@state.sd.us

Tennessee
Tennessee Department of Education
Office of Educator Licensure
9th Floor, Andrew Johnson Tower
710 James Robertson Parkway
Nashville, TN 37243–0377
615–532–4885
615–532–1448 (fax)
www.tn.gov/education/licensing
Educator.Licensure@tn.gov

Texas
Texas Education Agency
Educator Certification
WBT 5–100
1701 North Congress Avenue
Austin, TX 78701–1494
512–936–8400
tea.texas.gov/Texas_Educators/
    Certification/
educatorcert@tea.texas.gov

Utah
Utah State Board of Education
    Educator Licensing
250 East 500 South
P.O. Box 144200
Salt Lake City, UT 84114–4200
801–538–7740
801–538–7973 (fax)
www.schools.utah.gov/curr/
    licensing

Vermont
Educator Licensing Office
Vermont Agency of Education
1 National Life Drive, Davis 5
Montpelier, VT 05620–2501
802–828–3440
education.vermont.gov/educator
    -licensure
aoe.licensinginfo@vermont.gov

Virginia
Virginia Department of Education
Office of Licensure

Mailing Address:
P.O. Box 2120
Richmond, VA 23218–2120

Physical Address:
James Monroe Building
101 North 14th Street
Richmond, VA 23219
804–225–2022
804–530–4510 (fax)
www.doe.virginia.gov/teaching/
    licensure/index.shtml
licensure@doe.virginia.gov

Washington
Office of Superintendent of Public
    Instruction (OSPI)
Professional Certification Office
Old Capitol Building
P.O. Box 47200
Olympia, WA 98504–7200
360–725–6400
360–664–3631 (TTY)
360–586–0145 (fax)
www.k12.wa.us/certification
cert@k12.wa.us

West Virginia
Office of Certification
WVDE
Building 6, Suite 550
1900 Kanawha Boulevard East
Charleston, WV 25305–0330
304–558–7010
304–558–7843 (fax)
wvde.us/certification/certification
    -info/

Wisconsin
Teacher Education, Professional
    Development & Licensing
Department of Public Instruction

Mailing Address:
P.O. Box 7841
Madison, WI 53707–7841

Physical Address:
125 South Webster Street
Madison, WI 53703
608–266–1027
800–266–1027
dpi.wi.gov/licensing
licensing@dpi.wi.gov

Wyoming
Professional Teaching Standards
    Board
State of Wyoming
1920 Thomes Avenue, Suite 100
Cheyenne, WY 82001
307–777–7291
307–777–8718 (fax)
wyomingptsb.com/
wyoptsb@wyo.gov

Appendix 2

Addresses for Certification Information for US Possessions and Territories

American Samoa
American Samoa Department of
Education (Utulei)
Pago Pago, AS 96799
Phone: (684) 633–5237
Fax: (684) 633–4240
https://www.doe.as/
asdoetq@doe.as

Commonwealth of the Northern Mariana Islands
Jessica Estrada, Certification &
Licensure Officer
Capitol Hill
P.O. Box 501370 CK
Saipan, MP 96950
Phone: (670) 237–3061
Fax: (670) 664–3045
www.cnmipss.org/state-boe
-certification
boe.certification@cnmipss.org

Federated States of Micronesia
FSM Department of Education
P.O. Box PS 87, Palikir
Pohnpei, FM 96941
Phone: (691) 320–2609
Fax: (691) 320–5500
http://national.doe.fm

Guam
Guam Commission for Educator
Certification
Office: University of Guam School
of Education, Room 105 (1st
Floor)
Mail: 303 University Drive SOE
Building, Room 105
Mangilao, GU 96913
Fran-Nicole Camacho, Certification
Officer
francamacho@gcec.guam.gov
Phone: (671) 735–2554
Fax: (671) 735–2569
gcec.guam.gov

Marshall Islands
Embassy of the Republic of the
Marshall Islands
2433 Massachusetts Avenue, NW
Washington, DC 20008
Phone: (202) 234–5414
Fax: (202) 232–3236
www.rmiembassyus.org
info@rmiembassyus.org
See also www.gooverseas.com/
teach-abroad/marshall-islands

Palau
Emery Wenty, Director, Ministry of
Education
P.O. Box 189
Koror, Palau 96940
Phone: (680) 488–2489/2567/4220
Fax: (680) 488–8465
palaugov.org/bureau-of-education/
ewenty@palaumoe.net

Puerto Rico
Council on Education of Puerto
Rico
P.O. Box 19900
San Juan, PR 00910–1900
Phone: (787) 722–2121
Fax: (787) 641–2573
www.ce.pr.gov

Virgin Islands
Virgin Islands Board of Education
(St. Thomas)
P.O. Box 11900
60B, 61 and 62 Dronningens Gade
St. Thomas, VI 00801
Phone: (340) 774–4546
Fax: (340) 774–3384
https://www.myviboe.com/
certification/apply-certification
stt@myviboe.com

Virgin Islands Board of Education
(St. Croix)
1123 King Street
Christiansted, VI 00820
Phone: (340) 772–4144
Fax: (340) 772–2895
stx@myviboe.com

**United States Department of
Defense Education Activity**
Educator Recruitment and Staffing
DoDEA Headquarters
4800 Mark Center Drive
Alexandria, VA 22350–1400
www.dodea.edu/offices/hr/
employment/categories/index.cfm
(571) 372–0576